Gourmet's Guide
to
New Orleans

CREOLE COOKBOOK

AND DIRECTORY OF NEW ORLEANS RESTAURANTS

by

Elaine Douglass Jones

Illustrated by
Robert Seago

Baton Rouge
CLAITOR'S PUBLISHING DIVISION

TWENTY-SIXTH PRINTING
1988
ISBN No. 87511-620-5

Copyright
1933, 1939, 1940, 1941, 1945, 1947, 1949, 1951, 1955, 1957, 1959, 1960, 1964, 1965, 1967, 1969, 1972, 1975

by

ELAINE DOUGLASS JONES
in collaboration with
Mrs. W. Elliott Laudeman
Miss Elaine Friedrichs Jones

Illustrated by
Robert Seago

Published and for sale by:

CLAITOR'S PUBLISHING DIVISION
3165 S. Acadian at I-10, P.O. Box 3333
Baton Rouge, La. 70821

DEDICATION

For Gram

Mrs. Caroline Merrick Jones, the original author of "Gourmet's Guide to New Orleans"----

For her undying interest in the delicious cookery of the old and the new Southern Cuisine----

For her originality and dedication which has made possible the continuation of this grand melange of ideas and recipes which are a tribute to our heritage.

Gourmet's Guide to New Orleans

FOREWORD

A FOREIGN critic once described America as a country which had one sauce and twenty different religions. Evidently he did not reach New Orleans in his travels, or else he would have discovered that its gravies are even more varied than its theology, and that good cooking is one of its religions.

In this thrice blessed city where the art of living has even been esteemed the chief of the fine arts, and where dining is a function instead of a chore, cooking has reached a degree of perfection that it has not attained anywhere else in this country, and tourists come as definitely to New Orleans to eat as they go to New York to see the plays, or to Washington to behold the seat of government, or to Hollywood to gape at the movie stars.

Many things have contributed to make New Orleans a shrine to which gourmets make reverent pilgrimages. One is that it has what an old colored cook once described as the "ingrejuns" necessary to good cooking, for you cannot make omelets without having eggs. No other place in the world has such a market, for lying as it does with one hand in the marshes and bayous of this coastal region and the other grasping the packing houses of Chicago, as it were, and its head in a perennial market garden and its feet almost touching the tropics, it has a super-abundance all the year round of sea foods par excellence, the finest cuts of butchers' meats, fresh vegetables and the exotic fruits that swift steamers bring in from Central American ports.

To properly prepare these gifts of the gods for human consumption there has slowly evolved through the past two hundred years a school of cooking that is part inspiration and sheer genius, and part a happy adaptation of the dishes of many races and lands. Founded originally on the French cuisine, it was pepped up, so to speak, by the Spanish, given body and strength by the New England influence, a bit of warmth by the hot breads of Virginia, and finally glorified by the touch of the old Negro mammies who boasted that they had only to pass their hands over a pot to give it a flavor that would make your mouth water.

Thousands of hands have stirred and been subtle with onion and garlic, and pinched their thyme and bay leaves, and been spendthrifts with oil and miserly with vinegar, and have tested and tasted to make its incomparable sauces, and its oysters Rockefeller and its shrimp remoulade, and its crabs timbale, and its gumbo filé and its courtbouillon, and it is the secrets thus discovered of these sophisticated dishes that this little book offers you.

Try them, and Heaven send you luck.

DOROTHY DIX

ACKNOWLEDGMENTS

The present edition is a tribute and in some cases a memorial to the authors on the local and national scene who, over the years, have contributed their favorite recipes to the interest of this book:

Ella and Stanley Arthur	Grace King
Roark Bradford	E. P. O'Donnell
Barbara Brooks	Fulton Ousler
Hermann B. Deutsch	Virginia Shaw Putnam
Mr. and Mrs. Olin Downes	Eleanor Riggs
Charles ("Pie") Dufour	Helen Pitkin Schertz
Laurraine Goreau	Natalie Scott
Weeks Hall	Grace Thompson Seton
Hilda Phelps Hammond	Julian Street
Harnett Kane	Geneviève Trimble
Frances Parkinson Keyes	President and Mrs. Woodrow Wilson

These, and others, have made unique contributions, the thoughts of which will savor the appetites and interests of the ûsers of this volume, for which I am very appreciative.

Caroline Merrick Jones

Caroline Merrick Jones

Gourmet's Guide to New Orleans

INTRODUCTION

A gourmet—discerning admirer of fine food—is to New Orleans a native son, whatever his origin. In this New Orleans is a true offshoot of France, where culinary excellence was deemed worthy once of royal, and still of governmental, recognition. New Orleans likewise regards culinary creation with a high seriousness.

Here old culinary traditions are treasured like old masters and new ones are correspondingly acclaimed. In the following pages, the museums are thrown open, the chefs d'oeuvres stand for review. Only those that have assuredly met the critics' approbation have been chosen, and many of them are released here for the first time by formerly jealous guardians.

Such a collection is only possible, of course, through the generosity of celebrated hostesses and renowned restaurateurs. And such hostesses and such restaurateurs are only possible in the atmosphere of interest and appreciation which New Orleans, in fact, all Louisiana, affords. See for yourself!

Go to Antoine's and sense the ceremonial aura that attends the offering of the matchless productions there. You will find Roy Alciatore, third of the line, heir to the family tradition as his own dishes prove. Like his renowned ancestors, he went to Paris to study. His *Filet of Flounder Louis XIII* was his "thesis" that assured his place among the masters. Many New Orleanians affectionately remember his father, Jules, tall, erect, well-tailored, with eyes always as keenly blue as when in his boyhood in Strassbourg he was given the honor of making the pâté de foie gras for Bismarck. Antoine, first of the line, is still a figure in the city's proud traditions. The walls of some of the simple quiet old rooms are covered with affectionate eulogies signed by figures internationally as well as nationally famous.

Luxuriate at Arnaud's. There is no true artist who does not love his art, no restaurateur worthy of the name who lacks the fine perception of subtle flavors that makes the gourmet. Arnaud, the "Count," was an example: a genial bon viveur transplanted from his native France, he recreated it about him in his cuisine. The tranquilly busy rooms where he presided are delicately pervaded by an adulation. Habitués claim that the presence of the master spirit still persists, not only in the menu, but in the perfected service of an integrated organization. Eugène, grown old in the service, will sometimes substitute his son to serve a favored client, for instance, and expand with pride at the patron's approval. The staff's old loyalty is put at the service of the "count's" daughter, Germaine.

Seek out the Galatoire brothers in their sanctum, bright and shining. Perched high at one end of the room is the cashier, as in any proper French restaurant, while one of the brothers stands nearby, suavely courteous, watching unobtrusively but all-observing, as the smoothly moving waiters glide by with the Trout Marguéry, the canapè, the oysters ravigote. A younger scion of the house receives you deferentially, and the room is full of the unique expansiveness which only a pleased palate can produce. There, too, is the integrated service that time and loyalty evolve. In the First World War five of the waiters volunteered for service in France. When the war ended they returned to their home, several of them with the Croix de Guerre; one, Albert, now at Antoine's, with the Croix de Guerre with four palms, and the Medaille Militaire, the highest French decoration for bravery.

For New Orleanians, these restaurants are "home." A gracious dowager, a great-grandmother, will wait patiently for her chosen waiter. "I always ask for him," she explains composedly. "He has always taken care of us, since I used to come here as a young girl with my father."

Find the Broussard brothers, of course, Robert and Josef César. Several generations of Louisiana are behind them, but their speech has the French stamp, their cuisine fortunately even more so: such creations as their canard en papillote, or their crabmeat Broussard are French inspired, and of so savoury an individuality!

Tujagues, an old favorite, across from the French Market should not be missed.

Visit Josef's pleasant courtyard in the old French Quarter. You will find that he has taken with him the skill and understanding of the culinary arts which formerly took him to the top ranks among the chefs chosen by his former employer "the Count" Arnaud.

Recent, too, and likewise approved, is the Caribbean Room of the Pontchartrain Hotel. Here again, a wide choice of excellent dishes, each one tempting, is available: the "lump crab-meat" has attained a special fame.

Find your way to the great mirrored room at La Louisiane, where the ordered hosts of white tables await you. Changes of management have taken place, since the time when M. Fernand Alciatore, the brother of Jules, brought it to fame; but it still preserves the legacies of distinctive dishes.

The Patio Royal will be on your list. There, the background in itself is essentially of old New Orleans, with its sunny patio—in its dignified beauty it is eloquent of its once proud position as the "First bank of the City." Now it is equally distinguished as a restaurant.

It was started on its culinary career by one of the city's social favorites, Mme. Jeanne Castellanos, volatile with the French and Spanish of her ancestry, and with a noteworthy gourmet's outlook. Then her "right-hand man," Sherry, carried on worthily.

Now the Brennan family has taken over, the same family which brought the old Vieux Carré restaurant to its apogee. There is a constantly varying table d'hôte and constantly enrichened menu a la carte. In the easy traquillity of the rooms and patio (and, importantly, in the kitchen as well) one of the Brennans is quietly vigilant. And the Absinthe Suissesse, an old New Orleans favorite which they retrieved from oblivion, is just the right touch to ready the palate for the feast.

Everywhere the French atmosphere is dominant. But New Orleans has the French tolerance for worthy productions of other countries—as witness the popularity of Kolb's, who brilliantly asserts the German excellence of Wienerschnitzel, Pigs' Knuckles, Sauerbraten, worthy of old Leipzig or of Munich.

Italy is recognized with spaghetti and ravioli brought to their apogee by the Turcis (one of them once sang in the Old French Opera House here) and by Montalbano who looks out with a hearty face, as round as one of his cheeses, with a smile for his visitor's delight as he prepares an antepasto in the best Italian tradition—cheeses as big as cartwheels and graceful straw-girt Chianti bottles for his background. And notably in the upper part of the city by Commander's, Irwin's, Manale's, and many others.

But on the whole, the French atmosphere prevails, even in unpretentious little places that have misleading Anglo-Saxon names. Scattered throughout the city are such places, favorite resorts for New Orleanians of a Sunday night, or just any night. Some of them have the air of clubs—like Manale's, Commander's, and many others.

Even the cuisine of the hotels is genuinely affected: the French names that are flaunted on the menus are not, as in so many places, a camouflage for some ploddingly conscientious production, but have the character to match their names.

The fine fire of culinary genius burns not only in these numerous but sporadic formal restaurants. Home-cooking has its own spark as surely as have the restaurants. Even this you may easily—and pleasantly—sample, though you be "just a tourist." An apotheosis of it on lavish scale is to be found at Corinne Dunbar's. But there, mom ami, you will have to "make a date." There, you will be received in a handsome old house furnished in the best Creole tradition with silver and napery at which our proudest grandmothers would not have cavilled, and a home-cooking that is of the essence of Louisiana. At the Gumbo Shop, on St. Peter Street, you will find a gumbo worthy of any private home, choice salads, special ices and at the Quartres Saisons for perfect French pastries, cakes and ices; nearby the Coffee Pot, and various other cozy spots in the Quarter.

By no means must you omit a visit to the quiet little bars—not to be confused with the more garish and less distinctive night-clubs. And the Ramos Bar which, in new premises, serves still its deservedly famous gin-fizzes (did you know that Ramos Gin Fizz is inscribed full across the great mirror in the bar at Monte Carlo?) And the Old Absinthe House—perhaps you have heard of Josh Ferrer, who served there for so long—the same Josh Ferrer whose ancestors held the Absinthe House as a royal grant. There the notables drank elegantly through the years, and M. Josh filled countless glasses for them with the clouded green liquid. Now, the naughty absinthe is replaced acceptably by Herbsaint, or other modified versions, as savory but not so disastrous as the prototype—and the notables still patronize, as thousands of their cards attest.

And of an afternoon or evening, what more pleasant than the Pontchartrain's garden bar with its little fountain echoing the discreet tinkling of ice in the glasses?

In all of these, as many others, you will rejoice in the authentic versions of the city's own distinctive drinks—the gin-fizzes, the Suissesse, and other presentations of our reformed "absinthe," the Sazeracs—that find favor with the French-bred palates that are as difficult for drinks as for food. As to both, says the "proper New Orleanian," only the discerning attain the heights of enjoyment.

You may note the fervor with which our most cultured voices pronounce upon the sacrilege of over-boiling a fish, or of losing the juices of liver by piercing it with a fork. The erudite dwell lovingly upon their favorite dishes, discuss the various manifestations of them and their origins.

Thus, jambalaya, they tell you, is derived from the arroz paella, which has appeared on every proper Spanish menu from time immemorial. Quite often here as in Spain, a touch—no more—of saffron is added for color and savor as well. A nationally renowned doctor will tell you that it is the ideal food, combining with beautiful accuracy perfect nutriment in perfect proportion (his logic is well-supported by the inspired genius of his excellent cuisine!) Courtbouillon is so-called, according to tradition, because the earliest inspiration produced it as soup, then genius flashes again and it became "courtbouillon," a "short soup," a stew.

As to bouillabaisse, shades of Thackeray flutter at the name. That critic, so often difficult towards the United States, proclaimed that only in Marseilles and New Orleans could the dish be known in its perfection, a perfection that roused him to the supreme tribute of a poem. As for the name, the story is that in the first days of its glory, as the chefs hovered over it, when one saw that the rich brew was bubbling too rapidly, he shrieked a warning: "bouillit: baisse!" (it's boiling lower the fire).

And there's the story of oysters Rockefeller. When our Jules Alciatore offered them with just pride for a group of his most favored patrons, one of them exclaimed: "Mon Dieu, how rich! How are they called?" The world was at that time just blinking its best at Rockefeller's new millions, and the chef retorted quickly—"Rich, are they? Eh bien, oysters Rockefeller you have."

Read the press of other cities, and you will find now and again an exiled New Orleanian deploring with genuine emotion the crimes against the delicate palate committed in the name of Creole cooking. The thin savorless water that proclaims itself Creole gumbo. The viscous mass made to travesty jambalaya. One such plaintiff arraigns the dictionary: "a gumbo is any soup with okra in it,"—yes, but not a Creole gumbo.

Creole cooking it is true, is an art, and as such is mysterious in its origins and inspirations. But its technique can be acquired. Prime rule, each dish must be a harmony, its central feature predominant but subdued by the effect of its accompanying ingredients, so that not it, nor any one of them is perceptible for itself—a blend to unity. And, in contrast to the white pastes of other parts of the country, and even to the excellent French originals, Creole cooking emphasizes rather the brown roux, point of departure in so many savory directions.

Almost all soups, to meet approval in New Orleans, must have a bay leaf, thyme, a wee bit of onion, and meat or chicken broth; garlic, a bit of mace, are frequently included, garlic almost always.

Here it is common knowledge that the insipid carrots and peas of this country must be helped slyly with just a touch of sugar; that the least possible modicum of water must be used in cooking vegetables so that the flavor of them may be conserved. In fact, many deft lords and ladies of the cuisine steam their vegetables instead of boiling them, whenever it is possible. But enough for details, you must follow through the pages to come.

Thus the sources, thus the background. Our culinary history is old. Derived from France and from Spain chiefly, it is truly Creole. But it is never static, it grows. A language that is live enriches itself by borrowing and adaptations. So must a lusty cuisine. Stranger dishes arrive among us; our chefs and our beloved mammies deal with them!—they are naturalized, the strangers are the same and more so, they are Creoles!

All, fellow gourmet, are yours—for he who reads may cook.

Joy is one of the duties of life. And the refined discernment that is culture makes any enjoyment more exquisite, more keen. The worthy one of good eating is here with us. And so, bon appetit!

CONTENTS

Dedication iii
Foreword v
Acknowledgements vi
Introduction vii
Guide to Restaurants xiii

                                                        Page

I   Coffee, tea and beverages 1

II   Appetizers and Hors d'oeuvres 15

III   Eggs, cheese and grits 30

IV   Hot breads, pancakes and waffles 38

V   Salad and salad dressings 52

VI   Bisques, gumbos and soups 67

VII   Fish and shellfish 87

VIII   Poultry, game and dressings 111

IX   Meats 128

X   Vegetables, pastas, jambalayas and
         casseroles 149

XI   Sauces for meats, poultry, fish and
         vegetables 175

XII   Desserts, candy and ice cream 187

XIII   Cakes, small cakes, cookies, frostings, pies
         and pastries 210

XIV   Conserves, preserves and pickles 234

XV   Children's recipes 242

FINEST OF THE NEW ORLEANS RESTAURANTS

ANDREW JACKSON RESTAURANT
221 Royal Street
Telephone 529-2603
Closed Sunday. Hours 11 A.M. to
10:30 P.M.

Delicious seafood appetizers; combination of local and French cooking. Fine selection of wines, reasonable prices.

ANTOINE'S RESTAURANT
French Quarter
713 St. Louis Street
Noon till 9:30 P.M. Closed Sundays.

Excellent seafood dishes, sauces, excellent everything. Very fine wines. Prices not too high for the quality of food and the gourmet manner in which it is prepared and served.

ARNAUD'S RESTAURANT
French Quarter
813 Bienville Street
Telephone 523-5433
Open daily 11 A.M. to 12:30 A.M.

One of the fine old restaurants. Traditional cooking, traditional atmosphere. A lot of charm. Fairly reasonable.

BRENNAN'S FRENCH RESTAURANT
French Quarter
417 Royal Street
Open daily 9 A.M. to 2:30 P.M.

Noted for their fine and original ways with breakfast foods. Loaded with atmosphere. Fairly reasonable.

BROUSSARD'S RESTAURANT AND NAPOLEON PATIO
French Quarter
819 Conti Street
Telephone 523-4800
Closed Wednesdays – Hours, 6 to 10:30 P.M.

Very entertaining. Stick with the seafood. Reasonable prices.

COMMANDER'S PALACE
Garden District
1403 Washington Avenue
Open every day 11 A.M. till 11 P.M.

Located in the heart of the Garden District, now under management of the Brennan family. Fine New Orleans cuisine. Fun on Saturday & Sunday mornings, with jazz band entertaining.

CORINNE DUNBAR'S RESTAURANT
1617 St. Charles Avenué
Telephone 525-2957
Closed Sunday & Monday
Hours, noon till 2:30 P.M., and 6 till 9 P.M. By reservation only!!

No menu; dishes vary from day to day. Old family recipes that are cherished by New Orleanians. Perfect place for a lovely brunch. Reasonable.

ELMWOOD PLANTATION
Jefferson Parish
5400 Riverroad
Telephone 733-6862
Open every day -- hours 11:30 A.M. till 11 P.M.
Be sure of reservations, as this is a good thirty minutes from the New Orleans proper.

Setting in original plantation home of Louisiana Governor W. C. C. Claiborne. Try oysters or shrimp Mosca – good with game birds. Nicely varied menu. Reasonable and very atmospheric.

GALATOIRE'S RESTAURANT
French Quarter
209 Bourbon Street
Telephone 522-7261
Open every day, 11 A.M. till 12:30 A.M.

Big favorite of locals. Par excellence on fresh sea-food. Try the Trout Marguery or the Trout Meuniere Amandine. Atmosphere not exotic, but knives and forks mean more here than the candlelight. UNEXCELLED. (No reservations, one must wait their turn.)

KOLB'S GERMAN RESTAURANT
Central Business District
125 St. Charles Avenue
Telephone 522-8278
Closed Sunday, hours 11 A.M. till 10 P.M.

Combination of local and German Cuisine. Try the marinated crab salad, and the roast duckling. Very reasonable.

LE RUTH'S RESTAURANT
636 Franklin Street
Gretna, La.
Telephone 362-4914
Closed Sunday and Monday
Hours 5:45 till 10 P.M. Reservations necessary.

(Le Ruth's Restaurant continued)

French cuisine from first to last course at its very finest. Mr. Le Ruth's selection of wines is also excellent. Not over priced for the outstanding quality.

LOUIS XVI RESTAURANT
French Quarter
829 Toulouse St.
Closed Sunday, hours 6 P.M. till midnight.

The combination of local Creole and French cooking is superb. Seafood is highly recommended. Elegant wine list. Prices slightly high, but worth every penny.

MAISON PIERRE
French Quarter
430 Dauphine Street
Telephone 529-5521
Closed Monday and Tuesday, hours 6 P.M. till midnight.

Beautiful atmospheric surroundings. Imaginative Creole and French cuisine at its finest. Exceptional, charming and delicious. Very well chosen wines. Expensive, but understandingly so.

PASCAL'S MANALE RESTAURANT
Uptown
1838 Napoleon Avenue
Closed Tuesday, hours 11:45 5o 10:30 P.M. -- Sat. and Sun. 4-10:30 P.M.

Favorite with the tourists. Outstanding BBQ Shrimp. Specializes in Italian dishes. Very good wines. Expensive.

MASSON'S RESTAURANT FRANCAIS
Lake
7200 Ponchartrain Blvd.
Telephone 283-2525
Open daily, hours 5-11 except Sunday's from noon on.

Elegant decor. Delicious cuisine leans more to the French, but local cookery mixed in. Good wines, reasonable prices.

MAYLIE'S RESTAURANT
Central Business District
1009 Poydras Avenue
Telephone 525-9547
Closed Sundays, hours 11:30 A.M. till 9:30 P.M.

Completely charming. Steeped in old New Orleans tradition and exceptional food reflects the same. Good idea for a delightful lunch. Extremely reasonable.

SAL & SAM'S
4300 Veterans Memorial Highway
Telephone 885-5566
Open 11 A.M. till 2 A.M.

Varied menu. Great prime steaks, seafood, and Italian specialties. Try the seafood dishes. Reasonably priced.

PONCHARTRAIN HOTEL
Carribean Room
Garden District
2031 St. Charles Ave.
Open every day, noon to 2 P.M. and 6 to 10 P.M.

Most popular with the locals. Outstanding seafood dishes. Fine selection of wines. Relatively inexpensive for the fine quality of the cuisine and the expert service rendered.

SCLAFANI'S
Metairie
1315 North Causeway Blvd.
Telephone 835-1718
Open every day 11 A.M. till midnight.

Combination of expertly prepared dishes, both Creole and Italian. All seafood dishes highly recommended. Informal. Very good wines and extremely reasonably priced for everything.

TCHOUPITOULAS PLANTATION RESTAURANT
West Bank
6535 River Road
Waggaman, La.
Telephone 776-1277
Open every day 11 A.M. till 10 P.M.
Reservations necessary.

Very good varied menu, mostly traditional southern cooking. Setting is in an old plantation house and the atmosphere is fabulous. Well worth a visit, and reasonably priced. Wonderful for a relaxed luncheon.

TUJAGUE'S RESTAURANT
French Quarter
823 Decatur Street
Telephone 523-9462
Open every day 11 A.M. to 3 P.M. and 5 to 9 P.M.

One of the oldest New Orleans restaurants. Complete Creole cooking. Informal atmosphere. Brisket (or soup meat) highly recommended. No menu, and dishes vary from day to day. Unusual treat, don't miss it. Extremely reasonable prices.

T. PITTARI'S RESTAURANT
Uptown
4200 S. Claiborne Ave.
Telephone 891-2801
Open every day, 11 A.M. until midnight.

Presents an extremely imaginative and varied menu. Unusual types of wild game are available for the asking, fresh Maine lobsters, steaks and also local cuisine. Perfect place for the gourmet. Delicious every day lunches are offered at a very reasonable price. Otherwise, rather expensive, but well worth it.

TURCI'S ITALIAN RESTAURANT
Uptown
3218 Magazine Street
Telephone 899-3463
Open every day 6 P.M. till. . .Sunday 11-2:30, closed Monday.

One of the best! Salads and pastas are excellent, and menu is varied. Fine wines and reasonable prices.

BEST LOCAL SEAFOOD HOUSES

ACME OYSTER HOUSE
French Quarter
724 Bienville Street
Telephone 523-9828
Hours -- 7:30 A.M. till 8:30 P.M.
Closed Sunday.

Very informal atmosphere. If you have a taste for oysters on the half-shell, this one of the best. Always cold, always fresh. Also delicious fried oyster loaves and other good Po-Boys. Reasonably priced.

BRUNING'S RESTAURANT
Lake
1870 Orpheum Avenue
Hours 11 A.M. till 11 P.M. Closed Wednesdays.

One of the oldest seafood restaurants in New Orleans, catering especially to the seafood lovers. Very reasonable, informal atmosphere.

CASAMENTO'S RESTAURANT
Uptown
4330 Magazine Street
Telephone 895-9761
Hours 11:30 A.M. to 1:30 P.M. and 5:30 to 9 P.M. Closed Mondays.

One of the oldest oyster bars in the city, and one of the best. Very informal and relaxing. Menu offers other seafood offerings, Po-Boys, etc. Salads are great. Reasonable.

COMPAGNO'S RESTAURANT AND BAR
Uptown
5961 Magazine Street
Telephone 897-2061
Hours 11 A.M. till 11:30 P.M. Closed Monday.

(Compagno's Restaurant continued)

Neighborhood restaurant featuring marvelous fried trout and soft shelled crabs (when in season), and their freshly shucked oysters are delicious. Very reasonable.

FELIX'S RESTAURANT
French Quarter
739 Iberville Street
Telephone 522-4440
Hours 10 A.M. till 4 A.M.

Very informal atmosphere. Oyster lovers, this is oyster heaven! Also good – Oysters Rockefeller, Bienville (hot on the shell with sauce), or the fried oysters. Have these with a cold draft beer. Very reasonable.

FISHERMAN'S WHARF (ROCCA-FORTE'S)
Uptown
1135 St. Mary Street
Telephone 525-1701
Open daily except Sunday, hours 10 A.M. till 11 P.M.

One of the best all round New Orleans seafood houses. Heaping platters of fresh seafood in season. Informal, and reasonable.

FITZGERALD'S SEAFOOD RESTAURANT
Lake
West End Park
Telephone 282-9254
Open daily 11 A.M. till 11 P.M.

One of the oldest and best New Orleans seafood places. Picturesque view; the restaurant is set out over the lake. All kinds of fresh seafood served in every way. Delicious eating. Informal atmosphere.

FONTANA'S SEAFOOD RESTAURANT
Lake
West End Park
Telephone 282-9398
Closed Monday and Tuesday, hours 11 A.M. till 11 P.M.

Excellent for all kinds of seafood. Crabs prepared in many ways and all are delicious. Very informal.

MESSINA'S RESTAURANT AND OYSTER BAR
French Quarter
200 Chartres Street
Telephone 523-9225
Open daily except Mondays, hours 9 A.M. till 10 P.M.

Extremely informal, a great place to eat delicious raw oysters at the oyster bar. Other seafood dishes, plus a selection of very good sandwiches. Most reasonable. Really a typical seafood house, do not miss.

PAPA ROSELLI'S
Lake
1904 West End Park
Telephone 282-9275
Closed Monday, hours 11:30 A.M. till 11 P.M.

Excellent seafood, plus an array of fine Italian dishes. Delicious. Informal.

THE PEARL RESTAURANT
119 St. Charles Ave.
Central Business District
Telephone 525-2901
Open 24 hours every day.

Perfect place to end a long night with a cold ½ dozen on the half shell. Also features very good sandwiches. Reasonable.

PETROSSI'S
Uptown
901 Louisiana Ave.
Telephone 895-9114
Closed Monday and Tuesday, hours 11 A.M. till 11 P.M.

Neighborhood restaurant; excellent with all seafood. Other specialties offered, all very good. Reasonable and informal.

VISKO'S
West Bank
516 Gretna Blvd., Gretna, La.
Telephone 368-4899
Closed Sunday, hours 11 A.M. till 10 P.M., Saturday till 11 P.M.

Absolutely magnificent seafood! Served in many ways, and the service is very good. Reasonable and highly recommended.

BEST NEW ORLEANS STEAK HOUSES

BULL'S CORNER RESTAURANT
Uptown
4440 Magnolia St.
Telephone 895-7422
Open every day, hours Monday thru Thursday 11 A.M. till 10:30 P.M., Fridays and Saturdays 11 A.M. till midnight, Sundays 5 till 10 P.M.

RUTH'S CHRIS STEAK HOUSE (AND LOBSTER)
1100 North Broad
Telephone 822-1114
Open daily except Monday, hours 4 P.M. till 11 P.M.

CHARLIE'S STEAK HOUSE
Uptown
4510 Dryades St.
Telephone 895-9705
Closed Sunday, hours 10:30 A.M. to 11:30 P.M.

CRESCENT CITY STEAK HOUSE
Mid-City
1001 N. Broad Ave.
Telephone 922-9908
Open every day 11:30 A.M. till 11:30 P.M.

CHRIS STEAK HOUSE
711 North Broad
Telephone 821-4853 or 482-9278
Open every day 11:30 A.M. till 11:30 P.M.

RIB ROOM (ROYAL ORLEANS HOTEL)
French Quarter
621 St. Louis Street
Telephone 529-5333
Open every day, hours Monday – Saturday 11 A.M. till 3 P.M. and 6 P.M. till midnight. Sunday 10:30 A.M. till midnight.

BEST NEW ORLEANS SANDWICH SHOPS
Specializing in New Orleans Po-Boys, Muffuletta's, etc.

CENTRAL GROCERY COMPANY
French Quarter
923 Decatur Street
Telephone 523-1620
Closed Sunday, hours 9 A.M. till 6 p.m.
Muffuletta's specialty.

MARTIN'S PO-BOY RESTAURANT
Downtown
1940 St. Claude Ave.
Telephone 949-5201
Open daily 24 hours.

MOTHER'S RESTAURANT
Central Business District
401 Poydras Street
Telephone 523-9656
Closed Sunday and Monday. Hours 6 A.M. till 5 P.M. Saturday until 2 P.M.
Po-Boys.

PARASOL'S BAR AND RESTAURANT
Uptown
2533 Constance Street
Telephone 899-2054
Closed Tuesday and Sunday, hours 11 A.M. till 1:30 P.M. and 5 till 10 P.M.
Po-Boys.

PROGRESS GROCERY COMPANY
French Quarter
915 Decatur Street
Telephone 525-6627
Closed Sunday, hours 9 A.M. till 6 P.M.

BATTISTELLA'S
French Quarter
1000 Decatur Street
Telephone 522-3266
Open every day 5:30 A.M. till 10 P.M. (Extra Note)*** Check with the management here for the packing and shipping of fresh seafoods.

TALLEY HO COFFEE SHOP
French Quarter
400 Chartres Street
Telephone 523-0251
Closed Saturday and Sunday, hours 6:30 A.M. till 3:30 P.M.
Po-Boys.

BEST NEW ORLEANS PIZZERIAS

CIRO'S PIZZA AND SPAGHETTI HOUSE
Uptown
7918 Maple Street
Telephone 866-9551

DOMINO'S
Central Business District
701 St. Charles Ave.
Closed Tuesdays, hours 10 A.M. till 1 A.M.

4-- ROBERT M. SEAGO

coffee, tea and beverages

The history of coffee has been worldwide and colorful. It has been a favorite public beverage, stimulating to conversation and camaraderie in every country of the Orient and of Europe. Bienville and the early French settlers brought it to New Orleans and the habit found fertile soil amongst the Creoles. The habit persists today and is firmly embedded in the life of the city. Whether you prefer "Southern" coffee -- coffee with chicory and served with the cup half filled with hot milk -- or the "pure" variety, coffee you will learn to drink in unprecedented quantities if you linger long in New Orleans.

First thing in the morning.
Last thing at night.
All through the day.
With friends.
Alone.
A cup for when you're sad.
A cup for when you're happy.
To wake you up.
To put you to sleep.
Happiness is a steaming cup of cafe au lait.

-Terry Flettrich-

CREOLE COFFEE

The good cook never boils her coffee, but drips it very slowly until all the flavor is extracted. Use four cups of boiling water to one cup of ground coffee, (Dark Roast Chicory)

To make good Creole or French coffee, the water must be freshly boiled. Pour first about ten tablespoonfuls of boiling water on the coffee grounds, or sufficient water to settle the grounds. Wait about five minutes and pour a little more water and allow it to drip slowly through, but never pour water the second time until the grounds have ceased to puff or bubble. Continue to pour boiling water until all is used.

Cafe Au Lait is the pouring of hot cream (or hot milk) and hot coffee at the same time, filling rhe cup about a 50-50 mixture.

CAFE AU LAIT
Editors

4 cups dripped Creole coffee
4 cups homogenized milk

Heat coffee and milk in separate containers to scalding point. Simultaneously pour equal quantities of each into cup. Serve immediately. Add sugar to taste.

CAFÉ BRULOT
Terry Flettrich

There are probably as many ways of fixing Cafe' Brulot as there are New Orleans hostesses fixing it. One of the best Cafe Brulots is prepared with great flair and festivity by Mrs. Edward Preston Munson, owner and manager of the Lamothe House on Esplanade Avenue, a small inn of great beauty, charm and tradition.

1 cup brandy
2 lumps sugar per cup
1 quart coffee
   thin peel of ½ orange
   thin peel of ½ lemon
2 whole cloves
1 stick whole cinnamon broken into bits

Brulot Bowl:

In Brulot bowl, add spices, peelings, brnady and sugar. Pour a little alcohol in the tray under the bowl and light it. Stir contents of bowl and light it. Allow to burn only a few minutes, so as not to destroy all the flavor of the brandy. Pour in hot coffee slowly. Stir immediately.

CAFÉ BRÛLOT
Mrs. Stanley Arthur

1 cup cognac
2 lumps sugar per cup of coffee
   and 20 over
40 whole cloves

1

½ orange, very thin peel
¼ lemon, very thin peel
2 sticks whole cinnamon, broken
1 qt. coffee

Put the spices and the peel into the brandy in the brûlot bowl, with the sugar. Pour a little alcohol in the tray under the bowl and light it. Stir the contents of the bowl until it ignites. Let it burn only a few minutes, so that it may not destroy all the alcohol.

Pour in the coffee slowly.

For any Brûlot recipe the amount of sugar may be varied to taste.

Note:—If you have no brûlot bowl, you may light the contents of the bowl this way: take a tablespoon of the cognac, light a match, hold it underneath the spoon, and then light the cognac in the spoon, and light the contents of the bowl with the burning cognac in the spoon. The quantity of sugar may seem excessive: this is essential for the brûlot should taste like a very rich fruit cake.

CAFÉ BRÛLOT
Mr. Jules Alciatore
Antoine's

1 after dinner coffee cup of coffee
1½ lumps sugar
2 cloves, 2 allspice, 1 small cinnamon stick
½ after dinner coffee cup of cognac
   very thin piece of lemon rind
   very thin piece of orange rind

Use process above. Increase quantity as desired.

CAFÉ BRÛLOT
Mr. David D. Duggins
Café Brûlot Restaurant

chafing dish or silver revere bowl and ladle
4 cups strong drip coffee or extra strong regular coffee
1 peeled rind of one orange
1 peeled rind of one lemon
4 whole allspice
8 whole cloves
2 sticks cinnamon, broken up
½ cup sugar (or to taste)
1½ cups brandy (warmed)

Put all ingredients, except coffee, into chafing dish. Take a ladle full of sugar and brandy mixture, ignite with match and flame well; return down the

side of the chafing dish. When mixture ignites flame well, mix and crush the peels and spices to extract oils and flavor. When flame dies down add hot coffee, mix well and ladle into demitasse cups. Serves 8.

CAFÉ BRÛLOT
Mrs. Carl E. Woodward

6 jiggers brandy
6 coffee spoons of sugar
3 small pieces of cinnamon, 5 cloves
½ each orange and lemon rind slivered
6 cups of coffee (after dinner cups)

Put all ingredients with exception of coffee in brûlot bowl, putting the brandy last. Take a spoon of brandy, light it and dip it down in bowl, lighting up the bowl. Stir it up and down for a few minutes and then pour in the hot coffee and serve at once.

CAFÉ DIABLE
Mr. Fulton Oursler

1 qt. double-strength coffee
1 good sweet apple, the peel
1 orange, the peel, ½ lemon, the peel
   butter, size of small goose-egg
3 cinnamon sticks, 8 to 10 whole cloves
   Java coffee beans, fresh ground,
      or halved or split, 1 handful
½ cup cointreau
1½ cups brandy

Scald the brûlot bowl with boiling water first,—or any good chafing dish with an alcohol burner will do.

Put in about a tablespoon of butter, and as it cooks, add the coffee beans. Coax it, gradually, adding more butter for texture. Add the cloves and the cinnamon sticks. Add the sugar, 2 lumps for each person (as you will probably serve 2 cups to each one). Then the parings of the apple, orange, and lemon. The longer you coax, and stir, and cook, the stronger your bean essence will be. Grate in a dash of nutmeg.

Pour in gently the cointreau, and the brandy, mixing gently.

Light the brew, as directed in Café Brûlot, above. Pour your coffee, strong and very hot, slowly into the brûlot bowl. The more slowly you pour your coffee, the longer the flames will last—dramatic as they are!—and the more perfect your blend will be.

Ladle your coffee into demi-tasses.

This masterpiece is equal, we feel sure, to any other produced by The Reader's Digest, of which Mr. Oursler was one of the Senior Editors.

IRISH COFFEE
Editors

This should be the beginning and the end of the way to spend every evening in San Francisco or New Orleans. . .

Pre-heat Irish coffee cup in very hot water. (Any stem glass will do if Irish coffee cups are not available.) Empty. Immediately fill cup 3/4 full with hot black coffee. Add 3 cubes sugar. Stir till dissolved. Add jigger of Irish whiskey.

Gently pour lightly whipped cream over back of spoon to crest coffee without mixing.

Sit, sip, and call a cab!!!

IRISH COFFEE
(Such as they never served in Ireland)
Mrs. James Selman

TOPPING -- CREME CHANTILLY
    1 pt. whipping cream
    1 tablespoon vanilla
    1 tablespoon sugar

Whip cream, add vanilla and sugar. Put in refrigerator and keep cold.

COFFEE
    1 qt. strong coffee (strong drip)
    4 ozs. brandy
    4 ozs. Wild Turkey Bourbon whiskey
    4 heaping teaspoons sugar

Heat coffee in saucepan. Add brandy, bourbon whiskey and sugar. Heat a little longer. Pour into heavy stemmed water goblets, such as "Old Williamsburg", and top with the cold Creme Chantilly.

"MICKEY SPECIAL"

    1 cup good hot coffee
    2 generous scoops vanilla ice cream

Whip together thoroughly. This is important.

Pour into tall glass half filled with ice. Let stand for a few minutes before drinking.

This cannot be made on a quantity scale. To be really good, each serving must be made separately.

ORANGE BRÛLOT
Mrs. Joel Harris Lawrence

Take a thin skinned orange, run a sharp knife around the center only cutting the skin. Insert the edge of a thin spoon between the skin and pulp, thus separating them. Then carefully roll the skin back from the pulp, turning it inside out, the upper half making a cup, and the lower half, a stand. Fill cup with cognac, take a small lump of sugar, put it in a teaspoon filled with cognac, light, then put with the cognac in the cup, setting fire to the whole thing. The heat extracts the oil from the orange peel, making a delicious liqueur.

Any one of these delicious brûlots will round out a perfect meal.

CAFÉ ROYALE AU RHUM

Just place a lump of sugar on a teaspoon, drench it with Jamaica rum and, after warming the spoon with a lighted match or cigaret lighter, ignite the rum. When it has burned out, drop it into the demi-tasse for a flavorful drink of coffee.

RUM COFFEE

Blend in a cup two teaspoons honey and two tablespoons cream. Pour in one cup boiling hot coffee and stir. Combine in a warm saucepan ½ teaspoon each powdered all-spice and powdered cinnamon, four strips of orange peel, and as much Jamaica rum as you think necessary and set fire to it. Stir while it burns and pour, still flaming, into the coffee.

ICED TEA
Comdr. and Mrs. Phillip Yeatman

Heat teapot thoroughly. Add three teaspoonsful of tea, and pour six cups of boiling water over it. Let it stand a minute, and then pour into a large bowl, add a little mint, and let it cool. When cold, add one small cup of sugar, the juice of three lemons, and plenty of ice. Just before serving, add one small bottle of ginger ale and a little cherry juice.

MR. J'S SPICED ICED TEA
Mr. Joseph M. Jones, Jr.

2 family sized bags tea (or 5
  regular bags)
3 cups boiling water
1¼ cups fresh lemon juice
1 can frozen orange juice (regular
  size)
1 stick cinnamon
1 - 1½ cups sugar, or to taste
  water to make 2 quarts

Steep tea in boiling water. Add
sugar and cinnamon to the hot water
with the tea while it is steeping. Put
lemon juice and orange juice in 2 quart
pitcher and add the tea mixture. Serve
over lots of ice in tall glass.

JAMAICA AFTERNOON TEA

Simplicity itself: In each cup use
a slice of lemon, a teaspoon of sugar,
and a teaspoon of Jamaica rum, then
add a little more rum and ignite it,
which will add to your reputation as
a hostess with original ideas.

RUSSIAN TEA
Mrs. Mamie Saunders Cobb

1 quart boiling water
3 level tablespoons tea
1 cup sugar
1 quart cold water
  juice and rind of 3 lemons

Add tea to boiling water. Steep.
Dissolve sugar in cold water with
juice and rind of lemons. Let stand
a few minutes. Strain before serving
and fill glasses with crushed ice.
Most delicious when served with
tablespoon of pineapple sherbet on top.

SPICED TEA
Mrs. Joseph M. Jones, Jr.

5 tea bags
2 cups boiling water
1½ cups fresh lemon juice
1 small can frozen orange juice
2 cups sugar
2 qts. water
1 stick cinnamon

Steep tea in 2 cups boiling water.
Add cinnamon stick to tea while
steeping. Add sugar to the hot tea
mixture and stir until dissolved. Add
lemon juice and orange juice to
mixture, and then add 2 quarts water,
or less if stronger taste is desired.

TAGLIO LIMONI

Place 2 tablespoons of lemon sherbet in an iced tea glass and add
charged water to fill. Stir with spoon
and serve with a straw. In Milan,
whence we have imported this solace
for a summer day's heat, they frequently add more seltzer until the
sherbet is dissolved, and so prolong
this most refreshing beverage.

TEA À LA RUSSE

tea, sugar
4 oranges, 2 lemons

Make a good strong tea, to serve
about eight glasses. Add the juice of
four oranges and two lemons, sweeten
to taste and add cracked ice. Garnish
with a few sprigs of mint.

STANDARD BAR MEASURES

1 quart	32 ounces
4/5 quart (Fifth)	25.6 ounces
1 pint	16 ounces
4/5 pint (Tenth)	12.8 ounces
1 wine glass	4 ounces
1 jigger	1½ ounces
1 pony	1 ounce
1 teaspoon	⅛ ounce
1 dash	1/16 ounce

ABSINTHE FRAPPÉ
Dr. Erasmus D. Fenner

2 oz. absinthe
½ oz. rock candy (or simple syrup)

The trick for absinthe is to have
the ice crushed as finely as possible.
The glass should frost.
Mix well and pour slowly over a tall
glassful of finely crushed ice.

ABSINTHE SUISSESSE
Brennan's Restaurant

½ oz. orgeat syrup
1 oz. absinthe
¼ oz. maraschino
2 dashes orange flower water
1 egg, white
1 dash of anisette
1½ oz. water

Shake well with lump ice for three
or four minutes then strain in chilled
glass.

AIR MAIL SPECIAL

Shake up your favorite **Side Car**—say equal parts brandy, lemon juice and triple sec. Use champagne glasses and fill half full with **Side Car**. Then fill with champagne.

Invented in Shanghai by some of the aviators from the HOUSTON when she was flagship of the Asiatic Fleet, and given us by "Zondie" who guarantees it will create a furor.

ALEXANDER COCKTAIL

2 oz. gin
1 oz. crème de cacao
1 oz. sweet cream

Be sure to shake vigorously with ice.

ANCHORS AWEIGH

4 applejack
1 grenadine
1 lemon juice

... "Army you steer shy-y-y." ...

From the "Mixed Drink 'Compilec-tion' " of Lieutenant Winstan Folk, U. S. N.

ASH BLONDE COCKTAIL

5 parts chilled dry vermouth
1 part sweet vermouth
  twist of lemon

Mix above ingredients and pour over ice.

AUDUBON COCKTAIL

2 parts whiskey
1 part lemon juice
¾ part peach brandy
  dash of grenadine

Put in glass with ice. Stir, but do not shake.

BERMENDANIA COCKTAIL
Dr. Emile Naef

1 teaspoon sugar
1 dash Angostura bitters
2 strips lemon peel
2 ounces best Bourbon

Use plenty of cracked ice and stir until sugar is dissolved then add bourbon.

BERTA

Recently imported from **Taxco** is the Berta, sometimes known as the Dos Pasos, as that writer conceived it in a moment of non-literary inspiration. It consists of adding a jigger of tequila to a strong limeade. The ambitious make it two jiggers. Lemonade gives results, also, though of lesser excellence.

This drink is at its best in "Doña Berta's Cantina" in Taxco. Rumor says that the secret lies in her own syrup which she uses: she will not give nor sell the syrup or the sugar. However, the addition of a drop or two of honey to an ordinary sugar syrup improves the drink, and we suspect that Berta's secret lies in that.

BLACKBERRY CORDIAL
Miss Emily Bobb

1 qt. blackberries
1 lb. white sugar
1 pt. brandy, or
1 pt. whiskey
3 or 4 cloves

Strain the juice and dissolve the sugar thoroughly in it, and let it stand for about two hours with the cloves. Then add the brandy, or whiskey.

BLACKBERRY WINE
Southdown Plantation

1 gal. blackberries or dewberries
½ gal. water
3 lbs. sugar

Wash and mash the berries well. Let them stand with the water for 24 hours. Strain once or twice through cheese cloth, wringing as you strain. To gallon of juice add sugar and let stand in glass container for six weeks in a cool dark place. When all fermentation is over, bottle and seal well.

BLOODY BULL
Cookie Keenan

Equal parts Tomato juice and beef broth (bouillon) and vodka. Season with Worcestershire sauce, celery salt, Tabasco, and lemon juice.

Pour into tall glass with ice and stir. Garnish with celery stick.

BLOODY MARY SPECIAL
Mr. James K. Wadick III

Fill salt-rimmed double old-fashioned glass 2/3 with ice cubes.

ADD:
1½ jiggers vodka
  8 shakes Worcestershire sauce
  ¼ lime, well squeezed

Fill with Mott's Clamato juice. Stir with celery stalk.
  **   Optional: Tabasco to taste.

BLOODY MARY

2 ozs. vodka
4 ozs. tomato juice
1 oz. clam juice
1 oz. lemon juice
1 teaspoon horseradish
  dash celery seed
  Tabasco and Lea & Perrins to taste
  salt

BLOODY MARY
Mrs. E. V. Benjamin

2 ozs. vodka
2 ozs. Mr. & Mrs. T Bloody Mary Mix
2 ozs. beef bouillon (Campbell's)
1 teaspoon Lea & Perrins
¼ teaspoon celery salt
1 teaspoon pepper sherry
¼ - ½ of a teaspoon lime's juice
2 fresh oysters

Fill a double old-fashioned glass with ice and add vodka. Add other ingredients in the order listed and stir till well blended. Serve with a cocktail fork so the oysters can be eaten when desired.

BLOODY MARY
Lucius K. Burton

A morning eye opener! -- or a delicious cocktail to serve before lunch:

1½ ozs. vodka
  3 ozs. tomato juice
  ¼ lime or lemon -- juice only
  1 teaspoon of Worcestershire sauce
    dash of Tabasco
    pinch of salt

Serve in double Old-fashioned glass filled with ice.

BULL SHOT

1½ ozs. vodka
  3 ozs. bouillon
  ¼ lemon - juice only
    dash of Tabasco
    pinch of salt

Serve in double Old-fashioned glass filled with ice.

CAMEO KIRBY COCKTAIL

½ gin
½ Italian vermouth
2 teaspoons raspberry syrup
½ lime, the juice

Named for a famous Mississippi River character.

CANDADO RUM DRINK
Mrs. Paul B. Lansing

Serves: One or (eight)
1½ ozs. (1 qt.) rum
  1 oz. (24 ozs.) orange juice
  1 oz. (24 ozs.) pineapple juice
  5 dashes (4 ozs.) lemon juice
  5 dashes (4 ozs.) grenadine
  5 dashes (4 ozs.) bitters

Serve over ice and have one-half slice of orange, cherry, and fresh pineapple cube on toothpick in tall glass. Very refreshing and not too sweet.

CHAMPAGNE COCKTAIL

In a cocktail glass put 1 lump sugar, 2 dashes angostura bitters on sugar. Fill glass with very frapped champagne, twist a lemon peel on top and have the best of luck.

CHERRY BOUNCE -- LIQUER DE MERISE
Mrs. J. T. Bringier

Among the papers of the gracious chatelaine of the live-oak guarded old plantation of Tezcuco, is one in courtly French yellowed with age, beginning, "Madame and Friend, if you fear in any way whatever that you may not succeed in your first attempt, I can present to you all the quantity of liqueur de merise that you desire. The doctor has always been so kindly to my mother that this little savoir faire is only a feeble tribute of my gratitude." And concluding, "with the respectful homage of a grateful person." You will find it worthy, for its concrete form was the following recipe:

1 gal. wild cherries
1¼ gal. rye whiskey
1¼ (or 1½) lbs. sugar

Wash the cherries in two waters, and be sure that they are free from stems or leaves. Then put them in an earthenware container. Iron or tin will not serve. Put the whiskey with them and let them soak 18 to 24 hours. Mash two cupfuls of cherry seed in a mortar. Mash the cherries in the whiskey and add the seeds.

Boil the sugar in enough water to make a thick syrup. Let it cool, and add it to the alcohol mixture until the bitterness disappears. It must preserve, however, a piquant tang.

Strain the liquid three times through a closely woven cotton cloth.

CHERRY BOUNCE
Mrs. George Villere

wild cherries
alcohol
simple syrup

Half fill jug with wild cherries, then fill it with alcohol. Cork it and leave for six months, then drain off the first cherry bounce, reserving the cherries in the jug. The cherry bounce may be sweetened, when ready to serve, with simple syrup. Creole tradition has it that the unsweetened cherry bounce is an infallible cure for intestinal difficulties.

Into the cherries reserved from the cherry bounce in the gallon jug pour syrup to fill to the top. Cork and leave for three months. It will be ready to serve as it is and is almost as good as the first thick Cherry Bounce. This is called Piquet.

COCKTAIL SÉLINA
Mrs. J. N. Roussel

1 gal. whiskey
1 punch-glass Peychaud bitters
½ lemon, the peel
½ mandarin, the peel
1½ glasses simple syrup

Let stand three weeks, strain, and bottle. Be sure to use mandarins, not satsumas, as the flavor is entirely different. This keeps indefinitely. This is the first revelation of an old family secret of those **bons viveurs**, the Dugués.

A FAMOUS NEW ORLEANS DRINK—THE CONTRADICTION
Stanley Clisby Arthur

1 barspoon sugar
½ lemon—juice only
1 jigger rye whiskey

Mix in a barglass. Fill with cracked ice. Clap on the shaker and shake vigorously before straining into cocktail glass.

This is the drink a Frenchman had in mind when he walked into a New Orleans cocktail lounge and said to the man behind the bar:

"Mix for me, s'il vous plait, a contradictions."

"A which?" demanded the puzzled barkeep.

"Never heard of it, mister . . . how's it made?"

"You use whiskee to make eet strong; water to make eet weak; lemon juice to make eet sour, an' sugar to make eet sweet," explained the French visitor. "Zen you say: 'Here to you,' an' you drink eet yourself! Zat, sar, ees zee contradictions."

Whereupon the barkeep mixed the drink—which you will have no difficulty in recognizing as the old reliable, time-tested Whiskey Sour.

DAIQUIRI

2 limes, the juice
4 teaspoons sugar or four teaspoons grenadine
4 jiggers rum

Squeeze limes into cocktail shaker, add sugar and stir until well mixed, then add rum. Add crushed ice, shake until outside of shaker is frosted. Pour into cocktail glasses. Serves four.

1 teaspoon curacao for each jigger of rum is an excellent addition.

GEORGE WASHINGTON EGG-NOG
from my "Southern Christmas Book"
Harnett T. Kane

1 quart cream
1 quart milk
1 dozen eggs
1 dozen tablespoons sugar
1 pint brandy
½ pint rye
¼ pint sherry
¼ Jamaica or New England rum

Combine the liquors, then separate the eggs into yolks and whites. To the yolks, when beaten, add the sugar, and mix. To this slowly add the combined liquors, very lightly while you beat very slowly. Then add the milk and cream, again working slowly. Beat the egg whites until they are stiff and fold into the mïxtures, then set for hours in a cool place until ready to serve.

EGG-NOG
Mrs. David T. Merrick

12 eggs
1 qt. heavy cream
1 qt. best whiskey
1 qt. milk
8 tó 12 oz. rum
12 tablespoons sugar (level measurement)

Beat egg yolks very ligḥt, sift in 8 tablespoons sugar and beat vigorously. Stir ın whiskey, cream, and milk. Fold in the stiffly beaten egg whites to which the remainder of sugar has been added. Put in refrigerator until ready to serve. Extra whiskey may be used if flavor of rum is not desired. This may be made the day before using. Keeps well in refrigerator or freezer.

APRICOT FIZZ AU GEORGES

1 oz. apricot brandy
½ each lemon, lime, the juice
ice

Fill glass with White Rock.

DIAMOND FIZZ HIGHBALL
Col. Frank H. Lawton

1 jigger gin
1 teaspoon lemon juice
1 small lump sugar
champagne

Fill a tall glass with ice cubes and pour in the above and stir. Now fill with champagne. This is a sure cure for weariness.

½ champagne and ½ Baccardi rum makes a delicious and potent cocktail!

GIN FIZZ
Famous Ramos Style

The real art in making a Gin Fizz is in proper shaking. Don't just shake it up a few times and think you have done the job, because it is only started.

You need plenty of ice and you should shake until the contents of the Fizz have become so creamy that you won't be able to hear the ice tinkle against the sides of the shaker. Don't forget that, because your Gin Fizz won't be a real New Orleans concoc-

tion unless you follow these directions. Here's what goes into a Gin Fizz:

a dash of orange flower water
½ jigger lemon juice
½ tablespoon of simple syrup
2½ oz. of gin
2 oz. of cream
half of a white of one egg

These are the proportions of one drink.

GIN FIZZ "RAMOS"
Mr. S. A. Dobbs

1 teaspoon powdered sugar
½ teaspoon orange flower water
1 jigger Old Tom Gin
½ lemon, the juice
½ lime, the juice
1 egg white, beaten well
½ glass crushed ice
2 teaspoons rich cream
1 oz. seltzer water

Mix in this order: crushed ice, fruit juices, sugar, cream, orange flower water, gin, seltzer. Shake vigorously. Add beaten egg and shake until tired. Shake again!

GREEN FIZZ

1 teaspoon sugar
1 lemon, the juice
5 drops of crème de menthe
1 white of an egg
1 jigger gin

Shake with ice and serve in tall glasses.

FLAMING YOUTH

1 part honey
2 parts cream
2 parts gin (or whiskey)

Shake vigorously as for a gin-fizz. The result is smooth light cream gone snappy!

FOLKLORE COCKTAIL

2/3 gin
1/3 French vermouth
1/6 applejack
2 dashes orange bitters

Shake thoroughly with ice. Put a pearl onion in glass before serving.

This is a Martini with a little applejack added, and is one of the author's favorites.

GALATOIRE'S SPECIAL
Justin Galatoire
Galatoire's Restaurant, Inc.

½ ounce of Peychaud bitters
3 ounces of sugar syrup
6 drops of absinthe
1 lemon peel
28 ounces of good bourbon whiskey

Makes one quart. Bon appetit and good luck.

GARDEN OF EDEN HIGHBALL

This is a creation of the author's and is as good and refreshing as it is simple. It consists of applejack and sherry in equal parts, ice and soda.

An ordinary highball should have a genuine jigger (1 or 2 ozs.) of spirits. In this one, because of the relative weakness of sherry, use ¾ of a jigger each of the applejack and sherry. It is a good idea to keep a bottle of the applejack and sherry ready mixed. Put two cubes of ice in the highball glasses, three ounces of the mixture and fill with soda.

GUERRERO COCKTAIL

2 parts habañera
1 part orange juice
1 part lime juice
  sugar syrup to taste

Put the habañera in a saucepan on the fire until it steams.

Make a syrup of the sugar as usual. Put with other ingredients in a cocktail shaker with finely crushed ice and shake well. It adds point to the good-neighbor policy.

HONDURAS COCKTAIL

8 oz. gin
5 oz. vermouth
5 drops bitters
1 lemon, the juice
1 dessertspoon sugar
1 oz. absinthe
1 oz. crème de cacao
½ oz. Benedictine

Shake! Will serve eight.

LOUISIANA COCKTAIL

1 part Bourbon
¼ French vermouth
½ Italian vermouth
1 dash curacao

And swing into that "Bengal Swing."

MANHATTAN COCKTAIL

6 jiggers Bourbon Whiskey
2 jiggers sweet Italian Vermouth
4 dashes Angostura bitters
4 Maraschino cherries

Put several ice cubes in Cocktail shaker. Pour in cocktail. Stir till well chilled and pour into chilled glasses. Add cherries and serve.

KICK-OFF

2 dashes anisette
2 dashes Angostura bitters
2 dashes Benedictine
½ glass French vermouth
½ glass gin

Stir well and strain into a cocktail glass, add a twist of lemon peel.

MILK PUNCH
Mr. Stanhope Hopkins

1 cup milk
1 jigger Puerto Rico Rum
1 jigger brandy
1 teaspoon sugar
  sprinkle of nutmeg

Put in blender or shaker with 2 to 3 cubes of cracked ice. Shake or blend 3-4 minutes. Pour into Old Fashioned glasses. Sprinkle with ground nutmeg.

MINT JULEP BEAUREGARD
Mrs. David T. Merrick

2 teaspoons simple syrup or less
6 tablespoons whiskey
  sprigs of mint
  powdered ice

Have the mint fresh and dry. Let it soak in the whiskey an hour. Crush the ice to powder with a wooden mallet. Fill each glass to the top with ice, add the simple syrup, stir. Then add the whiskey. Stir again (never shake). Lastly, put a sprig of mint in the glass. Each glass should be made separately, and should frost.

MINT JULEP TO KEEP ON HAND
Mrs. John R. Peters

1 fifth bourbon
1/3 cup sugar
mint

Fill a quart bottle with mint and pour in bourbon. Add sugar. Shake to be sure sugar is dissolved. Put top on bottle, save bourbon bottle and set aside for 1 week. After a week, mint will be wilted, and bourbon will have strong mint flavor. Strain. Squeeze extra bourbon out of mint leaves, and throw leaves away. Return to bourbon bottle and place in freezer. Keeps indefinitely. When ready to serve, pour over crushed ice in Julep cup. Decorate with sprig of mint.

ST. REGIS MINT JULEP
Stanley C. Arthur

    1 teaspoon sugar
    1 teaspoon water
    1 dozen mint leaves
    1 jigger rye whiskey
    1 pony rum
    1 dash grenadine syrup

In a tall glass crush the mint leaves in the water and sugar with a long handled spoon. When dissolved pour in the jigger (1½ ozs.) of rye whiskey, then the pony (1 oz.) of rum, and the dash of grenadine syrup. Stir well, crushing the mint leaves. Fill glass to the top with finely crushed ice and jiggle well with the spoon. When properly frappéd decorate the top with sprigs of mint leaves.

Many people who know their liquor claim it is rank heresy to use anything but Bourbon in a mint julep because that's the only way a julep was ever made. Unfortunately these mint-flavored experts are not up on julep history or they would know that the original julep was made of rum, and the use of corn liquor was only a Kentucky afterthought. Mixed drinks can sometimes be improved upon and in consequence there are, besides whiskey juleps, those which have, as the spirit of the drink, rum, cognac, or peach brandy.

Unquestionably the best julep I have ever drawn through a straw is the one given above. Note that the recipe departs in three important ways from the usual—the whiskey is rye and not Bourbon, it contains a pony of rum and a dash of grenadine syrup. It is the masterpiece served in the good old summer time by John Swago at the St. Regis restaurant bar in New Orleans. If ever a saint was honored it is Saint Regis—whoever he was.

NEW IBERIA COCKTAIL

    2 parts brandy
    1 part French vermouth
    1 part sherry
    2 or 3 drops Tabasco.

Shake!

NEW ORLEANS COCKTAIL

    1 part whiskey
    1 teaspoon syrup
    2 dashes Peychaud's bitters
    1 dash absinthe

While these are getting acquainted frappé an old fashioned glass, throw out the ice and rinse glass with absinthe; then strain the cocktail into it and serve with ice water on the side.

O'JEN
Mrs. H. Waller Fowler

    ½ gal. alcohol, 198 proof
    1 qt. boiling water
    1 qt. simple syrup
    120 drops oil of anise
    12 drops oil of caraway

Drop the oils into the alcohol, and let stand 24 hours in a gallon jug, so that the essential oils may have time to blend thoroughly. Mix the water and the syrup together. Then pour the alcohol into the syrup-and-water mixture, and shake well. Allow to stand 48 hours.

Bottle, and age at least 60 days.

If the liquid becomes somewhat cloudy or murky, it makes no difference; when the ice is added to serve it, it always clouds anyway.

When serving, a few drops of Angostura bitters may be added, if desired.

ORANGE COOLER
Mrs. Victor H. Schiro

    1 bottle orange wine
      same amount bottled soda
      water
    2 ozs. fruit brandy
    2 ozs. curacao or triple sec

Pour liquid ingredients over ice into a large pitcher or other container and stir until cold. Garnish with curled pieces of orange or lemon rind, one to each glass.
Serves 10.

ORANGE FLOWER SYRUP
Mrs. Irene Keep Hughes

It was a pleasant old custom on the Louisiana plantations to serve afternoon callers with a drink made from this syrup. The recipe is copied from the original which I found among my mother's papers. She says, "A teaspoonful in a glass of water is an excellent tonic for the nerves." The drink was made by using a small quantity of the syrup in a tall glass filled with crushed ice and seltzer water. Orgeat syrup, made from almonds, was used in the same way, and also syrups made from strawberries, raspberries, or blackberries.

Select and wash without bruising 1 pint of white petals of the orange flavor. While they drain on a cloth prepare a rich syrup of granulated sugar and water, the same as for any fruit syrup, allowing 1 quart of syrup for each pint of petals. After skimming carefully drop in the petals and simmer two minutes. Stir gently, strain and bottle. Seal while hot. It will be a delicate sea green color and retains all the fragrance of the flower. It may be used to flavor custards, icings, or pudding sauces.

PEACHES A-GLOW
Mrs. William J. Bentley

6 large luscious peaches
simple syrup
champagne

Remove seeds from peaches, cover with simple syrup, chill in refrigerator, when ready to serve place a peach in a large glass, fill glass with very cold champagne.

This can be served before a meal or it serves as a delicious finish to a dinner.

PLANTER'S PUNCH
Reginald W. Titmas

This is an excellent drink developed in the tropics by the sugar cane planters. It has nothing to do with the drink served at bars under the same name—an impossible sweet concoction loaded down with slices of pineapple and orange and other trimmings to disguise the absence of rum.

In the old days each plantation had its own crude sugar mill and made brown sugar of indifferent quality. The money crop was rum. As the sugar was poorly refined there was a large quantity of molasses of excellent quality left over which went down to the still house to be turned into the famous Jamaica Rum. Limes grew or were planted no doubt when it was found that a combination of lime juice, sugar, rum and water, made a palatable and cooling drink. Due to the extreme heat planters are early risers. Four a.m. saw them up and about. By ten a.m. a drink was definitely indicated. Hence the Planter's Punch!

All the ingredients were nearby. Ice was not available but water was kept cool in a stone pitcher. It was mixed by rolling between the palms of the hands, a "swizzle stick." Planter's Punch should never be shaken.

In Jamaica, where the writer enjoyed his first drink of this nectar he was taught the rhyme of the recipe which is as follows:

One of sour (lime juice)
Two of sweet (brown sugar)
Three of strong (rum)
Four of weak (water)
A little nutmeg you must add
Then the mixture isn't bad.

Apparently this rhyme was made to help the sale of sugar. The writer finds that one of sugar makes a better drink. As for nutmeg, he believes this was added later by a limerick addict. However, some people have been known actually to like nutmeg.

In America the best liked drink is as follows:

For each person:
1 jigger lime or lemon juice
2 teaspoons brown sugar
3 jiggers rum (expensive rum is not necessary)
3 jiggers water (the melting ice will supply the fourth jigger of water)

Put the sugar and water into a pitcher and stir until dissolved. Add lime juice and sufficient cracked ice to chill thoroughly. Add the rum and stir with a swizzle stick, or large spoon. When it is well blended and chilled remove the ice and serve in small tumblers or cocktail glasses. One to a person is enough though the writer has never turned down a second helping.

SAN DOMINGO JULEP
Terry Flettrich

This seems to be the original mint julep that came to Louisiana away back in 1793, at the time the white aristocrats, who were expelled from San Domingo by the uprising of the blacks, settled in New Orleans. In the United States, especially those states south of the Mason and Dixon line, Bourbon whiskey gradually took the place of sugar cane rum as the spirit of the drink.

    1 piece of loaf sugar
    1½ jiggers rum
        sprigs of mint

Into a tall glass (preferably a metal goblet) drop the sugar and moisten with a little water. Take several mint leaves and crush while the sugar is being muddled with the barspoon. Fill with shaved or finely crushed ice. Pour in the rum. Jiggle to frappe the mixture. Set a bouquet of mint leaves on top before serving. A slice of orange peel for garnish is ritzy but not strictly necessary.

SANGRIA
Pam Hayne

    ½ gal. red wine (burgundy)
    ½ cup sugar (more if you
        like it sweeter)
    1 cup brandied fruit

Mix together and chill. Serve over ice and garnish with a sprig of mint. Good for a picnic.

SAZERAC COCKTAIL
Terry Flettrich

    1 teaspoon simple syrup
    1 jigger Bourbon whiskey
    2 or 3 dashes Angostura bitters
        ice cube
    2 or 3 drops Peychaud bitters
        few drops absinthe
        outside rind of lemon
        avoiding white skin

Place syrup in tumbler. Add whiskey and bitters. Place cube of ice in glass and stir ½ minute or so. Pour the whole into cold tumbler, inside edges of which have been "perfumed" with absinthe. (This is done by placing a few drops of absinthe in glass, and twisting until edges are coated.)

Before serving press juice of lemon rind into cocktail. Serve while cold.

SIMPLE SYRUP

The simple syrup referred to in many of the recipes in this section is made by mixing sugar and water together in the proportions of two parts of sugar to one part of water. It should be brought to a good boil and may be kept indefinitely in the refrigerator.

GOODNIGHT STINKERS
Editors

Mix equal parts brandy and white creme de menthe. Put in blender filled with ice and whirl until frapped.

Size of serving container depends upon weight of guest and previous consumption. Serve. . .place guest on stretcher and top with empty brandy bottle.

STRAWBERRY COCKTAIL

One part gin and one part fresh strawberry juice slightly sweetened. Shake well. Makes summer a triumph.

SUGAR BOWL COCKTAIL

    ¼ sloe gin
    ¼ French vermouth
    ¼ rum
    1 teaspoon sugar
    1 dash Peychaud's bitters

Named after New Orleans' New Year's Day Football Classic.

A SUMMER SPECIAL

    2 measures gin
        a dash of simple syrup
        a dash of lemon juice
        mint, crushed

Put mint in a tall glass, then gin and other ingredients, plenty of crushed ice, fill with seltzer. Stir until glass is frosted as in a mint julep.

THE TENDER TRAP
Fred Otell

In a blender put (for each drink):

1½ ounces light Bacardi Rum
1 teaspoon frozen limeade
1 teaspoon frozen grapefruit juice
1 teaspoon reconstituted lime juice
1 maraschino cherry
2 cubes ice, crushed

Run blender until thoroughly mixed. Pass through strainer (coarse) into 5 oz. glasses and serve.

TOM COLLINS (FIREMAN COOLER)
Mrs. W. E. Laudeman III

1 jigger frozen pink lemonade
1 jigger of gin or vodka
  soda to fill

One will ring your bell, two will definitely alarm you. . .

HOT TOM AND JERRY
Dr. Emile Naef

6 eggs
2 teaspoons sugar
6 jiggers brandy
6 jiggers rum, dark
  Puerto Rican
  nutmeg
  hot water

Separate whites and yolks of eggs. Add sugar to egg yolks and beat thoroughly. Beat whites until stiff, fold into yolks when ready to serve.

For serving fill one third of a Tom and Jerry mug with the above mixture. Add a jigger of brandy and a jigger of rum. Add the hot water (the hotter the better) stirring vigorously all the time. Sprinkle with nutmeg. This recipe serves six. Wonderful for a cold night!

TROPIC COOLER

6 or 8 sprigs mint
1½ cups sugar
5 lemons
3/4 cup water
3 bottles ginger ale

Put the sugar and water on the stove long enough to melt the sugar thoroughly. Cool. Add lemon juice and the crushed mint. Place in the refrigerator. When ready to serve, strain. Fill the glass with ice, fill each glass a quarter full of the mixture, and fill the remainder with ginger ale. Stir.

WHISKEY SOUR

1 lemon, the juice
2 teaspoons sugar
3 dashes bitters
2 jiggers of Bourbon Whiskey

Dissolve the sugar in the lemon juice with bitters. Add the whiskey. Shake well with chopped ice. Strain and serve with an orange slice.

WHISKEY TODDY BELLE CHASSE

2 teaspoons simple syrup
½ teaspoon orange flower water
1 twist lemon peel
1 jigger Bourbon, or rye whiskey
  ice, nutmeg

To a glass of cracked ice, add the simple syrup, orange flower water, and the lemon peel. Stir with a spoon till the glass is well chilled. Never shake. Then add the whiskey, and a dash of nutmeg. Make each glass separately. Drink, and the world assumes a brighter hue.

UNIVERSITY COCKTAIL

½ brandy
¼ anisette
¼ French vermouth
2 dashes Peychaud's bitters
1 dash absinthe
1 dash orange flower water

"Here's a song for the Olive and Blue."

ZEPHYR

1 part Italian vermouth
1 part Dubonnet
1 part orange juice

Serve with crushed ice. A refreshing apéritif of the French mode.

appetizers and hors d'oeuvres

ANCHOVY CANAPES
Miss Julie Folwell

1 can anchovy filets
2 hard boiled eggs
parsley, mustard and salt and
  pepper to taste

Make rounds of toast, spread with sweet butter, season with salt, pepper and mustard to taste. Arrange anchovy filets on these in form of a rosette or across. Garnish with finely chopped parsley. Press the yolk of a hard boiled egg, and some little of the white as well, through a sieve and arrange in a ring around the edges of the rounds.

SMALL JELLIED APPETIZERS
Mrs. R. C. Tipton

2 cans beef consomme
2 packages Lipton's dried onion
  soup
1 cup water
3 envelopes Knox's gelatine
3 cups meat, chicken, or fish, well
  chopped
1 tablespoon Worcestershire sauce
  few drops garlic juice, salt,
  pepper, to taste

Cook Lipton's soup according to directions on package. Soak gelatine in water a few minutes and add to the hot onion soup. Add consomme, meat, and seasonings. Fill tiny ice cube molds and put in icebox to set. Turn out and serve on small crackers.

STUFFED ARTICHOKE
LEAVES
Mrs. W. E. Laudeman III

6 large artichokes
1 pt. fresh mushrooms, minced
3/4 lb. boiled minced ham
1/3 cup olive oil (May need more)
3 cloves garlic, minced
3 shallots, minced

3 tablespoons fresh minced parsley
1/2 teaspoon oregano
3/4 cup fresh grated parmesan
  or Romano cheese
1 cup cracker crumbs
1½ teaspoon garlic juice
  salt and pepper
  butter

Boil artichokes until tender and leaves pull easily in very salty water to which 1 tablespoon olive oil has been added. Remove firm outer leaves and set aside. Scrape vegetable meat from remaining leaves and mince hearts.

Saute garlic and mushrooms in olive oil. Add ham, oregano, parsley and grated cheese, 2/3 cup crumbs, salt and pepper to taste, and the artichoke meats. Cook, stirring over low heat, until mixture becomes very thick in consistency.

Combine remaining crumbs and grated cheese. Add water and olive oil until stuffing consistency. Stuff leaves with artichoke mixture and roll leaves in the cheese crumb mixture. Dot each leaf with butter and drizzle with olive oil.

Place in oven for 30 minutes or until cheese melts. Serve hot as an hors d'oeuvre.

BACON WRAPPED CHICKEN
LIVERS, OYSTERS, SHRIMP
OR OLIVES
Editors

1 lb. chicken livers
1 lb. peeled and deveined shrimp
1 pt. oysters, OR
1 can pitted or stuffed
  (almond or anchovy) olives
1 lb. bacon
  garlic salt and pepper

Wrap each chicken liver, etc., in ½ strip of bacon. Secure with toothpick. Sprinkle with garlic salt and pepper. (Sliced water chestnuts are a nice addition to these appetizers, as they provide a crunchy taste.)

Broil in a 350° oven until bacon is cooked. Serve immediately.

BEURRE D'ANCHOIS

Mrs. Alfred T. Pattison

½ lb. best quality salt anchovies
(Use nothing but salt anchovies in brine)
½ lb. unsalted butter

Soak anchovies in water for half hour, changing water three times. Remove, wipe with a cloth to rémove all scales. Split in half lengthwise and remove bones and fins. Wipe with a dry cloth to insure absence of fins, bones or scales. Put anchovies in a bowl and mash until a perfect pulp is obtained. Then mix with butter. Serve cold but not as hard as butter which is used at the table. It should neither be too soft nor yet too hard. Never use anchovy paste. The secret is in reducing the anchovies to a pulp and in having them free from bones and scales. This is a very recherché hors d'oeuvre in France.

BOUCHÉES D'ANCHOIS

pie crust
tube of anchovy paste

Make a nice pie or biscuit crust, cut into rounds with small biscuit cutter. Into each round, squeeze a small quantity of anchovy paste. Fold over the round and press down the edges with a fork. Prick the top with the fork and bake in a hot oven.

BOUCHÉES SURPRISES

½ lb. chipped beef
4 Philadelphia cream cheeses
a few shallots, chopped fine
1 cup shelled walnuts, chopped fine

Get the chipped beef freshly sliced so it will not be dry.

Cream the cheese. Add the walnuts and the white tender part only of the shallots.

Take a slice of chipped beef, lay it on the biscuit board, put in a small quantity of cheese mixture and roll. Trim off the ends. When finished, each roll should be the size of a thin

finger. These are better after staying a few hours in a cold place.

If the flavor is preferred the cream cheese may be mixed with horseradish and cayenne pepper to taste.

CANAPÉ EGYPTIAN

Mrs. Edgar H. Bright

1 jar chipped beef
2 teaspoons catsup
3 teaspoons mayonnaise
cayenne pepper
toast rounds or crackers

Add a dash of cayenne pepper to chipped beef. Cut in small pieces; mix catsup, mayonnaise. Serve on toast rounds or crackers.

CELERY FARCI

Mr. Fred Otell

¼ lb. Roquefort cheese
½ lb. cream cheese
2 lemons
1 teaspoon Worcestershire sauce
½ cup mayonnaise
paprika

Blend with a silver fork the cheeses and the mayonnaise. Add the lemon juice, the Worcestershire Sauce and the paprika. Put in a pastry tube and stuff in short tender stalks of celery, and your guests will drink their cocktails with more relish.

ADMIRAL'S GOLDEN BUCK

1 lb. grated American sharp cheese
1 egg
1 tablespoon butter
½ teaspoon salt
1 tablespoon Worcestershire sauce
¼ coffee spoon cayenne pepper
2 doz. rounds of thinly sliced bread

Mix cheese, butter and raw egg together. Add seasoning, cover and put in refrigerator. When ready to serve, toast the rounds of bread to straw color. Spread the mixture on the rounds and run under the flame of the gas stove for 3 minutes until cheese melts. The mixture will keep for days.

It may be spread on the toasted **bread** rounds some time before serving if desired, and the whole heated just before serving.

PIERRE'S CHEESE ANCHOVY APPETIZER

1 Philadelphia cream cheese
1 small can anchovies, mashed
1½ teaspoons capers, mashed
½ teaspoon grated onion
½ teaspoon Worcestershire sauce
2 or more tablespoons cream or milk
cayenne to taste

Cream cheese with cream. Add other ingredients. Serve on round salted crackers. This mixture keeps well.

CHEESE BALLS
Mrs. Richard Adler

½ lb. sharp cheese
1 cup flour
1 stick butter
salt
paprika

Soften butter and cheese; add other ingredients. Roll into small balls. Refrigerate overnight.
To serve, warm in oven pre-heated to 450° for 10 minutes. Makes approximately 50 servings.

SARA'S CHEESE BITS
Mrs. J. W. Thompson
Paris, Kentucky

1 cup flour
1 cup strongest cheddar cheese, grated
1 stick butter
1 cup Rice Crispies

Work dough with hands until completely soft. Make into small balls and put on cookie sheet. Mash each one down with a fork. Bake at 350° for 10-12 minutes. These can be frozen.

CHEESE BALL
Mrs. Walter Hagestad

6 ozs. Bleu Cheese
2 5-oz. jars Old English Cheese
4 3-oz. packs Philadelphia Cream Cheese
2 teaspoons onion puree
1 teaspoon Lea & Perrins
½ teaspoon Accent
¼ cup chopped parsley
½ cup finely chopped pecans

Let all ingredients soften for several hours in large bowl. Mix thoroughly. Put in refrigerator to harden enough to handle. Form into one large ball, or two small ones. Roll in finely chopped pecans. This freezes beautifully. Have at room temperature when ready to serve.

BOUCHÉES SOUFFLÉES

Use very small muffin tin. Line each mold to height of ½ inch with pastry or thin slices of bread and bake. Half fill each with cheese soufflé mixture, and run in the oven. Bake about ten minutes and serve piping hot.

CHEESE CHILI CON QUOTIS
Editors

1 lb. Velveeta cheese (or any other processed cheese)
2 onions, finely chopped
1 garlic toe, finely minced
1 can Ro-Tel tomatoes (Green tomatoes and chilies), drained
1 tablespoon cornstarch or instant blending flour
¼ stick margarine
1 tablespoon Lea & Perrins sauce

Saute onions and garlic in the margarine. Add the Lea & Perrins. Melt cheese separately in top of a double boiler. Add Rotel mixture to the melted cheese. Serve in heated chafing dish. Fritos or tortilla chips may be used for dipping.

CHEESE CRESCENTS
Editor

1 cup water, cold
1 stick butter or margarine, cut in small pieces
1 teaspoon salt
½ teaspoon cayenne pepper
1 cup sifted flour
4 eggs
¼ lb. Swiss cheese, finely diced
¼ teaspoon Coleman's dry mustard

In saucepan, bring water, butter, salt and cayenne to a boil. Add at once the sifted floor. Cook this paste over low flame, stirring constantly until it forms a ball and leaves the side of the pan. Turn off heat and add eggs one at a time, heating well after each addition.

Add diced cheese and dry mustard. Allow mixture to cool.

Fill pastry bag fitted with No. 5 tube with pastry mixture and pipe it into crescent shapes on a cookie sheet. Brush crescents with milk and bake 10 minutes in a 425° oven. Lower heat to 375° and bake an additional 20 - 25 minutes until puffed and golden. Cool on wire rack.

Slit crescents and fill with pate de foie gras or ham filling just before serving. Best served warm.

HAM FILLING
Combine in mixing bowl:
  2¼ cups finely chopped ham
  1½ tablespoons grated onion
  1 teaspoon homemade mayonnaise
    pinch dry mustard
    sour cream, enough to bind the mixture

After slitting the warm crescents, stuff about 1 teaspoon (or as much as you can fit without an overflow) into the slit. If crescents are warm enough, serve as is. If not, reheat with filling in on the cookie sheet.

CHEESE CRUMBLES
Mrs. Ward Freeman

  ½ lb. butter or oleo
  ½ lb. sharp cheddar cheese, grated or ground
  3 cups flour sifted with
  ¼ teaspoon red pepper, salt
  1 egg

Cream the butter and cheese together. Add sifted flour and pepper, a little at a time, kneading until it will hold together. Roll out as for cookies and cut into small attractive shape with a cookie cutter. Dilute one whole egg with a little water and brush the top of each cookie. Bake about eight minutes in a 350 degree oven watching carefully as they burn easily. After taking from the oven sprinkle liberally with salt. Allow to cool in the pan.

CROQUETTES DE CAMEMBERT

  3½ ozs. flour
  5½ ozs. butter
  5½ ozs. Camembert cheese
  2 egg yolks
  1 pinch cayenne
  1 pinch paprika
  1 egg, bread crumbs

Mix the ingredients on a marble slab. Knead the paste three times and make it into a ball. Let it stand for 2 hours, then roll it out and cut into any desired shape. Dip the pieces of paste into the beaten egg and roll them in fine bread crumbs. Fry in hot fat and serve on a serviette.

They can be speared with toothpicks and served with cocktails and they are delicious, too, with salads.

GALETTES AU ROQUEFORT
Mrs. Walter Torian

  1 cup butter
  1 cup Roquefort cheese
  2 tablespoons Worcestershire sauce
  5 drops of Tabasco

Cream the butter and cheese together, add seasoning. Spread as appetizer on salted crackers. It can keep in the icebox for a week.

CHEESE-OLIVE APPETIZER
Mrs. Frank C. Moran, Jr.

  25 medium size stuffed olives
  1 cup shredded cheddar cheese
  2 tablespoons butter
  ½ cup flour
    cayenne to taste

Cream butter and cheese. Add flour and cayenne. Wrap teaspoonful of dough completely around an olive. Bake on wax paper, ungreased, in a hot oven for 15 minutes. Serve warm.

OLD FAITHFUL CHEESE AND ONION PUFFS
Mrs. Joseph Merrick Jones, Jr.

  16 ozs. grated sharp American cheese
  4 - 5 shallots with tops, finely chopped
    Hellman's mayonnaise, enough to bind the mixture
    cayenne pepper to taste

Blend all together by hand. Be sure to use the Hellman's mayonnaise, as the others do not puff up. Put about a teaspoon on Melba toast rounds, and heat in 350° oven until bubbly and the cheese has melted.

This is called old faithful because it will keep in a closed jar in the refrigerator for weeks, and is perfect for last minute guests.

MABEL'S SUPERB CHEESE PECAN WAFERS

Mr. H. W. Rhodes

1 lb. grated sharp cheese
½ lb. butter
2 cups all-purpose flour
1 cup finely chopped pecans
1 teaspoon salt
    red pepper

Cream cheese and butter, add flour, salt, red pepper and nuts. Roll and wrap tightly in wax paper and put in freezer for at least 24 hours. When ready to serve, cut in ¼ inch slices and bake in 350° oven for 12 minutes. Roll should be about 1¼ inches in diameter.

Can also be served with salad.

CHEESE PUFFS

Mrs. Robert Brehm

2 small jars (5 oz.) sharp cheese spread
1 stick of butter or margerine
1½ cups all-purpose flour
    teaspoon of Worcestershire sauce
    generous dash of cayenne pepper

Blend butter and cheese then add flour and seasonings and mix well. Roll into balls the size of a walnut and let stand in refrigerator for several hours. Bake in a hot over (400°) for about ten minutes or until slightly brown. These keep well in the refrigerator and can even be frozen then baked.

CHEESE ROLL

Mrs. Charles L. Cox

1 lb. pecans
1 large onion
3 packages Philadelphia cream cheese
3 packages Old English cheese
½ lb. Blue cheese

Leave cheese out of refrigerator for 7 or 8 hours—until soft. Grind pecans and onion through meat grinder, using the smallest disc. Add to cheese and mix thoroughly. Mold with hands into one large ball and place in refrigerator for several days before using. When wanted remove for a little while, roll in chopped parsley and watercress. Serve with rye crackers. The cheese can be made in small rolls and stored in deep freeze until needed. Good snack at Christmas time or to serve with cocktails.

ROQUEFORT CHEESE MICHEL

½ cup butter, unsalted
2 cups Roquefort cheese
2 tablespoons Worcestershire sauce
3 drops Tabasco
4 white shallots, cut very fine

Cream butter until soft. Mash the cheese well and add. Mix well, then add Worcestershire, Tabasco, and finely chopped shallots. This mixture will keep well in the refrigerator. Serve on crackers.

ROQUEFORT ROLL WALDORF

¼ lb. Roquefort cheese
2 small packs Philadelphia cream
    cheese
1½ tablespoons soft butter
1 stalk celery, chopped fine
½ green pepper, chopped fine
3 sprigs parsley, chopped fine
4 tablespoons chopped walnuts
1 teaspoon dry sherry
3 drops Tabasco

Reserve 3 tablespoons chopped walnuts.

Form rest of mixture in a small ball or roll and chill at least 4 hours in the ice box. Sprinkle with finely chopped nuts and serve, cut in slices with a green salad.

HOT CHEESE STRAWS

Mrs. Walter J. Barnes

1 cup flour (sifted)
1 pound of sharp cheddar cheese
    (grated)
1 stick of butter
1 pinch of salt
1 teaspoon of cayenne pepper or
    Tabasco

Cream cheese, butter, salt and pepper together. Add flour. Mix well. Place in cookie press and roll out in long ribbons. Bake in medium oven eight to ten minutes. Cool and break, or cut to desired size. Will last a month in cookie tins.

CHEESE STRAWS

Mrs. John C. Calhoun

7 ozs. extra sharp grated cheddar
    cheese
3/4 stick butter
1 cup sifted, self-rising flour
½ tablespoon cayenne pepper
    dash of salt

Cream cheese and butter. Add flour, salt and pepper. Mix until well blended. Place in a cookie press. Roll out on a cookie sheet. Bake in a 275° oven about 30 minutes, or until firm.

CHEESE STRAWS
Mrs. R. E. Tipton

¼ lb. butter
2 cups grated sharp cheese
1½ cups flour, sifted
1½ teaspoons baking powder
1½ teaspoons salt
½ teaspoon red pepper

Cream the butter, add grated cheese. Cream well together and mix in dry ingredients. Roll out to ⅛ of an inch thick, cut in strips ½ inch wide and bake in a moderate oven until delicately browned.

Do not grease or flour cookie sheet. Bake about fifteen minutes. Do not allow to get brown.

CHEESE STRAWS
Mrs. Gordon Francis Wilson

1 stick butter (softened)
¼ lb. sharp cheese (grated)
1 cup and 2 tablespoons of flour
    (after sifting)
⅛ teaspoon salt
¼ teaspoon cayenne pepper

Mix all ingredients, stirring only until all blended. Put through press onto cookie sheet in long strips. Bake in 350°-375° oven for 10 minutes. Cut into desired lengths when cool.

CHEESE STRAWS
Mrs. Harry Winters

1 cup flour
2 cups grated sharp cheese
½ teaspoon salt
1/3 teaspoon red pepper
3 tablespoons melted butter

Mix well and work with hands until it forms a soft ball. Use cookie press, and turn out using star-press plate. Bake in moderate oven 400 degrees until brown.

Note—All recipes for Cheese Straws may be served with salads.

TULANE FOOTBALLS
(Cheese Dates)
Mrs. Herbert Eugene Longenecker

1 box seeded dates (filled with any
    kind of nuts and rolled in sugar)
¼ lb. oleo
½ lb. cheese, medium sharp
1½ cups flour
    pinch of salt
    paprika

Grate cheese. Pour melted oleo over cheese, add salt and flour. Mix. Work with hands around dates. Sprinkle with paprika. Bake 300° ½ hr. to 40 minutes. Do not brown.

CHICKEN BITS IN BEER BATTER
Mrs. Charles Richards

6 chicken breasts, de-boned and
    cut in bite size pieces
2 cups flour
1½ cups beer
1 tablespoon paprika
1 tablespoon salt
1 tablespoon pepper

Mix batter made of flour, beer, salt, pepper and paprika by hand, or whirl all together in a blender. Dip chicken pieces in batter and fry in deep fat. Makes about 24 bits.

This may be used for shrimp or fish bites as well and is delicious. Use dips of your own choice.

AVOCADO OR GUACAMOLE DIP
Mrs. Joseph Merrick Jones, Jr.

2 large avocadoes or 3 small, ripe
    juice of 2 small lemons
2 tomatoes, peeled
2 tablespoons garlic salt
1 teaspoon cayenne
5 shallots, chopped fine
1 teaspoon salt
1 teaspoon black pepper
¼ cup olive oil
¼ cup mayonnaise

Coarsely mash avocadoes with potato masher or fork. Chop tomatoes and shallots and add to mashed avocadoes with the rest of the ingredients. Mix together and serve with chips of your liking.

AVOCAT TARAMA OUVÉ
Dr. George Davis Gammon

1 avocado (very ripe)
2 tablespoons homemade mayonnaise
2 tablespoons of lemon juice
small amount of chopped shallots
2 tablespoons Italian carp roe caviar
salt to taste

Mash avocado with mayonnaise, lemon juice, shallots and salt. Stir in caviar. Mound in bowl and heap small amount of carp caviar in center. Serve with crisp crackers, toast rounds or potato chips.

BROCCOLI DIP
Editors

1 medium onion, finely chopped
3 stalks celery, finely chopped
1 medium can mushrooms (stems and pieces)
1 package frozen chopped broccoli
1 can cream of mushroom soup
1 roll garlic cheese

Saute celery, onions and mushrooms in butter. Cook broccoli according to package directions and drain well. Combine above and add mushroom soup, undiluted. Melt cheese in top of double boiler. Combine all in chafing dish and serve.

Use Fritos, toast rounds, or favorite crackers to serve.

C'EST LA VIE WHIP
Mrs. Laurraine Goreau
Women's Editor, N.O. States-Item

4½ oz. can of shrimp
1 lemon—juice of
2 tablespoons mayonnaise
½ teaspoon yellow mustard
½ teaspoon dry mustard
½ teaspoon hot horseradish (fresh)
½ teaspoon paprika (fresh)
2/3 cup cottage cheese
2 heaping tablespoons prepared chives—Philadelphia cream cheese
1 3-oz. package Philadelphia cream cheese

Combine all ingredients and whip with handbeater for salad stuffing or sandwich spread. Electric beater is preferable for creamy dip.

For the hurried hostess, C'Est La Vie Whip can assume as many guises as you have ingenuity to vary it. It is perfectly at home as a salad when spooned over fresh or canned pears; over leafy lettuce, crisped in the refrigerator; over fresh (cooked) or canned asparagus; as a fill in avocado or tomato centers. It is also an excellent tea-sandwich spread. To switch identity to an excellent dip, add to the above recipe the following:

Onion salt and garlic salt to taste, and thin a trifle with sour cream to smooth, almost flowing consistency.

Basic recipe may be divided into 3 or 4 portions, and distinctive flavor additions introduced into extra portions for easy party preparation.

VEGETABLE DIP FOR HORS D'OEUVRES

2 cups mayonnaise
1 lemon, juice
6 drops Tabasco
1 tablespoon Lea & Perrins
2 tablespoons horseradish
red pepper to taste
2 tablespoons mustard seed
2 tablespoons celery seed
1½ tablespoons onion juice

This recipe makes about 2 cups. It may be used as a salad dressing, especially good with crab or shrimp.

SPINACH DIP (FOR FRESH VEGETABLES)
Editors

2½ cups sour cream
1½ cups finely chopped raw spinach
1/3 cup chopped scallions or chives
1/3 cup chopped parsley
1½ teaspoons salt
dash Tabasco
cracked pepper to taste
½ teaspoon garlic chips
1 teaspoon Parmesan cheese

Wash spinach. Wring dry with linen towel. Combine ingredients. Garnish with chopped parsley (an extra teaspoon). Chill and serve with carrot sticks, shallots, cherry tomatoes, cauliflower florets, sliced raw mushrooms, radishes, sliced raw broccoli or celery. Take your pick!! Cooked, peeled shrimp are also good with this.

TANGO CREAM
Mrs. Wm. Callon

4 Philadelphia cream cheeses
3 teaspoons horseradish
3 teaspoons Worcestershire sauce
3 teaspoons onion juice
1 teaspoon salt
4 tablespoons heavy cream
10 shakes Tabasco sauce

Mash the cheese with a fork until creamy, add all other ingredients except cream, blending together smoothly. Then add the cream. Mix an hour or more before using. Do not 'put in refrigerator as it hardens quickly. Serve with crisp potato chips, which are dipped into the mixture. This sauce keeps well in refrigerator.

EGGPLANT APPETIZER
Alex Ficklen

2 eggplants
2 onions
2 sweet peppers
2 small cans tomato sauce
1 cup vinegar
½ cup sugar
3 pods of garlic
2 2-oz. jars of capers

In your largest iron pot, uncovered, brown in olive oil two diced eggplants, two minced onions and two minced sweet peppers. Then pour in two cans of tomato sauce, one cup of vinegar and a half cup of sugar. Add several pods of garlic, minced, and simmer, still uncovered, till eggplant is soft and all is well blended. Then add two bottles of capers from which the vinegar in which they have been pickled is drained.

This must be kept in the icebox.

LIVER PASTE
Hermann B. Deutsch

1 lb. beef liver (venison if possible)
1 lb. ham fat
4 medium onions
1 tablespoon of oregano or
   marjoram
salt and pepper to taste

To one pound of beef (or venison, if possible) liver add one pound of ham fat, four medium onions, a little salt, and a heaping tablespoon of marjoram or oregano (they are both the same

thing). Cut them all in pieces that will go through a food grinder, and put the mixture through the food grinder twice, after which, if you really want to do a job, put it a little at a time through an electric blender. Pour the resulting batter-like blend into a baking pan, and bake in a 350-degree oven for three quarters of an hour. Set it aside to cool and refrigerate, serving it cold.

COCKTAIL SIZE ITALIAN MEATBALLS
Mrs. W. Elliot Laudeman III

1½ lbs. ground beef
½ cup freshly grated Parmesan cheese
2 cloves minced garlic
1 onion, finely chopped
1 cup Italian bread crumbs
1 teaspoon oregano
1 teaspoon salt
½ teaspoon pepper
2 tablespoons chopped parsley
2 slightly beaten eggs
   olive oil

In large mixing bowl combine meat, cheese, bread crumbs and seasonings. Saute onions and garlic in small amount of olive oil. Add to meat mixture. Add egg for binding and mix thoroughly. Form into bite size balls and brown in olive oil.

SAUCE:
1 onion, finely chopped
2 cloves minced garlic
1 bell pepper, diced
2 packages Lawry's Italian spaghetti
   sauce mix
1 can tomato paste
1 8-oz. can tomato sauce
3 tablespoons freshly grated
   Parmesan cheese
1 teaspoon crushed oregano
½ teaspoon sugar
   salt and pepper to taste

Saute onions, bell pepper and garlic in olive oil. Add remaining ingredients and simmer for five minutes. Pour sauce over meatballs in a chafing dish. Serve with toothpicks.

COCKTAIL SIZE SWEDISH MEATBALLS
Mrs. W. Elliott Laudeman III

1 lb. ground beef
½ lb. ground pork

½ cup grated sharp cheese
2 cloves garlic minced
1 onion finely chopped
2 shallots finely chopped
¼ bunch parsley - finely chopped
1 cup French bread crumbs,
    more or less
1 teaspoon salt
½ teaspoon pepper
2 eggs, slightly beaten
1 pinch of thyme
1 pinch of oregano
    olive oil
1½ stalks celery, finely chopped

Saute onions, garlic, and celery in small amount of oil. Add parsley, stir. Combine other ingredients and seasonings and add sauted mixture to this. Add more or less bread crumbs until a good consistency is obtained for making bite-size meatballs. Evenly brown meatballs in small amount of oil in heavy skillet. Keep warm in oven on paper covered platter till ready to serve.

Swedish Meatball Sauce:

2 jars of your favorite barbeque
    sauce
2 cans cream of musroom soup

Combine barbeque sauce and soup in saucepan and heat. Pour over meatballs in chafing dish and serve with toothpicks.

CHEESE STUFFED MUSHROOMS

Anne Gsell

12 large fresh mushrooms
3 tablespoons onion, finely minced
3 tablespoons shallots, finely minced
2 tablespoons butter
1 tablespoon oil
¼ cup Madeira wine (or Vermouth)
3 tablespoons bread crumbs
¼ cup grated Swiss cheese
¼ cup grated Parmesan cheese
4 tablespoons parsley, minced
½ teaspoon tarragon
2 - 3 tablespoons whipping cream
    salt and pepper

Wash and dry mushrooms. Carefully remove stems and chop them. Brush mushcroom caps with butter and sprinkle with salt and pepper. Place hollow-side up in roasting pan. Saute minced onions in 2 tablespoons of butter and one of oil. Add minced shallots and chopped mushroom stems. In a few minutes add wine and boil until almost evaporated. With heat off, mix in bread crumbs, cheeses, parsley, tarragon, salt and pepper and whipping cream. Fill caps and sprinkle with grated Swiss cheese and a few drops of melted butter. Bake in 375° oven until lightly browned, about 15 minutes.

CRABMEAT STUFFED MUSHROOMS

Mrs. Joseph Merrick Jones, Jr.

3 lbs. large fresh mushrooms
8 ozs. grated American cheese
1 lb. fresh lump crabmeat
1 small grated onion
3 tablespoons minced parsley
    stems from mushrooms, finely
    chopped
    Hellman's mayonnaise, enough to
    bind mixture together
    cayenne pepper to taste

Remove stems from mushrooms, and chop finely. Mix gently with rest of ingredients, being careful not to break up crabmeat.

Drizzle mushroom caps with butter and bake in 350° oven for 10 - 15 minutes. Remove, and stuff with mixture. Put in 350° oven for 10 - 15 minutes, or until heated through and cheese has melted.

ITALIAN STUFFED MUSHROOMS

¾ cup Italian style bread crumbs
¼ cup grated Parmesan cheese
¼ cup grated onion
1 teaspoon minced garlic chips
½ teaspoon salt
1 pinch oregano
1 stick melted butter
1 lb. fresh mushrooms

Wash and dry mushrooms. Remove and chop stems. Mix all ingredients together, except butter, and spoon mixture into mushroom caps. Spoon butter over mushrooms in shallow baking dish and bake in 350° oven until lightly browned (about 20 - 25 minutes).

MARINATED MUSHROOMS
Mrs. E. V. Benjamin III

1 lb. fresh mushrooms

Marinade:

½ cup olive oil
½ cup wine vinegar
2 garlic cloves (crushed)
1 teaspoon salt
1 teaspoon oregano
½ teaspoon crushed red chili
  peppers

Wash mushrooms in cold water and drain. Drop them into well-salted boiling water and simmer for 5 minutes (without boiling). Drain; cover with cold water and drain again. Place them on paper towels and dry them.
Combine ingredients of marinade.
Put mushrooms in a bowl and pour marinade over them. Let stand at least one hour before serving. They may be put in jars and refrigerated.

OYSTER STUFFED MUSHROOMS
Mrs. W. Elliott Laudeman III

2 lbs. large fresh mushrooms
½ bunch chopped shallots,
  tops included
¼ bunch chopped parsley
1 clove garlic, minced
1 stick butter
2½ dozen oysters, chopped
  Italian bread crumbs, for
  binding mixture
2 eggs, slightly beaten
  salt and pepper to taste

Remove and chop stems from washed mushrooms. Saute mushroom caps and garlic in butter. Remove caps and set aside. Saute shallots, parsley and chopped stems in remaining garlic-butter mixture.
Drain oysters, reserving liquid. Add chopped oysters to mixture and cook for 5 minutes. Add bread crumbs, eggs, salt and pepper. Thicken to desired stuffing consistency with more bread crumbs and a little oyster liquor. Fill caps and arrange in shallow baking dish. Bake in 350° oven until lightly browned, about 25 minutes.

PICKLED MUSHROOMS
Mrs. John Dart

1 large can mushroom buttons or
  freshly cooked mushroom buttons
  wine vinegar
1 large bay leaf
1 heaping tablespoon each of onions
  and shallots, finely chopped
3 whole cloves
  salad oil (cooking oil)
  pepper and salt to taste
1 clove of garlic
1 dash of Tabasco sauce

Drain liquid from mushrooms. Place in bowl, cover generously with wine vinegar. Put in refrigerator for 1 hour or longer. Put mushrooms in jar, now add onions, shallots, bay leaf, cloves, oil (barely enough to cover), pepper, Tabasco, salt and garlic. Close jar tightly and put in refrigerator for two days.

MUSHROOM ROUNDS

1 doz. slices bread
1½ cups fresh mushrooms
1 tablespoon butter
2 teaspoons cream
  salt, pepper to taste

Slice the bread as for Melba toast. Sauté the mushrooms in butter, chop them and add cream and seasoning.
Lightly butter the bread, spread it with the mushroom mixture, roll and hold together with toothpicks. Toast, and serve with tea or cocktails.

TOOTHPICK MUSHROOMS
Mrs. Joseph Merrick Jones, Jr.

3 lbs. medium fresh mushrooms
3 tablespoons frozen or fresh
  chives, minced
1 cup sour cream
1 stick margarine
  garlic, salt, & pepper to taste

Saute mushrooms over high heat, stirring constantly until golden brown. Remove from heat and add rest of ingredients. Heat gently, but do not boil, as sour cream will curdle. Serve hot on toothpicks.

MUSTARD BUTTER TOAST

2/3 parts creamed butter
1/3 part prepared mustard
  dash of A-1 sauce

Cream all together and spread on bread. Run in the oven to toast. Very good with hot tea or coffee.

DEVILED OYSTERS
Mrs. Paul Lansing

3 hard boiled eggs
1 qt. oysters, drain and save juice
1½ cups celery, chopped
1 cup white onions, chopped
1/3 cup green onions, chopped
½ cup parsley, chopped
4 cloves garlic, minced
½ cup butter
1 teaspoon salt
½ teaspoon freshly ground
   black pepper
1/8 teaspoon cayenne
   Tabasco, 2 - 3 dashes
2 tablespoons arrowroot, dissolved
   in 2 tablespoons Worcestershire
   Monosodium Glutamate, to taste

Saute celery, onions, parsley, garlic in butter until limp. Add seasonings except for Worcestershire and arrowroot. Add grated eggs and then drained oysters. After oysters have cooked about 10 minutes, add dissolved arrowroot to sauce and stir until thick. Do not boil or overcook. The whole cooking time should not be more than 25 minutes. This may be served in cocktail patty shells from a chafing dish, or in large patty shells as a main course, or as a side accompaniment to roast beef.

DEVILED OYSTERS
Mr. John R. Peters

¾ stick of butter
1 qt. of oysters, ground *
1 tablespoon flour
2 large shallots, chopped fine
½ cup Lea and Perrin
2 cups toast crumbs
1 cup milk
2 eggs
2 lemons, juice of
4 doz. cocktail patty shells,
   topless

Melt butter and brown well with flour. Add shallots and oysters. Cook until oysters water, then add Lea and Perrins sauce, lemon juice, crumbs (more if necessary), milk, and well beaten eggs. Place in double boiler to keep hot. Add salt and lots of pepper

(red and a little black). Serve in chafing dish with patty shells on side.

* Preparation of Oysters: Place pan under food grinder to catch juices. Pass oysters through grinder after fingering each to detect and remove particles of shells.

"FRIED OYSTER PO-BOY HORS D'OEUVRES"
Mrs. Loy Austin Everett

1 pint oysters, drained
   Yogi or Zatarain Fish Fry
   (corn meal)
1 loaf long thin French bread
3 cloves garlic, minced
1½ sticks butter
3 tablespoons dehydrated parsley
   flakes
3 tablespoons Parmesan cheese
   sliced pickles
   seafood cocktail sauce (tomato
   ketchup, lemon juice, horseradish,
   lemon, Tabasco, salt and pepper)

Slice French bread in half lengthwise. Prepare garlic-butter sauce by melting butter over low flame and adding garlic and parsley until well blended. Spoon over the interiors of the French bread halves. Lightly sprinkle bread with parmesan cheese. Bake in 400° oven until edges slightly brown. Slice into 1 - 1½" horizontal slices.

Meanwhile fry oysters according to "Fish Fry" package directions.

Place one fried oyster on each slice of garlic French Bread and top with pickle slice. Serve as Hors D'oeuvres on platter with cocktail sauce and lemon wedges.

OYSTERS ROCKEFELLER

2 doz. small oysters
1 pt. Rockefeller sauce (see
   index under sauces)
2 doz. toast rounds

Heat oysters in their own juice until they curl. Drain and pat with paper towels. Place one oyster on each toast round, cover with Rockefeller sauce and heat in a 350° oven.

SMOKED OYSTER HORS D'OEUVRE
Mrs. Dora Harris Jackson

Season 2 large Philadelphia cream cheeses with onion juice, Tabasco, and

Lea & Perrin. Drain and chop 6 cans of smoked oysters. Combine oysters and one cup minced fresh parsley.

Line a mold with saran wrap -- layer cream cheese mixture and oyster mixture -- cheese on bottom of mold -- pack tightly.

Refrigerate or freeze. To serve, unmold and serve on plate with crackers.

PÂTÉ DE FOIE GRAS BISCUIT WITH BACON

small biscuits
bacon
pâté de foie gras
cream

Make the biscuits very small and light, preferably the size of a half dollar.

Broil the bacon very crisp, chop.

Mix the pâté de foie gras with a little cream to moisten it.

Open the biscuits and spread one side with bacon bits, the other with the pâté. Press the halves together and it can share the honors of any cocktail.

EPICURE'S PÂTÉ

¾ pound calf's liver
4 hard-boiled eggs, chopped
4 large onions, thinly sliced
½ cup bread-crumbs
¾ cup chicken (or goose) fat, rendered
1 tablespoon lard
salt

Simmer the onions in the lard until they are transparent, beginning to brown. Add the liver: it should not cook more than 10 minutes, by which time the onions should be as browned as possible without burning.

Put the onions and liver in the blender to make them into a paste. Remove and beat and mash into them slowly first the eggs, then slowly and thoroughly the chicken fat; salt, and last of all bread-crumbs, mashing to a smooth paste.

Shape this with the hands into a rounded mound and set in the ice-box for 24 hours. Pâté de foie gras must look to its laurels.

PÂTÉ IN JELLY

2 cans of consommé
2 pounds of smoked goose liver, unsalted
½ pound cream cheese
¼ cupful Madeira
1 tablespoon brandy
1 envelope plain gelatine
2 tablespoons cold water

Work the liver and cream cheese into a smooth paste, adding half of the Madeira and all the brandy. Warm the consommé and add gelatine which has been dissolved in the cold water and the rest of the Madeira. Set the consommé to cool. Pour about ¾ inch of consommé into a mold and place in refrigerator, when stiff, remove, and with a knife, carefully place the pâté into the mold. Then cover pâté with the rest of the consommé. Chill.

PÂTÉ PAYSAN

½ pound calf's liver
3 hard cooked eggs
4 tablespoons mayonnaise
salt, pepper, cayenne

Cook the liver and chop it very fine. Chop the hard boiled eggs, mix both with the mayonnaise, season highly. Spread the mixture on thin crispy toasted rounds of bread, garnishing with powdered egg yolk.

It might be a twin to pâté de foie gras.

PETITE QUICHESA LA RED
Mrs. Ann Pitts Corrigan

4 eggs
2 packages shredded cheddar cheese
2 jars marinated artichoke hearts
¼ cup Progresso Italian style bread crumbs
1 medium onion, chopped
½ teaspoon garlic powder
salt and pepper to taste

In large mixing bowl, beat eggs by hand. Drain marinade from artichoke hearts, reserving the marinade from one jar and discarding the marinade from the other. Finely chop artichoke hearts and add to eggs. Saute onions in reserved marinade in skillet. Add onions and remaining ingredients to mixing bowl thoroughly stirring all together. Pour into greased 10" rectangular Corningware container, or reasonable facsimile. Bake in 350° pre-heated oven for 30 minutes. Let cool slightly then cut into hors d'-oeuvres size squares and serve.

BOULETTES DE SAUCISSON
Mrs. Walter Torian

2 lbs. sausage meat, well seasoned
3 cloves garlic
red pepper, sage, flour
onion, parsley, minced

Marinate the sausage meat with the garlic, red pepper, sage: let it stay in the ice-box with these seasonings at least all night.

Mold into balls, dredge in flour and fry in piping hot lard.

Remove the sausage onto a warm platter, and make a roux, stirring into the fat a teaspoon of flour, the chopped onion and parsley.

Served with yellow hominy, they make one of those good old "light" southern breakfasts, calculated to start a Sunday in the right direction.

PORK SAUSAGE
Mrs. David Merrick
Bel Air Plantation

8 lbs. pork, the lean
2 lbs. pork, the fat
3 tablespoons salt
1 tablespoon each red pepper, black pepper, sage

Grind the pork very fine, and mix with seasonings.

PINWHEEL SAUSAGE ROLLS
Mrs. Harry Merritt Lane, Sr.

2 cups biscuit mix (Bisquick)
½ cup cold water
1 lb. ground pork sausage

Prepare biscuit mix. Add water as for rolled biscuits. Knead and place on lightly floured surface. Roll out in rectangle (15 x 18) and 1/8 inch thick. Spread the entire surface with sausage. Roll up jelly roll fashion on aluminum foil or waxed paper. Chill or freeze.

When ready to use, slice into ¼ - ½ inch slices. Place slices on baking sheet and bake at 450° for 15 minutes. Serve hot as an appetizer.

CROQUETTE DE SAUCISSE
Mrs. Walter Torian

The sausage meat is left overnight to marinate with a little vinegar and spices, and garlic. The next morning it is seasoned highly and ½ cup of sherry is added. After that pleasant touch, it is shaped in croquette form and fried in sizzling hot lard.

SHRIMP APPETIZER
Mrs. Frank H. Lawton

1 lb. boiled shrimp, chopped
sour pickles, chopped
grated sharp cheese
Hellman's mayonnaise

Mix the chopped shrimp with the chopped pickles and add enough mayonnaise to bind the mixture. Spread on toast rounds and sprinkle generously with grated cheese. Before serving put in 350° oven and let the cheese melt.

MARINATED SHRIMP
Mrs. James Selman

3 lbs. peeled, cooked, and de-veined shrimp
Courtbouillon, made of:
2 quarts water
2 large quartered onions
2 quartered lemons
1 tablespoon dried or fresh red pepper
1 tablespoon cayenne
3 tablespoons salt
4 bay leaves
4 cloves

Bring courtbouillon to a boil. Add shrimp, bring to a boil again. IMMEDIATELY turn off shrimp and let sit for 10 minutes, leaving in the hot liquid. Remove them from this liquid and marinate shrimp in the icebox overnight.

Marinade:

1 cup olive oil
1 cup Wesson oil
1/3 cup lemon juice
1/3 cup cider vinegar
1 teaspoon grated lemon peel
1 tablespoon salt
½ teaspoon fresh ground pepper
5 shakes Tabasco

5 shakes Worcestershire
4 bay leaves
2 large white onions, sliced
2 large garlic toes, sliced

Serve in bowl with toothpicks available. (They look nice in fluted white souffle dish.)

eggs, cheese and grits

EGGS BENEDICT
Mrs. Joseph Merrick Jones, Jr.

6 eggs
3 English muffins
12 slices Canadian bacon
1 can Emilio's Hollandaise
  sauce (base mix)
butter

Make Hollandaise sauce according to directions on can. Set aside over warm water.

Butter halved English muffins and put in 350° oven to heat, having placed two slices of bacon on each.

Poach eggs, adding 2 teaspoons vinegar to the simmering water; this holds the eggs together.

Take the hot buns and the bacon from the oven, top with an egg, then pour the sauce over. Garnish with paprika and parsley if you are in a festive mood.

EGGS BENEDICTINE
Mrs. Donald Rafferty

8 English muffins or Holland Rusks
8 eggs, poached
2 cups cream sauce
2 beaten egg yolks
½ - 1 cup grated cheddar cheese
1 jigger sherry
8 thin wafers of Virginia ham
8 slices tomatoes
salt and pepper to taste

Prepare sauce by adding to basic cream sauce the cheese, beaten egg yolks, sherry, salt and pepper.

Arrange 8 toasted English muffins or Holland Rusks which have been buttered in an oven-proof serving platter. Top each with a slice of broiled Virginia ham. Place in slow oven to keep warm. Meanwhile poach eggs and saute tomatoes in butter. Place a slice of tomato and a poached egg on top of each ham-covered muffin and top with

heated sauce. Serve at once. Serves four.

EGGS IN BLACK BUTTER

1 raw egg
1 oz. butter
1 teaspoon chopped parsley
5 drops vinegar

Warm butter in frying pan until it turns brown. Add parsley and cook for one minute more controlling the heat carefully to prevent its turning too dark. Add vinegar. Pour over a raw egg in a small individual casserole and run into the oven until the egg sets.

EGG CASSEROLE FOR BRUNCH
Mrs. Joseph Merrick Jones, Jr.

15 eggs, finely chopped, or put
  through the biggest blade of
  your meat grinder
1½ cups ground ham
4 - 5 cups thick white cream sauce
  to which 2 teaspoons cayenne and
  2 teaspoons garlic salt have been
  added
2 packages (16 oz.) grated sharp cheese
10 large fresh mushroom caps

Mix ground eggs, ham and cream sauce together. Add enough cream sauce to bind mixture. Top with grated cheese. Saute mushroom caps in butter until brown. Lay caps on top of cheese and bake until bubbly.

EGG AND CHEESE CASSEROLE
Mrs. William Hine

4 cups chopped hard-boiled eggs
2 cups crushed saltine cracker
  crumbs
3 cups medium cream sauce
2 cups grated sharp cheese
1 cup chopped pimentos
butter for topping

30

Butter casserole. Start first layer with cracker crumbs. On top of crumbled cracker pour 1/3 cream sauce. Add layer of grated cheese, pimentos and hard-boiled eggs. Repeat layers in same order until dish is full. Top with bread crumbs, and dot with butter.
Serves 6 - 8.

CREOLE EGGS
Mrs. Lucius K. Burton

¼ cup salad oil
½ cup flour
1 large onion, sliced
1 10-oz. can tomatoes
1 bay leaf, crumbled
4 hard-boiled eggs, sliced or
   quartered
2 small stalks celery and tops,
   finely chopped
½ cup water
1/8 teaspoon allspice
2 green peppers, chopped
2 shallots, chopped
1 thin slice lemon
   parsley

Make roux with oil and flour. Add onions and brown. Add tomatoes, and cook for 5 minutes. Add egg halves or quarters to sauce just before serving.
ALTERNATIVE: Make alternating layers of tomato sauce and eggs in casserole. Top with bread crumbs and bake until bubbly at 350°.

EGGS EN COCOTTE

Warm individual small pyrex bowls, cover bottoms with warm cream—slide two eggs in each dish—season with salt and pepper and a tiny piece of butter. Put bowls in a pan of boiling water, cover but leave opening for steam to escape. Put in oven and cook slowly until set. A good luncheon dish.

DANISH ROE EGGS
Mrs. Donald Rafferty

Hard boil the desired number of eggs, halve lengthwise. Take out the yolks, which should be mashed to a paste, and softened with a little mayonnaise and a few drops of Worcestershire sauce, put in halved eggs. Cover with a mixture of tomato paste, thinned with mayonnaise until it takes on a pretty pink color. Then add some rich roe and spread over the eggs. Shad roe is especially good.

FRIED EGGS PROVENCE

Half fill a skillet with cooking oil. Heat very hot. Drop in eggs, immediately lowering heat, and tightly cover skillet. Cook until done. Remove top, pour off fat and turn eggs out on platter. Salt and pepper. Eggs will be plump and delicious!

EGGS A LA KING

1 teaspoon lemon juice
2 tablespoons butter
¼ lb. sliced mushrooms
½ green pepper, shredded
2 tablespoons flour
1½ cups rich milk
2 beaten egg yolks
½ cup cream
8 hard-boiled eggs, sliced
   salt, pepper to taste

Put the eggs in a pan of boiling water. Cover, turn off heat and let stand thirty minutes. (This makes the yolks very soft, mealy, and digestible, and the whites easily crumbled.) Remove the eggs and cover them immediately with very cold water. Remove the shells and press the whites through a vegetable press, keeping them separate from the yolks.
Rub the flour and butter together, add the cold milk and stir this over the fire until it just reaches the boiling point, then add the salt, pepper, and the whites of the eggs. Heat over hot water.
Toast the slices of bread and arrange them neatly on a platter. Pour the mixture with the whites of eggs over them, sprinkle the top with the grated yolks of the eggs and stand them at the oven door for two minutes until thoroughly heated.

EGGS DE LUXE

2 ozs. Roquefort cheese
1 doz. hard-boiled eggs
¼ cup each finely chopped celery,
   onions
2 teaspoons finely chopped parsley
2 teaspoons butter or mayonnaise
½ cup bread crumbs
1 raw egg
¼ cup water
   salt, pepper

Slice eggs lengthwise, remove yolks and work together with the cheese, butter or mayonnaise, onions, celery, parsley, salt and pepper. Refill the egg cases with the mixture and press the halves together. Dip eggs into the beaten raw egg to which the water has been added. Roll in bread crumbs and fry in deep fat until light brown in color. Serve at once with a tomato sauce, and garnish with a pepper ring, stuffed olives and sprig of parsley. A rich treat.

HUEVOS RANCHEROS
Mrs. George Douglass

6 eggs
1 large bell pepper, chopped
1 large onion, chopped
2 stalks celery with tops, chopped
2 cans tomatoes (medium cans)
½ lb. bacon, chopped
2 toes garlic, chopped
½ - 1 Jalapeno pepper, according to hotness desired

Saute bacon, set aside. In remaining grease saute the bell pepper, onion, celery and garlic.

Add the tomatoes, Jalapeno pepper finely chopped, and the bacon. Let simmer 10 minutes. Drop eggs into hot sauce and poach hard or soft, as desired, basting frequently with the sauce. Serve on English muffins or toast rounds.

EGGS A LA PURGATOIRE
Mrs. J. N. Roussel

4 hard-boiled eggs
4 pieces buttered toast
1 cup tomato ketchup
2 tablespoons Worcestershire sauce
1 teaspoon pepper-vinegar
½ teaspoon each salt, black pepper
1 tablespoon butter
1 teaspoon mustard

Hard boil eggs, peel and stand on ends on hot buttered toast ½ inch thick with a hollowed center. Pour over this a sauce made out of the other ingredients. This must be poured over the eggs and toast while very hot. Delicious and so simple.

RUSSIAN EGGS

6 eggs
1 small jar caviar

2 tablespoons anchovy paste
1 teaspoon butter
1 cup Hollandaise sauce
6 rounds lightly toasted bread
salt, pepper

Poach eggs until firm. Sprinkle with salt and pepper. Butter toast, spread it with anchovy sauce and put an egg on it. Cover with the Hollandaise sauce and top with caviar.

EGGS ST. DENIS

1 cup chicken livers (raw) ground fine
½ cup mushrooms, minced fine
¾ cup cooked ham (lean) minced fine
1 pony sherry wine
1 dash Lea and Perrin's Sauce
½ cup purée of tomatoes
1 pt. Espagnole Sauce (brown roux moistened with strong beef broth)
salt and pepper to taste

Proceed as follows:
Sauté raw chicken livers in one-half butter and one-half olive oil until done. Add the ham, cook some more, add the mushrooms. Add Sherry wine, dash of Lea and Perrin's Sauce, and then add the purée of tomatoes. Cook all together and then add the Espagnole or Brown Sauce. Season to taste. Cook slowly at least a half hour or until sauce has the proper consistency.

Cut triangular pieces of toast and cover with slices of broiled ham cut in same shape.

Place one egg which has been fried in deep fat and well rounded on each slice of toast on top of the ham slices. Then cover eggs entirely with the luscious sauce.

EGG SARDOU GALATOIRE'S

1 doz. large artichokes
enough creamed spinach to fill hearts
1 doz. poached eggs
Hollandaise sauce

Boil artichokes. Remove outside leaves and spikes over heart. Fill cavity in artichokes with creamed spinach. Cover each cavity with a poached egg and pour Hollandaise sauce over each.

SCRAMBLED EGGS BENOIT

Break six eggs into a bowl. Melt a tablespoon of butter in double boiler.

Pour in the well beaten eggs. Lower heat, add 3 tablespoons of water. Scrape from the sides of the pot as they cook. The slower they cook the more delicate. Handle lightly. Serve on buttered toast.

EGGS SHIRRED À LA STANFORD
Mr. Stanford Eaglin

16 eggs
24 cleaned chicken livers
1 cup tomato sauce
¼ cup sherry
1 stick butter
8 tablespoons grated sharp cheddar cheese (or more to taste, this is topping)
salt, cayenne pepper or black pepper

Butter ramekins well. Set aside. Saute chicken livers in stick of butter, making sure they are well done, and season with salt and cayenne, or black pepper if you prefer. Add tomato sauce and sherry and simmer for a few minutes. Put 3 chicken livers with a little sauce in the bottom of each ramekin. Break 2 eggs carefully on top of the livers. Sprinkle with 1 table-spoon cheese each, and put a few dots of butter on each so they will not dry out. Bake in pre-heated oven (350°) until eggs are set. Watch carefully so they do not get overcooked. Serve in the remakin.
Serves eight.

OLD ENGLISH SHIRRED EGGS
Mrs. Walter Stauffer

6 eggs
3 tablespoons each butter, flour
1½ cups milk
¼ cup of Old English Cheese
salt, pepper, buttered bread crumbs

Melt the butter and work in the flour to a smooth paste, adding the milk slowly. When thick and smooth add the cheese and stir until the cheese is melted. Season to taste with salt. Pour sauce into a shallow dish (a Pyrex pie plate is excellent) and drop into the sauce the eggs. Season, cover with bread crumbs and bake in a moderate oven (325 degrees) until the egg white is set. The eggs can be cooked in ramekins just as well.

SNOWDRIFT EGGS

Use a glass or porcelain baking dish about two inches deep. Butter it generously. Beat the whites of eggs to super stiffness, add salt and pile in the dish with as many hills and valleys as possible. Allow one tablespoon of cream to each egg and pour gently over the egg whites. Now slip the yolks into the crevices where they fit best. Run into the oven until the yolks are just set and the whites tipped with brown. This is a particularly good way to serve eggs to an invalid as they are attractive to look at and most digestible, being prepared without fat.

VENETIAN EGGS
Mrs. Stanley Arthur

1 tablespoon butter
1 tablespoon finely chopped onion
1 pt. fresh or canned tomatoes
1 tablespoon grated cheese
1 level teaspoon salt
1 saltspoon paprika
4 eggs

Put butter in saucepan. When hot add onion, cook about five minutes but do not brown, add tomatoes, cover, and when simmering add cheese, salt and paprika. Slip in four unbeaten eggs, and pick up white with a fork as it thickens. When coagulated break yolks and stir all together.
Serve on round pieces of toast lightly buttered. This quantity will cover six slices of toast. Fine for Sunday night supper, and so quickly and easily prepared.

OMELETTE AU FOUR

1 cup soft bread crumbs
1 cup milk
6 eggs
salt, pepper to taste

Soak the crumbs in milk five minutes. Beat the eggs until light, add seasoning, then the crumbs, and milk mixture. Bake in a greased shallow pan in a moderate oven, for 25 minutes. Serve with jelly, or with creamed mushrooms or meat. Yesterday's bread here comes to a noble end. One may mix a little grated cheese with melted butter, sprinkle it over the omelette just before it is done, and let it brown before serving.

BACON-MUSHROOM OMELET
Mrs. Joseph Merrick Jones, Jr.

1 cup sliced fresh mushrooms
½ cup chopped celery
½ cup diced cooked bacon bits
½ cup butter
1 tablespoon flour
½ cup cream
  salt and pepper to taste
8 eggs

Cook bacon, drain and dice. Saute mushrooms and celery in butter. Sprinkle flour over and stir. Add cream and stir until slightly thickened. Add bacon to mixture.

Make a plain omelet, and when set, pour the mixture in the center and fold.

If you have trouble with omelets, I suggest that you divide your eggs and mushroom mixture in half, and make two smaller individual omelets. This is a hearty breakfast for two.

CRAB OMELET

8 eggs
3 teaspoons water
1½ cups milk
2 cups crab meat
1½ tablespoons each flour, butter
½ teaspoon onion
1 teaspoon minced parsley
  salt, pepper to taste

Make a cream sauce by mixing flour, butter and milk and cooking in double boiler. Add crab meat, salt, pepper, a little grated onion and minced parsley. Beat eggs separately, add water to yolks and fold in whites. Turn into a hot skillet, reduce heat. When done, pour over it one-third of crab meat and sauce, fold over and turn on hot platter. Pour balance of crab meat and sauce over omelet.

MUSHROOM OMELET

1 cup button mushrooms
1 tablespoon butter
½ cup cream, or milk
1 teaspoon flour
8 eggs, salt, pepper to taste

Cut the mushrooms fine. Melt the butter and add the mushrooms with salt, pepper, and cream. Thicken with flour dissolved in a little water or milk,

and set to boil gently for 10 minutes. Make a plain omelet, and just before folding, pour some of the mushrooms in the center. Serve hot, with the rest of the mushroom sauce poured over.

SUNDAY MORNING KILN OMELET
Mrs. Joseph Merrick Jones, Jr.

10 eggs
½ cup minced or ground ham
¼ cup shallots
1 cup sliced fresh mushrooms
1 cup chopped drained oysters
  (optional)
1 - 2 tablespoons flour
1 teaspoon garlic salt and pepper
  to taste
1 cup Half and Half

Saute ham, shallots, mushrooms and oysters in butter. Sprinkle flour over and mix in. Slowly add Half and Half until mixture binds together. Keep warm.

In separate pan, cook eggs as you would for a plain omelet. It is easier to divide the eggs and mixture in half and make two separate omelets, but one big one looks so pretty on the platter.

Garnish with parsley and toast points that have been sauteed in butter.

OYSTER OMELET
Mme. Ludo d'Arcis

4 doz. oysters
1½ tablespoons each celery, onion,
  parsley
2 tablespoons flour
2 tablespoons butter
1 cup each rich milk, oyster liquor
7 eggs
  salt, pepper, to taste

Skin the oysters and remove the hard part. Heat in their own liquor till they curl. Remove, cut in halves and set aside. Save also one cup of the oyster liquor.

Fry the celery, onions and parsley, chopped fine, in the butter, then make a cream sauce stirring in the flour slowly and adding the milk a little at a time. Set aside.

Beat the eggs, yolks and white separately, until very stiff, combine, fold in about two-thirds of the oysters, add salt and pepper and turn all into a very hot skillet in which a tablespoon of butter has been melted. Lower the heat and allow to cook slowly till set and brown on the bottom. Then slip into a warm oven for three minutes. Double over, turn out on a hot platter and pour over the sauce to which the remainder of the oysters has been added.

OYSTER OMELETTE PASCUAL MANALE
John Wyeth Scott

    9 eggs well beaten
    ¼ cup each cream, water
    1 doz. oysters
    1 onion, 2 cloves garlic
    8 shallots, the green part
    ½ stick butter
    salt, pepper

Boil the oysters in their liquor until they swell. Take them out and drain thoroughly and chop, not too fine. Chop the onion, garlic, and shallot tops, very fine, and fry them in butter. Next add the chopped oysters, taking care that they do not burn. Finally, add the well beaten eggs, to which have been added the water and the cream. Mix all well and quickly, add salt and pepper and allow to cook for the minimum of time required to set. Turn out in omelet form on a hot platter and garnish with finely cut parsley.

RUM OMELET
Mrs. T. S. Behre

    1 whole egg
    ¼ teaspoon sugar
    ¼ cup rum

This is best made in individual servings. Set the rum to heat slightly. Make omelet by beating the egg till well mixed, adding salt, sugar and two tablespoons of cold water. Cook until set in a small well buttered skillet. Turn out on a piping hot plate, pour warm rum over, light, and rush to the table.

WOOTIE'S WIENER OMELET
Mr. L. P. Lebourgeois

    4 eggs, well beaten
    4 large shallots, chopped fine

    2 wieners, well cooked
    1 cold small potato, firmly cooked and diced
    salt, pepper and Tabasco
    2 tablespoons butter
    2 ozs. milk

Beat eggs well. Add milk, salt, pepper, tabasco and blend together. Place butter in skillet. Heat until nearly brown. Pour in egg mixture. When cooked on one side add shallots, wieners, potatoes, Fold over and flip and cook until done. Add the Tabasco, salt and pepper to taste, and enjoy with a good Rose.

QUICHE LORRAINE
Mrs. Walter Cook Keenan III

    ½ lb. bacon, fried crisp, drained & crumbled
    8 ozs. good quality Swiss cheese, grated (Cheap cheese will be stringy when cooked)
    3 eggs, at room temperature, slightly beaten
    2 cups whole milk or light cream, at room temperature
    1/3 - ½ cup onion, minced
    1/3 - ½ cup fresh mushrooms
    2 tablespoons butter
    salt, pepper, Lea & Perrins to taste
    paprika for garnish, as desired

Brush 10" pie crust, unbaked, with egg white. Pre-heat oven to 350°. Place crumbled bacon in crust. Cover with cheese. Mix eggs, milk or cream, and seasonings. Set aside.
Saute mushrooms and onions in butter until onions are transparent. Add to egg mixture; pour over bacon and cheese. Garnish with paprika.
Bake at 350° for 45 minutes, or until silver knife inserted near the outside of the crust comes out clean.
Serve lukewarm. Do not let custard cool completely or it will be too firm.

CHEESE SOUFFLÉ

    1 pt. milk
    4 eggs
    2 tablespoons each butter, flour
    5 tablespoons grated cheese
    1 teaspoon salt
    1 pinch cayenne pepper
    ½ level coffee spoon soda
    1/3 coffee spoon paprika

Mix flour, milk and butter thoroughly and boil, stirring until the mixture becomes creamy. When cool, add the well beaten yolks, then the cheese and seasoning; fold in the stiffly beaten whites. Turn into a well buttered baking dish and place in hot water in slow oven 30 to 50 minutes. Fish, shrimp, ham, or chicken may be added.

Long, slow cooking insures that the soufflé does not fall.

SOUFFLÉ AU FROMAGE (CHEESE SOUFFLÉ)

Comtesse de Toulouse-Lautrec
Head of Maxim's Cooking
Academie, Paris, France

Serves 5.

    4 eggs
    3½ ozs. Swiss cheese
    2 tablespoons flour
    2 cups milk
    ¼ cup butter
    salt, pepper

Prepare a thick Bechamel with the butter, flour and milk. Season with salt and pepper (use salt sparingly as cheese will bring in its own salt).

Remove from heat. Add the egg yolks, one at a time, stirring constantly, then add the grated cheese. Continue stirring until mixture is smooth. Let it cool.

Beat egg whites until stiff and add to mixture. Pour into a buttered soufflé dish and bake in hot oven for about 25 minutes.

Serve immediately—'un soufflé n'attend pas'—a soufflé will not wait.

FROMAGE

Mrs. W. J. Bentley

    1 lb. grated cheese
    2 eggs, the yolks
    ½ pt. milk and cream
    cayenne, salt

Beat the eggs very light, and add the cream, then the cheese. Pour into buttered ramekins and bake 15 minutes or until set.

CHEESY FRIED GRITS

Mrs. Joseph Merrick Jones, Jr.

    4 cups cold cooked grits
    1 stick margarine

    6 eggs, beaten
    salt and pepper to taste
    1½ cups grated sharp cheese
    ½ cup minced parsley

Slice cold grits into ½ inch slices. Dip into beaten eggs that have been seasoned with salt and pepper.

Cook in melted margarine until brown on both sides.

Arrange on oven-proof platter in one layer. Sprinkle with grated cheese and parsley and crisp under broiler.

GARLIC GRITS

    1 cup Quick cooking grits
    ½ stick butter
    ¼ cup milk
    1 roll garlic cheese, about 6 oz.
    size
    1 egg
    Tabasco

Cook grits according to directions on package. Remove from heat. Add butter, milk, cheese and egg and a dash of Tabasco. Mix together. Transfer to baking dish and bake at 375° for 30 minutes. This is an excellent substitute for mashed potatoes or rice and goes well with breakfast sausages.

SOUFFLED GRITS

Mrs. Walter Cook Keenan III

    4 servings Aunt Jemima Quick Grits, cooked and still warm
    2 eggs, separated, at room temperature
    1 cup milk, warmed
    2 tablespoons butter
    salt, at least ½ teaspoon
    Tabasco and white pepper to taste

Stir egg yolks, milk and 1 tablespoon butter into grits; blend well. Beat egg whites until soft peaks form, fold into grits, and pour into 1½ quart baking dish sprayed with Pam. Top with 1 tablespoon butter and bake at 350° for one hour.

These grits are bland to serve with hash, but when serving with eggs, add ½ cup grated cheese with egg yolks and milk. Use larger baking dish. Be sure cheese is at room temperature when added.

hot breads, pancakes and waffles

BEATEN BISCUITS
Mrs. David T. Merrick

1 qt. sifted flour, 1 teaspoon salt
1/3 cup each hog lard, butter
1 cup ice water
1 teaspoon sugar, heaping

Mix the dry ingredients. Add the water, sweetened with the sugar and work until there is life in the dough, about 15 minutes (longer takes the life out of the dough). Then beat with rolling pin or use a machine until the dough blisters. Roll, cut with biscuit cutter and prick the centers with a fork. Bake in a moderate oven. If the above is too hot, the biscuits will begin to blister.

MITTIE'S CHEESE BISCUITS

1 lb. sharp American cheese
1 cup butter or half and half with lard
1 to 2 tablespoons ice water
1½ cups flour
½ teaspoon each salt, cayenne pepper
pecans

Work up on marble slab without handling much. Roll out thin, cut with biscuit cutter. Place a pecan half on each biscuit. Bake in a slow oven.

FOUR O'CLOCK BISCUITS

2 cups flour
4 teaspoons baking powder
½ teaspoon salt
4 tablespoons shortening
2/3 cup milk

Mix and sift the dry ingredients. Work in the shortening with the finger tips till it looks like a coarse meal. Make a well in the center, and pour in the milk all at once. Stir until well mixed. Dough should be soft. Turn on a well floured board. Knead it quickly and lightly for a few minutes.

Pat or roll to ½ inch thickness and cut with a small biscuit cutter. Bake in a very hot oven about twelve minutes. Instead of rolling out, one may drop them from a spoon, avoiding the kneading process. They are toothsome morsels for tea.

STICKY BISCUITS
Mrs. Eli W. Tullis

12 day-old biscuits
½ cup melted butter
½ cup syrup

Lightly toast day old biscuits. In casserole dish layer biscuits that have been toasted; coat generously with butter, then coat with syrup. Repeat until biscuits are used up, and bake at 350° for about 30 minutes. Serve as a breakfast sweet.

BANANA BREAD

2 eggs, well beaten
1 cup sugar, 1 teaspoon salt
2 tablespoons sour milk
½ cup butter, 2 cups flour
3 ripe bananas
1 teaspoon soda, level

Sift flour and measure. Add soda and salt, sift 3 times. Cream sugar and butter, mash bananas and add. Beat eggs well, add to banana mixture. Then add flour and sour milk. Bake in loaf pan ¾ to 1 hour in slow oven (325°F).

BATTER BREAD

1 qt. sweet milk
1 cup cornmeal
3 eggs
1 teaspoon each baking powder, salt
1 tablespoon Crisco, rounded

Heat a pint of the milk with meal, stirring all the time until it thickens to consistency of mush. Then take off the fire, and add salt, Crisco, and the rest of the milk. Add the beaten yolks and then fold in the whites of the eggs well beaten. Blend well and pour into hot earthenware or glass baking dish, greased with Crisco. Bake 40 minutes.

CHEESE BRIOCHE
Mrs. James Selman

1 cup water
½ stick butter, (4 ozs.)
1 teaspoon salt
3 shakes Tabasco
1 cup flour
3 eggs
3 ozs. Swiss or Gruyere cheese, diced
1 well-buttered baking sheet

Pre-heat oven to 350°. Bring water, butter and salt to boil in saucepan. Add Tabasco; lower heat and carefully and slowly add flour, stirring all the time. You should get a nice smooth ball of flour which should be stirred around over low heat for about 5 minutes. Remove from heat and allow to cool. Add eggs, one at a time, beating well after each addition. A-chieve smoothness each time. Then add diced cheese.

Butter or oil hands and form dough into a ring on a cookie sheet. Bake in moderate oven (350°) for ½ hour until puffed and golden.

To serve, loosen with spatual and place on large chopping board. Cut into wedges. Excellent hot or cold. This is well complimented when served with a fine Chablis wine.

BROWN BREAD
Mrs. Gerald Derks

1½ cups water
1 cup large seeded muscat raisins
2 tablespoons shortening
1 beaten egg
½ cup chopped nuts
2 teaspoons baking soda
2¾ cups flour
1 teaspoon salt
1 cup sugar

Boil raisins in water. Let cool. Mix together other ingredients. Add raisins and one cup of raisin liquid. Bake at 350° for one hour in four No. 2 cans.

(Delicious with butter or Philadelphia cream cheese.) This freezes well.

CARROT BREAD
Mrs. George Douglass

1 cup sugar
¾ cup Wesson oil
1 cup grated carrots
2 whole eggs
1 teaspoon soda
1 teaspoon cinnamon
¼ teaspoon salt
1½ cups sifted flour
1 cup chopped nuts

Mix all ingredients together. Bake in loaf pan at 350° for one hour.

DILLY CASSEROLE
Mrs. Mims Gage

1 package active dry yeast
¼ cup warm water
2 tablespoons sugar
1 cup cream-style cottage cheese heated to lukewarm
1 tablespoon butter
1 teaspoon salt
½ teaspoon baking soda
1 tablespoon instant minced onions
2 teaspoons dill seed
1 egg
2¼ - 2½ cups flour

Dissolve yeast and sugar in warm water in small bowl.

Combine in large bowl: cottage cheese, butter, salt, soda, onion, dill seed, egg and softened yeast. Mix well. Gradually add flour, beating well after each addition. Dough may have to be worked with hands after each addition of flour. Place dough in greased bowl and cover with a tea towel. Let rise in warm place for 1 hour. Stir down and turn into greased casserole dish. Cover and let rise in warm place until light (about 30 minutes). Bake at 350° for 35 - 45 minutes.

This bread is foolproof!

ENGLISH NUT BREAD
Mrs. Petrie Hamilton

2 eggs, 2 cups milk
3¾ cups flour, ½ cup sugar
1 cup chopped pecans
3 teaspoons baking powder, heaping

Pour into buttered bread pans and set in a warm place to rise for ½ hour. Bake in a moderate oven 30 to 40 minutes.

MEXICAN CORN BREAD
Mrs. Preston S. Herring

1 cup yellow corn meal
1 cup cream style corn
1/3 cup Wesson oil
¾ cup milk
½ teaspoon baking soda
½ teaspoon salt
2 eggs
1 can (4 oz.) hot green chili peppers, chopped
1 cup Kraft Old English Cheese, grated

Mix all ingredients except last two. Pour ½ of mixture in greased Pyrex dish and add a layer of grated cheese and peppers. Then pour on the rest of mixture and top with remaining peppers and cheese. Bake 40 minutes at 400°. Good served with a meal or as a hot hors d'oeuvres (cut in very small squares).

ORANGE BREAD
Miss Ethel Forman

2 cups whole wheat flour
2 cups white flour
3 teaspoons baking powder
1 teaspoon salt
¼ cup melted shortening
½ cup syrup, made by boiling the skins of two oranges in four cups of water with two cups of sugar until reduced to ½ cup
1 cup milk
3 eggs
1 cup orange peel, cut fine

Mix the dry ingredients including the orange peel. Add the syrup and the milk and shortening. Fold in the well beaten eggs and bake in a loaf pan slowly for a half hour or longer.

PUMPKIN BREAD
Anne Romaine
(Through
Terry Flettrich)

2½ cups and 4 tablespoons flour
3 cups sugar
2 teaspoons soda
1 teaspoon nutmeg

1½ teaspoons salt
2 cups canned pumpkin
4 eggs, beaten
1 cup Wesson oil
½ cup and 3 tablespoons water
½ cup chopped nuts

Mix well together the first 5 ingredients and then add the next five ingredients, putting chopped nuts in last. Pour mixture into greased loaf pans. Bake 1 hour in 350° oven or until done.

QUICK DELIVERY HOT BREAD
Elsie Roussel

1 pullman loaf or square bread
½ lb. butter

Cut the crust off the two sides and ends of the pullman loaf. Cut the bread in two, lengthwise. You now have two halves.

Cut each half into squares. In cutting your squares, be sure not to cut through the bottom crust. Run one of these halves in the oven until very hot and toasted on top. Have the butter melting and pour generously on the bread, so that the butter runs down the sides of the squares. Serve one-half loaf of squares with early part of the meal and toast the other half for the latter part.

SOUTHERN EGG BREAD

2 cups white cornmeal
3 eggs, well beaten
1 level teaspoon salt
1 tablespoon melted shortening
3 level teaspoons baking powder
1½ cups milk
1 cup cold boiled rice

Sift the cornmeal, salt, and baking powder together; add the well-beaten eggs, then the shortening, milk and rice. Beat well. Pour into a shallow, well greased pan and bake half an hour in a hot oven. For cornmeal sticks, use the same mixture pouring it into greased iron cornbread stick pan.

SPOON BREAD
Mrs. Petrie Hamilton

3 eggs
1¼ pts. milk, 1 teaspoon salt
½ cup cornmeal
½ teaspoon baking powder
1 heaping tablespoon butter

Heat 1 pint of milk to the boiling point. Stir in cornmeal gradually, and cook until the consistency of mush. Then add the rest of the milk, butter, salt, baking powder and the well beaten egg yolks. Fold in the egg whites beaten stiff. Pour into a buttered baking dish and bake 30 to 40 minutes. Serve at once.

STEAMED BROWN BREAD

Mrs. Dora Harris Jackson

½ cup corn meal
½ cup graham flour
½ cup rye flour
    little less than ½ cup molasses
1 teaspoon soda in 1 cup of sour
    milk

Pour in round buttered mold and steam 2 hours. (½ cup seedless raisins may be added.)
This is a must with Boston Baked beans and cod fish cakes every Saturday night.

SQUAW BREAD

John Mecom

2 tablespoons baking powder
1 qt. lukewarm water
1 teaspoon salt
1 tablespoon melted butter
    flour

Combine dry ingredients using enough flour in proportion to water to make a biscuit-like dough. Roll and cut any shape desired. Fry in kettle of boiling water.

Syrup for Squaw Bread

1 qt. corn syrup
1 lb. brown sugar
1 tablespoon mapeline
½ cup bacon grease
    red pepper

Boil corn syrup and brown sugar together using no water. Add mapeline, take from fire, and beat into mixture the bacon grease and 1 tiny pinch of red pepper.
This is very good with fried chicken and tossed salad.

MITTIE'S WHOLE WHEAT BREAD

2 cups milk
1 Fleischman's yeast cake
4 rounded tablespoons lard
3 level tablespoons sugar
2 teaspoons salt
4 cups white flour
3 cups whole wheat flour

Heat the milk lukewarm. Dissolve yeast in it, then the lard and sugar. Add 3 cups of white flour and place in a warm place to rise twice its size. Then add the whole wheat flour, salt and the other cup of white flour. Knead well, set it to rise again until twice its bulk, then roll out and cut.
This quantity makes one loaf and 21 rolls.

BRIOCHE

(French Parisian Brioche)

Mrs. René Salomon

Through Mrs. John R. Chessworth

Make a sponge of:
    ¾ cup of milk;
    3 cups of sifted flour
    1½ yeast cakes, dissolved in ¼ cup
        of water
    1 tablespoon of sugar
Let rise until bubbles burst on top. Then add:
    1 stick of butter, creamed well
    ½ cup of sugar
    1-1/3 (approximately) cups of flour
    ½ teaspoon of salt
    4 egg yolks, 2 whole eggs

Beat all thoroughly. Put in refrigerator overnight. Make into small rolls, drop into melted butter. Brush with yolk of egg and sprinkle sugar. Let rise.
Bake at 375 degrees, but first slit each roll before cooking and remember to sprinkle sugar before baking.

BUTTERED BREAD CRUMBS

Mrs. Clifford Stem

1 tablespoon butter or oleomargarine
½ cup sifted bread crumbs

Put butter in skillet and let it soften. Then put in crumbs, and toss them around in butter. Turn them out on board or platter and mush with spoon.

DANISH EGG CAKE
Mr. Thomas Farrar

½ lb. bacon
7 or 8 eggs·
1 cup of cream (or ¾ cream, ¼ milk)
box of soda crackers
chives (or minced shallot tops)
sliced bread (very thin)
salt, pepper, paprika

Mince the bacon and set to cook on a slow fire.

Meanwhile crumble the crackers and make a paste of them, softening them with water. Add part of the cream. Beat the eggs well, adding liberally, salt, pepper, and paprika, then add them to the cracker mixture and pour all this over the bacon.

When the mixture is nearly hard, add the chives, or shallot tops, with a liberal hand. The bread must be made ready meanwhile, the edges of some of the slices trimmed, so that the slices can be made to cover neatly all the contents of the pan (remember the bread must be very thin).

After the chives are added, the bread is fitted over the contents of the pan, dotted liberally with butter, and then the remainder of the cream is added. This is run under the broiler flame for a few minutes. The whole process takes about an hour; and at the end, the egg-cake should be hard enough so that it can cut like a cake. Sunday morning breakfast is a triumph with this.

CALAS CHIFFON
Mrs. S. A. Fortier

½ cup cooked salted rice
1 cup rice water
½ yeast cake
2 cups flour
2 teaspoons powdered sugar
½ teaspoon salt
3 eggs

Mash the rice. Add the yeast which has been dissolved in the lukewarm rice water and 1 cup flour. Let set twelve hours. Then add the eggs, well beaten, and the other cup of flour. Drop by tablespoonfuls into deep hot fat and fry till a golden brown. Drain and dust liberally with powdered sugar. This fritter may be served for breakfast as a hot bread, or for tea, made somewhat smaller, and is also a delicious dessert with coffee.

SCOOP KENNEDY'S
CALAS TOUT CHAUD
Courtesy of
Terry Flettrich

Scoop is a great cook -- a great gourmet -- a great jazzologist -- a great traveler and boulevardier. He is also an Irish Creole who grew up in the French Quarter, traveled the world over, has a chest full of cookery and bon vivant medals, a book shelf of Kennedy by-lined cook books -- the most recently called "Cook Along with Scoop" -- from which comes this one with comments by Kennedy.

In the old days in New Orleans (I'm told) rice fritters were sold on Sunday mornings outside almost all Catholic Churches. The fritters were called "Calas Tout Chaud."

After each Mass hungry worshippers who had received Communion and couldn't wait until they got home to eat would gather around the iron pot, full of boiling fat, and buy a batch of Calas, wrapped in brown paper.

They were so delectable that members of "other faiths" would haunt Catholic Church neighborhoods, looking for the "Calas Lady," who invariably was stout, colored and wore a tignon, which was a red bandana headpiece.

These "other faiths" perforce didn't enjoy Calas as much as Catholics because the latter hadn't eaten since going to Confession the evening before. Catholics, you should know, "go to" Confession (generally) on Saturday evening and do not eat again until after receiving Communion at Sunday Mass.

Thus, you can imagine what the aroma, sight and anticipation of the crisp fritters did to Catholic gastric juices, which I like to think are somewhat more whimsical than those of the alteram partem.

All right, now let's go into the kitchen and try doing 18 Calas:

Combine two cups of mushy cooked rice, three beaten eggs, ¼ teaspoon of vanilla, one half teaspoon of nutmeg.

Sift together ½ teaspoon of sugar, ½ teaspoon salt, 6 level tablespoons of flour and 3 teaspoons of baking powder.

Stir the two mixtures together, then drop by tablespoons full into a frying pan loaded with hot (360°) fat.

Fry until crisp and brown, sprinkle with powdered sugar, and hollar.

Until you've digested the moral principle involved in making Calas, you could fail. That is to say the fritters may disintegrate in the pan.

To assure success you should wear a tignon, go to church regularly, and disapprove of white buildings with no windows.

"CALAS TOU' CHAUDS"

Mrs. Albin Provosty

½ cup salted rice, 3 eggs
3 cups boiling water
¼ cup sugar
½ cake compressed yeast
½ teaspoon grated nutmeg
3 tablespoons flour

Boil rice until soft in the water. When soft set aside to cool. Mash and mix with the yeast which has been dissolved in a half cup of lukewarm water. Set to rise for twelve hours. Then beat three eggs thoroughly and add to the rice, beating well. Add the sugar, the flour and nutmeg, beat to a thick batter. Have ready a deep frying pan with sufficient boiling hot lard for the cakes to swim in. Drop the batter by spoonfuls into the lard and fry to a nice brown. Drain on brown paper, keep in a warm place. Pile on a hot dish and sprinkle liberally with powdered sugar.

The musical cry of portly mammies in "tignons" and guinea blue dresses, "Calas! Calas tout chauds!" as they peddled these dainties through the streets of the town was one of the distinctive street songs of old New Orleans. It is still heard on fête days.

COFFEE CAKE

Mrs. Harry Davis

¼ cup soft butter, 1 cup sugar
1½ cups flour, 1 teaspoon baking powder
2 eggs, ½ cup milk
sugar, cinnamon, chopped pecans

Cream butter and sugar, add egg yolks well beaten. Then add milk and flour which has been sifted with baking powder, alternately. Fold in beaten whites. Pour into oblong tin, spread, dot with butter and sprinkle with sugar, cinnamon and chopped pecans.

Bake in moderate oven. Cut in small pieces when cool.

TANTE MATHILDE'S CORNBREAD

Mrs. Walter Torian

2 cups sifted yellow cornmeal
3 eggs, 2 tablespoons lard
2 teaspoons baking powder
½ teaspoon salt, 1 coffeespoon sugar
1 cup flour, 2 cups milk

Beat the eggs, yolks and whites separately. To the cornmeal add the baking powder, salt, flour, and milk, then the beaten yolks, and the sugar and fold in whites.

Put the lard into a pan and set it into the oven, until very, very hot. Pour the bread mixture into this. The pan should be small enough so that the bread mixture may be fairly deep. Cook until done.

CORN DODGERS

Mrs. David T. Merrick

2 eggs
1 tablespoon each milk, lard
1 teaspoon salt
2 cups cornmeal
½ teaspoon baking powder
boiling water

Mix salt, lard, and meal, and pour water over it, sufficient to wet dough. Beat the yolks of the eggs well, add milk, and baking powder and pour into meal that has been cooled. Fold in well beaten whites of eggs.

Drop by teaspoonfuls on a well-greased baking sheet, two inches apart. Bake in a hot oven 15 or 20 minutes.

PLANTATION CORN MUFFINS

2 cups cornmeal
1 cup cooked grits or rice
2 or 3 eggs
1 teaspoon salt
1 cup milk
1 teaspoon each lard and butter
½ teaspoon baking powder

Scald the meal by pouring over it about 1½ cups of boiling water, add salt and beat until it is very smooth. Add the butter, lard, rice or grits and milk, and continue beating. Beat eggs slightly and stir them in. Then the baking powder, beat again. Have well greased rings smoking hot and pour in the batter. Bake in a very hot oven.

INDIAN PUMPKIN CORN PONES

Mrs. Herbert M. Shilstone

2 tablespoons oleo
1 cup of sugar
2 eggs, beaten together
7 large kitchen spoons of cooked
     mashed pumpkin (canned is
     just as good)
2/3 cup of water
1½ cups yellow cornmeal
2 tablespoons flour
2 teaspoons baking powder
1 teaspoon cinnamon

Mix in order given. Put in greased biscuit pan. Bake until straw or toothpick comes out clean. Cut in squares. Serve warm or cold.

OLD FASHIONED CORN PONES

Mrs. Rachel Bunting Wilmot

2 cups meal, scalded
½ teaspoon each salt, soda
1½ teaspoons, level, lard or bacon
     grease

Make into pones. Just fill the center of your hand with batter. Batter should be stiff in order to form pones.

Put on a very hot greased baking sheet. Put melted butter on top of the pones so they will brown nicely.

Bake at 400 degrees. They should have a hard crust.

CORN PUFFS

Mrs. Joseph Merrick Jones

4 egg whites
1 teaspoon salt
5 tablespoons white cornmeal

Beat 4 egg whites very stiff. Add 1 teaspoon salt. Scald 5 tablespoons of white cornmeal with enough boiling water to make soft mixture—not too soft. When mixture is warm fold in egg whites with salt. Drop from spoon on cookie sheet. Bake ½ hour in very slow oven.

ACADIAN "COUSH-COUSH"

Mrs. Walter Torian

2 cups cornmeal
2 teaspoons baking powder
½ teaspoon each salt, lard
1½ cups boiling water
3 eggs, beaten together

Scald meal and salt. When cool, add baking powder and beaten eggs. Have iron skillet piping hot, put lard in it, pour meal mixture in and allow it to cook 5 minutes. Scrape lightly from the bottom with spatula, reduce heat and place another hot iron skillet on top and steam 10 minutes longer. A rare treat, served with bacon or hash and coffee for breakfast.

CROISSANTS PARISIAN

Mrs. Olga Hirsch

1½ cups butter **or**
  1 cup butter and ½ cup margarine
1/3 cup sifted enriched flour
  2 packages active dry yeast **or**
  2 cakes compressed yeast
¼ cup each water, milk (scalded), sugar
  1 beaten egg
3¾ to 4 cups sifted enriched flour
  1 tablespoon milk, 1 egg yolk

Cream butter with 1/3 cup flour. Pat or roll butter mixture between 2 sheets of waxed paper to form a 12 x 6 inch rectangle. Then chill thoroughly. Soften active dry yeast in **warm** water or compressed yeast in **luke-warm** water. Combine milk, sugar and salt. Cool to lukewarm. Add softened yeast and egg. Mix well. Add 3¾ cups flour (or enough to make soft dough). Knead dough on lightly floured surface until smooth and glossy, about 5 minutes. Roll dough in a 14 inch square on lightly floured surface. Place chilled butter mixture on half the dough. Fold over other half of dough, sealing edges with heel of hand. Roll on lightly floured surface in a 20 x 12 inch rectangle. Repeat the folding and rolling 2 more times. Then fold in thirds to form rectangle about 12 x 7 inches. Chill ½ hour.

Next cut dough crosswise in fourths. On lightly floured surface roll each part of dough, keeping remainder in refrigerator in 22 x 7 inch rectangle. (Dough will be thin—about ⅛ inch.)

Cut into 10 pie-shaped wedges 4 inches at base and 7 inches long. (See sketch below.)

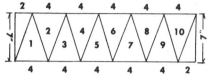

To shape croissants, begin with end opposite point (if dough has shrunk back, pull wedge to original size) and roll up loosely, toward point. Place 3 inches apart on ungreased baking sheet with center point down, curving ends to form **crescents.** Cover and let rise—Dainty crescent rolls, rich and flaky like puff pastry.

CORNSTARCH FRITTERS
Mrs. Frank Rose

Boil one pint of milk with one inch stick of cinnamon. Stir together one-half cup sugar, two tablespoons cornstarch and one tablespoon flour; add one-fourth cup of cold milk and yolks of three eggs well beaten. Add the boiling milk to this, also saltspoon of salt. Stir well.

Strain into double boiler and cook 15 minutes, stirring often. Take from the fire and add 1 teaspoon butter and 1 teaspoon vanilla.

Pour into buttered bread pan (about 1 inch deep) and set to cool. When very hard, sprinkle a bread board with fine bread crumbs. Turn the mixture out on this and cut into strips 2½" long and 1" wide, or in diamonds. Cover these in crumbs; dip in beaten egg, then in crumbs again. Fry 1 minute in smoking hot lard.

Sprinkle with sugar and serve hot. It is better to make the cream the night before. (They are delicious and very delicate.)

RICE FRITTERS
Mrs. Albin Provosty

1 cup cooked rice
3 eggs
½ cup flour
1 teaspoon baking powder
   sugar to taste

Mash the rice. Mix all ingredients together and beat to a light thin bat-

ter. Drop by tablespoonfuls into hot boiling lard. Fry to a nice brown, drain on brown paper and dust with powdered sugar. This is a sweet entremets and also a nice breakfast dish.

LUTIE'S "HUSH-PUPPIES"
Charlotte Farms
on the Jordan

½ cup sifted enriched flour
2 teaspoons baking powder
1 tablespoon sugar, ½ teaspoon salt
1½ cups white cornmeal
1 small onion, minced
1 beaten egg, ¾ cup milk

Sift dry ingredients together. Add onion, beaten egg and milk stirring all lightly. Drop batter by small spoonfuls into hot deep fat. Fry to golden brown. Drain on absorbent paper.

POLK MUFFINS
Mrs. Leonidas Polk

3 eggs
1 pt. milk
3 tablespoons flour, 1 teaspoon salt
1 tablespoon melted butter or lard

Beat the eggs. Mix rest of ingredients and add to beaten eggs and blend well. The batter should be about as thick as thick cream.

Bake in muffin pans in a very slow oven.

A real treat for Sunday breakfast.

NUT STICKS
Mrs. O. LeR. Goforth

2 cups flour, 1 teaspoon salt
2 teaspoons baking powder
4 tablespoons shortening
¾ cup nuts, chopped fine
   butter, milk

Sift dry ingredients, cut in shortening, add enough milk to make a soft dough. Roll out dough to ½ inch thickness or less, brush with melted butter. Spread half dough with nuts, fold other half over it. Cut into strips 1 inch by 3 inches. Brush with melted butter. Bake 20 minutes at 400°. Twice during baking brush with melted butter.

OWENDAW
Mrs. J. T. Bringier

2 cups cooked hominy
1 heaping tablespoon butter or lard
4 eggs, 1 pt. milk
½ pt. cornmeal, salt to taste

Have the cooked hominy hot and
mix into it the butter (or lard). Beat
the eggs very light and stir them into
the hominy. Next the milk, stirring
in very gradually. Lastly the cornmeal. The batter should be the consistency of thick boiled custard. If
thicker, add a little more milk.

Bake in a casserole at 375° to 400°
and enjoy a treasured plantation
legacy.

PAIN PERDU
Mrs. Walter Torain

sliced bread
orange flower water or vanilla
milk, 2 eggs
grated nutmeg
lard and butter

Soak the slices of bread a few minutes in milk to which a few drops of
orange flower water and a very little
sugar have been added. Remove, press
lightly and set aside for a few moments. Beat the yolks and whites
separately. Add the yolks to the whites
and put in a little grated nutmeg. Dip
the slices of bread in this, then fry in
the mixed lard and butter. Take out,
sprinkle powdered sugar and cinnamon over them and serve hot.

PETIE'S PAIN PERDU
Mrs. Jefferson Davis Hardin, Jr.

1 egg, ¼ cup sugar
1 cup of milk, 1 tablespoon vanilla
6 slices fresh Bond bread

Beat egg and sugar together, add
milk and vanilla. Cut each slice of
bread in four pieces (round or square)
removing crust. Dip in mixture, place
on plate to drain a moment, then fry
in frying pan in rather deep, hot fat.
Turn and brown on both sides being
careful not to burn. Place on brown
paper and sprinkle heavily with sugar
while hot. Goody, goody, yum, yum!

PAIN PERDU (LOST BREAD)
Mrs. Joseph Merrick Jones, Jr.

1 cup flour
3 teaspoons baking powder
1 egg
1½ tablespoons light syrup
1 cup milk plus 2 tablespoons
¼ teaspoon salt

Put all ingredients in blender on low
speed. When thoroughly mixed, transfer to shallow pan. Trim bread slices,
dip in batter, and fry in hot cooking
oil. Let brown and puff, and drain on
paper towels.

Serve with sifted confectioner's sugar, syrup, and melted butter.

PANCAKES
Mrs. Emile Kahn

8 eggs beaten separately
4 cups milk, salt (pinch)
8 tablespoons sifted flour
2 oranges, only the grated rind
1 cup of sugar, mix with the rind
Crisco to grease the skillet
butter to put on hot pancakes
maple syrup, hot

Stir yolks in milk, sift in the flour
and salt. Beat until smooth, fold in the
stiffly beaten whites. The griddle 7 to
8 inches, heat, grease, pour a cup of
batter which is thin on skillet for cakes
to be the same size. Butter each cake
and cover with the orange-sugar mixture and continue until the desired
number are cooked. Stack them in a
pyrex dish, place in a warm oven
leaving the door open, cover with
crystallized fruit. Cut as you would a
cake. Pass hot syrup and serve.

CAKES AU BAYOU TECHE
Mrs. Walter Torian

2 cups buttermilk or clabber
1 coffeespoon soda, scant
1-1/3 cups sifted flour, pinch of salt
2 tablespoons melted butter
1 tablespoon cane syrup

Sift the soda with the flour. Stir in
the buttermilk or clabber, add salt,
butter and cane syrup. The batter
must be very thick. Drop one tablespoon at a time on a very lightly but-

tered griddle. Serve with home-made sausage and good coffee for a perfect breakfast.

BUCKWHEAT CAKES
Mrs. Rachel Bunting Wilmot

½ cake yeast in
2½ cups tepid milk or water
2 cups buckwheat flour
2 tablespoons meal

Cover and place in a warm place to let rise overnight.
Next morning, beat the batter hard, add:

1 teaspoon salt, 1 tablespoon sugar
1 tablespoon lard
1 egg (whole) beaten
½ teaspoon soda (dissolved in a little warm water)

If batter is too thick, add a little tepid milk.
Cook on griddle.
Serve with melted butter and maple syrup or cane syrup.
Good with turkey hash or sausage.

BUCKWHEAT CAKES
Mrs. H. W. Waterfall
Baton Rouge

2 cups buckwheat flour
1 cup white flour
6 teaspoons baking powder
1½ teaspoons salt, 2½ cups milk
2 tablespoons melted butter
2 tablespoons molasses
2 eggs (beaten)

Sift baking powder, salt and both flours together twice. Add milk, melted butter, molasses and add beaten eggs last. Beat a little after adding eggs.

CREOLE PANCAKES

1 lb. flour
3 eggs
½ tablespoon lard, or lard and butter
1 teaspoonful sugar
milk to make a thin batter, or milk and water

This will serve eight or ten people. Crumble the shortening into the flour. Beat the eggs without separating, add the sugar and stir into the flour. Then add sufficient milk to make a thin batter. Use a heavy aluminum skillet so that no grease is necessary to fry them in. Heat the skillet but keep the fire low, and pour in enough batter to cover the skillet with a very thin coating. Turn like pancakes when both sides are browned roll into cylinders. Keep hot until all are prepared and serve with melted butter and sugar or with syrup. To turn them into a simplified version of crepes suzette, flavor the batter with grated orange rind. They may be served with a sauce made of ½ curacao and ½ brandy. This is lighted just as they are taken to the table. If no curacao is available, be more liberal with the grated orange peel in the batter and add a few drops of orange juice to the brandy sauce before lighting it.

FRENCH PAN-CAKES
Mrs. Emile Kalen

8 eggs, separated
4 cups milk
8 tablespoons sifted flour
2 oranges, grated rind only
sugar, same amount as grated orange
maple syrup, glazed fruit

Beat egg yolks thoroughly, add milk, then the flour. Beat until smooth, Fold in the stiffly beaten egg whites. The batter will be thin. Pour batter on hot griddle, greased lightly with Crisco. Spread very thin. When done butter each cake lightly and dust with the orange rind and sugar which have been mixed together. Stack in a pyrex dish and keep warm either in oven with door open or over hot water.
When ready to serve, cover top with glazed fruit cut portions as you would a cake. Serve with maple syrup.

FRENCH PAN-CAKES BRINGIER
Mrs. Edna Waldo

2 eggs, 1 cup flour
¼ teaspoon each sugar, salt
1 cup milk

Beat the ingredients well together. Pour the batter carefully on the griddle, just enough to cover, and as each cake is lightly brown, remove it to a hot plate, spread the center with any filling desired, and roll the pan-cake in the traditional cylindrical form.

If jam or jelly or sugar is to be used, the cake should be spread first with butter. An unusual and savory filling is grated American cheese.

GRIDDLE CAKES AUX MIETTES
Laura May

1½ cups fine stale bread crumbs
1½ cups scalded milk, 2 eggs
2 tablespoons butter
½ cup flour, ½ teaspoon salt
2 teaspoons baking powder

Mix the milk and butter with the crumbs and blend well.

Now add the eggs, well beaten, to the flour with the salt and baking powder sifted with it. Add to first mixture, stir well, and the batter is ready for the skillet. Use a minimum of lard in the latter.

PECAN LOAF
Mrs. Alton Ochsner

3 cups bread crumbs
1½ cups milk
½ cup each chopped onions, celery
½ cup melted butter
1½ cups chopped pecans
2 eggs, well beaten

Soak crumbs in milk. Fry the onions till soft, in a little butter. Put celery and nuts through the meat chopper. Mix all together and add the beaten eggs. Place in a mold and set mold in another pan partly filled with water. Bake for three quarters of an hour in a medium oven. Serve with creamed mushroom sauce.

POPOVERS
Miss Hilma Johnson

4 eggs
1 pt. milk, 1½ cups flour
2 tablespoons melted butter
salt to taste

Beat eggs lightly, then add milk and flour and beat until smooth. Bake in hot, well greased iron muffins pans about 35 minutes. Reduce the heat after twenty minutes baking. This will make nine popovers. There are two musts for successful popovers—first, a very thorough beating of the ingredients; second, do not open oven for 20 minutes.

ROLLS
Mrs. Thomas Fields
(Through Mrs. George Frierson)

1 cup each boiling water, cold water
1 cup lard, ½ cup sugar
½ teaspoon salt
1 yeast cake, 2 eggs
6 cups unsifted flour
1 tablespoon or more butter

Put lard, sugar and salt in a large bowl. Pour boiling water over. Mix well until lard dissolves. Add cold water, eggs well beaten, and yeast cake. Blend flour in until all is used. Set aside to rise. When double in bulk store in refrigerator until ready to use. Roll dough out not too thin. Cut with cutter. Have melted butter ready. Butter pans and top of rolls and fold over pocket-book style. Butter tops of rolls again after folded. Let rise for 1 to 1½ hours. Bake in hot oven.

ROLLS
Mrs. Paul Saunders

6 cups flour, 2 yeast cakes
2 eggs
2 cups sweet milk, scalded and cooled
1 tablespoon sugar, 2 teaspoons salt
4 kitchen spoons melted lard or oil

Mix the dry ingredients and sift. Add lard. When milk is tepid add yeast cake and whole eggs. Pour into flour mixture and mix well. Place in a covered vessel, and let rise 2 hours. Pour on a bread board which has been floured, roll and cut into rings and let rise another hour. Keep covered. Brush tops with butter and bake in a rather quick oven about 20 minutes.

CINNAMON ROLLS
Mrs. John E. Hurley

½ cup lukewarm milk
½ cup sugar, 1 teaspoon salt
2 packages yeast
½ cup lukewarm water
1 cup (2 sticks) butter or oleo
4½ to 5 cups flour, 2 eggs
Ingredients for spread:
1½ cups brown sugar
¾ cup (1½ sticks) butter
1½ tablespoons cinnamon

During first rising of dough, cream together sugar, butter and cinnamon.

Allow to stand at room temperature until ready for use.

Directions:
Mix together milk, sugar and salt. Soak yeast in water for about 5 min. without stirring. Then stir well and add to milk mixture. Add eggs and shortening. Add flour in two additions, using only amount necessary to make it easy to handle. Mix in first with spoon, then with hands. When dough begins to leave sides of bowl, turn out onto lightly floured board or marble and knead until smooth and elastic and does not stick to board. Place in greased bowl, turning once to bring greased side up. Cover with damp cloth and let rise in warm draft-free spot of 80°-85° until double in size, about 1½-2 hrs.

Then thrust fist into dough, pull edges into center and turn completely over in bowl. Let rise again until almost double in size, about 30-45 min.

Divide dough into two portions, round up, cover and let rest 15 min.

Roll each portion into oblong about 9 in. x 24 in. Spread with butter mixture. Roll up tightly, beginning at the wide side. Seal well by pinching edges of roll together. Cut each roll into 32 slices, ¾ in. Place a little apart in a greased pan 17 x 11. Cover and let rise until double in bulk, 35-40 min.

Bake in 375° oven for 25-30 min.

SALLY LUNN

Agnes Thompson
(through Mrs. T. S. Behre)

2 eggs, separated
½ cup sugar, scant
1 tablespoon butter
3 cups flour, ¼ teaspoon salt
2 teaspoons baking powder
¾ to 1 cup milk
2 tablespoons melted butter

Beat the sugar and the egg yolks together, add milk alternately with the flour, which has been sifted with the salt and baking powder. Beat till smooth and free from lumps. Add the melted butter, and fold in the whites of the eggs which have been beaten stiff. Pour into a well greased stem pan and bake in a moderate oven for about ½ hour. As it begins to brown brush with melted butter. After removal from the oven, brush again

lightly with butter and sprinkle liberally with sugar and cinnamon. Run in oven a second. Serve hot.

CINNAMON TOAST

Mrs. Jefferson Davis Hardin, Jr.

½ cup granulated sugar
¼ stick of butter, pinch salt
1 level teaspoon cinnamon
1 large loaf of fresh bread cut in rounds

Cream butter, sugar, salt and cinnamon thoroughly. Pile sugar mixture high on bread like a cone. Place in pan and put in hot oven and bake about 10 minutes keeping it low and let bread brown. Take out and lay on baking sheet and dust with granulated sugar. Serve immediately.

CHOCOLATE WAFFLES

6 tablespoons sugar
2 tablespoons melted butter
3 teaspoons baking powder
1 cup milk
1¾ cups flour, ½ teaspoon salt
2 squares chocolate, melted
2 eggs

Sift flour, baking powder, salt and add sugar, eggs, milk, butter and chocolate. Cook in waffle iron.

PLANTATION WAFFLES

1 cup each milk, flour
1 tablespoon cornmeal
1 teaspoon salt, level
2 teaspoons melted lard
2 tablespoons melted butter
2 eggs
1 teaspoon baking powder

Beat the yolks of the eggs and the milk together and add the shortening. Sift the flour, salt, and baking powder; add it to the milk and eggs. Just before cooking, fold in the well beaten whites. If electric iron is used add 3 tablespoons cooking oil.

SOUR MILK WAFFLES

Mrs. W. E. Winship

3 eggs, 2 cups flour
2 cups thick sour milk
2 teaspoons baking powder
¾ teaspoon each soda, salt
6 tablespoons melted butter

Separate eggs. Beat yolks. Add one cup sour milk. Sift dry ingredients, add to yolks. Add other cup sour milk, then butter and stiffly beaten whites. Bake in hot greased waffle iron, unless an electric waffle iron is used, when no grease is necessary. Serve with butter and hot maple or cane syrup.

WHEAT FLUFF

Mrs. Robert A. Laird

1½ cups cooked Cream of Wheat
3 eggs

1 cup grated American cheese
¼ teaspoon ground black pepper
1 teaspoon Worcestershire sauce
1 dash Tabasco sauce
  salt to taste

Mix together cooked Cream of Wheat, and well-beaten eggs. Add grated cheese, pepper, Worcestershire and Tabasco sauce. Pour into buttered casserole. Sprinkle additional cheese on top. Place in hot oven for about twenty minutes, or until top is golden-brown. This is an excellent dish for breakfast, lunch, or dinner. Serve hot.

salad and salad dressings

TOMATO ASPIC
Mrs. J. C. Greenoe
Vicksburg, Mississippi

1 qt. tomato juice
2 cloves garlic, crushed
½ teaspoon dry mustard
2 teaspoons salt
2½ tablespoons sugar
5 tablespoons lemon juice
1 teaspoon paprika
1/8 teaspoon red pepper
4 envelopes plain gelatin
2 ozs. beef bouillon
3 ozs. cream cheese
2 tablespoons grated onion and
    juice (or to taste)
    Tabasco to taste

In 1½ quart saucepan mix tomato juice, garlic, dry mustard, salt, sugar, lemon juice, paprika and red pepper. Bring to a boil, uncovered, and boil 3 minutes. Remove from fire and add gelatin, which has been softened in beef bouillon. Stir until dissolved. Pour into mold and refrigerate. Mix softened cream cheese with grated onion and Tabasco and refrigerate until ready to add to aspic.

When aspic gets thick but has not completely jelled, add cheese which you have rolled into little balls as you go along. Place cheese balls in the center of the aspic mold as you desire.

ARTICHOKE ASPIC
Mrs. Miriam W. Laudeman

2 large boiled artichokes
1 can Swanson's clear broth
1 envelope Knox gelatine
    (dissolved in small amount of
    water or cold broth)
lettuce
mayonnaise
capers
salt and pepper to taste
celery salt

Scrape artichoke leaves and cut hearts into small pieces. Season chicken broth with salt, pepper and celery salt and heat to boiling. Add dissolved gelatine. Separate artichoke meats into four individual molds. Fill with broth mixture. Cool and refrigerate until jelled.

Separate and serve over lettuce (from mold). Top with mayonnaise and capers.

ARTICHOKE MOUSSE
Mrs. Edward B. Poitevent

4 artichokes
3 pkgs. Philadelphia cream cheese
2 cups of milk
2 stalks of celery
1 teaspoon of onion juice
    dash of Lea & Perrin, cayenne,
      black pepper, salt
1 can of consommé
1 can of pimentos
3 envelopes gelatine

After boiling artichokes, separate leaves from hearts, removing chokes. Cut hearts in quarters. Scrape leaves. Take scrapings, cream cheese, chopped celery, onion juice, Lea & Perrin, salt, cayenne and black pepper, and mash thoroughly together. Then add consommé and one cup of milk. Place on stove to warm, then add gelatine dissolved in the other cup of milk. Remove from stove and pour into well greased ring in which the hearts and pimentos have been arranged. Let congeal. Serve with mayonnaise in center.

ARTICHOKE MOUSSE
Mrs. Robert Moore Parker

8 boiled artichokes
1 cup celery, chopped

1 cup mayonnaise
1 tablespoon gelatine
    salt, cayenne, Worcestershire

Scrape the artichoke leaves and add to the hearts which have been cut in small pieces. Add gelatine, which has been soaked in cold water, (use as little water as possible). Fold all ingredients including mayonnaise together and pack in a mold. Chill until firm and turn out on lettuce leaves. Serve with mayonnaise.

ARTICHOKES SHARON

Mrs. Charles L. Seemann

8 medium artichokes
1 can consommé or green turtle soup
1 envelope gelatine
1 tablespoon Worcestershire sauce
¾ cup of water
1 lemon, the juice
2 teaspoons French dressing
    salt, pepper, to taste

Boil the artichokes in salt water until tender. Separate leaves from hearts and remove chokes. Scrape soft part from leaves and mash well. Mix with the French dressing, fill the hearts and chill.

Soften gelatine in ½ cup water and dissolve in ¼ cup boiling water. Combine with the soup, season with salt, pepper and lemon juice and Worcestershire sauce. Chill till slightly thickened. Pour a small amount of the soup into each of eight muffin tins. Place the stuffed artichoke hearts stem up, one in each, and fill with the remaining soup. Chill in the refrigerator until firm. Turn out on lettuce leaves and serve with mayonnaise.

ARTICHOKE IN TOMATO ASPIC

6 artichokes
1 qt. can tomatoes
    grated onion, a little
1 bay leaf, 2 cloves
½ cup boiling water
½ cup cold water
1 tablespoon gelatine

Cook the tomatoes and the seasoning 15 minutes. Dissolve the gelatine in cold water and add the boiling water to it. Strain the tomatoes and add the gelatine. When cool, put a little in the mold to set. Next, add the boiled artichoke hearts, cut up,

and the tender part of the leaves that have been scraped off with a silver knife, into the tomato juice. Pour all into the mold to set. Serve on hearts of lettuce, with mayonnaise.

AVOCADO

Take ripe avocados, cut in halves, remove seed, scoop out the meat with a teaspoon, mix with pieces of tomato, and marinate with a sharp mayonnaise seasoned with Worcestershire sauce and grated onion. Put back in shell. Chill. This makes a good beginning for a summer luncheon.

AVOCADO ASPIC

Charles L. Dufour

Pie Dufour's à la Mode

1 soft avocado
2 tablespoons of mayonnaise
1 can of consommé
1 package of gelatine
    salt and pepper to taste

Macerate the avocado into a creamy consistency. Add mayonnaise and seasoning.

Add softened gelatin to hot consommé.

Pour into mashed avocado and mix thoroughly. Allow to cool, and when tepid, pour into molds and place in refrigerator.

Makes eight individual servings or one mold.

AVOCADO MOUSSE

1½ tablespoons gelatine
½ cup cold water
½ cup boiling water or stock
1 teaspoon salt
1 teaspoon onion juice
2 cups avocado
2 teaspoons Worcestershire sauce
½ cup whipped cream
½ cup mayonnaise

Cream avocado, add salt, Worcestershire sauce and onion juice. Soak gelatine in cold water. Add boiling water. When cool pour it into cream and mayonnaise, that have been well mixed. Now combine this with the avocado and turn into a mold. Serve with tomatoes, hearts of lettuce and mayonnaise.

CHICKEN SALAD
Mrs. Grace Stevenson

Stew one chicken slowly with one quart of water to which one tablespoon of tarragon vinegar and three cloves of garlic have been added, also salt and pepper. When tender cut from bones and cube. Add one cup mushrooms, ¼ cup diced green and red peppers—return to stock and season highly.

Core and pare eight medium sized apples leaving one inch band of peel around the centers. Fill each apple with the chicken mixture and place them in a roasting pan with some of the chicken stock. Bake until the apples are tender but not falling apart. Baste several times. When done, chill. Serve on nest of endive with mayonnaise.

CHICKEN SALAD
Mrs. James Selman

1 4-6 lb. baking hen

Stock for Cooking Hen:

3 quarts water
2 teaspoons salt
 freshly ground pepper
2 celery stalks, with leaves
2 carrots
1 large onion, quartered
3 parsley sprigs
½ lemon (optional)

Simmer chicken in stock, covered, for 2½ hours, or until tender. Allow chicken to cool in stock. (This makes the dish.) When cool, remove bird from stock. Pull meat from carcass and cut up into rather large dice with a pair of scissors. (Use only white meat, reserve dark meat for another dish.)
Mix cut up meat with:

½ cup minced celery
½ cup minced parsley
¼ cup minced shallots, green part only
¼ cup chicken stock

Toss all together.
Make a homemade mayonnaise (blender type), adding to the mayonnaise while blending, ½ cup coarsely chopped shallots, green part included

and 1-2 tablespoons Creole (black) mustard.
Add enough of the mayonnaise mixture to the chicken mixture for consistency desired. Serve on lettuce leaves and pass the mayonnaise dressing on the side.

CLUB SALAD
Mrs. Paul B. Lansing

This salad is excellent as a main course served with hot bread and iced tea in the summer. Men adore it, and I have never served it when men (and women) didn't go back for seconds! Great for ladies luncheons, also.

¾ lb. garlic salami cut into 1/8 inch slivers, ¼" thick
¾ lb. ham cut as above
½ lb. American cheese cut in cubes
2 bunches shallots, chopped
1½ lbs. cleaned and boiled shrimp
1 head lettuce, broken in bite size pieces
4 hard boiled eggs, sliced

Dressing:

½ part Kraft French dressing
½ part Miracle Whip

Combine salad ingredients in large salad bowl and toss with salad dressing.

COLE SLAW
Mrs. William McClean

3 cups cabbage, shredded
1½ cups crisp celery, chopped
1 small can grated pineapple, drained
1 small green pepper, chopped
½ cup blanched almonds, cut in slivers

Cabbage should be put in a bowl of ice water after cleaning. Drain after ½ hour, and put on ice. When ready to mix, dry thoroughly. Then put in a bowl which has been rubbed with garlic. The chopped celery, pepper, and almonds are then added and the pineapple. The whole must be well mixed and dressed with boiled dressing.

CRAB MEAT, ROQUEFORT DRESSING

1 doz. hard crabs, or 1 lb. lump crabmeat

6 tomatoes
3 hard-boiled eggs
French dressing
Roquefort cheese dressing
salt, pepper, crab boil

Boil the crabs with crab boil, salt. Pick crab meat when cold and season. Slice the hard-boiled eggs and the tomatoes. Pour French dressing over them and set aside. Later, put the sliced hard-boiled eggs and tomatoes around the crab meat and pour the French dressing over it, then pour over all Roquefort cheese dressing.

CRAB SALAD

Mrs. Wilson Jones

1 tablespoon gelatine dissolved in
   ¼ cup cold water
½ cup hot water added, when cool mix
   with 1 pt. crab meat
½ cup each celery, green pepper,
   chopped
2 tablespoons olives (chopped fine)
1 teaspoon salt, and a little red pepper
¼ teaspoon paprika
2 tablespoons lemon juice or vinegar
¾ cup mayonnaise

Pour into fish mold, set in refrigerator until firm.

MARINATED CRAB SALAD

Mrs. W. Elliott Laudeman III

8 hard shell boiled crabs
3 ribs celery, diced
3 carrots, peeled and diced
1 bell pepper, slivered
1 small fresh red pepper whole (hot)
1 lemon, sliced
6 raw cauliflower florets
¾ cup oil cured black olives or
   Greek olives
1/3 cup pickled onions
½ cup green olives
8 rolled anchovies
6 garlic toes, peeled

Marinade:

2 cups olive oil
2/3 cup lemon juice or tarragon vinegar
2 teaspoons salt
2 teaspoons coarse ground pepper
1 teaspoon garlic salt
½ teaspoon prepared yellow mustard
½ teaspoon oregano
4 teaspoons grated parmesan cheese

Using a gallon screw top jar or other large covered container, fill container

with salad ingredients. Crabs are prepared by removing outer shell and deadmen (lung portion). Break crab bodies in halves or quarters, leaving legs and claws attached to bodies. Save yellow crab fat to add to marinade. Shake jar vigorously to evenly distribute various ingredients.

Prepare marinade. Shake well. Pour over crab salad mixture and again shake vigorously. Refrigerate.

About every hour for at least 8 hours, turn and shake jar alternating letting jar stand on its top and bottom. This will keep for several days in the refrigerator.

CRAB MEAT SALAD

1 lb. lump crab meat
1 medium onion (grated fine)
7 pieces celery cut in tiny pieces
1 tablespoon Worcestershire
1 teaspoon mustard, salt, pepper
2 tablespoons mayonnaise
   lettuce

Cut ½ inch thick slice of iceberg lettuce and spread mayonnaise on both sides. Mix all the other ingredients well and pile on sliced lettuce. Garnish with celery, parsley and ripe olives.

Serve with crackers, sliced date and nut bread (very hot and buttered).

CRANBERRY SALAD

Mrs. Thomas Garner

1 pt. fresh cranberries
1 cup each water, sugar
1 tablespoon plain gelatine
½ cup canned crushed pineapple
½ cup diced peeled apples
½ cup chopped celery
½ cup chopped nuts

Wash and pick over cranberries. Put sugar, water and cranberries on fire and boil for 5 minutes. Remove from fire and cool. Now soak plain gelatin in ¼ cup cold water. Add gelatin to cranberries while hot. Let cool and then add the pineapple, apples, celery and nuts. Stir well. Turn into a mold. Place in refrigerator. Serve with mayonnaise. This serves 8. Whole Ocean Spray cranberries may be substituted if fresh cranberries are not available.

CREAM OF CUCUMBER SALAD

Frances Parkinson Keyes

1 cucumber cut in small cubes
½ pt. whipped cream
2 teaspoons gelatine dissolved in water
½ sweet pimento
½ teaspoon Tarragon vinegar
  salt and lemon juice to taste

Mix, mold, and let stand for twelve hours. Serve with lettuce and French dressing.

CUCUMBERS WITH SOUR CREAM DRESSING

Mrs. T. S. Behre

2 firm cucumbers
½ pt. commercial sour cream
2 tablespoons cider vinegar
2 tablespoons minced green onions
1 tablespoon minced parsley
1 scant teaspoon sugar (optional)

Slice the cucumbers paper thin and cover with water to which 1 teaspoon of salt has been added. Place in the refrigerator for thirty minutes or so. Drain and dry on a towel, patting away as much moisture as possible. In a large bowl mix the sour cream, onions, parsley, vinegar and sugar to taste. Add the cucumbers. This can be kept refrigerated for several days and should be served with very thin slices of pumpernickel.

DESSERT SALAD

Mrs. John Barry

1 large can sliced pineapple
½ lb. marshmallows
½ lb. blanched whole almonds
½ teaspoon each salt, mustard
3 teaspoons flour
2½ tablespoons vinegar
½ tablespoon each sugar, butter
½ pt. whipped cream
½ cup thick cream
3 egg yolks

Drain pineapple overnight, or several hours before using. Mix sugar, salt, flour, mustard and vinegar in double boiler. Cook until it begins to thicken. Add the beaten egg yolks and butter, stirring all the while. Let cool, then thin with the cream. Cut the pineapple in small pieces, quarter the marshmallows and add. Pour the dressing over this. Mix thoroughly and place in refrigerator to get very cold.

Before serving add almonds and the stiffly whipped cream. Serve on hearts of lettuce. Cheese biscuits or cheese straws make an excellent accompaniment.

EGG MOUSSE

1 doz. eggs, hard boiled, chopped
1 cup milk
1¼ tablespoons gelatine
1 cup mayonnaise
  salt, pepper
2 cups shrimp or crab salad

Mix eggs and mayonnaise. Soak gelatine in ½ cup cold milk, then dissolve in ½ cup hot milk. Pour into eggs and mayonnaise and mix. Season. Pour in ring mold and place in refrigerator to set. Turn out on a platter, fill center with shrimp or crab salad, garnish and serve.

FROZEN SALAD TENERIFFE

Mrs. Hugh DeLacey Vincent

1 cup each mayonnaise, whipped cream
1 Philadelphia cream cheese
1 cup canned pineapple
2 to 3 tablespoons sugar
1 small bottle Maraschino cherries

Mash the cherries and add them gradually to the whipped cream keeping the mixture smooth. Drain all the juice from the fruit and fold lightly into the mixture. Blend the cream cheese to the mayonnaise and add to the other mixture blending well.

Place in a melon mold, or freezer, cover with waxed paper, pack in ice and salt for 3 hours, (two parts ice to 1 part salt).

FRUIT SALAD WITH HONEY DRESSING

Mrs. Gerald Derks

Salad:
  Mandarin sections, canned
  Tokay grapes, split and seeded
  Canned pineapple chunks
  Toasted slivered almonds
  Lettuce, any mild type
  Fresh spinach

Dressing:

½ cup sugar
1 teaspoon salt
½ teaspoon paprika
½ teaspoon celery seed
½ teaspoon poppy seed
¼ cup vinegar
1 teaspoon dry mustard
1 teaspoon onion juice
1 cup Wesson oil

Beat all ingredients except honey at high speed. Add honey very slowly. Beat until consistency of thick syrup. Toss salad just prior to serving.
Note: Dressing can be beaten again before using, if necessary.

GAZPACHO SALAD
Mrs. W. Elliott Laudeman III

2 cucumbers, peeled and finely diced
2 bell peppers, seeded and finely slivered
4 Creole tomatoes, seeded and finely diced
1 onion, finely diced
2 carrots, peeled and thinly sliced crosswise
1 can black olives
1 can rolled anchovies
2 toes of garlic, minced
¼ cup vinegar
½ cup olive oil
1 tablespoon finely chopped parsley
2 teaspoons finely chopped shallots
1 pinch of ground cumin seed
1 pinch of ground oregano
salt and pepper to taste, one lemon

In glass jar arrange alternate layers of cucumbers, carrots, bell peppers, onions, and tomatoes. Lightly sprinkle each layer with salt and pepper and intersperse the layers of vegetables with black olives and rolled anchovies. Make salad dressing of other ingredients. Pour dressing over salad layers and chill for at least 3 hours, occasionally turning jar upside down to marinate layers.
Serve the vegetables in chilled bowls and sprinkle with the juice of one lemon or top with lemon slice.

GROUND ARTICHOKE MOUSSE

1 lb. ground artichokes, boiled and mashed through a colander
1 heaping tablespoon gelatine softened in ½ cup cold water
½ cup boiling water
1 teaspoon each salt, onion juice

2 teaspoons Worcestershire sauce
½ cup each, whipped cream, mayonnaise

Add salt, Worcestershire, and onion juice, to the mashed artichokes. Dissolve the soaked gelatine in the boiling hot water and add to above mixture. When cool fold in the cream and mayonnaise which have been well mixed. Mold and chill and serve with tomatoes, hearts of lettuce and mayonnaise.

JELLIED BARTLETT - BEET SALAD
Mrs. George Douglass, Jr.

1 package jello (small) each raspberry, strawberry, and cherry
3 cups boiling water
1 cup sweet pickle juice
2 teaspoons vinegar
dash salt
1 can cut beets, drain well
1 can pears cut, drain well

Dissolve jello in boiling water. Add juice, vinegar and salt. Add beets and pears.
Serve with vegetable sour cream dressing.

Vegetable sour cream dressing:

½ cup mayonnaise
¼ cup sour cream
1 teaspoon each: chopped green onions, celery, and green pepper
salt and pepper to taste

JELLIED BORSCH
Mrs. Charles L. Seemann

1 can small whole beets (diced)
2 tablespoons Tarragon vinegar
1 package lemon jello
1 cup boiling water
1 dash onion juice
2 tablespoons horseradish
¾ cup celery chopped fine
½ pt. sour cream, seasoned with pepper
salt, pepper to taste
¾ cup drained beet juice

Dissolve lemon jello in boiling water, add cold beet juice, salt, vinegar, horseradish. Put in refrigerator until it begins to set. Then add diced beets, celery and onion juice. Stir well. Put in greased muffin pans (8) and chill six or more hours. Turn out and garnish with lettuce and top with sour cream.

FISH ASPIC SALAD
Mrs. May Westerfield Born
Orleans Club

6 filets of trout, tenderloined
  (save head and bones for
  stock)
salt, cayenne, thyme, 4-5 bay
  leaves, few cloves
few allspice, juice and rind of 1
  lemon
½ glass vinegar
4 egg whites
2 tablespoons gelatin
½ cup cold water

Make cooking broth for fish; boil heads and bones with seasonings and vinegar in 2 quarts water. Strain this broth and poach the filets in it until they flake with a fork (about 10 minutes, depending on the size of the filet). Remove fish and let cool. Add the 4 beaten egg whites to the broth and let boil 4-5 minutes. Strain this through cloth.

Soak the gelatin in the cold water, and add 2 cups of the hot broth to this. Place fish in ring mold and cover with the gelatin-broth mixture, adding enough broth to this to make the broth cover the fish in the mold. Place mold in the icebox until it jells.

Editor's note: serve with homemade mayonnaise.

ONION BEGUE SALAD
Begue's Restaurant
(Through Mrs. Walter Torian)

6 large onions
2-3 cups French dressing
1 chopped hard boiled egg

Pare and boil the onions. Remove from the water, cool, and drain. Season with French dressing, sprinkle with the chopped egg, and serve.

JELLIED ORANGE
Mrs. Edward Rightor

1 envelope Knox gelatine
½ cup water
1 cup orange juice
1 cup sugar
1 tablespoon lemon juice
1 cup pineapple, shredded
2 large carrots, grated

Soak gelatine in ¼ cup cold water and add ¼ cup boiling water. When cool add orange juice, lemon juice, sugar, pineapple and carrots.

Put in mold and place in refrigerator.

Serve with mayonnaise, that has had a cup of whipped cream added.

LEEK SALAD

Boil and chill leeks. Serve with either French dressing or a mayonnaise. It is supposed to be one of the most tasty salads in the world.

LETTUCE CHAPON

½ teaspoon each salt and pepper
2 tablespoons vinegar
6 tablespoons olive oil
1 clove garlic
  crusts of stale bread
  lettuce and other greens

Make a dressing by adding vinegar to salt and pepper then add the oil, slowly, stirring till well blended. Rub a salad bowl with garlic. Break up the greens and place in the bowl. Rub the bowl and the crusts of bread with garlic which has been dipped into coarse salt. Cut crusts into small pieces and add to the greens. Pour dressing over and toss with a fork till all is well coated with the dressing.

LOBSTER MOUSSE
Mrs. Seth Miller

Chop meat of two lobsters weighing about 1½ pounds each (or 1 pound of shrimp). Soak 1 tablespoon of gelatine in ½ cup of cold tomato sauce. Heat. When cool, mix with ½ pint of whipped cream and ½ cup of mayonnaise. Pepper and salt to taste. Mix together and fill mold. Chill. Serve on lettuce, center filled with mayonnaise.

LOBSTER MOUSSE
Mrs. Sterling Parkerson

1 can tomato soup
3 Philadelphia cream cheese
2 tablespoons gelatine
¾ cup each finely chopped celery,
  chopped green pepper

2 tablespoons grated onions
1 large can lobster
1 cup mayonnaise
lettuce, salt, Tabasco, Worcestershire sauce

Mash the cream cheese in the tomato soup, and heat in a double-
boiler until the cheese is melted and
very hot. Soak the gelatine for five
minutes in a cup of cold water and
add to the soup mixture. As soon as
this begins to congeal, add the celery,
green pepper, and onions, and the lobster, which has been broken into small
pieces. Add the mayonnaise and season highly with salt, Tabasco, and
Worcestershire sauce.

Place in a wet mold and when set,
serve on a bed of lettuce leaves, garnished with mayonnaise.

Note: This is a rich and filling salad.
It should not be served at dinner or
when other heavy food is served. But
it is a thing of perfect grace for a
Sunday night supper, or for a light
luncheon. Shrimp can be used instead
of lobster.

MANDARIN ORANGE SALAD

Mrs. Walter Hagestad

2 regular size packs orange jello
2 cups boiling liquid (which includes
juice from fruits
1 pint orange sherbet
1 No. 2 can crushed pineapple, well
drained
1 small can mandarin orange segments,
drained
2 large bananas, diced (optional)

Dissolve jello in hot liquid. Melt
sherbet in hot mixture. Add other
ingredients and pour into oblong dish.
Cover tightly with Saran Wrap. Stir
once or twice while it is congealing.

MIRLITON (Vegetable Pear)

Choose mirlitons about the size of
a duck egg, or very little larger. Wash
them and boil until tender. When
cool, pare and take out seed. Give
them a few hours in the ice-box to
marinate with French dressing.

On a bed of shredded lettuce put
two halves for each serving. In the
seed cavity put a filling of Neufehâtel
or cream cheese, moistened with a little cream if necessary. Add salt and

pepper to taste. Garnish with mayonnaise and sprinkle with paprika.

FRESH MUSHROOM SALAD

Mrs. Mims Gage

1½ lbs. fresh mushrooms, sliced
2 bunches watercress
10 green onions, chopped
1 bunch parsley, chopped
2 heads of Romaine lettuce
2 tomatoes (for garnish)

Dressing:

1 cup wine vinegar
3 cups olive oil
2 teaspoons dry mustard
1 teaspoon horseradish
1 egg yolk

Mix all dressing ingredients in blender and blend for 2 - 3 minutes.

PEAS AND SOUR CREAM

Mrs. Fleur Hampton

1 package frozen peas
1 small onion
½ top basil
salt and pepper

Cook all ingredients until tender,
then chill. Add to peas:

½ cup celery
½ cup sour cream
½ tablespoon lemon juice

Cut fresh green onions for the top.
Chill 24 hours.

PÂTÉ DE FOIE GRAS ASPIC

Mrs. Alfred T. Pattison

2 to 3 calf's feet
(chicken feet and heads add to flavor)
1 qt. water
1 lb. piece shin bone, broken
½ soup bunch
1 small clove garlic
2 eggs, the whites
1 can bouillon
1 can pâté de foie gras
salt, pepper, to taste

Boil all of this except the pâté, the
egg whites and bouillon until calf's
feet boil to pieces, at least 2 hours
cooking. Strain and let cool, then

clarify with white of eggs. When clear, add bouillon and 1 pint water. Season to taste and set in molds to harden. This amount makes about 3 pints of jelly. It can be kept in the ice box, and used for several days. The pâté can be put in individual molds of this jelly or in a large ring of it. It is delicious served with hearts of lettuce salad and French dressing.

Note: The calf's feet may be put to use, instead of wasting them, the meat picked from the bones and made into a stew with brown gravy; or served "en poulette" with a cream sauce thickened with the yolk of an egg. This makes a delicious dish.

PEGASUS SALAD

Mrs. Joel Harris Lawrence

2 large boiled potatoes
2 hard-boiled eggs, chopped
1 small onion, chopped fine
1 teaspoon dry mustard
4 tablespoons olive oil
2 tablespoons vinegar
1 teaspoon anchovy paste, or sauce
    salt, pepper, garlic salt, to taste

Boil the potatoes and press through a ricer. Add the chopped eggs, and minced onion. Make a dressing of the other ingredients, using a rotary egg beater. Stir into the potato mixture. Serve on lettuce leaves.

HOT POTATO SALAD

2 lbs. small Irish potatoes (the red variety)
2 tablespoons each minced onion, green pepper, minced parsley
    French dressing

Have the seasonings ready when the potatoes are boiled and thinly sliced. Add them immediately to the hot potatoes and stir well and lightly. Have savory French dressing ready, pour over, and if liked add small bits of crisply fried bacon.

RASPBERRY JELLY SALAD

Mrs. William James Kearney III

2 packages raspberry jello
2 packages frozen raspberries
2 No. 303 cans of pears

2/3 cup port wine
4 tablespoons lemon juice

Drain pears. Use juice plus water to make 1½ cups. Heat and add to Jello, add wine and lemon juice. Cool to syrup consistency then fold in berries and pears.

SHRIMP MOUSSE

Mrs. Wallace E. Sturgis
Ocala, Florida

1 can tomato soup
    pinch baking soda
9 ozs. cream cheese
2 envelopes gelatin
¼ cup chicken stock, or bouillon
1 cup homemade mayonnaise
1½ lbs. cooked shrimp, cut up
1 tablespoon grated onion
½ cup celery, finely chopped
½ of a green pepper, finely chopped
    juice of 1 lemon or 1 lime
    salt and cayenne to taste

In a double boiler heat soup and add soda. Add cream cheese and melt. Beat until smooth.

Soften gelatin in stock and add to mixture. Stir when dissolved, allow to cool, then add mayonnaise, shrimp, onion, celery, green pepper, lemon juice. Season to taste with salt and cayenne. Pour into mold and refrigerate.

CONGEALED SHRIMP SUPREME

Mr. Lucius K. Burton

1 lb. fresh shrimp (in shells)
1 can Campbell's beef consomme
1 eight-oz. can Rialto asparagus tips
4-oz. bottle salad olives, broken
1 cup chopped celery
2 packages gelatin
½ cup liquid from asparagus tips
6 pieces of pimento, chopped
1 teaspoon Worcestershire sauce
1 teaspoon lemon juice
    salt and red pepper to taste

Boil shrimp in seasoned water. Cool and peel. Line bottom of 6 cup mold with shrimp. Soften gelatin in asparagus water. Add to heated consomme. Add chopped celery, pimento, asparagus tips, rest of shrimp. Place in mold, or in individual molds. Serve on lettuce and top with homemade mayonnaise.

SOUR SWEET SALAD

Mrs. Mabel Goetter Godchaux

6 cucumbers, sliced thin
2 cups celery, cut in small pieces
½ cup each vinegar, sugar, water
2 cups stringbeans
2½ cups shredded cabbage

Let vinegar, sugar and water come to a boil. Drop in the celery, cook 5 minutes, then add cucumbers and cook 15 minutes.

Stringbeans, cooked in plain water, and shredded cabbage, may be used with the same salad dressing, putting in stringbeans first, then adding cabbage, cook 15 minutes.

THREE STAR SPECIAL

Mrs. Gordon Reddy

1 head lettuce, 1 clove garlic
1 hard boiled egg
3 oz. Roquefort or Bleu cheese
½ teaspoon salt
¼ teaspoon each white pepper, dry
     mustard
½ cup olive oil, vinegar

Make a dressing of the salt, pepper, mustard, and oil. Add enough vinegar to make ½ cup.

Rub a mixing bowl with garlic (cut in half). Cut lettuce, which has been chilled, into small pieces. Add chopped egg, then cheese, crumbled fine. Pour over lettuce and serve.

TOMATO DILL ASPIC WITH ARTICHOKE HEARTS

Mrs. Robert Moore Parker

3 envelopes Knox gelatin
5 cups tomato juice
⅓ cup lemon juice
1 tablespoon grated onion
1 clove garlic, crushed
2 teaspoons dried dillweed
2 teaspoons salt
1 teaspoon basil
1 teaspoon oregano
1 bay leaf, crushed

Soften gelatin in ½ cup of tomato juice. Simmer all ingredients together for 10 minutes, stirring occasionally. Remove from heat and strain hot

tomato juice through cheesecloth. Add softened gelatin, stir until dissolved. Cool. Drain one 19 oz. can artichoke hearts and slice in half. In the bottom of a 2-quart ring mold arrange a design of artichoke hearts. To seal in design, carefully add enough of the tomato mixture to measure about ¼" deep in bottom of mold. Chill until gelatin is thickened, but not firm. Add remaining artichoke hearts and tomato juice mixture and chill until firm. Unmold, garnish with crisp greens and serve with Caviar Mayonnaise. Makes 6 to 8 servings.

RESTACKED TOMATO SALAD

Mrs. John R. Peters

6 tomatoes
2 green onions, finely chopped
½ cup minced parsley
   French dressing
6 large lettuce leaves

Peel tomatoes, slice thin, keeping slices in order. Place bottom slice on lettuce leaf, sprinkle with onion and parsley and add some French dressing. Continue this with each slice until the tomato has been placed back together. Dribble French Dressing over each and sprinkle with a little parsley. Marinate in refrigerator several hours before serving.

SPICED TOMATO À LA JONES

Created in honour of Mrs. Hamilton Polk Jones by Roy L. Alciatore Antoine's Restaurant

Cut top from a real Creole tomato. Spear tomato with a fork and hold it over a gas flame until skin cracks. Remove all of the tomato skin. Hollow it out.

Mince some celery and mix it with anchovy paste and a little puréed garlic.

Stuff tomato with the minced celery and garlic and anchovy paste.

Sprinkle the top with chopped egg and place a thin slice of sweet pepper around the chopped egg. Insert a seeded black olive in center of chopped egg. Douse with French dressing and serve very cold.

TURKEY SALAD
Miss Charlotte E. Mitchell

15 lb. turkey
12 hard-boiled eggs, chopped
6 stalks celery, finely chopped
1½ green peppers, finely chopped
1 red pepper pod
1 tablespoon minced parsley
12 bay leaves and some stems
2 sprigs thyme
½ teaspo n minced shallots
1 lemon, sliced
1 small bottle capers
well seasoned mayonnaise
dash of Tabasco, salt, pepper

Boil turkey until legs pull off easily, in water to which has been added salt, bay leaves, thyme, celery leaves, green pepper, red pepper and lemon. Remove skin and fat while hot. When thoroughly cooled, remove meat from bones and cut into large cubes. Add to meat celery and some tender leaves, green peppers, parsley. Mix thoroughly with just enough mayonnaise to moisten the meat. Let stand 2 hours in ice box. Before serving add eggs, shallots, parsley and Tabasco to taste. Never stir or mash the salad, lift it from the bottom with a pancake turner. Serve in lettuce cup with a heaping spoonful of stiff mayonnaise on top with three or four capers. Garnish with tomatoes if desired. Serve with a large kitchen spoon—never mold. This is a service for 25 people.

A fine addition to this salad is to make an aspic of the turkey soup and serve with mayonnaise on side.

Chicken salad may be made in the same way.

CAVIAR MAYONNAISE
Mrs. Robert Moore Parker

Mix well together ½ cup mayonnaise and 1 cup sour cream, tablespoon lemon juice and 2 teaspoons French's Yellow Mustard. Now fold in the contents of one 1-oz. jar of imported black caviar. Makes about 1¾ cups..

CREOLE FRENCH MUSTARD
Mrs. James Selman

1/8 cup lemon juice
1/8 cup cider vinegar
½ cup Plaignol olive oil
½ cup Wesson oil
salt and freshly ground pepper to taste
dash each of Tabasco and Lea & Perrins
1 tablespoon Creole mustard

Shake well and pour over favorite greens. This is also good over seafood salad.

FRENCH DRESSING
Mrs. E. V. Benjamin

2 tablespoons water
2 - 4 tablespoons dry mustard
1 teaspoon paprika
1 cup wine vinegar
3 cups oil (olive, Wesson, Peanut)
salt and freshly ground pepper to taste
2 cloves garlic, crushed

Put water in large mixing bowl. Add eggs, dry mustard, paprika, salt and pepper. Mix with a French whip.

Boil vinegar and add very slowly, beating constantly with whip. Let cool. Add oil gradually, beating constantly.

Put 1 or 2 cloves crushed garlic into container as you pour in dressing. This makes a bit more than a quart. Keep refrigerated.

Good on everything, artichokes, salads, seafood, cold meats, etc.

FRENCH DRESSING
Mrs. H. Merritt Lane, Jr.

½ cup olive oil
½ cup salad oil
1/3 cup tarragon vinegar
1 teaspoon salt
1 teaspoon fresh ground pepper corns
½ teaspoon sugar
¼ teaspoon prepared yellow mustard
1 clove garlic

Mix ingredients in cruet. Shake well before using.

FRENCH DRESSING–UNUSUAL
Through Mrs. John R. Chesworth

2 heaping tablespoons powdered
  mustard
2 tablespoons or less sugar
1 tablespoon salt, pepper to taste
1 cup warm water
¼ cup vinegar

Mix all in Waring blender. Add ¼ cup of vinegar. Add Wesson or olive oil until thickened; taste and add more water and oil until blender is full. Taste for salt, sugar and vinegar.

FRUIT SALAD DRESSING
Mrs. Hughes P. Walmsley

1 cup sour cream
1-6 oz. can orange juice, thawed
½ teaspoon minced onion

Combine and chill.

GREEN GODDESS DRESSING
Mrs. C. Nolte DeRussy, Jr.

Mayonnaise:

1 egg
½ teaspoon salt
¼ teaspoon dry mustard
2 tablespoons tarragon vinegar
1 cup Crisco oil

Into blender container put egg, salt, mustard and ¼ cup of the oil. Cover and turn motor on low speed. Immediately remove cover and in a steady stream, pour in remaining oil.

Add to mayonnaise in container:

5 coarsely cut green onions with tops
½ cup parsley clusters
1½ tablespoon lemon juice
1 tablespoon tarragon vinegar
1 clove garlic
2 anchovy fillets
1 teaspoon coarsely ground pepper

Cover and blend on high speed for 15 seconds. Fold in ½ cup sour cream.

GREEN GODDESS SALAD DRESSING
Mrs. E. T. Merrick III

1 clove garlic—pressed
½ pint sour cream

1 can anchovies or 1 tube of anchovy
  paste
3 tablespoons finely chopped green
  onion tops
1 tablespoon lemon juice
3 tablespoons vinegar
1 cup mayonnaise
⅓ cup finely chopped parsley
  salt and pepper to taste

This is best made in a blender, but can be done in electric mixer. If using mixer, a paste is best.

KOLB'S DRESSING
Kolb's Restaurant
Courtesy Mr. W. W. Martin, Manager

2 cups salad oil
2 cups Creole mustard (black
  mustard)
1 cup water
1 cup cider vinegar
3 tablespoons sugar

Combine all ingredients and mix well. Quantity of Creole mustard and/or sugar can be increased or decreased as to taste. (This is marvelous with a seafood salad or just as good with a plain green tossed salad.)

HONEY POPPY SEED DRESSING
Mrs. Morrell Trimble

½ cup honey
1 teaspoon dry mustard
1 teaspoon salt
1/3 cup vinegar
½ teaspoon onion juice
1 cup Wesson Oil
½ cup poppy seed

Mix and add honey, mustard and salt. Add vinegar, onion juice, Wesson Oil and poppy seed. Beat until well blended. Put in jar and refrigerate. Sugar may be substituted for honey (1/3 cup sugar).

QUICK MAYONNAISE

5 tablespoons salad oil
2 tablespoons lemon juice
½ teaspoon each sugar, salt
1 raw egg
½ pt. salad oil

Beat the first 4 ingredients well together with a rotary egg beater. Then
add the whole egg. Beat well, add the
salad oil and beat again until very stiff.

WARING BLENDER MAYONNAISE

Mrs. Edwin T. Merrick III

1 whole egg
1 teaspoon prepared mustard
1 teaspoon salt
2 tablespoons of lemon juice
5 drops of Tabasco
1 teaspoon of Worcestershire
½ teaspoon of paprika
1 cup salad oil

Put all ingredients except oil into
blender. Add ¼ cup of oil to ingredients. Cover and blend at high speed
for a few seconds, until smooth. Switch
to low speed and add remaining oil in
a steady stream. Switch to high speed
and blend a few more seconds, until
mixture is thick and smooth.

"MIGNON" SALAD DRESSING

½ cup granulated sugar
1/3 cup catsup
¼ cup cider vinegar
1 cup salad oil
¼ teaspoon salt
1 teaspoon Worcestershire sauce
1 medium sized onion
1 small clove garlic, 6 cloves
dash of Tabasco sauce

Rub bowl with garlic and salt. Grate
garlic, and onions, add all other ingredients. Strain into quart bottle.
Shake well. Make day before using.
Keeps indefinitely.

MRS. SEL'S DRESSING

Mrs. James Selman

¼ cup cider vinegar
½ cup Plaignol olive oil
½ cup Wesson oil
1 teaspoon Dijon mustard
salt and freshly ground pepper to
taste

Shake well and pour over your
choice of greens, etc.

POPPY SEED DRESSING

Mrs. Preston Herring

½ cup sugar
1 teaspoon dry mustard
1 teaspoon salt
½ teaspoon onion juice, optional
1/3 cup vinegar
1 cup salad oil
1 teaspoon poppy or celery seed

Combine sugar, mustard, salt, onion
juice and half the vinegar. Add oil
gradually, alternating with remaining
vinegar. Beat well with a whip until a
stable emulsion is formed.
Delicious over fruit salads! (Grapefruit, cantaloupe, etc.)

ROQUEFORT CHEESE DRESSING

Mrs. Petrie Hamilton

¼ cup Roquefort cheese
4 tablespoons olive oil
1 hard-boiled egg, yolk only
2 tablespoons whipping cream
2 tablespoons vinegar, Tarragon
salt, pepper, cayenne

Rub the cheese with the olive oil to
a cream. Add slowly the sifted yolk
of the egg, beating constantly. Add
the cream and the vinegar, drop by
drop, beating constantly, or it will
curdle. Season with salt, pepper, and
cayenne.

RUSSIAN DRESSING

2 egg yolks
½ teaspoon sugar
1 tablespoon Tarragon vinegar
1 teaspoon prepared mustard
1 cup olive oil, added by spoonful
salt and pepper to taste

Assemble the above and beat with
egg beater. Then add

1 large pimento, chopped
3 or 4 large olives, chopped
3 tablespoons catsup

SALAD DRESSING

Mrs. J. Gordon Reddy

1 cup mayonnaise
1 cup Roman cheese
(American cheese may be used)
3 tablespoons tomato catsup
1 tablespoon Worcestershire sauce
1 lemon (juice)
¼ teaspoon Tabasco sauce

2 teaspoons each sugar, salt
1 teaspoon white pepper
¼ teaspoon dry mustard

Place mayonnaise in bowl, add lemon juice, salt, pepper, sugar, Worcestershire sauce, Tabasco, catsup, mustard, stirring well and last fold in cheese.

SALAD DRESSING A L'ITALIEN

1½ cups Italian oil
½ cup each vinegar, tomato catsup
¼ cup sugar
  clove of garlic
  salt, pepper, paprika to taste

Mix all ingredients in a bowl well rubbed with the garlic. Beat well with an egg beater. Put dressing in a glass jar in the refrigerator until ready to serve.

It is better after a day or two, when the flavorings have become blended.

COOKED SALAD DRESSING

Mrs. Petrie Hamilton

5 egg yolks
1 tablespoon mustard
1 teaspoon salt
2 tablespoons sugar
3 tablespoons melted butter
¼ teaspoon cayenne pepper
1 cup vinegar
¼ teaspoon celery seed
  one onion, the juice

Put all ingredients except the onion juice in double boiler and cook until it thickens, stirring constantly. When done, add the juice of one onion. Particularly good for potato salad.

SALAD DRESSING PASTORAL

Mrs. Walter Torian

2 hard-boiled eggs
2 cloves garlic, minced
3 tablespoons olive oil
3 tablespoons Tarragon vinegar
1 teaspoon powdered sugar
1 sprig of celery, minced
  lettuce, salt, red pepper, paprika

Mash the egg yolks fine with the minced garlic. Add the olive oil drop by drop, then the minced celery, salt and red pepper. Thin with the vinegar. Shred the lettuce with scissors and put into salad bowl which has been well chilled. Toss the salad dressing into it. Chop the white of eggs very fine and sprinkle over this, following with the powdered sugar and a little paprika. Serve very cold.

Note: The breath of the Arctic must blow on the ingredients, everything thoroughly chilled.

VINAIGRE AROMATISE

Mrs. Louis Perrilliat

1 pt. claret vinegar
1 large onion, minced
2 cloves garlic, a little mint
1 oz. elder blossom
1 shallot
2 ozs. Tarragon leaves
2 teaspoons each celery, mustard seeds
1 teaspoon each sugar, whole black
  pepper, allspice

Add the spices, onion, shallot and seasonings to the vinegar. It will keep indefinitely and add interest and flavor to any dressing calling for vinegar. A tablespoon of tomato catsup may be added if liked.

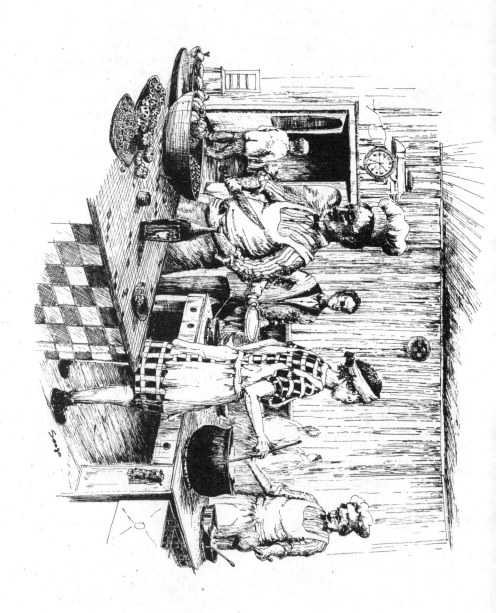

bisques, gumbos and soups

ROUX
Mrs. Joseph Merrick Jones, Jr.

IF YOU DON'T KNOW HOW TO MAKE A ROUX, LEARN!!!

This is the base for all of your soups, stews, gumbos, bisques, or anything that you are doing with leftover that requires a good, rich, brown gravy. The thickness of your gravy can always vary, according to the amount of water, stock, or bouillon that you will eventually add to the basic cooked roux mixture.

Here is the procedure for the basic roux, and it will require approximately 20-30 minutes of your time, because you must stand watch over this, stirring religiously all the while. This may sound like trouble, but it will either make or break your dish.

STEP 1:

Keep warm in separate pot the water, stock, or bouillon that you are eventually going to use as your liquid additive.

STEP 2:
1 cup oil
1¼ cups flour
1 iron pot, or the heaviest skillet
   that you own

Thoroughly mix flour and oil together in a cold pot or skillet. Place over medium heat, and start stirring, scraping all browned bits from the bottom of the pan. When the glorious moment has come, and it begins to turn brown, then dark brown, remove the pot from the fire immediately. Slowly incorporate your water, stock or bouillon into the roux, STIRRING STILL all the time.

Return to low heat and add liquid needed for consistency of dish in the making.

Keep in mind that vegetables give off water and will tend to thin sauce over long period of time. It is better to keep a rather thick consistency, and towards end of cooking, thin to desired consistency with your water, stock, or bouillon.

AVOCADO BISQUE
Mrs. John O'Reilly

1 (10½ oz.) can condensed cream of chicken soup
1½ soup cans of rich milk
1 tablespoon instant minced onion or ¼ cup finely chopped green onion
1 teaspoon chili powder
1 tablespoon lemon juice
2 medium sized avocados
   salt

Combine soup, milk, and onion in a double boiler. Heat slowly. Puree avocados with one teaspoon water, lemon juice and chili powder. Blend into hot soup, heat a few minutes longer. Be careful not to overheat or boil. Add salt to taste. This makes about one quart of unusual soup delicately colored and flavored.

CRAYFISH BISQUE
Mrs. Lester Lautenschläger, Jr.

20 lbs. crayfish

Stuffing for heads
2 white onions, chopped
1 clove garlic, chopped
6 green onions, chopped
1 stick butter
½ crayfish tails
   crayfish fat
2 cups fresh French bread, crumbed
1 egg
1 tablespoon Worcestershire sauce
2 teaspoons tabasco
   flour
   salt and pepper to taste
The Bisque:
1½ sticks of butter or 12 tablespoons bacon grease
12 tablespoons flour
3 onions, chopped
1½ cups celery, chopped
1 clove garlic, minced
1 green pepper, chopped

1 28-oz. can tomatoes
½ can tomato paste
2 qts. water that the crayfish were boiled in OR crayfish liquor*
Worcestershire sauce
Tabasco
Salt and pepper to taste
small fresh hot pepper, chopped (optional)

*Crayfish liquor: To make crayfish liquor, put about 15 claws through the coarse blade of a meat grinder. Boil the crushed claws with 2 qts. water seasoned with salt, pepper and the juice of 1 lemon. Strain.

Purge crayfish in salted cold water for 20 minutes prior to boiling. Boil crayfish in seasoned salted water (crab-boil, onions, lemons, cayenne, etc.) for 20 minutes. Strain and reserve at least 2 quarts of this stock or make crayfish liquor.* Drain crayfish. Peel tails and clean heads, reserving the yellow fat for the stuffing. Reserve 30 of the largest heads for stuffing.

To prepare the stuffing for the heads, saute white onions, green onions and garlic until soft. Add crayfish fat, ½ of crayfish tails, French bread crumbs, egg, Worcestershire sauce, Tabasco, salt and pepper. Stuff mixture into heads and roll them in flour.

The bisque: Make a very dark roux using butter or bacon grease and flour. When quite dark, add onions, celery, garlic and green pepper. Saute a few minutes. Add canned tomatoes and tomato paste. Next add 2 quarts water in which the first batch of crayfish were boiled or crayfish liquor. Season the bisque to taste with Worcestershire sauce, Tabasco and salt and pepper. The color of the bisque should be brown with only the hint of tomato coloring. Add here a small finely chopped pepper if you have any fresh handy.

Heat stuffed heads in 300° oven and place remainder of crayfish tails in soup bowls. Fill with hot bisque, sprinkle with chopped parsley and drop a few of the stuffed heads into each bowl. White fluffy rice may be passed around and Hot French Bread is a must! Serves 10.

CRAYFISH BISQUE
Mamie Isadore

20 lbs. fresh crayfish, cooked
1 cup crayfish fat

cleaned heads from cooked crayfish
2 cups chopped onion
1½ cups chopped celery
4 stale buns soaked in water
1 stick butter
1¼ cups chopped parsley
2 toes garlic
1¼ cups chopped green onion tops
4 hard cooked eggs
salt, black pepper and cayenne

Peel crayfish tails, reserve meat and fat. Boil heads until clean and pliable. Reserve 4 cups picked tails for bisque sauce. (The remainder of tails are to be chopped for the stuffing of the heads.)

Brown onions and celery in butter, using uncovered pot, and stir over medium heat until golden. Add parsley, garlic, and onion tops, and stir again. Add crayfish tails, chopped, and minced hard-boiled eggs. Squeeze water from buns and combine with mixture. Add salt, pepper, and cayenne to taste.

Fill cleaned heads with mixture, roll in flour, and brown in butter. Set aside.

Bisque Sauce:
3 tablespoons flour
1¼ tablespoons butter
1 large onion
4 tablespoons chopped celery
2 tablespoons green pepper
1 can whole tomatoes
1 can tomato sauce
4 cups reserved whole crayfish tails

Brown butter in flour. Add chopped onion, garlic, celery and green pepper. Saute for a few minutes, then add tomatoes, tomato sauce and 1 quart of water. Cook until all seasonings are well done, then add crayfish tails. Simmer for 15 minutes or until of thickness desired. Add heads, but do not boil after heads are added. Heat gently, and serve over cooked white rice.

MADAME BÉGUÉ'S BISQUE À L'ECREVISSE

40 nice crawfish
1 cup soaked bread
1 large spoon fried onions
  garlic, chopped parsley
  salt, red pepper, to taste
Soup:
  flour, butter
½ cup minced shallots
½ cup minced parsley, sprigs of thyme
2 bay leaves, chopped fine
  salt, cayenne pepper

Wash the crawfish very thoroughly, cleaning them with a brush and purge in salt water. Boil them well, remove from the fire, and drain. Save the stock, clean the heads, keeping 30 of the shells and also the remains which you will set to boil in a quart of water.

Peel the tails and chop them fine.

Make a paste with the meat, together with the soaked bread, the fried onions, garlic, parsley, salt and pepper. With this, fill the 30 shells, and set them aside while the soup gets under way.

The Soup: fry the shallots in butter, add flour for thickening, then the onions, parsley, thyme, and bay leaves. When browned, strain the stock from the crawfish remains and heads, and season with salt and pepper. Let this boil slowly for half an hour. Add more water if needed. When ready to serve, roll each of the stuffed heads in flour, fry in butter until crisp all over, and throw them in the soup. Let boil three or four minutes, and serve with very thin slices of toasted bread, or garlic bread.

This bisque was one of the reasons why a stretch of long bare rooms with sanded floors became one of the most famous and recherché restaurants in these United States.

CRAWFISH BISQUE
Mrs. C. A. Tessier

10 lbs. crawfish
6 large onions
6 slices dried out bread
2 cloves garlic
2 sprigs thyme, 4 sprigs parsley
1 small can of tomatoes
2 bay leaves, 4 cloves
¾ gallon water
1 pt. chicken broth or consommé
    salt, pepper to taste, dash of cayenne

Purge crawfish in salt water 10 minutes, then wash until water is clear. Boil crawfish until they turn red (about 5 minutes), strain, cool. Separate heads from tails. Now clean heads by pulling out the inside without losing too much of the fat. Place the heads in three quarts fresh water you are going to use to make your bisque. Break or crack each claw with a small hammer and boil with the heads to flavor the bisque. Let this

come to a boil, then set aside and let stand while you prepare the stuffing.

Chop onions fine and cook in a heaping tablespoon of butter until tender. Soak and squeeze out bread, add to onion and mix thoroughly. Let cook ten minutes, add crawfish meat that has been chopped fine and seasoned with red or black pepper, salt, garlic and parsley. You can be the judge of how long to cook. Make roux with two heaping tablespoons each butter and flour. When golden brown, add a small can of tomatoes strained into roux. Gradually add bisque juice, thyme, cloves, bay leaves and chicken broth (or shrimp consommé, if used on a fast day). Let this simmer for two hours.

Now go over the heads and clean thoroughly this time. When dressing cools, stuff heads and place in refrigerator over night (this will pack the dressing in the heads so that it will not come out into the juice). If you haven't time, then dot each stuffed head with butter and bake in oven ten minutes. Drop stuffed heads in bisque one-half hour before serving and heat slowly.

ONION BISQUE
Mr. Fred B. Otell

5 lbs. yellow onions
3 cups water
¼ cup vegetable oil
1 pint sour cream
4 cans beef consommé
3 cans clear beef bouillon
3 teaspoons Worcestershire sauce
3 teaspoons salt
1 teaspoon black pepper
    Romano cheese

Cut up onions and cook slowly with water and oil in a covered pot until soft. Do not brown. Mix sour cream with the canned soups using electric mixer, blender, or egg beater to prevent curdling. After onions are soft add all other ingredients and bring to a boil. Let cool and refrigerate, which improves the flavor. If a smooth bisque is desired run through the blender to dissolve the onion pieces. Serve hot with croutons or toast sprinkled with Romano cheese. This will serve sixteen people.

SHRIMP BISQUE
Mrs. Geo. W. Boutcher

2 lbs. boiled shrimp
3 slices stale bread
1 can condensed tomato soup
  bay leaf, onion, parsley
  salt, pepper to taste
  bacon grease

Peel the shrimp and cut them in half. Soak the bread in enough water to soften. Season highly with the bay leaf, chopped onion and minced parsley, salt, and pepper. Put in the frying pan with the bacon grease and cook as you would a dressing for chicken. When well blended add the can of condensed tomato soup and an equal quantity of water. Then add the shrimp. If too thick a little more water may be added.

TOMATO BISQUE

1 can tomatoes
1 onion, medium sized
1 teaspoon sugar
1 tablespoon butter
1 pint simmered milk
1 tablespoon flour
  pinch of soda, salt, and red pepper

Cook the tomatoes and onion in a double boiler with seasonings until they are thoroughly done. Sauté butter and flour. Add to mixture. In a separate pot bring the milk to a boil and combine with the first mixture. Serve immediately.

CHICKEN OKRA GUMBO

1 young chicken (3 lbs.)
1½ lbs. okra (sliced)
1 can tomatoes (large)
1 large onion (sliced)
2 tablespoons fat
2 qts. water
  salt, pepper to taste
1 teaspoon filé powder (optional)

Cut chicken in pieces and fry a light brown. Remove from frying pan, then put in okra and onions, stirring to prevent burning. Add tomato, chicken, water and seasonings. Cook until chicken is done. If desired add filé powder just before serving. Serve with rice.

Fifteen minutes before gumbo is done shrimp, oysters, and crabs may be added.

The carcass of turkey may also be used in gumbo.

Crabs, shrimp, ham, oysters, veal or chicken—any one of the above may be omitted if not desired.

CRAB GUMBO
Mrs. Edgar A. Fordtran

12 large hard shell crabs
1 lb. shrimp
1¼ lbs. fresh okra
3 large tablespoons lard or butter
1 large onion, 2 cloves garlic
1 medium sized green pepper
6 large fresh tomatoes
1 bay leaf, 1 sprig thyme, 3 sprigs
  parsley, salt, pepper to taste

Scald crabs and clean carefully removing all inedible parts. Cut off claws and crack. Cut bodies into quarters. Sprinkle with salt and pepper. Melt one tablespoon of lard or butter in the soup pot. Add crab and claws, cover closely and simmer for ten minutes. Set aside.

Peel the green pepper and remove the seeds. Place in a wooden chopping bowl with the bay leaf, thyme and onion. Chop all fine.

Wash the okra and dry well in a towel. Starting at the stem end slice thinly. If the okra is large quarter before slicing.

Melt remainder of the butter or lard in an iron skillet and when hot add the chopped okra and the contents of the chopping bowl. Then add the pulp of the six tomatoes which have been peeled, chopped, and strained. (Reserve the juice.) Cook, stirring until all is well blended then add the shrimp which have been cleaned, veined and salted. Cook until the shrimp turn pink. Then add all to the contents of the soup pot; add the tomato juice and two quarts of hot water. Simmer for one hour. Add salt and pepper to taste and the chopped parsley.

If so desired the crabs and claws may be removed a half hour before serving and crab meat which has been sautéed in a little butter may be substituted.

CRAB GUMBO
Weeks Hall

As prepared at the famous plantation home of Weeks Hall "Shadows of the Teche" in New Iberia.

1 doz. large crabs
2 lbs. okra
4 onions, medium sized
4 cloves garlic, minced
1 pod red pepper
5 tomatoes (or 1 small can)
3 ears tender corn
1 tablespoon sifted flour
1 kitchen spoon lard
1 tablespoon vinegar
   salt to taste

Wash the crabs thoroughly, then boil them in just enough water to cover and cook until done, (about twenty minutes after the water begins to boil) saving the water the crabs were boiled in.

Remove the shells, saving all the fat from the upper shells, and picking out all the meat of the crab.

Now put the lard in a large pot. Have the okra cut up in round slices and add it to the hot lard, to fry until dry. Add the onions, the chopped up tomatoes, and the minced garlic. Fry all this together, then add the water in which the crabs were boiled. Add salt to taste, and set it all to boil about 2 hours.

Meanwhile, add the flour to the corn, and about half an hour before serving, add the crab meat and the corn with the flour.

The gumbo must be thick and highly seasoned. Just before serving, add one tablespoon of vinegar to prevent the gumbo from being ropy. Serve with rice.

CREOLE SEAFOOD GUMBO
Pontchartrain Hotel

2 lbs. fresh shrimp (if possible with
   heads still on)
12 live bluefin crabs
3 slices bacon
4 large onions, minced fine
2 bay leaves
1 tablespoon finely chopped green
   pepper
   pinch of thyme
1½ teaspoons sugar
   salt and pepper to taste
2 lbs. fresh or frozen (not canned) okra
1 large ham bone
½ lb. chicken wings or same amount of
   any leftover chicken
1 lb. boneless stewing veal
1 heaping tablespoon lard
⅓ cup chopped parsley

1 large can tomatoes or 4 large fresh
   tomatoes dipped in hot water and
   peeled
3 or 4 liberal dashes Tabasco sauce
4 tablespoons Worcestershire sauce
   juice of ½ lemon
1 pint fresh oysters

Clean the shrimp, don't cut them up. Put the shells on to boil. Drop the live crabs into boiling water, cook for five minutes and clean by removing shells, "dead fingers" or lungs, and entrails in center. Break the bodies in half and twist off the fins. Scrape the shells and catch the juices and fat particles from the corners. This is very important for the gumbo. Save the claws.

Fry the bacon in a large pot until crisp, remove and set aside. Fry the onions until golden brown. Add bay leaves, green pepper, thyme, sugar, salt and pepper. Fry slowly until the green pepper is limp. Add the okra and continue cooking until the okra loses its gummy consistency. Put the ham bone, chicken and veal to brown in another pot with the lard. When the meats and the onion mixture have both browned well, pour off about half of the excess grease from each and then combine the two. Add the chopped parsley, tomatoes, Tabasco sauce, Worcestershire sauce and lemon juice. Add the crab sections with juice, claws, shrimp, oysters and bacon and fill the pot with liquid from the boiled shrimp shells plus extra water until the water covers the shrimp, crabs and meat well. At least 2 quarts of liquid are necessary.

Boil over slow fire for at least 2 to 2½ hours. Stir occasionally, overcooking will never hurt Creole Gumbo; it blends the flavors that much better. Remove the ham bone and chicken bones just before serving. Serve over fluffy white rice in soup plates. (This serves 6.)

GUMBO FILÉ
Mrs. Walter Torian

1 4-lb. hen
1 tablespoon hog lard
2 tablespoons flour
1 tablespoon parsley, minced
2 large onions, chopped
2 cloves garlic, chopped
1 pinch red pepper

2 qts. stock from hen
½ tablespoon filé powder
2 doz. oysters
    salt, pepper, to taste

Boil hen till tender in a quantity of water so that sufficient stock will be left when done. Cut the meat from the bones in medium sized pieces. Make a very brown roux. Add to it the stock from the chicken and the meat, seasonings and oyster liquor. Boil thirty minutes more and just before serving put in the oysters. Allow to boil up—and last the filé powder. Serve with rice.

This gumbo can also be made from a good beef stock and is subject to infinite variations. Raw ham can be boiled, chopped and added with the stock in which it is boiled, or a variety of seafoods may be used, a few shrimp or crabs and fewer oysters.

SCOOP'S IRISH CREOLE SATURDAY NIGHT GUMBO
Scoop Kennedy

4 tablespoons cooking oil
2 tablespoons flour
    Chopped: 1 large green pepper—1 onion—6 cloves garlic—6 sprigs fresh parsley—1 Chaurice sausage, skinned
4 thin slices Canadian Bacon
2 large live crabs
2 large cans shrimp
1 large can tomatoes
1 lb. fresh okra
¼ teaspoon powdered thyme
1 bay leaf
    salt to taste

Heat oil in a large heavy pot. After pot and oil are well heated, sprinkle flour into the hot oil. Now cook flour until brownish but not burnt. Stir often with a wooden spoon and keep an eye on it—it mustn't burn. Now add the onion, celery, green pepper and parsley, all chopped. Stir and cook for about ten minutes. Add the cut-up bacon and fry for about five minutes. Do not allow the bacon to become too crisp. Add the sausage and garlic and fry for an additional five minutes. Now add the okra which has been cleaned in cold water, both ends snipped off and sliced into rounds. Cook and stir (with wooden spoon) for about ten minutes or until okra stops being stringy when lifted with

spoon. Add tomatoes, a little at a time, on a fire that has been turned up from the low with which you started cooking previous ingredients. Cook and stir, and there's no use trying to cook this dish unless you're willing to keep an eye on it, stirring, smelling and watching. When the tomatoes are bubbling, add the liquor from the cans of shrimp. If fresh shrimp are used, save liquor when cooked and add. When this too is bubbling, add crabs. What you do with the crabs after parboiling is to break and clean thoroughly, leaving the large claws attached. Now add warm water, barely enough to cover crabs. The gumbo must not be too watery. If it becomes too thick while cooking, add a little more water. Cook slowly for fifteen minutes with the cover on. Now add about a teaspoon of salt, the bay leaf and the thyme, stirring a little, then taste to see if you need more salt. Another twenty minutes of slow cooking, and it should be almost ready. When almost ready, add the shrimp, cook for five minutes. Serve, of course, with rice.

OKRA, CRAB & SHRIMP GUMBO
Mrs. Wilkinson Roth

2 lbs. selected okra
4 heavy crabs
1 lb. med. sized shrimp
2 kitchen spoons shortening
1 kitchen spoon flour (level)
3 large Bermuda onions, chopped fine
1 small can Italian tomato paste
1 small can Italian peeled tomatoes
3 large bay leaves, 2 sprigs thyme
½ teaspoon Tabasco
1 tablespoon Lea & Perrin's sauce

Scald and clean crabs, saving any fat. Pick out all meat OR just remove claws and halve bodies. Clean and shell shrimp but do not cook.

Wash and thoroughly dry okra. Slice in thin disks. Fry in black iron skillet stirring and chopping constantly until all ropiness is gone. Take off flame and remove ALL excess fat.

Melt fat in black iron Dutch oven and blend in flour slowly to a smooth, dark roux. Add onions and sauté until soft. Add tomato paste, stirring and chopping constantly until dark red-brown in color and perfectly blended. This step determines brew's ultimate color and texture. Remove all excess fat and stir in seasoning: salt, crunched bay leaves, whole thyme sprigs, Tabasco. After blending well, slowly add peeled tomatoes, saving juice for later. Cook slowly until whole mixture is uniform, dark rich color.

Now, add fried okra. After thorough blending, add tomato juice and about two quarts cold water—not all at once. When bubbling gently again add crab claws, fat, and halves OR crab meat. Raise flame slightly then drop in raw shrimp. Cover and allow to simmer gently at least another hour. Whole cooking time. about 4 hours. Taste for seasoning before turning off fire. Allow to cool, if possible, before reheating slowly. One tablespoon Worcestershire sauce before serving.

Serve with cooked long grain rice.

OYSTER GUMBO

2 to 4 doz. oysters
1 full kitchen spoon of olive oil
  or other shortening
1 tablespoon flour
1 tablespoon chopped shallots
1 tablespoon parsley, 3 sprigs thyme
1 pt. oyster liquor
2 bay leaves

Put oil in pot, slowly sift in flour, stirring all the time. Brown slightly, add onions, seasoning, oyster liquor, salt and pepper to taste. Let oysters simmer slowly for a few minutes in another pot, and just before serving, add to first mixture.

QUICK GUMBO

Mrs. Harry Hardie

1 can Campbell's chicken gumbo
½ can water
1 pint of oysters with liquor

Heat well and when removing from stove, add enough fresh filé to thicken. Serve immediately. (4 servings.)

"GUMBO Z'HERBES"

Mrs. J. T. Simmons

almost any fresh, tender greens
pod of cayenne, salt to taste
herbs, savories, seasonings
3 tablespoons butter, lard or olive oil

Wash the greens thoroughly. To rid them of grit and insects, use salt water.

Drain, and strip them carefully of stems and tough midribs.

Put them in a large pot with enough water barely to cover them packed in loosely.

When the pot boils place it where it will simmer gently about 20 minutes.

Remove, pour off the water, saving it. Remove the greens to a wooden bowl, and put the water back in the pot. Chop the greens very fine, adding the herbs, savories and flavoring, with salt, and chop again.

Replace in the simmering pot liquor, adding the butter, (lard, or vegetable oil), set back to simmer for about 2 hours.

If desired, one may add part or the whole of a chicken, or just the giblets, or a few strips of bacon, or diced ham, or diced fresh pork, browned in butter, or fried shrimp (this last is a favorite Creole dish for fast days.)

The ingredients may be chosen from the following:

Greens: spinach, mustard greens, lettuce, beet tops, collards, carrot tops, water cress, radish tops, turnip tops, cabbage, kale, barcole, rape, Brussels sprouts, kohlrabi, endive, broccoli.

Savories: bay leaf, sage, borage, thyme, catnip, dill, tarragon, chives.

Herbs: parsley, celery, green onions, sweet pepper, sorrel, dandelion, fennel, cress, celeriac, shallots, leeks, chili, garlic roquette.

This Gumbo Z'herbes, so-called by the black slaves who served it to their Creole masters in the south's long-ago, probably originated in the Congo jungles of Africa. And no doubt it was modified by the friendly Cherokee and Choctaw Indians of the south, from their rudimentary knowledge of medicinal or "pot" herbs. Certainly many of the ingredients for making this delectable concoction were to be obtained from the Indian squaws who squatted with their baskets on the flagged entrance to the old French market.

Besides its savory taste, it has a highly salubrious quality, and, now that savories and simples are reappearing in favor, it finds a place in modern household magazines, recommended for its beneficial qualities.

BUTTER BALLS FOR SOUP

½ cup butter
1 cup flour
½ teaspoon salt

Mix with sufficient ice water to form into balls. Roll into flour and drop in soup ten minutes.

KATHLEEN'S FRUITS OF THE BAYOU

John Mecom

½ cup butter or margarine
2 green onions (or leeks)
1 cup sliced celery
1 onion, diced
2 cloves garlic, chopped
2 cup white wine or Lancer's
1 can (1 lb. 12 ozs.) tomatoes, chopped
2 cans (10½ ozs. per can) condensed chicken broth (or instant broth, which has less calories)
½ tablespoon saffron
1 or 2 bay leaves
2 lbs. assorted fish (red snapper, cod, haddock, sea bass)
2 lbs. shrimp - mussel
1 pkg. (9 oz.) frozen S. African rock lobster tails
18 mussels or little clams (whole or chopped)
salt and cayenne to taste
(I use Gumbo file & fish seasoning and I also add 1 can Rotel)

In a large kettle melt butter. Add leeks, onion and garlic; saute until golden then add wine, tomatoes, chicken broth, saffron and bay leaves. Bring to a boil, lower heat. Cut fish into 2 inch pieces and slice lobster (shell and all) into 1 inch crosswise slices. Add fish and lobster to soup. Simmer until fish becomes white, 10 or 15 minutes. Scrub the mussels, removing beards from mussels. Add to soup. Add at least 1 pint of oysters. Cover and simmer until shells open. Serve with garlic French bread.

BOUILLABAISSE

à la Nouvelle-Orléans

4 lb. red fish, red snapper, or trout
2 cloves garlic
4 tomatoes
1 tablespoon parsley
3 onions, 1 pinch saffron
½ cup olive oil
salt, pepper to taste, water

Put the olive oil in a saucepan, add chopped tomatoes, onions, garlic and parsley. Let all this simmer, then throw in a good pinch of saffron, season with salt and pepper to taste. Now put in sliced fish, cover with water and bring to a boil. Cover the saucepan well and allow the fish to boil gently for 12 to 15 minutes. Sprinkle the sauce and fish with parsley. Serve on slices of French toast.

FISH COURTBOUILLON

Terry Flettrich

It's divine! And you'd never guess that you pronounce it "koo-boo-yon." It may look complicated, but really, it isn't. And it's so very Creole-Cajun.

5 lbs. blue cat fish, cut in large pieces
¼ cup water
salt, black pepper, red pepper
3 tablespoonfuls high grade salad oil
2 buds garlic, minced
1 bunch parsley, chopped
1 large bay leaf
2 tablespoonfuls flour
¼ teaspoon thyme
3 stems celery, chopped
2 slices lemon
1 large bunch green onions (both white and green part) chopped
1½ cans tomato sauce
1 large bell pepper, chopped

Select a black iron pot that you can handle well enough to shake as you never stir the fish while it's cooking.

Rub the pieces of fish well with salt, black and red pepper. Put oil into cold pot. Arrange a layer of the fish on the bottom. Mix the bell pepper, garlic, celery, onion and parsley together. Sprinkle generously over fish. Sprinkle a tablespoonful of the flour over the vegetables and half of the tomato sauce and then repeat with a layer of fish, a layer of vegetables, then a tablespoon of flour and the remaining tomato sauce. Add the thyme, bay leaf, lemon and water. Place pot on very low fire and cook slowly for one hour or until tender. Shake pot often to keep from sticking. Never stir as this will break up the fish. When done taste for seasoning and add more if necessary.

COURTBOUILLON
Mr. E. P. O'Donnell
from "The Great Doorstep"
As made by Slavonian Fishermen in the Mississippi Delta

Put three tablespoons of olive oil in a heated pot. When hot put in two tablespoons flour and stir until brown. Into this put two medium sized onions finely minced and stir until onions are brown. To this add two large cans tomatoes, 1 tablespoon tomato paste, two minced sweet peppers, two minced cloves, garlic, two sprigs thyme, 1 tablespoon minced parsley, ¼ of a bay leaf, six allspice which have been previously crushed, and the tip of a red pepper minced. Allow this mixture to cook slowly about twenty minutes, then slowly add two and a half tumblers of water. When this boils, add four medium sized slices of red fish or drum fish, about an inch thick. Add one lemon, thinly sliced. Cook fifteen minutes. Add half a glass of sherry wine and serve over thinly sliced stale French bread which has been fried in butter. This serves four.

COURTBOUILLON BARATARIA
Mrs. Albin Provosty

3 lbs. redfish or red snapper (six slices)
1 tablespoon each lard, flour
12 mashed allspice
3 sprigs each thyme, parsley, marjoram
3 bay leaves
2 large onions, 1 clove garlic
1 qt. of water
6 large fresh tomatoes or 1 can
1 glass of dry wine
1 lemon (the juice)
salt and cayenne to taste

Make a roux by putting lard in a deep pot and when hot add flour, stirring to prevent burning. Throw in allspice, finely chopped thyme, parsley, marjoram, bay leaf, onions and garlic. Add tomatoes chopped fine. Pour in water and wine. Let simmer one hour. Add salt and cayenne to taste, then the sliced fish. Let all boil gently for fifteen minutes. Add the lemon juice and serve.

ALMOND SOUP
Mrs. Edward Butts Poitevent

1 qt. almonds
2 qts. white stock
1 teaspoon salt
1 tablespoon butter
2 tablespoons flour
1 cup mushroom liquor
2 pieces celery
1 teaspoon onion juice
1 sprig of parsley
1 cup button mushrooms
2 cups whipped cream
2 jiggers of sherry

Boil almonds in salted water for ten minutes. Peel, skin and chop. Then make a cream sauce of stock, mushroom liquor and finely minced mushrooms. Add celery, onion juice and parsley. Boil for fifteen minutes. Thicken with flour and butter melted together. Add sherry. Add almonds, serve with whipped cream on top. This serves 15 or 20 people.

BLACK BEAN SOUP

1 qt. dried black beans
2 tablespoons sherry wine
1 hard-boiled egg
1 small shin beef bone
2 stalks celery, minced
1 large lemon
few cloves, or allspice

Soak the beans overnight. Next morning, put the soaked beans on to boil with the beef shin and plenty of cold water. Boil till the meat leaves the bone. Take out the beans and mash them through a colander. Put the meat and the beans back into the pot and add the wine, the lemon, the egg, and the spice. Boil up once and serve.

Mrs. John B. O'Kelly suggests that with this soup a happy addition is 2 or 3 slices of avocado and sliced fresh limes.

FAMOUS HOUSE OF REPRESENTATIVES RESTAURANT BEAN SOUP

Cover two pounds of No. 1 white Michigan beans with cold water and soak overnight. Drain and re-cover with water.

Add a smoked ham hock and "simmer slowly" for about 4 hours until beans are cooked tender. Then add salt and pepper to suit taste. Just before serving, bruise beans with large spoon or ladle, enough to cloud. (Serves six.)

FAMOUS SENATE RESTAURANT BEAN SOUP

Take two pounds of small Navy pea beans, wash and run through hot water until beans are white again.

Put on the fire with four quarts of hot water. Then take one and one-half pounds of smoked ham hocks, boil slowly approximately three hours in covered pot. Braise one chopped onion in a little butter, and when light brown, put in bean soup. Season with salt and pepper, then serve. Do not add salt until ready to serve. (Eight persons.)

BORSCH CREOLE

V. M. Friede

2 cans of beets
1 can bouillon
1 cup sour cream
  salt

Use the juice from both cans of beets. Cut the beets from one can into fine strips. Reserve others for salad. Add cut beets to the juice with the canned bouillon. Season, and just before serving add the sour cream.

or

1 bunch fresh beets cut into strips, covered with water and allowed to stand for two or three days until a slightly fermented juice is formed. Then add stock or canned bouillon as above, salt and sour cream.

For serving in hot weather the bouillon may be omitted and finely sliced cucumbers added. It should be chilled and served with sour cream.

BOUILLON

Mrs. Rachel Bunting Wilmot

1 can Campbell's bouillon
1 can water
1 small can tomatoes
2 pieces celery
½ green pepper
1 bay leaf
1 sprig parsley

2 cloves
½ teaspoon salt
  dash red pepper

Cook for 15 minutes. Strain. Serve hot with slice of lemon. (Delicious and inexpensive.)

BRAIN SOUP BONNE FEMME

2 sets calf's brains
1 qt. boiling water
2 tablespoons lemon juice
1 tablespoon salt
1 qt. milk
1 tablespoon butter, heaping
1 slice breakfast bacon
  salt, white pepper to taste
  soda crackers

Wash and skin the brains and plump in ice water for one hour.

Next, plunge them into boiling water with the lemon juice and the salt. Boil gently 30 minutes.

In another stewpan, put the milk with the butter, bacon, salt and pepper. Heat this.

When the brains are done, chop them up and pour the milk into the stewpan with the brains and the water in which they were cooked. Let all come to a boil and pour over toasted soda crackers.

CHICKEN CURRY SOUP

Mrs. Philip Steegman

1 large onion, 1 apple
2 cups water
4 cups chicken broth
½ pt. whipping cream
3 to 6 teaspoons curry powder

Cut the onion and apple in half and boil in water twenty minutes. Strain. Add four cups strong chicken broth. Just before serving add curry. Top each cup of soup with whipping cream. Serves six.

CHICKEN SOUP ONORATO

1 three or four lb. hen
½ lb. blanched almonds
1 cup cream

Boil the hen until tender with a whole onion and a few pieces of celery and reserve the stock. Take the white meat and grind it, using the fine blade of the grinder. Grind the almonds.

Combine both. Add the cream to the meat and nuts. Stir until smooth, add the stock in which the hen was cooked and boil gently for about an hour. Season, strain and serve poured over thin slices of toast.

JELLIED CONSOMMÉ DE LUXE
Mrs. Robert B. Parker

Use Madrilene or a good canned, jellied consommé. Place in bouillon cups, three-quarters full, in refrigerator for several hours. Top this consommé with the following mixture: Mix homemade mayonnaise with chopped stuffed olives. Add a dash of Tabasco. Cover consommé with this mixture about ¼ inch deep. Hard-boil eggs. Grate. Cover the mayonnaise mixture with the grated egg. Serve ice cold.

ROYAL CONSOMMÉ
Mrs. Shaw Putnam

1 turkey or chicken carcass
1 each large soup bone, veal knuckle
3 calves feet
4 quarts water
  salt and pepper to taste

Boil these slowly with salt and pepper for 1½ hours. Skin. Add

1 stalk celery, 3 green peppers
6 onions, 6 carrots
½ bunch parsley, 2 bay leaves
½ teaspoon mace, 10 cloves
1 teaspoon Kitchen Bouquet
1 teaspoon Creole Seasoning
2 lemons, the juice and rind
1 orange, the rind
  several dashes of Tabasco

Boil two hours. Cool and skim carefully. Put back on fire, add shells of 3 eggs to clarify. Boil 5 minutes, remove and strain. When cold, strain through flannel bag dipped in ice water.

CORN SOUP
Mrs. Gene Jefferson

1 stick butter
2 tablespoons flour
1 large onion, chopped
1 medium bell pepper, chopped
2 cans whole kernel corn
1 can cream style corn

1 can Ro-tel tomatoes
  salt and red pepper to taste
3 lbs. shrimp peeled

Make slightly brown roux using butter and flour. Add onions and bell pepper. Saute 10 minutes. Add corns and Ro-tel tomatoes. Cook slowly for 1 hour. Add water as needed to maintain creamy consistency. Season. Add shrimp and simmer covered another 20 minutes.

CORN SOUP

2 cans creamed corn (yellow)
1 pint of half-and-half cream and milk
2 bouillon cubes (chicken or beef)
½ cup water

Put 2 cans of creamed corn through a sieve and then season to taste. Add 1 pint of half-and-half cream and milk. Place in double boiler and add 2 bouillon cubes dissolved in ½ cup of hot water. Cool and serve garnished with sour cream and chives.

CREAM OF CORN SOUP
Mrs. William Westerfield

1 can corn (golden bantam)
1/3 can water
1 large whole onion
1 pt. milk
1 tablespoon flour, heaping
2 tablespoons butter
  dash of Tabasco
  salt to taste
  whipped cream

Add the water to the corn, then put in the onion, set in a double boiler and cook 1 hour.

Make a thin cream sauce with the milk, flour and butter.

Press corn through a sieve, add the thin cream sauce, Tabasco and salt.

Heat, serve with a spoon of whipped cream on each cup.

CREAM OF CRAB SOUP
Mrs. David T. Merrick

8 crabs, boiled and picked, OR
  1 lb. lump crabmeat
1 tablespoon flour
1 tablespoon butter
1 qt. milk, ½ cup cream
¾ teaspoon salt
½ teaspoon grated onion

¼ teaspoon cayenne pepper
8 drops Tabasco sauce
1/3 cup sherry
    dash of nutmeg

Cream butter and flour—add milk and allow to simmer for 6 minutes. Put cream and seasoning and crab meat in a double boiler, heat and pour into milk. Add parsley and sherry last, if the flavor is desired. It is good without the wine.

SOUP GAULOISE

4 leeks chopped fine
1 onion (small) chopped fine
4 potatoes cut very thin
1 qt. chicken stock
1 tablespoon butter
2 cups boiled milk
2 cups light cream, 1 cup heavy cream
1 teaspoon butter
    chives, salt, pepper to taste

Put leeks in pot with sweet butter, brown lightly, add onion, potatoes and stock, (canned consommé can be used, if you haven't the chicken stock). Simmer one half hour until the vegetables are done—remove from fire, crush vegetables through fine sieve. Return to fire, add milk and cream and butter. Put more seasoning if desired, bring to a quick boil, cool and again rub through strainer. Add one cup chives on top when ready to serve. (For six.)

MUSHROOM SOUP

Mrs. Erasmus Darwin Fenner

1 lb. fresh mushrooms
2 tablespoons butter
1 tablespoon flour
5 drops Cream of Teche sauce or
    Tabasco
1 pt. milk, ½ pt. whipping cream
    salt, pepper to taste

Boil the mushrooms 20 minutes. Strain them and grind them in a fine food chopper. Put the butter in a saucepan, blend in the flour, add the liquid in which the mushrooms were boiled, and cook until thick. Then add the mushrooms. Season, and add the pepper sauce. Just before serving bring milk to boil and then add cream.

ONION SOUP

Served in Petits Marmites

Mrs. Herbert N. Cook

4 or 5 medium onions
2 tablespoons butter
1 qt. stock, chicken, beef
    bread, Parmesan cheese, grated

Slice the onions and fry until light brown, in butter.

Put onions in well seasoned stock and allow to simmer twenty minutes.

Cut bread in thin rounds, and toast. Place one round in each marmite, sprinkle lightly with cheese. Pour broth with onions over this, then cover with another round of toast, sprinkling it also with Parmesan cheese. Run in the oven under flames long enough to melt the cheese. Place covers on marmites and serve very hot. Thin slices of imported Swiss cheese added just before serving are a pleasant addition.

CREAM OF ONION SOUP

Mrs. William Perry Craddock

2 medium-sized onions
2 tablespoons butter or other fat
1 cup water
1 tablespoon rice
1 teaspoon meat extract or a
    bouillon cube
3 cups milk
    salt, pepper

Chop the onions and cook in the fat until slightly yellow. Add the water, rice and meat extract or bouillon cube, and cook until rice and onions are tender. Add milk, reheat, and season with salt and pepper.

OXTAIL SOUP À LA LUCIE

3 tablespoons, level, bacon drippings
2 oxtails
1 medium sized onion, 1 carrot
2 sprigs parsley, 1 bay leaf
1 stalk celery
1 quart cold water or stock
1 tablespoon pearl barley, a little flour
1 tablespoon cold water
½ cup sherry, salt, pepper to taste

Melt the fat and fry in it, the diced carrot and onion, then the oxtails which have been cut in pieces. When brown, add water, celery, parsley, and bay leaf tied together in small bag.

When it comes to a boil, put in the barley and let simmer four hours. Remove the largest bones, and the bag of seasoning, and thicken the soup with flour, rubbed smooth with a tablespoon of cold water. Season rather highly, add the sherry, and serve.

OXTAIL SOUP–For Eight Persons

Mr. Julian Street

This is a recipe given me by the late Charles Scotto, who, with his master, the late A. Escoffier, and Prosper Montagné, of Paris, forms one of a triumverate of historic chefs of our time. It is common practice now for self-advertising chefs to claim to have been "the favorite pupil of Escoffier," but Scotto actually was that, as Escoffier himself indicated to me. Scotto was chef at the Hotel Pierre, New York, when that hotel opened and during the lifetime of Monsieur Pierre. He was a culinary genius, and his productions and delightful personality are remembered with affection by countless gourmets.

Ingredients for the soup:

1 oxtail, 1 shin of veal
1 knuckle of beef
1 bay leaf, 1 pinch of thyme
2 stalks of celery
½ tablespoon whole white pepper
3 fresh tomatoes or equal quantity of canned tomatoes
1 clove of garlic, 1 leek, 2 onions
4 carrots, 2 turnips
a few sprays of parsley
a few green peas
1 tablespoon arrow root

Preparation: This to be done a day ahead of time:

Cut the oxtail into small piece and split the shin of veal and knuckle of beef. Put them all in a pot, cover them with cold water and parboil (about ten minutes). Run water over them until they are cold, then pour all water from the pot. Add one onion cut in half, one carrot, one stalk of celery, the bay leaf and the pinch of thyme, and place in the oven to brown. Pour out fat. Cover the contents of pot with water. Add the leek, the second onion, the second stalk of celery, one carrot, parsley, garlic, tomatoes and white pepper. Bring to a boil, skim and boil slowly for 4½ to 5 hours. Strain off the stock, let it stand until cool, and place in icebox.

Next day, an hour or so before serving, remove the fat, heat the stock, thicken with one tablespoon of arrowroot diluted in water, and strain again through fine cloth. Having previously cooked in water the few green peas, the two turnips and the two remaining carrots, dice the turnips and carrots and add them, with the peas, to the soup.

Put in one piece of oxtail for each person and add one full wine glass of dry Madeira or Sherry (preferably the former) or no wine.

Serve hot.

OYSTER SOUP

The Boston Club of New Orleans

4 dozen medium size oysters
¼ lb. butter ¼ lb. bacon, fried lightly and finely chopped
½ cup minced white onion
½ cup minced shallots
1 cup flour
2 bay leaves
2 quarts water

Boil oysters for 5 minutes. Strain and save stock. In a large pan, melt butter and saute shallots and onion until tender. Stir in flour and cook 3 - 5 minutes. Add oyster stock and bay leaves and cook slowly for 20 minutes. Stir in bacon and oysters. Salt and pepper to taste and simmer 10 minutes. Remove from heat.

OYSTER SOUP

Mrs. Joseph Merrick Jones, Jr.

3 doz. oysters
1 stick butter, not margarine
1½ cups chopped green onions with tops included
1 cup finely chopped celery
3 pints Half & Half cream
2 teaspoons Maggi seasonings
1 tablespoon Mei Yen seasoning
2 teaspoons ground white pepper

Saute onions and celery in butter until tender. Add oysters and juice and cook until oysters curl (over low heat). Add seasoning and cream and heat gently. DO NOT BOIL!

Alternate: This is just as delicious if you substitute 2 lbs. lump crabmeat for oysters. You may want to add a cup or so of milk if extra guests arrive!

OYSTER SOUP

Mr. Francis J. Selman

½ cup (1 stick) butter
1 cup diced celery
1 cup finely chopped shallots
1 tablespoon flour
1 clove garlic, minced
6 cups liquid, all of oyster water (add additional water to make 6 cups)
2 dozen oysters
2 bay leaves
   salt and pepper

Melt butter in saucepan; saute celery and shallots until tender. Blend in flour and cook over low heat, stirring occasionally. Add remaining ingredients and simmer for 25 - 35 minutes. Remove bay leaves and serve. Makes 1-1½ qts.

OYSTER BOUILLON

Mrs. Frank H. Lawton

4 doz. oysters
3 pts. breakfast cream
1 pt. oyster liquor
1 dash Tabasco
1 stalk celery, grated
½ small onion, grated
1 tablespoon parsley
½ cup whipped cream
   butter the size of an egg
   salt, black pepper to taste

Cook oysters in liquor very slowly until they curl, add celery and onion. Heat cream and mix with oysters and let simmer 5 minutes in double boiler. Season just before serving. Strain into cups, top with a teaspoon whipped cream.

OYSTER BROTH

Mr. Albert Aschaffenburg

Pontchartrain Hotel

3 green onions
1 tablespoon butter
1 tablespoon flour
1 dozen oysters
1½ pints oyster water
½ teaspoon Accent
   salt and pepper to taste

Sauté the onions in butter gently for 3 or 4 minutes. Add flour and stir constantly for 3 minutes. Then add oysters, oyster water and Accent. Let simmer for 15 or 20 minutes. Add salt and pepper and strain through a fine sieve. (Serves 6.)

OYSTER SOUP
CRESCENT CITY STYLE

Terry Flettrich

Oysters are marvelous in New Orleans; fresh, baked, casseroled, sauced, fried or made into a hearty, easy, quicky, scrumptious oyster soup.

1/3 cup olive oil
4 slices of French bread
2 sprigs of parsley, chopped
3/4 cup red wine
1 tablespoon ketchup
1½ doz. oysters with liquid
1 clove garlic
1 cup oyster juice
¼ teaspoon pepper
½ teaspoon oregano

Heat 2 tablespoons oil in saucepan; add bread and brown on both sides. Remove bread and add garlic to oil; cook 2 or 3 minutes, then remove garlic. Add remaining ingredients to oil and simmer a few minutes. Put a slice of bread in each bowl and pour in soup. Makes 1 quart or 4 servings.

OYSTER SOUP LAFAYETTE

Mrs. Walter Torian

2 doz. oysters and 1 pt. liquor
3 shallots, 2 cloves garlic
1 tablespoon butter, heaping
1 tablespoon flour, heaping
1 sprig celery
⅛ cup minced parsley
2 eggs
   salt, red pepper

Melt the butter in a saucepan, and stir in the flour carefully, to make a light roux. Add the onions, celery, and garlic, chopped fine.

With the chopping knife, cut the oysters in three pieces, add salt and red pepper, and pour them with the liquor into the roux. Cover, and let cook three minutes. Beat the eggs lightly, and pour the soup into them, whipping all the time. A golden color is the result.

Note 1: 1 teaspoon of cold water in the eggs, and they will never curdle.

Note 2: Lessen the amount of liquor used and a delicious stew, instead of soup, results, that will do credit to a luncheon.

RED BEAN SOUP
James Plauché, Dunbar's

Each section of the country has its staple, week after week dish—delicious economical, and filling. With the Creoles, it was and is today red beans and rice. From this everyday meal Dunbar's devised a soup that retains all the flavor, but is ideally light as a summer soup.

½ lb. red kidney beans
1 small onion, 2 cloves garlic, chopped
2 strips celery (chopped)
2 bay leaves, 2 sprigs thyme
¼ stick of butter
1 teaspoon Worcestershire sauce
½ lb. ham (ground fine)
   water
   salt and pepper to taste
   Claret wine, sieved hard boiled egg,
      lemon slice

Brown onion in butter
Simmer beans for about 3 hours in water with seasoning
Strain mixture through coarse strainer—mash with large spoon
Add ham, salt, pepper
Place 1 tablespoon claret wine in bottom of each bouillon cup
Pour soup. Garnish with sieved egg and lemon slice.

SPLIT PEA SOUP
Mrs. James Selman

½ lb. pickled pork
½ lb. Andouille sausage, thickly sliced
2 lbs. sliced beef marrow bones
½ cup bacon grease
2 large chopped onions
2 small whole garlic cloves, unpeeled
2 small chopped celery stalks
¼ cup chopped celery leaves
¼ cup chopped parsley
1 lb. bag split peas
3 quarts water plus 2 or 3 cups
1 tablespoon salt
1 teaspoon pepper
1 teaspoon thyme
1 bay leaf

2 cloves
¼ teaspoon Tabasco (optional)
4 sliced carrots
¼ cup freeze chives
½ cup barley

Use large soup kettle. Render the meats in grease. Remove meats. Add next 5 ingredients, and cook 10 minutes over low heat. Replace meats. At this point, take out garlic, skin and mash back into the soup. Add rest of ingredients except barley. Boil hard, uncovered for ½ hour. Add barley, simmer partially covered for 2 hours. Remove bay leaf and clove if possible. To serve, give each person a slice of marrow bone and andouille and bit of pickle pork. This makes a nice looking soup, with the barley and carrot slices contrasting with the green of the broth.

SPLIT PEA SOUP
Mrs. David T. Merrick

2 qts. water
2 cups green split peas
4 pieces celery, 2 carrots, 1 onion
¼ teaspoon thyme, 1 bay leaf
   salt, pepper, cayenne to taste

Boil hard for 20 minutes—then slowly until peas are done.
Strain through colander.

TOMATO SOUP FRAPPÉ

1 cup cream
3 cups tomato juice
1 onion grated
2 stalks celery grated
½ coffeespoon Tabasco
   salt to taste

Put in cocktail shaker filled with ice and shake well. Serve very cold in cups. This is delicious frozen.

TOMATO SOUP MARTIN

1 can tomato bouillon
1 can plain bouillon
½ cup sherry
   salt and pepper to taste

Heat bouillon and just before ready to serve, add sherry. This serves four people.

TURTLE SOUP
Mamie Isadore

1 lb. turtle meat, cut in 2 inch pieces
2 large toes garlic
1 large onion, diced
1 can tomato sauce
1 or 2 lemons
4 hard boiled eggs
1 tablespoon parsley
3 tablespoons green onion tops
1½ tablespoons flour
2 tablespoons oil
2 tablespoons butter
½ cup sherry (or more to taste)
6 cloves
1 tablespoon Lea & Perrins
 salt and pepper to taste
1 tablespoon paprika
6 or more cups water, for desired
 consistency

Salt and pepper the diced turtle meat. Brown flour in oil and butter until golden. Add diced turtle meat, onion and garlic and saute until all is golden brown. Add tomato sauce and water, and simmer until meat is tender. Add parsley, chopped onion tops, sliced hard boiled eggs, cloves, and lemon. Cook over low heat for about ½ hour. Add paprika for color. The longer it stands the better the flavor!!

TURTLE SOUP
Mrs. Jesse Penrose Wilkinson
through
Mrs. Wilkinson Roth

1½ lbs. turtle meat
2 large Bermuda onions, 1 small onion
1 kitchen spoon shortening
1 level kitchen spoon flour
1 small can Italian tomato paste
2 hard boiled eggs
3 lemons
3 bay leaves, sprig of thyme
 few drops Tabasco
1 tablespoon Lea & Perrin Worcestershire sauce
 small cluster curly parsley
½ cup dry sherry

Boil until tender diced turtle meat with 2 bay leaves and small quartered onion. Drain meat and save stock. In large black iron Dutch oven blend flour into melted shortening into a smooth, dark roux. Add the 2 larger onions, finely chopped. Sauté until soft. Now add tomato paste, stirring constantly to avoid sticking until dark red-brown in color. Lower flame

—add salt, 1 crunched large bay leaf, sprig of thyme, Tabasco, tablespoon grated lemon skin (oily, thin-skinned lemon). Slow-cook awhile longer. Spoon out ALL excess grease before combining with turtle meat. Now slowly add 1 or more qts. cold water. Allow to simmer, stirring frequently—with cover ON for at least 1 hour. Preferable to allow to cool before reheating slowly. Add water, if necessary, for right consistency. Only the experienced can determine this. Just before serving remove from flame, add Worcestershire sauce and sherry. Garnish with minced hardboiled egg, finely chopped parsley (never cook parsley) and thinnest lemon slices.

Serve with melba toast or favorite hot bread with unsalted butter curls —a perfect green salad (French dressing only)—and preferred wine (rouge, rosie or blanc) slightly chilled.

In lieu of fresh turtle meat, a fine-quality canned turtle soup (clear), combined with basic substance described above, results in a mock turtle soup to delude all but the most canny gourmet.

TURTLE SOUP
Mrs. Curran Perkins

1 small turtle
1 large onion
4 hard-boiled eggs, yolks only
4 bay leaves
1 qt. water
6 cloves, a little flour
1 tablespoon sherry, each plate

Boil the turtle with cloves and bay leaves till soft. Keep the stock. Take out the bones of the turtle. Fry the onion in butter, then thicken with flour. Pour the stock over it and add the meat. Cream the yolks of the eggs, and add them with the sherry when ready to serve. If there are many eggs in the turtle, the yolks of two hen eggs only need be used.

LOCKPORT TURTLE SOUP
Mr. Louis Perrilliat

5 lbs. good turtle meat, fresh or frozen
 (snapper or loggerhead, no white meat
 or neck, preferably leg)
5 lbs. yellow onions

1 gallon skinned whole tomatoes
4 fourteen-oz. cans tomato sauce
1 lb. flour
5 bay leaves
2 tablespoons cloves

Cut and clean turtle meat in bite size pieces (about ¾ inch cubes). Brown in oil until almost burned in large saute pan or stock pot. Remove and reserve cooked meat. Saute coarsely chopped onions on slow fire . . . until amost mush consistency. Add additional oil if desired. Combine meat and onions and continue simmering for ½ hour. Drain whole tomatoes and retain liquid. Remove seeds from tomatoes and mash whole tomatoes to a pulp. Add to meat and onion. Add tomato sauce. Add tomato liquid and fluid to suit. Brown flour in oil, DO NOT BURN, and add to mixture. Add salt, bay leaves and cloves. Simmer slowly for 4 or 5 hours, stirring regularly. Add Tabasco and Lea & Perrins to taste. Garnish with finely chopped hard cooked eggs, chopped parsley, thinly sliced lemon, and good quality sherry.
**For freezing soup, add juice.

TURTLE SOUP A LA MARDI GRAS

The Editors

15 lbs. turtle meat, cut in ¼ inch cubes
5 tablespoons garlic salt
1 tablespoon ground cloves
1 tablespoon ground cinnamon
1 tablespoon cayenne
4 teaspoons black pepper
2 sticks butter, not oleo

Put turtle meat in pan. Bake in 350° oven, after sprinkling with seasonings and dotting with butter. Cook 1 hour stirring frequently.

Make Roux:
4 cups oil
6 cups flour

Stir together over medium high heat until it is as dark a brown as you can get it without burning it. Remove from heat and add:

12 cups chopped onions
12 celery stalks and tops, chopped
5 carrots, put through grinder, or minced
2 small bunches curly parsley
2 whole lemons, put through the grinder, or minced, rind and all

Stir all of this together into roux and cook over medium heat for about ½ hour.

Now Add:
8 l-lb. 12-oz. cans Progresso peeled tomatoes, chopped
9 ozs. B. V. Beefer Upper, Wilson's
4 tablespoons Lea & Perrins
2 tablespoons Maggi seasoning
5 teaspoons black pepper
30 cups water
5 tablespoons plain salt
2 tablespoons garlic salt
2 15-oz. cans tomato sauce
cooked turtle meat and juices from pan

Cook all together for about 2 hours on a slow flame. When good, thick consistency, add four cups sherry, and 26 chopped hard-boiled eggs. Slice three to four lemons thinly and float on top of garnish. Serve with extra sherry for individual tastes. Makes about 10 gallons.

If you like extra thick soup, add to the soup during the final cooking 1 cup of Wondra (or other instant blending flour) which has been mixed with 2 cups cold water until it is a paste. Stir in gradually.

MOCK TURTLE SOUP

Mrs. Odette J. Hemenway

2 lbs. round steak or soup meat
1 qt. tomatoes
2 onions
½ cup flour
2 quarts water
1 cup sherry
3 bay leaves, cloves to taste and thyme, tied in a cloth
salt and pepper to taste
3 hard-boiled eggs

Fry meat and onions in a little lard until brown. Remove them from the fat and stir in the flour and brown well. Return the meat and onions to the fire, add the tomatoes, stirring constantly to prevent lumping. Add water and spices and simmer for three or four hours. Strain through a colander, add sherry, and serve a thin slice of lemon and a slice of hard boiled egg in each bowl.

VEGETABLE SOUP

Mrs. James Selman

7 quarts cold water
5 lbs. beef shank slices

½ cup bacon grease
2 large onions, sliced
1 lb. bag carrots, peeled and sliced
2 diced celery ribs
1 cup parsley, chopped
2 green onion stalks, chopped
1 tablespoon chives, freeze dried
plenty black pepper
3 tablespoons salt
1 teaspoon cayenne
1 can tomato paste

Bouquet garni: Make by tying in cheese cloth:
2 cloves unpeeled garlic
2 cloves
1 bay leaf
1 teaspoon thyme

2 big Irish potatoes (large dice)
2 big turnips (large dice)
head cabbage, sliced
1 teaspoon Italian seasoning
¼ lb. fresh spinach, torn up
¼ lb. red beans

Brown shanks on grease. Remove and place in soup pot with 7 quarts of cold water, and the bouquet garnie. Begin cooking. Fry onion in grease and add to soup. Do same with carrots. After 1 hour add pepper, cayenne, shallots, and parsley, chives, celery and tomato paste. After 2 hours, add red beans. After 2½ hours, add cabbage, spinach, turnips, Italian seasoning and salt. After 3 hours, add potatoes. After 3 hours, turn off flame. Fish out the bouquet garnie and squeeze and discard. Take out all meat and trim gristle. Allow soup to cool in pot, covered. With each serving serve a shank slice.

BELAIR VEGETABLE SOUP
Mrs. David T. Merrick

a large beef soup bone with plenty
  of meat on it
a small veal knuckle
1 stalk celery, cut fine
1 bunch carrots, cut fine
6 onions, chopped fine
1 qt. can tomatoes
thyme, bay leaf, 8 cloves

Wash meat, cover with 1½ gals. cold water and allow to stand for an hour or longer. Then place on fire and bring to a quick boil, and boil for fifteen minutes. Skim. Reduce the heat, simmer for three hours, then add the seasonings and the vegetables, salt

and pepper. Simmer one hour longer. Strain some and color, by adding one teaspoonful of sugar which has been caramelized. An oxtail added to this soup improves the flavor. This is delicious hot or cold.

DEEP SOUTH VEGETABLE SOUP
Mrs. Clave E. Gill

1 lb. shin beef with bone and marrow
2 lbs. beef brisket
½ lb. salt pork
4½ qts. cold water
4 tablespoons salt
1 teaspoon cayenne pepper
4 large onions
2 cups diced celery
1 cup diced carrots
1 cup diced string beans
1 cup green peas
1 cup whole grain corn
1 cup minced parsley
1 cup tomato paste
½ cup diced turnips
½ cup egg pastina, a very fine spaghetti

Place shin bone, brisket and salt pork in large kettle. Add salt, pepper, and whole onions. Cover and simmer 4 hours. Then skim. Remove onions, bone and meat. Shred the beef and salt pork, return to stock. Then add all the other remaining ingredients, except the pastina. Re-cover and simmer 2 hours. Add the pastina and cook 30 minutes longer.
This makes a very thick, nutritious mixture, suitable for a one dish meal with a salad.

VICHYSSOISE
Mrs. Carl E. Woodward

2 bunches of leeks
1 cup celery
2½ tablespoons butter
1 qt. milk
2½ cups of potatoes
2 tablespoons each butter, flour
  chives, salt and pepper

Cut leeks and celery in very fine slices crosswise and cook in butter, stirring constantly for ten minutes. Add milk and cook in double boiler for forty minutes.
Cut potatoes in slices and cut slices in small pieces then cook in boiling salted water for ten minutes. Melt 2

tablespoons of butter, add flour and milk with vegetables and potatoes. Cook until potatoes are soft, push through sieve. Serve hot or cold in bouillon cups, sprinkling each cup lightly with chopped chives.

COLD VICHYSSOISE

Mrs. Rufus Foster

4 leeks (white part)
1 medium sized onion
2 ounces of sweet butter
5 medium sized potatoes
1 quart of chicken broth
1 tablespoon of salt
2 cups of milk
2 cups of medium cream
1 cup of heavy cream
chives or water cress

Slice very fine the leeks and onion and brown lightly in the sweet butter, then add the potatoes sliced fine. Now add broth and salt. Boil from 35 to 40 minutes. Mash and rub through a fine strainer. Add milk and medium cream. Season to taste and bring to a boil. Cool and rub through a fine strainer. When soup is cold add heavy cream. Chill thoroughly before serving. Add finely chopped chives.

QUICK MOCK VICHYSSOISE

Mrs. John Newton Pharr

1 can Campbell's green pea soup
1 can milk
2 tablespoons shallots, chopped fine
2 strips bacon, crumbled
1 tablespoon parsley, chopped fine
1 teaspoon or more Worcestershire sauce

5 drops of Tabasco
1 pinch of salt
1 tablespoon of heavy cream

Run in blender for about two minutes the soup, milk, one teaspoon of shallots, Worcestershire sauce, Tabasco and salt.

To chill quickly place in freezing compartment about one-half hour before serving. Stir in heavy cream.

Sprinkle bacon, shallots and parsley on top of each soup cup.

CRABMEAT STEW

The Boston Club of New Orleans

2 1-lb. tins of fresh lump crabmeat
2 tablespoons vegetable oil
1 cup coarsely chopped onion
1 cup coarsely chopped bell pepper
2 cups canned tomato
1 cup canned tomato puree
2 cups crab stock or boiling water
2 tablespoons roux
2 cloves garlic, minced
½ teaspoon thyme
2 bay leaves
2 teaspoons minced parsley

In 2 tablespoons vegetable oil saute onion and bell pepper until tender. Stir in tomato and tomato puree and simmer slowly for 25 minutes. Stir in roux and crab stock or boiling water, simmer for 15 minutes more. Add crabmeat, garlic, parsley and thyme and bay leaves. Salt and pepper to taste. Cook 20 minutes and remove from heat.

Serves 6 - 8.

fish and shellfish

CODFISH CAKES
Mrs. Frank H. Lawton

3 cups shredded codfish (B and M)
3 cups mashed potatoes
3 teaspoons onion juice
2 eggs
½ stick butter
black pepper

Buy codfish by the pound, soak in cold water. Put in fresh cold water and boil for several hours until easily shredded. Boil potatoes and mash, adding a half stick of butter.

Mix cod fish and potatoes, adding onion juice and eggs, beating in one egg at a time and black pepper, salt if necessary.

Both the codfish and potatoes must be warm when mixed. Shape the cakes suitable for a portion. Flour well on both sides, set aside to cool and cook in deep fat. The cakes should be creamy inside and brown on the outside. Serve with crisp bacon and tomato catsup. Canned cod flakes may be substituted, in which case the freshening and cooking process is omitted.

COD ROE AND BACON
Mrs. Alfred T. Pattison

1 tin fine cod roe, Crosse & Blackwell
½ lb. butter
1 lemon, the juice
½ lemon
1 tablespoon parsley, chopped fine
6 slices very thin bacon

Remove roe from tin carefully so as to keep it whole. Cut into thick rounds. Sprinkle with a little lemon juice. Fry in butter until a light brown, being careful not to break rounds. When done pour over these rounds a maître d'hotel sauce made with 3 tablespoons butter, 2 tablespoons lemon juice and 1 tablespoon chopped parsley. Serve with curls of bacon.

CRAB CHOPS À LA NOUVELLE ORLÉANS

1½ doz. crabs, or 1 lb. meat
1 cup sweet milk
4 tablespoons flour, level
2 tablespoons butter
2 egg yolks
1 teaspoon minced parsley
1 tablespoon Worcestershire sauce
  salt, pepper to taste, bread crumbs

Mix the flour with part of the milk. Put the rest of the milk to boil, then stir into the flour a tablespoon of butter. Cook until a stiff paste, add crab meat to get well heated. Have the egg yolks beaten, then stir them into the hot mixture. Put back into double boiler, add another tablespoon of butter, the minced parsley, pepper, and salt. After it cools, place it in the refrigerator. When cold, form in chop shape. If too soft, use a little fine bread crumbs to help mold chops. Dip each one first in bread crumbs, then in egg, then back in bread crumbs. They must stand several hours in the refrigerator to harden before frying. Pull the little claw with the teeth from the foot claw. When your chops are fried stick a claw in each one. Serve with mushroom sauce. (A cup of crab meat may also be added to the sauce.) Lobster or salmon may be used in the same way.

CRAB FRICASSEE

2 sweet peppers, chopped
8 large fat crabs
1½ lbs. peeled raw shrimp
2 tablespoons butter
2 tablespoons flour
3 cloves garlic, minced
4 shallots, minced
3 tablespoons parsley, minced
2 stalks celery, minced
3 tablespoons sherry
  season highly with red pepper,
  and salt to taste

Boil crabs 15 minutes without seasoning. Put butter in iron skillet, melt, add flour and make a dark roux. Add shallots, garlic, and sweet peppers, and cook five minutes, then add four crabs quartered and two cups of the crab water, cover and cook ten minutes. Now add two more cups of water, season highly and put in the raw shrimp and cook 15 minutes. Now add parsley and picked meat from crab claws and the white meat of the four other crabs and cook 5 or 6 minutes. When removed from fire put in sherry. Serve with boiled rice. This with a salad makes a delicious luncheon.

CRAB MEAT AU GRATIN

Mrs. Yvonne Galatoire Wynne Galatoire's Restaurant, Inc.

Sauté lightly in butter some finely chopped green onions; then make a cream sauce using a little milk to this sauce, you add the crab meat, and cook it on a very slow fire for 3 minutes. Remove from fire and then place crab meat in a pyrex dish, over it sprinkle bread crumbs, grated cheese and a little melted butter. Place in a hot oven. Remove when golden brown.

BAKED CRAB MEAT

Mrs. David T. Merrick

1 lb. lump crab meat
1½ cups milk and cream
½ cup bread crumbs
4 eggs
½ onion grated
1 lemon (grated rind)
1 tablespoon Worcestershire sauce
2 tablespoons sherry
1 tablespoon butter
  salt, pepper

Cream yolks of eggs with seasoning; add bread crumbs, butter, milk, cream and sherry. Fold in well beaten whites. Turn in well greased mold. Bake one-half hour in moderate oven. Serve with mushroom sauce; shrimp and oysters may also be added. Serve immediately.

LUMP CRAB MEAT WITH SAUCE

Pearl Carter

¼ lb. butter
3 tablespoons flour

½ cup each finely chopped celery, shallots
2 tablespoons finely chopped green peppers
1 cup finely chopped mushrooms
1 cup milk
½ pt. whipping cream
1 cup sherry
3 lbs. lump crab meat
2 tablespoons finely chopped parsley
  salt, pepper, Worcestershire sauce, Tabasco to taste

Put flour and butter in pot, sauté but not brown, add onions, celery, green peppers and mushrooms, juice from mushrooms and milk. When this has cooked, add the whipping cream and sherry, salt, pepper, Worcestershire sauce and Tabasco. After sauce is thoroughly cooked, add crab meat and parsley. This can be served on rosettes or toast and will serve 12. It can also be served as an appetizer for cocktails on rounds of toast.

CRAB MEAT NEWBERG

Miss Grace King

1 lb. crab meat, or shrimp
1 tablespoon butter
2 egg yolks
1 cup cream
½ teaspoon salt
  dash hot pepper and Tabasco
  sherry to taste

Put butter in sauce pan, when just melted add crab meat or shrimp, salt and pepper.

Cover and simmer for 5 minutes add 1/3 cup sherry, cook for 3 minutes, have the egg yolks and cream beaten together—pour over the crab meat. Shake in sauce pan until mixture has thickened and follow directions carefully or failure will result. Serve immediately.

CRABS ST. JACQUES

Miss Virginia Fassman

1 doz. large crabs, or 1 lb. can lump crab meat
1 can mushrooms
1 tablespoon flour
1 tablespoon butter
2 egg yolks
1 teaspoon salt, pepper to taste
1 pt. milk

Cream butter, flour, and eggs. Add gradually to hot milk in a double boiler, and cook until the mixture thickens. Cut the mushrooms in four and season with salt and pepper, a little butter, and boil them in their own juice. Pour this over the crab meat, then add the salt. Put in shells or baking dish, sprinkle with bread crumbs, dot over with butter, and bake until brown in a hot oven.

CRABMEAT SYCAMORE
Mrs. Frank C. Moran, Jr.
Mrs. Anthony Vizard

2 pounds white lump crabmeat
¾ pounds diced Swiss cheese
2 packages frozen artichokes
  (cooked and drained)
1½ cups cream sauce
1 tablespoon chopped green onions
  (shallots)
1 teaspoon parsley
3 tablespoons butter
2 tablespoons flour
1¼ cups milk
2 tablespoons dry sherry
  Tabasco, Worcestershire sauce,
  salt and pepper to taste

Place alternate layers of crabmeat, cheese and artichokes in greased casserole. Spoon cream sauce evenly over top. Sprinkle with bread crumbs and bake 30 minutes until bubbly. Garnish with thin lemon slices and parsley. Serves 6 - 8.

CRAB MEAT TIMBALE
Ella Brennan Martin
Brennan's French Restaurant

1 chopped pimento
4 chopped anchovies
½ cup mayonnaise
3 tablespoons unflavored gelatin
1 cup vinegar
½ teaspoon pepper
½ teaspoon salt
1 can crab meat

Dissolve gelatin and vinegar in cup. Mix chopped pimento and chopped anchovies, mayonnaise in a bowl. Add salt and pepper, and crab meat. Then add gelatin and vinegar mixture in the same bowl. Mix well. Put in cup or casserole. Refrigerate for 1 hour.

HARD SHELL CRAB HALVES IN WINE SAUCE
Mrs. Joseph Merrick Jones, Jr.

1 dozen crabs, cooked
1 cup olive oil
1 cup white wine
1 tablespoon Rosemary
1 - 2 tablespoons cracked pepper
4 - 6 cloves garlic, minced

Clean crabs and break in halves. Heat all other ingredients in saucepan. Stand crabs up with meat side down in bowl. Pour warm sauce over and let marinate for a few hours. Serve as an hors d'oeuvre with small plates and plenty of napkins. If you want to serve these warm, marinate in an oven proof dish and heat in low oven.

UPSIDE-DOWN CRABS
Mrs. H. C. Ehrenfels

1 lb. crab meat
1 cup bread crumbs (soak and drain)
1 large onion cooked soft in butter and
  minced
2 eggs, well beaten
1 teaspoon Worcestershire sauce
2 heaping tablespoons mayonnaise
  nutmeg, salt and pepper

Mix all together well and fill shells. Toast a little bread crumbs and spread over the top, patting firmly. Drop in deep hot fat to fry with filled side down. Then turn and do shell side. Will take about 5 minutes to brown well.

CRABBY ELIZABETH
(Fried Soft Shell Crab)
Mr. David D. Duggins

8 medium to large soft shell crabs
2 lbs. medium shrimp - peeled raw
2 cups dry vermouth
2 teaspoons salt
½ teaspoon black pepper
½ teaspoon red cayenne pepper
½ pint sour cream
3 cups onion, chopped fine
3 cloves garlic, chopped fine
2 sticks butter
4 tablespoons flour
3 eggs
½ cup milk
2 cups flour for crab breading

Boil peeled shrimp in vermouth, salt and pepper for 8 minutes, drain and cool, reserving stock. While shrimp are boiling saute onions and garlic slowly in butter on low heat until very clear (about 30 or 40 minutes). Add 4 tablespoons flour, stir to make a light roux, add heated shrimp stock gradually to roux to make a medium thick white sauce (water may be added to thin).

Slice cooled shrimp lengthwise in order to have a thin slice of shrimp to stuff into the crab -- insert slices of shrimp in a slit in the center of the crab as well as in each point, after the dead man has been removed. Use as many shrimp to stuff crabs as possible -- add remaining shrimp to sauce.

Roll stuffed crab in beaten egg and milk mixture (add salt, pepper and cayenne to egg batter to taste). Roll stuffed crab in flour after coating with egg mixture. Fry in oil until golden brown.

Just prior to serving, add ½ pint sour cream to white sauce. Heat, but do not boil, and pour over crabs. Serve with lemon wedges. Will serve eight.

BOILED CRAYFISH
Mr. James Gundlach

For 1 sack of 40 to 50 pounds add to ½ filled No. 3 tub of water:

3 boxes salt (1 lb. 10 ozs. each)
1 pack bay leaves
1 dozen lemons, cut and squeezed
1 dozen onions, cut in quarters
2 buds garlic, peeled and cut in pieces
4 ozs. cayenne pepper
1 bottle of Louisiana Hot Pepper Sauce
3 boxes crab boil
1 dozen large potatoes (to be eaten with crayfish)

Bring mix to a rolling boil, add crayfish. Return to boil and cook for 20 minutes. Do not overcook. Remove from fire, and let soak in seasoned water for 10 to 15 minutes, sampling as they soak. Drain off water. Let cool, and eat with vigor!!!!

CRAWFISH CARDINALE
Mrs. J. Mort Walker, Jr.

3 lbs. boiled crawfish
1 large can B & B sliced mushrooms

2 level tablespoons flour
1 stick butter
3 shallots—chopped fine
2 tablespoons parsley—chopped fine
½ cup dry sherry

Peel crawfish. Brown flour in butter until dark brown, add shallots and simmer until soft; add parsley, mushrooms with liquid, and sherry and simmer in double boiler ½ hour. Add crawfish, heat and serve in sea shell with buttered toast.

LES ÉCREVISSE DE GAULLE
Mr. Seymour Weiss
The Roosevelt Hotel

1 lb. crayfish tails
6 shallots, chopped
3 tablespoons chopped chives
½ cup white wine
2 cups chicken broth
1 cup cream
4 tablespoons roux (flour browned in butter; see SOUPS, GUMBOS, & BISQUES)
3 tablespoons chopped pimentos
salt, tabasco, paprika

Saute shallots and chives; add the white wine and a little paprika. Make sauce of the roux, chicken broth and cream. Add wine mixture, crayfish tails, salt and Tabasco and chopped pimentos. Fill ramekins or casseroles. Top with parmesan cheese and brown in oven.

This recipe was concocted especially for President Charles de Gaulle in 1963 when he visited New Orleans. Seymour Weiss, then the owner of the Roosevelt Hotel hosted a gourmet luncheon and this dish was served.

CRAWFISH ETOUFFE
Terry Flettrich

Perhaps you have never seen a crayfish, and couldn't care less whether you do or not, but if this is going to be a collection of Cajun Creole recipes, there has to be a crayfish recipe. Etouffe means cooked down, or smothered with onions. This was given to me by a well padded cook in the crayfish capitol of Pierre Part, La.

30 lbs. live crayfish
¼ cup oil
½ green pepper
5 medium chopped onions
onion tops, parsley
1 stalk celery, chopped

Wash and cull crayfish. To approximately 10 gallons of boiling water add crayfish and scald for 5 minutes or until half cooked. (This is very important because they will break up and become mealy when cooking if they are not scalded long enough.) Cool and peel at once, separating the fat from the tails.

Heat oil, add onions and celery, cook until tender. Add crayfish fat and cook over low heat stirring constantly until fat comes to the top. Add tails, pepper and season to taste. Simmer for 30 minutes. Add parsley, onion tops and serve. Serves 8 people.

LOBSTER, CRAB MEAT OR CRAYFISH A LA NEWBURG

Mrs. Alfred T. Pattison

2 cups cooked lobster, crab meat or crayfish cut into small pieces. Crayfish should be left whole
1 cup whipping cream
3 egg yolks
1 cup cooking sherry
2 green onions or shallots
    dash of cayenne and paprika, salt
    heaping teaspoonful butter
    sprigs of parsley tied into a bouquet

Put meat, butter, salt, cayenne, paprika and bouquet of shallots and parsley in a double boiler, preferably a chafing dish. Let cook for five minutes. Add cooking sherry and cook until sherry begins to simmer. Remove bouquet of shallots and parsley. Mix egg yolks thoroughly in cream. Add to mixture. Stir constantly, without allowing to boil. As soon as mixture begins to thicken serve immediately, as the sauce will curdle if cooking is continued too long after adding cream and eggs. The secret of success is in the seasoning.

BOILED FISH

3 or 4 lbs. red fish or red snapper
3 bay leaves, thyme
½ onion
2 tablespoons salt
½ lemon sliced with peel

Tie the fish up in a piece of bobinet. Into enough water to cover the fish, put all the ingredients. Let it come to a boil, put in fish and cook until thoroughly tender, about 20 to 30 minutes.

Remove and drain well. It may be served hot with egg sauce with capers, oyster sauce, drawn butter, or, cold with mayonnaise and garnished with lettuce, quartered tomatoes, asparagus ringed with green peppers, or something of the sort.

BROILED FISH CHARPENTIER

3 lbs. red snapper or trout, tenderloined
3 tablespoons olive oil
1 lemon, the juice
    salt, pepper, garlic

Rub the fish with the garlic and season with salt and pepper. Pour over it the olive oil and the lemon juice. Place on the broiler and cook under the flame, turning once and allowing ten minutes to each side.

Serve with the following sauce:

1 cup each shrimp and crab meat
1 onion, minced
1 tablespoon lard
½ cup sherry wine
    salt, cayenne pepper
    thick white sauce

Fry the finely minced onion in the lard, add the crab and shrimp meat. Season with the salt and red pepper. Add all to the thick white sauce and thin with the wine. Pour over the broiled fish and garnish with thin slices of lemon and fresh parsley. Serve very hot.

CREAMED FISH

Mrs. Edgar Bright

3 lbs. trout
4 ozs. butter
2 eggs, the yolks
¼ pt. thick cream
    salt, pepper

Bone the raw fish and pound to a pulp. Add the butter and yolks, well beaten, pound again, and season with salt and pepper. Rub through a hair sieve into a bowl, work the mixture with a wooden spoon until quite light, adding the cream gradually. Put mixture in greased mold and set it into a pan of water to steam, but not to boil, for 20 minutes. Serve with mushroom sauce, with a few shrimp or oysters added.

FILET OF FLOUNDER LOUIS 13th

Mr. Roy Alciatore, Antoine's

"Take some choice green onions, chop them very fine and sauté them in the finest butter. Then take some fresh mushrooms, chop very fine and add this to the green onions, cook for about five minutes and then add a wine glass of the best dry white wine. Cook again for five minutes.

Then take a sole or flounder, remove the filet and cook in white wine, green onions, butter, and season with salt, pepper, and a bouquet of thyme, bay leaf and celery. Moisten with oyster water.

Take a silver dish, fill the bottom with the mushrooms cooked with green onions and white wine. Lay the filet of flounder on top of this.

Then to the sauce in which the fish was cooked add some rich cream and allow to cook a while longer. Cover the sole with this sauce and on top of this sprinkle some grated Parmesan cheese. Pass this under the salamander (overhead fire).

Garnish the sides of the dish with Duchesse potatoes sprinkled with chopped pistachio nuts and serve."

FILET OF FLOUNDER À LA MARSEILLES

6 to 8 filets of flounder
1 onion
2 tablespoons butter
3 cups rich soup stock
2 tablespoons flour, sifted
½ cup thick cream
½ cup Parmesan cheese
½ cup chopped almonds
    salt, white pepper to taste

Cut the filet in narrow strips, roll each strip and fasten with a toothpick. Fry the chopped onion in butter, add the stock, cook the filet in this until done, when it must be removed to a baking dish. The sauce is then thickened by stirring in slowly the flour which has been stirred to a thin, smooth paste with a little water. After it has cooked a few minutes add the cream and pour over the fish. The cheese and almonds are sprinkled over the top and the dish run under the broiler to brown.

STUFFED FLOUNDER

Mrs. Joseph Merrick Jones, Jr.

4 fresh flounders, 1 lb. each
1 lb. fresh crab meat (buy the
    white flaked crab meat or the
    dark claw meat; it is much cheaper
    and the lump breaks up anyway)
5 large fresh mushrooms, chopped
1 cup heavy cream
3 eggs, beaten lightly
1 stick butter
3 shallots, chopped
1 teaspoon salt, or more to taste
    (garlic salt may be used)
¼ - ½ teaspoon cayenne pepper
½ cup breadcrumbs to thicken, more
    if needed
    more butter to dot the flounder with
        when cooking, and about
1 cup of chicken broth for pan
    gravy

Gently mix the crabmeat, eggs and cream in bowl. Set aside. Saute the onions and mushrooms in the melted stick of butter until tender. Add the crabmeat mixture to the pan and season with the salt and cayenne. Cook over low heat for 10 minutes. Add ½ cup of bread crumbs, and if not thick enough, add a little more until of stuffing consistency.

Place flounders on baking pan, skin side up. With sharp knife, cut the fish down the backbone, cutting the whole length of the flounder. Run sharp knife carefully under each side, cutting from backbone out to the side of the fish. Flap sides open and heap inside high with the stuffing. Dot each fish with butter and add about 1 cup chicken broth to the pan. Bake at 350° for ½ hour. Baste constantly. Serves 4.

FISH MARTINIQUE

Mrs. Shaw Putnam

1 chicken carcass (Add water and bo
    down to 4 cups of broth)
6 lbs. filet of flounder
1 can truffles
1 can grapes, peeled and skinned
4 tablespoons butter
3 eggs
1 can mushrooms
1 cup cream
½ cup each sweet and dry white wine
4 tablespoons flour
½ cup lemon juice, ½ cup onion juice
    parsley, finely chopped
    salt, pepper, Tabasco

Soak grapes in wine for 2 hours before starting dish. Lightly brown
mushrooms in butter, add flour. When
smooth add the chicken broth and
wine. Cream the yolks of eggs and
butter. Add this and onion juice and
the cream, and grapes. Cook only a
few minutes. Remove from fire, add
lemon juice to taste, salt and Tabasco.
Lay in rows in a shallow pyrex baking
dish the filets of flounder which have
been boiled and carefully cleaned of
bones. Pour the sauce over fish, flood-
ing generously. Slice the truffles and
dot around in dish, pushing some
down into the fish. Dot liberally with
butter. Sprinkle lightly with powdered
parsley. Do not let dish get cold. Run
under hot flame only long enough to
get a rich brown.

Serve with thin, crisp, sliced ice-
cold cucumber salad with highly seasoned French dressing.

FISH GLACÉ
Mrs. Jefferson D. Hardin, Jr.

3 to 4 lbs. sheepshead
1 large onion, 2 cloves garlic
2 pieces celery
1 piece bell pepper, 1 small bay leaf
1 pt. or more bouillon
  salt, black pepper and cayenne
  onion juice, Worcestershire sauce,
  lemon juice, sherry, pimento to
  taste
2 envelopes gelatine

Boil fish with above seasoning, when
cooked use 1 cup of bouillon and
enough liquid from fish water to make
a quart. Season this with onion juice,
Worcestershire sauce, lemon juice and
sherry (or white wine) to taste.

Strain—and to one quart of this
hot liquid add gelatine. Skin and bone
fish placing the meat in 1 large (or two
medium sized) fish molds using round
piece of lemon peel for the eyes and
strips of pimento for the tail. Pour
liquid over fish and allow to "jell" in
refrigerator.

Place on garnished platter and
serve with butter, parsley potatoes
and cucumber vinaigrette.

A perfect summer dinner dish!

KEDGEREE
Mrs. Curran Perkins

3 to 4 lbs. red snapper, red fish, trout
1 cup boiled rice
1 small onion, chopped
2 tablespoons melted butter
2 hard boiled eggs, sliced
4 bay leaves, 6 cloves, parsley
  salt, pepper to taste

Boil the fish, with cloves and bay
leaves and break up the eggs, white
and yolks together and mix well with
rice, onion and parsley. A little mashed
potato mixed with it is an improve-
ment. Add the butter, then the fish,
put in a baking dish and bake quickly.
Garnish with sliced hard-boiled eggs.

FISH MOUSSE
Mrs. Frank Henning

2½ lbs. fresh fish filets, or frozen
  onion, parsley, bay leaf
  salt, pepper and lemon

Boil fish with seasonings about ten
minutes. Drain and flake. There should
be 1 quart of flakes.

1 cup blanched and toasted almonds,
  chopped
1¼ cups cracker crumbs
1 cup cream
¼ cup melted butter
2 tablespoons grated onion
2 lemons, the juice
6 eggs, whites and yolks beaten
  separately

Mix all ingredients with the flaked
fish, folding in the beaten egg yolks
and last of all the beaten whites. Butter a ring mold or bread pan and fill
with the mixture. Set in a pan of
water and bake in a 350 degree oven
from 1 to 1½ hours. Serve with the
following sauce:

2 tablespoons butter or margarine
2 tablespoons flour
½ cup milk
1 cup thick sour cream
  chives, parsley, paprika, water cress
  salt and pepper

Make a thick smooth cream sauce
of the butter, flour and milk. Just before serving add the chives, parsley or
other green herbs. Add salt and pepper. At the last moment stir in the
sour cream.

This dish may be served hot or cold.
It can be prepared ahead of time ex-

cept for adding the whites of eggs to the fish and the sour cream to the sauce.

POMPANO EN PAPILLOTE

3 medium sized pompano, cut into six filets
2 cups crab meat
2 eggs, the yolks only
1 pt. fish stock, made by boiling the heads and bones of the fish
1 large tablespoon butter
4 each onions, truffles, chopped
1 cup mushrooms, chopped
2 ozs. white wine
1 tablespoon flour
salt, white pepper

The filets are boiled for five minutes in salted water. The crab meat is sautéed in butter and a dash of white wine for five minutes. The sauce is prepared by cooking the chopped onions, truffles and mushrooms in the butter about five to ten minutes. The fish stock is added to them, a little being reserved to rub with the flour to a smooth paste. When the stock has simmered with the onions, mushrooms and truffles about ten minutes, the flour paste is slowly stirred in and it is allowed to cook down until quite thick, then add egg yolks. It is seasoned to taste with salt and pepper and the wine is added. It is immediately removed from the fire, not being allowed to cook after the addition of the wine. Each filet is then folded over with a generous spoonful of the sautéed crab meat in the fold and is placed in a paper cooking bag. It is liberally dressed with a sauce, some being placed within the fold as well as over the fish. The bag is securely folded and the whole baked for ten minutes in a hot oven. It is served piping hot in the bag in which it is cooked, which is cut open at the table.

RED FISH SHAH OF PERSIA
Mrs. Harry Williams
"Marguerite Clark"

7 to 8 lbs. red fish
2 qts. water
2 onions, 1 stalk celery
bay leaf, parsley, thyme
red pepper and salt to taste

Make highly seasoned stock using two quarts water, celery, onions and all seasonings. Place fish on rack, lower into hot stock and cook 20 to 25 minutes until done, keeping tightly covered. Remove fish and reduce stock to about two cups. Separate all fish from the bones and arrange in warm casserole from which it is to be served. Cover and place in warmer. Serve with Sauce "Marguerite Clark."

Sauce:
4 tablespoons butter
2 tablespoons flour
2 cups fish stock strained
2 egg yolks
¾ cup sherry wine
2 tablespoons chopped parsley
1 teaspoon lemon juice
salt, pepper

Blend butter with flour in top of double boiler, slowly add the fish stock and stir until smooth. Lower flame and add the slightly beaten egg yolks always stirring slowly, then add lemon juice. When sauce becomes quite thick, remove from fire and add salt, pepper, sherry and parsley. Pour over the fish and serve at once.
This will serve ten people.

VOL-AU-VENT BERCY
Mrs. Edwin French

large pastry shell
3 to 4 lbs. sheepshead, boiled and boned
2 lbs. boiled shrimp
1 lb. crab meat
1 lb. broiled fresh mushrooms
Sauce:
¼ lb. butter
2 tablespoons flour
2 cups cream
1 cup wine bercy or any other white wine or sherry

The fish should be boiled with ½ lemon, pod of red pepper, ½ cup freezing salt, bay leaf, thyme, and ½ clove garlic.

Make a cream sauce, using a double boiler with the butter, flour and cream and cook it until it begins to thicken, then add the other ingredients, the wine last of all. Season to taste. Put all in pastry shell and pass through a hot oven for 3 minutes.

Noteworthy, even in this New Orleans where there are so many noteworthy fish dishes.

COLD BOILED RED SNAPPER

Mrs. Albert C. Grace

4 lbs. red snapper
½ cup salt
1 tablespoon peppercorns
1 teaspoon ground white pepper
2 pieces celery
2 yellow onions, sliced
2 each bay leaves, sprigs thyme
1½ pts. tartar sauce or mayonnaise to which a tablespoonful of mustard has been added

Wash and clean fish leaving head and tail on. Wrap in a piece of cheesecloth and place in a baking pan. Add all seasonings above, cover with cold water and simmer for three quarters of an hour. Remove carefully from the pan with two spatulas, place on a long fish platter and remove the cheesecloth carefully and all the bones, leaving head and tail, however. When cold spread the mayonnaise over the whole fish, except the head and tail. Garnish with lettuce, sliced egg and carrot cubes. Place the heart of lettuce in the fish's mouth and on each eye a slice of stuffed olive. Serve with hot new parsley potatoes.

COLD FISH RING

Mrs. Helen Pitkin Schertz

2½ lbs. red fish or red snapper
½ cup celery, chopped fine
1 small bottle capers
1½ cups fish stock
1¼ cups mayonnaise
3 hard boiled eggs, chopped
2 teaspoons onion juice
1 lemon, juice
¼ cup cold water
1 envelope gelatine
3 tablespoons French dressing
1 onion, parsley, thyme
1 bay leaf, 8 cloves
1 small red pepper
1 tablespoon salt

Put sufficient water in a fish boiler to cover fish. Bring to a boil with all seasonings. When it has come to a good boil lay in the fish, reduce heat and boil very slowly about twenty minutes or until tender. Allow to cool, remove all skin and bones from the fish and toss the pieces in a bowl with the chopped eggs, celery and capers. Marinate with the French dressing, onion juice and lemon juice. Place in a mold. Soak the gelatine in the cold water and dissolve in the hot fish stock. When cool stir in the mayonnaise and pour over the fish. Put in icebox to set and unmold on crisp lettuce leaves. Garnish with slices of tomato and sprigs of parsley.

FILET OF SOLE VERONIQUE

Mr. Roy L. Alciatore
Antoine's Restaurant

Buy, beg or borrow a sole (flounder will do). Look at it straight in the eyes (you can do that with a flounder because both eyes are on one side) and if it stares back at you, it is decidedly FRESH.

The Fish

Remove the filets, there are four of these, but if you have never done that sort of thing before, just have the job done by your fishmonger. Season the filets with salt and pepper and lay them gently in a pan. In this pan place an onion cut in quarters, a piece of celery, the juice from half a lemon and the half lemon itself and a little white wine (dry). Add just enough water to cover the fish. Simmer slowly for 10 minutes. Remove from fire. Set aside.

The Stock

With the skin and bones of the flounder make a strong stock by simmering these with a little onion, celery, lemon juice and 1 bay leaf. Simmer for half an hour, strain out the bones, etc. and reduce this stock until it is very concentrated. Set aside.

The Stuffing

Mince finely some boiled shrimp, green onions and parsley. Sauté these in a pan with a little butter for a few minutes and then add a spoonful of fish stock and enough cream sauce to make a thick mixture. Season with salt and pepper. Allow to cool.

The Sauce

Make a roux with flour and butter in equal parts. (A roux is a mixture of flour and butter cooked slowly with continuous stirring so as not to burn or scorch.) Cook about 5 minutes. To this roux add a little of the fish stock and a little of the water in which the filets of flounder were poached. Stir well to avoid all lumpiness. Taste for seasoning and add salt if necessary.

Assemble The Dish As Follows

Take each filet of flounder from the water in which it was poached, dry it on a towel, add a quarter of an inch layer of the stuffing on top of each filet. Place the filets in a dish and heat under the broiler. When ready to serve, take two egg yolks and a half cup of cream and add this mixture which is well stirred together first, to the sauce. Place on fire to heat and mix but **do not let sauce come to a boil.** This would curdle the eggs and ruin the sauce. The cream makes the sauce rich and the egg yolks give it a fine color.

To Serve

Pour the completed sauce over the fish with the stuffing and spread over the top of the sauce some seedless grapes cut in half and previously heated in some dry white wine. Eat and enjoy!

FISH SOUFFLÉ

- 3 lbs. red fish
- ½ lemon, sliced
- 2 bay leaves, 1 pinch thyme
- 1 pod red pepper, ¼ teaspoon salt
- 2 cloves garlic
- 1 heaping tablespoon butter
- 1 tablespoon flour
- ½ cup milk
- 3 egg whites, well beaten
- 2 tablespoons minced parsley
- 2 teaspoons lemon juice
  - a dash of cayenne pepper
  - bread crumbs

Put the fish in a deep pan and cover with water. Add salt, red pepper, lemon, bay leaf, thyme and garlic to the water in which the fish is boiling. Cook the fish until done, about 20 minutes. Remove from water and take off the skin and bones and flake the fish. Put the butter in a saucepan and add flour and a little salt and the milk. Add minced parsley and a dash of cayenne pepper. Cook about 5 minutes, then add flaked fish. When well blended, take off the fire and add two teaspoons of lemon juice. Stir well and add stiffly beaten whites of eggs. Put in a buttered casserole, sprinkle with bread crumbs and put a little melted butter on top. Put the casserole in another vessel of hot water and bake for 15 minutes. Serve with following sauce:

- 4 tablespoons butter
- 2 tablespoons flour
- 2 cups fish stock, strained
- 2 egg yolks
- ¾ cup sherry wine
- 2 tablespoons chopped parsley
- 1 teaspoonful lemon juice

Blend butter with flour in double boiler, slowly add the fish stock and stir until smooth. Lower flame and add the slightly beaten egg yolks always stirring slowly, then add lemon juice. When sauce becomes quite thick, remove from fire and add the sherry and parsley. Pour over the fish and serve at once. This will serve ten people.

STEWED TERRAPIN
Mrs. D. D. Curran

- 3 terrapins
- ½ lb. butter
- 5 eggs, boiled hard
- 2 tablespoons flour
- 2 gills sherry
- 1 dessertspoon salt, cayenne to taste

Boil meat until tender; break into small pieces, adding liver and any terrapin eggs, the juices that have accumulated through the cutting up, and 2 gills of stock. Set in a china lined stew pan (or pyrex) over a moderate fire, rub flour and butter to a cream and stir it in. Rub the yolks of eggs to a smooth paste with salt, pepper and wine, then add the cream and serve immediately. It must not boil after the cream is added and must not stew more than 5 minutes after the time it begins to cook.

FISH TIMBALE

- 5 lbs. red snapper
- 1 stick butter
- 1 pt. cream
- 6 eggs
- 1 cup each cream sauce, mushrooms
  - salt, Tabasco sauce
  - celery, bay leaf, cayenne

Boil the fish with a piece of celery, a couple of bay leaves, salt and cayenne in the water. Carefully remove all bones and beat with a wooden spoon until light. Add the butter, cream, yolks of eggs, salt to taste, and Tabasco. Beat thoroughly then fold in the stiffly beaten egg whites.

Put in a well buttered mold, securely covered. Set in a pan of water,
taking care that there is not enough
water to seep into the mold, and bake
½ hour. This quantity will serve ten
or twelve people. Serve with a medium thick cream sauce to which a
cup of finely chopped mushrooms has
been added.

TROUT
Mrs. John R. Peters

6 filets of trout
  salt and pepper
12 thin slices of tomato
  capers
¼ cup minced parsley
2 garlic pods, minced
  olive oil or butter
  lemon juice

Place trout in individual pieces of
aluminum foil, large enough to wrap
foil completely around trout. Salt and
pepper filets, place 2 slices of tomato
on top of each filet, sprinkle with
capers and parsley. Add as much garlic
as desired. Pour about 1 tablespoon of
butter or olive oil over all, and 1
teaspoon lemon juice to each. Seal the
foil around the fish. Place on cookie
sheet and bake at 400° for 20 minutes. To serve, carefully unwrap each
filet and remove from foil to serving
plate.
Serves 6.

TROUT ALMONDINE
WITH SEEDLESS GRAPES
Mr. Francis J. Selman

Have the fish-monger filet and skin
the fish. Use one filet per person.
Saute trout in butter gently. Brown
both sides. When fish flakes when
pierced with a fork, remove to a warm
serving plate. Use canned white seedless grapes. In the same pan saute the
grapes until they wrinkle. On the other
side of the pan, saute slivered almonds
until they are brown. (Do NOT mix
the grapes with the almonds.)
With a spoon, put almonds around
both edges of the filet and the grapes
down the middle. Melt additional butter until hot but not brown, and spoon
over each filet. Sprinkle with salt and
pepper to taste.

BARBEQUED TROUT
Lester Lautenschläger, Sr.

6-8 trout filets
12-16 slices bacon
1 cup melted butter (2 sticks)
1/3 cup lemon juice
1/3 cup Lea & Perrins

Have trout tenderloined. Wrap tightly in extra thinly sliced bacon. Use
toothpicks if necessary. If filets are
large, 2 slices of bacon are necessary.
Grease fish racks heavily and place
trout in them. Place racks on open pit
and baste with sauce of butter, lemon
juice and Lea & Perrins.
Serves 6 - 8.

FILET OF TROUT DUGLERE
Pontchartrain Hotel

1 filet of trout
1 tablespoon butter
¼ cup fish stock
¼ cup white wine
¼ cup canned tomatoes, strained
1 tablespoon minced onion
1 tablespoon minced pepper
1 teaspoon minced parsley

Saute vegetables in butter then add
tomatoes, let cook for approximately
two minutes, then add rolled trout
and cook for fifteen minutes.
Garnish with watercress.

TROUT EMILY
Scoop Kennedy

2 fat filets of trout
¼ stick butter
1 lemon (juice only)
1 tablespoon water
3 tablespoons chopped parsley and
  shallots
1 cup heavy cream
3 tablespoons bread crumbs
  salt

Grease generously a baking dish
with butter. Place the filets in dish.
Sprinkle with salt, lemon juice, parsley, shallots and a tablespoon or two
of water. Bake for ten minutes, or
more, in a pre-heated 400° oven.
Meanwhile boil the heavy cream in
sauce pan, i.e., bring the cream to just
under the boiling point and hold it
there for no longer than three minutes.
Pour over the fish (after the fish has

baked for ten minutes), sprinkle with
commercial bread crumbs, slide under
broiler and keep it there until sauce
bubbles and top is brown.

TROUT MARGUERY

Mr. Justin Galatoire
Galatoire's Restaurant, Inc.

Tenderloin the trout, skin it and
fold. Place the folded fish in a pan to
which you add a tablespoonful of olive
oil and a glass of water. Bake in a hot
oven for 15 minutes. To make the
Hollandaise sauce, use the following:

½ lb. of melted butter
3 egg yolks
 juice of a strained lemon

Salt and cayenne and pepper to
taste. Place the egg yolks in a double
boiler, then gradually add the melted
butter; stir very slowly until thick.

To this sauce add:
12 lake shrimp
2 truffles
½ can of mushrooms

Cut all of these ingredients into
small pieces, then mix with your
sauce. Dress your fish on a platter
and pour sauce over it.

FILET OF TROUT EN
PAPILLOTE

6 or 8 filets of trout (pompano,
  flounder, or sole, may be
  substituted)
2 cups béchamel sauce
1 cup stock
1 cup chopped mushrooms
1 lb. shrimp, chopped
2 doz. oysters
1 stalk celery, chopped
¼ cup chopped shallots
  salt, pepper, bay leaf, thyme
  sherry

The fish is boiled with the seasonings. To the béchamel sauce add the
stock in which the fish was boiled.
Add the chopped mushrooms, shrimp,
oysters, and at the last a dash of
sherry.
Each filet is prepared and served in
a paper cooking bag as in "Pompano
en Papillote." No dish has contributed so largely to the culinary fame of
New Orleans.

TROUT MEUNIÈRE
AMANDINES

Count Arnaud

Filet of trout is dipped in milk, then
seasoned with salt and pepper. After
that it is dipped in flour so that both
sides are well covered. The next step
is a saucepan where butter has been
heated. The trout is dropped into
this, turned as it cooks, so that it may
brown evenly on both sides.
Remove it from the saucepan to a
warm platter, drop chopped almonds
a moment into the butter where the
trout was cooked, and sprinkle them
thickly over the fish. (Pecans may be
substituted for almonds.)

TROUT PLAUCHÉ

Mr. James J. Plauché
Dunbar's

3-2 lb. trout (split and filléted)
  shortening
½ lb. butter
2 hard boiled eggs (sieved)
½ can anchovy filets (mashed)
½ bottle capers
  juice of 1 lemon
2 teaspoons horseradish mustard
½ teaspoon Worcestershire sauce
1 clove garlic (minced)
2 teaspoons onion juice

(1) Wash filets well.
(2) Bake filets submerged in shorten-
    ing in shallow pan in 350° oven
    about 10 minutes.
(3) Melt butter in saucepan.
(4) Add all ingredients and simmer
    about 15 minutes.
(5) Remove trout from shortening and
    place on plate. Pour sauce over
    filets.
(6) Decorate with pimento strips and
    lemon quarters.

TROUT VERONIQUE

Mr. Albert Aschaffenburg
The Pontchartrain Hotel

1 filet of trout (from 1½ lb. trout)
½ pt. white wine
½ cup heavy cream sauce
½ cup very rich Hollandaise Sauce
8 seedless grapes

Poach trout in white wine in pan
that will cover trout, about 7 minutes.

Remove from poaching liquor and place on plate well drained. Then reduce the liquid over fast fire to 2 cooking spoons of liquid. Mix with cream sauce which is moderately hot. Add Hollandaise-Sauce and stir briskly. Place grapes on trout, then sauce, and glaze quickly in the broiler.

TROUT WITH WHITE WINE SAUCE

3 lbs. trout
3 tablespoons olive oil
2 chopped onions
6 tablespoons butter
2 tablespoons flour
1 lemon
1 doz. shrimp, cut fine
3 truffles, cut fine
½ can mushrooms
12 oysters
1 glass white wine
  bread crumbs, grated cheese
  salt, pepper to taste

Skin and bone trout, cut in six pieces, fold over and put in pan with olive oil, a few onions, salt and pepper to taste. Place in oven to cook. Take another pan, blend flour, butter and lemon juice over fire, add shrimp, mushrooms, truffles, oysters and wine. Pour all over fish. Sprinkle with bread crumbs and cheese, dot with butter and run in stove again to heat very hot.

TURTLE AU GRATIN

Mrs. E. M. Choppin

4 lbs turtle meat
½ cup butter, or lard
1 tablespoon flour
1 onion, 1 clove garlic, chopped fine
1 cup chopped olives
2 doz. stoned olives
1 wine glass sherry
1 hard boiled egg
1 lemon
  toasted bread crumbs
  salt, pepper, parsley, chopped fine

Remove all the fat from the turtle meat and boil until tender. Make a roux of the butter (or lard) and the flour, sprinkling in the flour after the butter is hot, letting it brown thoroughly. Add the onion, parsley, and garlic. Now put in the diced turtle meat, cover with water, add seasoning to taste, and let all simmer gently until very tender when the water will be reduced to a thick gravy. Soak the olives for chopping well in

water, otherwise the dish will be too salty. Add them to the simmering turtle meat with the sherry and pour all into a shallow pyrex baking dish. Cover the top with toasted bread crumbs and decorate with the stoned olives, the sliced hard boiled egg and sliced lemon. Serve very hot.

NOTE: it is not necessary to soak the olives for stoning, as they are not used in the cooking. To stone them, take a sharp knife and cut around and around the stone, leaving the olive meat in a spiral.

ABBEVILLE OYSTERS

Terry Flettrich

There's a beautiful cook book called "Cook with Marie Louise," one of Louisiana's great hostesses, Marie Louise Snellings, compiled primarily for her children and friends. Among her many oyster recipes, is this excellent one which she got in Abbeville, a charming town in Cajun Dairy Country.

First, you make a roux out of ¾ cup of oil, butter or bacon grease, and four heaping tablespoons of flour and you add to this 2 large onions chopped up and brown it. Then, you add about 5 of 6 cups of water to this, including your oyster water, then salt and pepper, about 2 tablespoons of Worcestershire sauce and a dash of Tabasco. To this you add 2 quarts of oysters, chopped or cup up, 2 large cans of mushrooms and about 6 green onions (that is, the tops). Add ½ cup chopped parsley and a bell pepper chopped up. Now, when you are heating this, after you have added the oysters, the mushrooms and the green onions, just about 10 minutes before you put it in the shells, you add about two-thirds of a loaf of bread, breaking it up fine in this and then you put the whole thing in the shell and top it with crumbs and bake it, and add dots of butter. You bake it about 30 minutes at 350° and it is delicious.

OYSTERS ALEXANDRIA

Mrs. Richard Franklin White

3 doz. oysters
1 tablespoon butter
2 tablespoons flour

1 medium sized onion
1 small can tomatoes
½ cup oysters liquor, or more
   parsley, green onion tops, sweet pepper, celery, salt, pepper, cayenne,
   Worcestershire sauce

Brown the flour in the butter, with minced onion and cook a few minutes, then add the tomatoes, slowly, stirring constantly. Add all green seasoning, chopped fine, also salt, pepper, cayenne, and Worcestershire. Add oyster liquor but do not make too thin as the oysters, which are added last, will thin the sauce somewhat. Cook three minutes and serve on a hot platter. Cover with croutons.

This dish may be varied by using one-third oysters, one-third crab meat and one-third shrimp.

OYSTERS AND ARTICHOKES SUNSET FARM

Mrs. George Calhoun

  6 artichokes
  6 dozen oysters
  1 pint oyster liquor, more if needed
  3 tablespoons flour, or less
  1 stick butter
2/3 cup shallots finely chopped
  1 large clove garlic, crushed
  6 thin rounds lemon with dash of
    paprika
½ cup parsley chopped fine
    pinch of thyme (oregano and
    marjoram if desired)
    salt and pepper to taste

Boil artichokes. When cool scrape the leaves and take out the heart and cut in thin slices. Put into buttered casserole. This can be put in refrigerator until needed. Put butter in a skillet to melt over low heat; stir in the flour slowly and constantly. Add the shallots and cook until soft. Add oyster liquor, thyme, parsley, salt and pepper and simmer for 20 minutes. Add oysters and cook slowly for 4 or 5 minutes until they curl. Pour this over the artichokes in the casserole, put lemon slices over all and put in a preheated oven and bake only until piping hot. This is a delicious dish.

OYSTERS AND ARTICHOKES

Mrs. Hughes P. Walmsley

4 artichokes, boil until tender,
  scrape leaves, chop up hearts

1 stick butter
4 green onions, tops too, chopped
2 toes garlic
2½ dozen oysters, cut in half
1 can cream of mushroom soup
1½ tablespoons Lea & Perrins
  dash Tabasco
  juice of ½ lemon

Melt butter in saucepan. Saute in butter, green onions with tops, chopped, and add 2 toes of garlic, chopped. Add halved oysters and simmer until edges curl. Add 1 can Cream of Mushroom soup, Lea & Perrins, lemon juice. Then put in artichokes and mix gently. Place in casserole or individual ramekins and top with bread crumbs and pats of butter. Bake until bubbly. (350° oven)

BAKED OYSTERS BOURGUIGNONNE

"La Louisiane"

Shallots, very little garlic, few anchovies, fresh walnut meat, all chopped fine and sautéed in butter. Pour over oysters on half shell, bake and serve with a piece of bacon on each.

BAKED OYSTERS EMIL

Put oysters on half shell on platter or pie tin half filled with rock salt. Cover with thousand island dressing, then plenty of grated sharp cheese on top. Put in very hot oven 5 or 6 minutes.

OYSTERS À LA BECHAMELLE

Mrs. Duncan Parham

2 qts. medium oysters
2 pts. heavy cream
2 tablespoons butter
2 teaspoons flour
2 teaspoons each shallots, parsley,
  chopped

Heat the cream lightly. Rub the flour and butter together, thin with a little of the warm cream and stir into the rest of the cream together with the seasonings. Simmer till it is a light beige color, then add the oysters and continue to simmer slowly until the mixture is thick. Do not use oyster liquor.

This recipe will serve eight when cooked in a casserole as a main dish, with petits pois and a salad, or if served in ramekins as a fish course it will serve twelve.

OYSTERS WITH BELL PEPPERS
Mrs. Shaw Putnam

4 doz. oysters
3 large bell peppers
1 lb. sharp cheese, grated
1 pt. each oyster liquor, milk
2 egg yolks
2 tablespoons corn starch
1 cup butter
1 teaspoon Kitchen Bouquet
  Tabasco, black pepper, salt

Strain the oyster liquor and put on to boil with the three green peppers ground through a meat chopper. After they have boiled until quite soft, add the oysters and salt to taste (and in correct salting lies the success of the dish). Cook for five minutes and add milk, corn starch, eggs and butter which have been creamed smoothly together, Kitchen Bouquet, a generous dash of Tabasco, and three-fourths teaspoon of black pepper. When the mixture has thickened, put in the cheese. Stir constantly. The cheese should be dissolved and smooth in less than five minutes. Serve on thin slices of very crisp buttered toast.

OYSTERS BENEDICT
Mrs. John B. Levert

6 slices of toast
6 slices of broiled ham
3 dozen raw oysters
¼ cup melted butter or oleomargarine
  salt and pepper to taste

Heat oysters in melted butter over low heat until edges curl. Arrange four or five oysters on ham and toast, and top with Easy Hollandaise Sauce.

BOHEMIAN OYSTERS
Mrs. Shaw Putnam

4 doz. oysters
1 lb. noodles
1 pt. each milk and oyster liquor
1 lb. American cheese, sharp, grated
2 egg yolks
2 tablespoons corn starch
1 cup butter
1 teaspoon Kitchen Bouquet
  dash of Tabasco, salt

Place a large iron skillet or Dutch oven on the fire, and let it get very hot.

Drain the oysters, and throw them into the pot so that they stick and appear to scorch.

Stir with a cake turner so as to scrape up that portion of the juice and oysters which have stuck to the hot pot, as this gives a delightful flavor to the dish.

Salt, and remember you are salting for the finished dish, not for a few .....rs in the pot.

At the end of five minutes, when the oysters are at least partially cooked, add the pint of oyster liquor and the pint of milk. When this is hot, add the eggs, corn starch and butter, which have been creamed together, Kitchen Bouquet and Tabasco.

When the mixture is thick and creamy, remove from the fire.

The noodles, in the meantime, should have been boiled with salt until very tender, and drained.

In a large casserole, place a layer of noodles, about an inch deep. Divide the oysters into three parts, and cover the noodles with one-third of the oysters. Flood liberally with the sauce, and then cover the layer thickly with grated cheese. Sprinkle with black pepper. Add another layer of noodles, a third of the oysters, sauce and cheese. Finally the third layer of noodles, the remaining third of the oysters, and enough of the sauce to flood the dish generously, sprinkle thickly with the cheese and dust with black pepper.

Put in the oven for 20 minutes before serving. All of the ingredients being cooked, the dish should not be allowed to remain in oven longer than this, as the cheese otherwise bakes into a crust, whereas it should only melt. Twenty minutes is sufficient to make the dish very hot when served.

OYSTERS BROILED IN BROWN SAUCE
Mrs. Lucius K. Burton

½ stick butter
2 dozen raw oysters
¾ cup oyster liquor
½ cup shallots, cut fine (about
  2 shallots)
2 tablespoons finely chopped parsley
1 tablespoon flour, rounded
  cayenne pepper, salt to taste

Melt butter in skillet, add flour gradually. Brown to tobacco color. Add shallots and saute. Add oyster liquor and cook to desired thickness. Oysters and parsley are to be added 5 minutes before serving. (Cook them in same sauce till oysters curl.)

For main luncheon course, serve with a salad and toast points garnish. Serves 4 as an appetizer; serves 2 as a main luncheon course.

OYSTERS CARIBBEAN

Mr. Albert Aschaffenburg
The Pontchartrain Hotel

1 qt. of oysters, drained
1 teaspoon chopped parsley
2 teaspoons Worcestershire sauce
1 pt. medium cream sauce
1 bunch of shallots (chopped)
2 ozs. butter

Melt butter in saucepan and add shallots; brown oysters on heavy grill and add to saucepan. Sauté slowly five minutes, then add other ingredients. Let simmer 5 minutes and serve with steamed rice.

COCKTAIL OYSTERS
A LA RASCAL

Mr. Larry Regan
W S M B Radio Station

3 dozen oysters
1½ cups tomato ketchup
3 teaspoons horseradish
juice of 2 lemons
salt and pepper to taste

Clean and drain oysters. Chill six oyster cocktail glasses. Drop six cold oysters into each glass. Keep cold. Mix remaining ingredients in a small pitcher and pour equal amounts into each of the six glasses.

Hey fellows!!! This recipe is an old New Orleans love potion!!!!!

OYSTERS AND CRABMEAT
À LA BONNE FEMME

Mrs. Richard Adler

1 lb. crabmeat
20 oysters and liquor
¼ lb. butter
1 cup white wine
½ cup cream
3 green onions
2 tablespoons parsley
2 generous tablespoons flour
breadcrumbs for topping

Put crabmeat, chopped onions and parsley in skillet with wine. Simmer gently 5 minutes.

In another skillet, blend butter and flour. When this begins to bubble (but not brown), add oysters and liquid and cream. When well mixed and simmered for 5 minutes, put in with crabmeat. Put all in buttered baking dish. Top with buttered bread crumbs. Put in pre-heated 450° oven for 5 minutes.

Can be served in ramekins as first course, or casserole as main course.

CURRIED OYSTERS

1 pint oysters
4 tablespoons butter or margarine
½ cup oyster liquor
½ cup milk
1½ tablespoons flour
¼ teaspoon salt, dash pepper
½ teaspoon curry powder

Drain oysters, reserving liquor. Sauté oysters very gently in two tablespoons butter or margarine until edges begin to curl. Remove. Melt remaining two tablespoons butter in saucepan, add flour and seasonings and blend. Add oyster liquor and milk gradually and cook over low heat until mixture is thickened, stirring constantly. Add oysters and heat thoroughly. Serve at once over fluffy rice. Serves four bountifully.

OYSTERS FAIRVIEW

Mrs. Joseph Merrick Jones, Jr.

4 dozen oysters
2½ cups cream sauce (made with oyster liquor and heavy cream)
3 tablespoons each minced chives, minced shallots
1 cup sliced fresh mushroom caps
⅛ lb. butter; white pepper and salt
2 tablespoons sherry

Sauté mushroom slices and shallots in butter until tender. Add oysters and cook until they curl a bit.

Mix chives, white pepper and salt together and add to oyster mixture. Pour into buttered casserole dish, top with buttered bread crumbs and bake in 350° oven till brown. Then add the sherry.

OYSTERS FARCIS
Mrs. Frank S. Walshe

3 dozen large oysters
1 cup each shallots, parsley, minced
½ cup celery, minced
1 stick of butter or bacon drippings
1 tablespoon flour
½ cup dried bread crumbs
1 egg
6 large oyster shells
cayenne, salt to taste

Heat the oysters until plump. Drain and cut into small pieces. Melt butter, cook onions, parsley, celery. Add the flour, oysters and bread crumbs. Season to taste. Remove from the fire. Mix in the beaten egg. When cool, fill shells, cover with bread crumbs and dot with butter. Put aside until a few moments before ready to serve, then run into the oven to brown, and serve piping hot.

FRIED OYSTERS

Take fine large oysters, free them from small particles of shell. Put them into a colander and pour over a little water to rinse them. Place in a clean towel and dry them. Have ready some cracker dust, seasoned with salt and pepper, or better use the commercial preparation known as "Fish Fry." Beat as many eggs and cream mixed as will moisten all oysters. Dip each oyster in the eggs and cream and lay them in the cracker dust and pat with the back of a spoon. Pack the cracker dust close to the oyster, lay them on a dish and so continue until all are done. Put in a frying pan equal portions of oil and lard. When boiling hot, put as many oysters as the pan will hold without their touching and fry quickly a light brown on both sides. A few minutes will cook them.

POACHED OYSTERS
Mr. Francis J. Selman

3 doz. oysters
1/3 cup butter or margarine
½ lb. sliced mushrooms
salt and freshly ground black pepper
2 tablespoons frozen chopped chives
1 cup (½ pint) heavy cream

Open oysters with an oyster knife, or have them opened at the market. Heat butter in a small saucepan. Saute mushrooms until soft and lightly browned. Add chives and cream. Heat until cream just starts to bubble. Lower heat and add oysters. Simmer about 5 minutes or until edges of oysters crinkle. Season to taste with salt and pepper. Serve in small bowls with toast or crackers.

OYSTERS POULETTES
Mrs. Edgar H. Bright

2 doz. oysters
¾ cup sherry
3 beaten egg yolks
1 tablespoon each parsley, green onion, chopped
1 pod garlic
¼ lb. butter
2 tablespoons flour, heaping
1 doz. whole cloves
salt and pepper to taste

First, drain oysters and save liquor.
Second, melt butter and stir into it the flour until smooth, gradually add oyster water, salt, pepper, and cloves.
Third, add oysters and chopped garlic. Let simmer until oysters curl.
Fourth, take out some of the cream sauce (about ½ teacup) and add ½ of the three beaten egg yolks and part of the sherry. Stir well and add to the oysters. Then take more of the sauce in cup and add to the remainder of egg yolks and sherry, and then add to the oysters. Add, lastly, onions and parsley, and serve. A very fine old French recipe. Garlic can be omitted if flavor is not desired.

OYSTERS ROCKEFELLER
Mr. Fred B. Otell

Take out the oysters, wash them, and drain them. Put them back in the shells, set on a pan of hot ice-cream salt, and run them under flames of the gas stove for five minutes, then cover them with the sauce described below, and run under the flame until the sauce melts and browns.

Large bunch spring onions
Large bunch parsley
¼ lb. butter or oleo

Chop above and cook slowly in covered pot until soft, in butter or oleo, about 20 minutes. Run through food blender, put back in pot and add:

4 cans strained baby spinach
1 tablespoon celery salt
¾ tablespoon anchovy paste
2 tablespoons Worcestershire sauce
2 tablespoons Louisiana Hot Sauce
1 tablespoon fresh ground horseradish
2 teaspoons basil
1 teaspoon marjoram

Bring to a boil then remove from fire and add:

2 tablespoons absinthe
1 tablespoon Peychaud bitters

Stir well—let cool—after which put in refrigerator until ready for use.

ROCKEFELLER SAUCE
Mrs. John William Moore

2 lbs. tub butter, cream soft
4 bunches of spinach
2 bunches green onions (tops only)
1 garlic
2 bunches of parsley
1 bunch of French celery or another bunch of parsley and heart leaves of regular celery

Cut all greens through fine cutter of food chopper, save all juices.

1 box (quart) Bond bread crumbs
1 large bottle Worcestershire sauce
2 or 3 tubes or small jars anchovy paste
1 large bottle tomato catsup
about 2 tablespoonfuls salt
pepper and paprika as desired
generous dashes of Tabasco

Use wooden spoon to blend all ingredients as you would blend and mix a cake. (Use electric mixer.) Store away in jars in ice box to use as desired. Clean shells and place oysters on shells. Cover with sauce, place shells on pie tins filled with rock salt and run in oven about 20 minutes. Use 350° oven. Then run under broiler for about ½ minute.

OYSTERS ROFFIGNAC
Ella Brennan Martin
Brennan's
French Restaurant

1 small bunch of shallots, chopped
4 ozs. mushrooms (stems and pieces) chopped
½ lb. boiled shrimp

1 clove of garlic (finely chopped)
4 ozs. red wine
1 oz. concentrated beef stock
2 doz. boiled oysters (save water)
1 tablespoon of corn starch

Let shallots saute in butter. Add mushrooms, then shrimp, let simmer and then add garlic and wine. Continue to simmer on slow fire. Add beef stock, strained oyster water, and corn starch. Cook for at least ten minutes.

Arrange the oysters on six half shells on pie plate covered with a bed of rock salt. Cover oysters with sauce and place in oven just long enough to curl edges of oysters.

SCALLOPED OYSTERS
Mrs. E. V. Benjamin

5 dozen oysters (drain and reserve liquor)
1 stick butter
2 tablespoons flour
1 cup green onions and some tops, finely chopped
1½ cups celery, finely chopped
1 teaspoon salt
½ teaspoon pepper
¼ teaspoon Tabasco
½ cup heavy cream
1 tablespoon lemon juice
1½ cups cracker crumbs, finely crumbled
½ cup parsley, finely chopped

Drain oysters and reserve liquor. Melt butter, add flour and cook 5 minutes, stirring constantly. Do not brown. Add green onions and celery and cook 5 minutes. Add ½ cup oyster liquor, salt, pepper, Tabasco, and cook rapidly 2 minutes. Add cream and stir. Take off heat. Add lemon juice and mix well.

Crumble crackers finely and spread 1/3 of them on the bottom of a shallow 1½ quart baking dish. Sprinkle with ½ of the parsley, ½ of the oysters and ½ of the sauce. Now make another layer with 1/3 of the cracker crumbs and the remainder of the parsley and oysters. Sprinkle the rest of the cracker crumbs on top of the casserole and pour remaining sauce over it.

Bake in a pre-heated oven (400°) until oysters are cooked and top is browned.

SCALLOPED OYSTERS, GRAND ISLE

2 dozen large oysters
2 large tablespoons butter
2 tablespoons Worcestershire sauce
½ teaspoon Tabasco sauce
1 tablespoon minced parsley
½ lemon, the juice
6 crackers, rolled fine
2 tablespoons sherry wine

Drain all liquor from oysters and melt butter with Worcestershire sauce, Tabasco, and lemon juice. Roll crackers fine and roll oysters in cracker crumbs. Put alternate layers of oysters and butter sauce into the casserole until it is filled, having crackers on top layer. Dot with butter. Put in hot oven and bake for 15 minutes or until brown. When done, remove from oven, pour over the oysters 2 tablespoons of sherry wine and serve immediately.

STEAMED OYSTERS

3 doz. oysters
1 tablespoon butter
½ teaspoon salt
1 tablespoon parsley

Put the oysters in a colander, and let cold water run through. Put them over a pot of boiling water and cover to steam until the edges curl. Turn them on a hot dish or platter, pour melted butter with parsley and salt over them and serve at once. They require about 5 minutes to cook. Serve with lemon.

STUFFED OYSTERS

Mrs. Lester Lautenschläger, Jr.

3 dozen oysters, cut up
1 small bunch shallots, finely chopped
2 ribs celery, finely chopped
¼ bunch parsley, finely chopped
2 small cloves garlic (or 1 large) minced
½ teaspoon thyme
1 teaspoon Lea & Perrins sauce
1/3 loaf French Bread
3/4 stick oleo
Tabasco, salt and pepper to taste

Soak bread in oyster liquid. Saute vegetables in oleo. Cook slowly and thoroughly. Add oysters and quickly cook for a few minutes. Add soaked bread and liquid seasonings. Stir well and cook a short time.

Stuff mixture into greased oyster shells. Cover with bread crumbs and paprika. Dot with butter and bake in 350° oven for about 15 minutes. Bon appetit!

STUFFED OYSTERS

Mrs. Robert Moore Parker

1 qt. oysters
3 or 4 stalks celery, chopped fine
1 tablespoon butter
1 tablespoon shortening or salad oil
1 egg
1 clove garlic, minced
1 bay leaf, crushed
½ teaspoon thyme
2 thin slices lemon, minced
1/3 to ½ cup oyster liquor
bread, about 4 to 6 slices

Drain oysters and save liquor. Free oysters from all bits of shell and chop fine. Melt butter in skillet and add celery and garlic. Simmer but do not allow to brown. Add bay leaf and all seasonings. Meanwhile the bread should have been soaked in cold water, squeezed dry and broken up with a fork. Add it to the seasonings and simmer about thirty minutes stirring and mixing until well blended. Add the chopped oysters and reserved liquor and simmer a few minutes stirring and mixing. When well mixed stir in the slightly beaten egg and stir briskly for two minutes over a very low flame. Fill oyster shells or ramekins with the mixture, cover with buttered crumbs, and bake about 20 minutes with the oven at 350 degrees. This will fill eight or ten shells.

OYSTERS AND SWEETBREADS

2 sweetbreads
2 dozen oysters
1 cup white stock
¼ cup butter, 2 tablespoons flour
1 wineglass cream
pepper, salt, nutmeg, bay leaf

The sweetbreads must be soaked, parboiled, and trimmed. Place in a saucepan with the white stock, strained oyster liquor and seasonings. Allow to simmer 20 minutes. Put the butter in a saucepan and stir in the flour slowly, add some of the stock in which the sweetbreads are cooking, slowly, stirring all the time to prevent lumping. Finally add the rest of the stock and the sweetbreads. After a few minutes cooking, add the oysters and cook until they curl. Just before serving add the cream. A touch of luxury is attained by adding a few truffles and mushrooms.

OYSTER AND SWEETBREAD PIES

Helen Duprey Bullock
From Harnett Kane's
"Southern Christmas Book"

2 lbs. sweetbreads
1 qt. small oysters

Put the sweetbreads in a pan with enough cold water to cover. Add the well-washed celery tops, 1 bay leaf, 2 tablespoons vinegar, (mild), 4 sprigs parsley, salt, white pepper. Bring to a slow simmer and cook about fifteen minutes. Drain and plunge into a bowl of water with ice in it to make them firm. After fifteen minutes remove outer membrane and tubes. Near serving time pull the small clusters apart and sprinkle each with flour and paprika. Sauté in a heavy pan with a generous amount of butter until a delicate brown. Sift flour over them and blend lightly, stir in milk or thin cream and stir until thickened and blended into a delicate cream sauce. Then add the oysters, with their liquor and cook gently until the "petticoats" on the oysters curl. Have ready fluted individual pie shells of rich pastry, warmed. Place on a large platter and fill with the creamed mixture. The secret of this dish is its delicacy—forget wine, dominant seasonings etc. and let it speak for itself. Garnish platter with parsley and have fresh mace in a silver shaker. Serves eighteen.

SEAFOOD,
WILDER THAN WHO????
Mrs. James Selman

1 lb. large shrimp
1 lb. lump backfin crab meat
½ lb. fresh mushrooms, large ones
½ stick butter
   salt and freshly ground pepper to taste

2 cups white sauce
½ cup aged cheddar cheese
½ cup Swiss cheese
¼ cup fresh parmesan cheese, grated
   Tabasco and salt to taste
1/3 cup Madeira

Peel and devein shrimp, salt and pepper and saute in butter until done. Don't overcook. Place in casserole and keep warm. Artfully arrange crabmeat around the shrimp. Saute mushrooms (caps only) and add to the shrimp and crab meat. Keep warm.

Make white sauce. Add cheeses and seasonings. When smooth and blended, add Madeira, and pour over the seafood and mushrooms. Serve over toast points.

BARBEQUED SHRIMP
Mr. W. Elliott Laudeman

2 lbs. shrimp with heads (as large as
   you can find)
5 sticks unsalted margarine
2 sticks butter
3 tablespoons medium grind black
   pepper
3 tablespoons crab boil
2 tablespoons Lea & Perrins
2 tablespoons A-1 sauce
1 tablespoon Pick-a-Pepper sauce
2 tablespoons Lawry's seasoned salt
3 teaspoons paprika
2 lemons
2 teaspoons crushed red pepper
2 teaspoons Accent

Pre-heat oven to 450°. Place shrimp in shallow baking pan in one layer. Pour sauce over and bake 15 - 20 minutes, basting with sauce frequently.

Crisp under hot flame in broiler. (Watch carefully when shrimp are under broiler.)

BARBEQUED SHRIMP
À LA MANALE
Terry Flettrich

Manale's is a magnificent restaurant in uptown New Orleans. I think their finest dish is Barbequed Shrimp. I have been trying to get it for years. (So has everyone else.) One night I had the identical shrimp at my daughter Patty's house. "How did you get this recipe?" I asked. Patty would only say that she got it from her sister-in-law Melanie who eats at Manale's often. Melanie is also a great cook. Whether Melanie had it so often that she finally figured out a way to fix it, or whether someone at Manale's gave it to her in a weak moment, we shall never know. But what difference -- Que sera, sera..

Wash and drain shrimp (1 hour) but
    don't peel
Line pan with shrimp 1½" - 2" sides
Each lb. shrimp - 1 lb. butter or ½ lb.
    butter and ½ lb. Oleo
To butter add loads black pepper,
    garlic salt, 1 teaspoon crab boil to
    each pound shrimp; bring to a boil
    on top of stove. Pour sauce over
    shrimp and immediately put in hot
    broiler about 20 minutes.

Serve lots of hot French bread to sop up lovely goo. Please pass many, many paper napkins.

SHRIMP CREOLE
Olga Petit

3 tablespoons oil
2 large onions (chopped fine)
1 tablespoon flour
4 lbs. shrimp, peeled, washed and
    salted
2 green peppers, chopped
1 can tomato paste, 6 oz. size
1 can tomatoes, 1 lb. size
1 cup each parsley and shallots,
    minced
3 cloves garlic, minced, 1 bay leaf
¼ teaspoon cayenne pepper
2 cups water

Heat oil, add onions and cook on low flame until they are light brown. Stir flour in well and add shrimp and peppers, cook a few minutes, stirring all the time. Add tomato paste, tomatoes, and garlic, stirring them in to cook until tomatoes turn a deep red (about 10 minutes). Add water (enough to cover shrimp), parsley, shallots, bay leaf, and cayenne. Salt and pepper. Cover and simmer about 30 minutes.

BOILED RIVER SHRIMP "BELAIR"

1 qt. shrimp
1 qt. water
½ cup coarse salt
2 pods red pepper
½ lemon, sliced
10 whole cloves, celery leaves

The shrimp must be thoroughly washed. Let the water with the seasonings and spices boil, then drop in the shrimp and let them cook 10 to 15 minutes. Drain and cool. To serve, cover with cracked ice.

The same procedure is followed for crabs, also for crawfish.

SHRIMP CREOLE (CREVETTES CREOLE, SE PREPARE ET QUIT AVEC VITESSE)
Mr. Francis J. Selman

2 lbs. raw shrimp
3/4 cup chopped onions
1 cup green pepper, chopped
1/8 teaspoon paprika
1 tablespoon salt
2 tablespoons butter
½ cup shallots, chopped
½ clove garlic, minced
1 pint stewed tomatoes
½ teapoon pepper
½ teaspoon oregano

Peel shrimp, wash and remove vein. Saute shallots, onions, green pepper and garlic in butter. Let simmer until pepper is tender. Add tomatoes and other seasoning and boil for 5 minutes. Add shrimp and boil for 10 minutes more. Serve over steamed or boiled rice. Serves 6.

Recommended wine: Aurora Sauterne.

FRIED SHRIMP

To one pound of boiled, peeled lake shrimp, add the yolk of one egg, one cup of cold milk. Take shrimp out, dip in bread crumbs or corn meal. Fry in deep hot lard.

SHRIMP AND MUSHROOMS

4 tablespoons butter
2 tablespoons olive oil
6 shallots, chopped
1 lb. mushrooms, sliced
4 tablespoons parsley, finely chopped
4 tablespoons Madeira wine
1 lb. shrimp
1 cup sour cream
    toast
    salt and pepper to taste

Melt butter with olive oil over mild

heat and in it saute shallots for 2
minutes. Add mushrooms, cook 5 minutes. Sprinkle with parsley and wine.
Bring to a slow boil and add shelled
and deveined shrimp. Cook until
shrimp turn pink. Stir in sour cream
and heat slowly but thoroughly. Season with salt and pepper and serve on
toast.

SHRIMP NEWBURG
Mrs. John Barry

3 lbs. shrimp
½ cup salt
1 pod cayenne pepper
1 pt. scalded sweet milk
1 tablespoon flour
1 heaping tablespoon butter
1 wine glass sherry
1 raw egg
  sprigs of thyme, 1 bay leaf

Boil the shrimp about 15 minutes
with the seasonings. Remove the
shells. Cream together the flour and
butter, put in a double boiler and add
the scalded milk very gradually, stirring constantly, and let it cook until
it thickens. Add shrimp, salt to taste
and a dash of red pepper. Remove
from the fire and add sherry. Just before serving add the egg well beaten.

"SHRIMP ORLEANS"
Mrs. Fleur Hampton

1 tablespoon butter
1 medium onion, sliced
1 clove garlic (crushed)
1 can cream of mushroom soup
1 cup sour cream
¼ cup catsup
2/3 cup broiled sliced mushrooms
2 cups cooked shrimp

Melt butter and cook onion and
garlic until tender, but not brown.
Combine soup, cream, catsup, mushrooms, shrimp, onion and garlic; and
just heat through. Serve. (You may do
all except the shrimp the day before, if
desired.)
This is delicious served over hot rice
with ham slices on the side; or even
over the ham.

SHRIMP PIE
(For Crawfish Pie substitute same amount)
Mrs. Victor H. Schiro

2 cups cooked shrimp well-seasoned
  (or crawfish)
3 slices bread, cubed
1 cup milk or white wine
3 eggs well-beaten
1 cup minced onion and celery mixed
2 tablespoons butter
2½ tablespoons Worchestershire sauce
  pinch of nutmeg or mace
  salt and pepper to taste

Soak bread in wine or milk.
Saute celery and onions in butter.
Add shrimp, eggs, bread and seasoning. Mix all ingredients. Add a little
liquid if necessary to make consistency
of thick custard. Bake in buttered
casserole at 350° for 20 minutes or until brown on top.
Serves 4-6.

SHRIMP REMOULADE
Mr. Justin Galatoire
Galatoire's Restaurant, Inc.

2/3 cup of olive oil
 5 tablespoons of creole mustard
1 bunch of green onions
2 tablespoons of paprika
1/3 cup of vinegar
1 stalk of celery
2 cloves of garlic
1 sprig of parsley
  salt and pepper

Grind all very fine, the vegetables,
then add the mustard, paprika, salt
and pepper. Mix all these ingredients
thoroughly with vinegar, then add
gradually the olive oil. After the
shrimp are boiled and peeled, let them
soak in this sauce for 3 hours. Makes
one quart. Shrimp should be served
on shredded lettuce as a garnish.

SHRIMP ROSSI
Mr. Francis J. Selman

2 lbs. shelled and deveined shrimp
1/3 cup olive oil
½ cup extra dry Vermouth (Italian)
2 cloves garlic, crushed
3/4 teaspoon salt
½ teaspoon freshly ground black
  pepper
3 tablespoons chopped parsley
3 tablespoons lemon juice

Brown shrimp in hot olive oil. Add Vermouth, garlic, salt and pepper. Cook until liquid is almost gone. Sprinkle with parsley and lemon juice and serve.

SHRIMP SOUFFLÉ

Mrs. Chas. Crawford

1½ tablespoons shortening
1 tablespoon curry powder
1 tablespoon flour
1 cup milk
1 small onion
¼ cup canned tomato soup
½ teaspoon salt, pepper to taste
1 cup fresh shrimp, cut up
½ cup cooked rice
4 eggs

Melt shortening in saucepan, add chopped onion and brown lightly. Add curry and stir well. Sift in flour, stir well and slowly add milk, salt and pepper, shrimp, yolks, and rice. Heat, remove from fire. Add beaten whites. Pour in greased baking dish, bake at 350 degrees.

SHRIMP SUPRÊME

1 cup boiled shrimp
¾ cup chopped celery
1 pimento chopped
1½ teaspoons grated onion

1 small bottle stuffed olives, sliced
1 heaping tablespoon gelatine
¾ cup mayonnaise
2 hard-boiled eggs, chopped
1 lemon, juice, salt to taste

Soak gelatine in 2 tablespoons cold water, melt over hot water and add lemon juice. Let cool, add mayonnaise, salt and pour this mixture over the other ingredients. Mix well and pour into molds. Place in ice box to congeal, and serve on lettuce with mayonnaise; canned tuna fish may be substituted for shrimp.

SHRIMP VICTORIA

Mrs. Frank Schick

3 lbs. raw shrimp, peeled and cleaned
¼ cup minced onion
5 tablespoons butter
  medium can mushrooms, cut up
1 tablespoon salt, pepper to taste
1½ cups sour cream
1 - 3 tablespoons flour

Saute shrimp and onion in 4 tablespoons butter until shrimp are pink. Add mushrooms and remaining tablespoon butter. Sprinkle in flour, salt and pepper and cook for 1 minute. Add sour cream and cook, carefully stirring until smooth. Serve with rice or noodles. Makes 4 - 6 servings.

poultry, game and dressings

CHICKEN ACADIAN

Mrs. Charles O. Noble

1 hen
2 small onions, 1 stalk celery
1 doz. eggs, boiled hard
1 cup green peppers, 1 large onion, minced
1 large can mushrooms
6 medium sized tomatoes
1 cup thick white sauce, ½ cup milk, ½ cup chicken broth
½ cup butter or chicken fat
    Tabasco, Worcestershire, red and black pepper, salt
    cracker crumbs

Boil the hen until tender with the small onions, leaves and outer stalks of the celery and seasonings. Dice the meat, melt the butter and brown in it the minced pepper, the rest of the celery, chopped, and the large onion. Turn in the tomatoes and white sauce, then the chicken, with salt, pepper, Tabasco and Worcestershire, to taste. Last of all add the hard boiled eggs. Stir as little as possible after the eggs are added. Arrange in a casserole, sprinkle toasted crumbs on top, dot with butter then set the casserole in a pan of hot water in the oven and bake until very hot.

CHICKEN AVOCADO

Split avocado pear and remove seed. Fill the cavity with creamed chicken or turkey. Run into the oven until the avocado is thoroughly heated. This makes a delicious and unusual luncheon dish.

BAKED CHICKEN

Mrs. E. V. Benjamin

1 five-lb. chicken
    salt and pepper to taste
4 tablespoons Wesson Oil (or bacon grease)

2 garlic cloves, minced
1 large onion, or 6-8 shallots, minced
4 ribs celery, cut in large pieces
4 fresh carrots, cut in large pieces
¼ cup parsley, chopped
1 medium bell pepper, cut in large pieces
½ - ¾ cups wine (white or red), OR
1/3 cup cognac
    herbs (sprinkle on your favorite or a combination, as you like)

Wash and dry chicken, and cut off all excess fat. Sprinkle generously with salt and pepper and brown on all sides in dutch oven. Remove excess oil from pot and leave chicken in the center. Put into the cavity and around the sides the garlic, shallots or onions, celery, carrots and parsley, and bell pepper. Pour wine or cognac over all and sprinkle with your favorite herbs. Cover tightly and cook in 350° oven until tender. Baste the chicken 2 or 3 times while cooking.

BAKED BROILERS, MUSHROOM STUFFING

Miss Grace King

Three broiler chickens split in half. Sprinkle with salt, brush with olive oil or melted butter. Broil, cavity side up until light brown. Fill cavity with following stuffing then place broilers in 350 degree oven and cook until brown and tender. Baste occasionally with one third each cup butter, water, and sherry.

Stuffing:

3 cups stale bread crumbs
1 cup poultry or meat stock
1½ cups mushrooms
1 beaten egg
6 tablespoons butter
1 tablespoon minced onion
1 tablespoon minced parsley
1 teaspoon each salt, celery salt

111

Put mushrooms through food chopper, melt butter, add mushrooms. Cook five minutes. Add seasonings, stock and cook three minutes. Cool and add lightly beaten egg.

CHICKEN BROILED IN WINE
Mr. Fred B. Otell

3 whole chicken breasts (or thighs)
  Adolph's tenderizer
  poultry seasoning
½ stick butter or oleo
1 medium onion
1 cup dry white wine
  salt, pepper

An hour and a half before cooking sprinkle chicken with tenderizer and rub in well. Keep at room temperature. Just before cooking rub chicken pieces plentifully with poultry seasoning, place in a shallow broiling pan flesh side down. Pour over wine, then butter or oleo melted. Grate onion over chicken pieces and sprinkle sparingly with salt and pepper. Broil 12 minutes about five inches below flame. Turn over and brown. Baste occasionally. Drippings make good gravy.

COQ AU VIN
Mrs. Robert C. Cutting

2 three or four lb. chickens
¼ lb. butter
12 small white onions, stick 3 with 3
  small cloves
1½ cups each red wine and consommé
1 clove garlic, 1 tablespoon parsley,
  minced
1 lb. mushrooms, halved
4 small carrots, diced
1 celery heart, diced
1 bay leaf, pinch thyme, salt, pepper

Cut chicken in pieces, brown lightly in butter, place in casserole. To butter left in pan add seasonings, brown lightly. Add wine and consommé gradually and when hot pour mixture over the chicken. Cover casserole, bake at 300 degrees for 1½ hours, or until tender.

CHICKEN CROQUETTES WITH BRAINS AND MUSHROOMS
Mrs. Wm. J. de Treville

2 cups minced boiled chicken
1 small set brains
1 small can mushrooms, chopped

3 tablespoons flour
1½ cups milk
1 teaspoon Worcestershire sauce
1 tablespoon chopped parsley
1 large spoon of butter
  salt and pepper to taste

Scramble brains in butter. Add mushrooms, mix well with chicken. Make a thick white sauce, creaming butter, flour and milk. Cook well and then add other ingredients.

Then fold in mixture of chicken, brains, and mushrooms. Set aside to cool. Mold into shape, roll in fine cracker crumbs, then in beaten egg, again in cracker crumbs and fry in deep fat.

CHICKEN CURRY
Mrs. Carl E. Woodward

1 4 lb. chicken cut up
4 cups water
1½ teaspoons salt, ⅛ teaspoon pepper
½ cup each butter, chopped onion
½ cup chopped apples (green apples)
3 tablespoons flour
1 tablespoon curry powder
¼ teaspoon cinnamon
½ cup light cream

Simmer chicken 2 to 4 hours or until tender. Remove chicken and simmer stock until reduced to 3 cups. Cut chicken from bones in large pieces —dredge in flour and brown in small amount of fat. Sauté onion in butter until golden brown. Add flour and when blended pour in hot stock, stirring constantly. Add apples, chicken and seasonings. Simmer about five minutes and add cream. Reheat and serve on fluffy boiled rice with curry accompaniments. Serves 6.

CHICKEN CURRY
Given by Knox Van Zandt to Phyllis Dart

1 large hen
1 large onion, whole
  celery tops, 1 bunch
  red pepper and salt
2 cups yellow onions, chopped
2 cups celery, chopped
2 cups cabbage, chopped
½ cup flour
1 large can mushrooms (stems and
  pieces)
1 large can Dietetic Apple Sauce
1 whole bottle Cross & Blackwell
  Curry Powder

In large pot, boil hen for three hours in water seasoned with whole large onion, celery tops, red pepper and salt. Hen is cooked sufficiently when meat pulls away easily from bones. Let cool and refrigerate. Next day skim off fat and reserve. Remove meat from bones.

In reserved chicken fat, saute till transparent, chopped onions, celery and cabbage. Add flour and mix till dissolved. Add chicken broth, mushrooms, applesauce, curry powder and cut up chicken. Cook 30 minutes. Taste and season with salt and pepper to taste. Cool and refrigerate overnight so curry flavor can permeate broth. Reheat and serve over rice with the following boys:

    1 can peanuts, large can
    10 hard boiled eggs, separated into
        whites and yellows and sieved
    1½ lbs. bacon, cooked, drained and
        crumbled
    1 can shredded coconut, browned in
        oven for 20 minutes
    1 large Bermuda onion, sliced
        paper thin and marinated all day
        in Tabasco and Wesson oil - drain
        before serving
    3 thin sliced tomatoes
    1 jar capers
    1 jar chutney
    6 bananas, sliced lengthwise
        (half banana per person). This
        is really a must, for it is
        what stabilizes the curry and the
        other ingredients, and prevents
        heartburn!

Serves 12.

HAWAIIAN CHICKEN CURRY

Mrs. Hubert Vos
Hawaiian Princess

    1 qt. milk from coconut
    1 large coconut grated, or 2 small
        ones—¾ not peeled
        fresh ginger root, piece about
        1 in. long
    1 or 2 cloves garlic
    2 or 3 onions
    1 to 3 tablespoons curry powder
        to taste

Grate ginger root, slice onions and garlic and fry in oil or Crisco with the curry powder (do not use butter, as it is apt to brown). Curry powder should always be cooked.

Add all these to milk and grated coconut, let cook in double boiler for an hour, being careful not to curdle.

Use broilers, fry slightly in oil or fat, when light brown, put on back of stove in covered pot (with several onions, sliced and browned). Cook until tender.

Strain coconut sauce through cheesecloth squeezing very thoroughly to get all flavor of coconut and curry. Add to chicken and serve.

Curry made the day before is better but in warming be careful not to let it curdle.

Salt should always be added last.

Shrimp or hard boiled eggs make a very delicious curry using the same sauce.

Rice and sambals are always served with curry dinner.

CURRY LUNCHEON
Barbara Brooks

A perfect one-dish meal.

    4 lb. chicken or duck
    ½ lb. rice boiled Creole Style
    2 tablespoons each flour, butter
    1 tablespoon brown sugar
    1 to 3 tablespoons curry powder
    1 each small onion, green pepper
    ½ cup seedless raisins
    4 or 5 cups stock from fowl
    1 tablespoon vinegar, 1 stalk celery
        black pepper, cayenne, bay leaf, salt

Simmer fowl until tender, in salted water with celery, bay leaf and vinegar. When done, remove skin and bones and cut meat in medium small pieces. Reserve 4 or 5 cups of stock for sauce.

Sauce:

In a large iron skillet, melt the butter and lightly brown the onion and pepper, finely chopped. Add curry powder, sugar and flour, blend together until smooth, and add hot stock, cup by cup. Let boil gently for about five minutes, until the consistency of thick cream. Add raisins and cut-up fowl, and simmer until ready to serve. Add more hot stock just before serving if necessary.

To serve, heap the rice on a large hot platter, make a depression in the middle of the pile and fill with the curry sauce. Serve individually in hot soup plates, with any or all of the following sambals: chutney, chopped roasted peanuts, chopped bacon, piccalilli, grated coconut, chopped fresh pineapple, and shrimp. These are stirred into the rice and curry sauce and the mixture eaten with a fork and a large soupspoon.

CHICKEN DE LUXE

Mrs. Ludo d'Arcis

4 large fryers, cut for frying
1 wine glass sherry
1 wine glass brandy
1 lb. fresh mushrooms, cut fine
3 shallots, chopped
½ lb. butter
4 eggs yolks, 1 pt. cream
1½ cups chicken stock
salt and pepper

Use breasts and second joints only, reserving other parts for a family dish. Boil giblets, necks, feet and heads in water, highly seasoned, to make stock.

Sauté chicken in butter or oil, after rubbing with salt and pepper. Remove to another pan, add more butter, pour over sherry and brandy and simmer till very tender.

Put another lump of butter in the first pan and turn in the mushrooms and shallots to fry lightly. Cover with the chicken stock and allow to cook slowly till tender. Combine with the chicken.

Heat the cream in a double boiler at the last minute and stir in the parsley and the egg yolks, that have been well beaten. Cook until thick, stirring constantly.

Pour over the chicken and serve at once.

COQUILLES DE VOLAILLES

A Favorite Dish of:
Judge and Mrs. Edwin T. Merrick

3 or 4 lb. chicken
1 cup milk
1 tablespoon flour
1 can mushrooms, chopped
1 small can truffles, chopped
½ cup sherry
1 tablespoon minced onion
2 tablespoons butter
salt, pepper, bread crumbs

Boil the chicken until tender and remove meat from the bones and cut into pieces, not too small. Season with salt and pepper and pour over the sherry. Make a cream sauce with the milk, flour and butter and add the

minced onion. Add the mushrooms and truffles to the chicken and combine all with the cream sauce. Put into baking shells, cover with bread crumbs, dot with butter and set in the oven to brown very lightly.

HONEY BUN'S CHICKEN AND DUMPLINGS

Mrs. Mirian S. Ruppel

1 large stewing hen, cut in pieces. (If a Springer is used instead of a hen, add 3 bouillon cubes to substitute for hen fat.)
2 large onions, chopped
2 cloves garlic, minced
½ bunch shallots, finely chopped
½ teaspoon thyme
cooking oil
flour and paprika
salt and pepper to taste

Dumplings:

2 eggs, well beaten
½ teaspoon salt
flour

Salt and pepper hen pieces. Dredge in flour to which paprika has been added for coloring. In heavy skillet of oil, fry hen pieces till golden brown. Drain hen pieces on paper towels. Pour off excess grease.

To about 3/4 cup of remaining fat add ½ cup of flour, continuously stirring to make a golden brown roux. Add onions, shallots, garlic, thyme, salt and pepper. Cook about 10 minutes, slowly. Place this mixture and hen pieces into large Dutch oven. Season with additional salt and pepper and cover with water. Simmer on low flame till chicken is tender and broth is of gravy consistency (allow pot to cook uncovered if gravy is too liquidy).

About 10 minutes before serving prepare dumplings. Beat two eggs, add pinch of salt and gradually pour in flour until mixture is very stiff and difficult to stir. Using two teaspoons, dip both in chicken gravy. Use one teaspoon to scoop up dumpling mixture and the other to spoon off mixture into gravy. Repeat process for each dumpling. Note: dumplings will swell as they cook in gravy so don't be concerned about their small initial size as you spoon them off teaspoon. Cook dumplings in gravy for at least ten minutes. Serve over egg noodles. Serves 4.

CHICKEN ESTHER
Mrs. Esther Breckenridge

6 salted and peppered chicken breasts
¼ cup Wesson Oil
¼ cup butter or more
1 box fresh mushrooms, sliced
3 stalks green onions, green part included, chopped
½ cup Hollandaise sauce
2 tablespoons tomato paste
1 can Bouillon (beef broth)
½ cup sherry
salt and Tabasco to taste

Brown the chicken breasts in skillet in the butter. Remove the skin and the bones from chicken when done, and place in serving dish and keep warm. In the same dish, cook the mushrooms and the green onions until tender, adding more butter if necessary. Set aside.

In another skillet make a dark roux with the oil and flour. Cool a little, then add the tomato paste and cook over low heat until the brightness is gone. Then add the bouillon and the sherry. When well heated and blended, add the Hollandaise. Add salt and Tabasco to taste. Combine with the mushrooms and the green onions, and pour over the chicken. DELICIOUS!!

CHICKEN FRICASSEE WITH DUMPLINGS
Mrs. J. B. Simmons

1 tender young hen, capon or 2 fryers
2 cups vegetable oil
1 tablespoon sifted flour
½ cup each of chopped onions, parsley, celery and green pepper, sprig of thyme, salt, pepper
5 tomatoes, large, ripe (or 1 qt. can)
hot water, dumplings

Disjoint the chicken, cutting as for frying. Put the oil into a large iron skillet, and when it boils, add the chicken (which has been rubbed with salt and a little pepper; add the giblets if desired). Let brown to rich café au lait color. Remove from the fire, pour off the surplus oil (about ½ the original quantity—it can be strained and kept for future use).

Now add the chopped ingredients, thyme, and bay leaf to the oil remaining in the pot, stir in slowly and carefully the flour and allow to cook, stirring constantly, until the chopped ingredients begin to melt into a rich brown gravy.

At this point, add the tomatoes. Set pot on a slow fire until the tomatoes begin to be absorbed in the bubbling gravy. Add enough hot water (1 qt. or more) to cover and let the pot simmer gently for at least 2 hours, stirring occasionally to prevent sticking. Next the dumplings (rich biscuit dough, cut into any shape desired), dropped in to plump in the fragrant gravy.

Long to tell of, but easy in performance. Serve hot.

FRIED CHICKEN À MERVEIL

1 chicken, disjointed
salt, pepper to taste
flour, sifted
lard or other fat
butter, size of egg

At the last minute, wash chicken in cold water. Do not wipe, but salt and pepper, then dip in flour. Have a large pan with very hot lard ready. Add butter.

Drop chicken in, never touching a fork to it; cover, and let it cook on slow fire twenty minutes.

Turn with spatula, cover and cook about twenty minutes more.

CHICKEN GANYMEDE
Mrs. Thomas Gardner

3 chickens, frying size
1 stick butter
2 cups dried bread crumbs
salt, pepper

Disjoint, or halve chickens and rub with salt and pepper. Melt butter and roll each piece of chicken in it, then roll in fine bread crumbs. Place pieces in a covered roaster and cook for one hour in a 300 degree oven.

BREAST OF CHICKEN HAWAIIAN
Mr. Albert Aschaffenberg
Pontchartrain Hotel

Sauté a boned chicken breast in butter. Place on a plate a cooking spoon of Sauce Espagnole, a piece of toast, a grilled pineapple ring and then chicken breast. Cover same with a sharp Bearnaise Sauce.

HOT JELLIED CHICKEN
Mrs. Paul Gorham

3½ lb. hen
1 can mushrooms, chopped
1 cup stock
1 cup cream sauce, thick
2 tablespoons parsley, chopped
1 tablespoon onions, minced
8 eggs
   salt and pepper to taste

Dice chicken, add mushrooms, parsley, onions and seasoning. Marinate with cream sauce and stock. Stir in eggs but do not beat. Put mixture in well-greased mold, place in hot water and steam very slowly until it sets. Turn out on hot platter, fill center with mushroom sauce and serve.

CHICKEN "LA LOUISIANE"

1 fryer, 2 to 2½ lbs.

Disjoint and fry the chicken to a golden brown. Keep it hot. Make a sauce by combining the following ingredients:

2 tablespoons butter
1 tablespoon flour
1 pt. consommé or stock
6 stoned olives
12 large fresh mushrooms, chopped
4 artichoke hearts
   salt, pepper and sherry to taste

Pour over the chicken and dress on a hot platter.

CHICKEN ORIENTAL
Mrs. Charles L. Brown

A quick adaptation of a very fine recipe.

2 5 oz. cans of boned chicken
1 can cream of mushroom soup,
   undiluted
1 can mushrooms, drained
1 small can pimento, chopped
1 can water chestnuts, sliced
½ cup blanched almonds
¼ cup sherry

Add all ingredients and heat well in a double boiler. Season to taste with salt and pepper. Serve over rice or noodles.

CHICKEN PAPRIKA
Mrs. John Minor Wisdom

Season three fryer breasts (cut in half to make 6 pieces) and six thighs with salt, pepper, poultry seasoning and lemon juice. Broil in heavy iron skillet, using butter and browning lightly. Add more butter, as it is needed to skillet while broiling. As pieces are cooked (about 20 minutes) remove from skillet and place in a small roaster. When the 12 pieces have been placed in roaster set the skillet aside and sprinkle the chicken with 2 oz. of sherry. Add butter (about one stick dotted over pieces) and place in covered roaster in low oven to keep hot, adding ½ warm chicken broth in small quantities to keep pieces moist. Turn occasionally.

Now, add to the skillet in which the chickens were cooked one small minced onion and 2 chopped shallots. Add butter if necessary and brown lightly. Add 2 tablespoons flour and brown lightly. Add slowly ¾ cup warm chicken broth. Mix in 2 tablespoons paprika and add paprika carefully as it is inclined to lump. When the gravy is made, strain well, or, better still, puree in electric blender. Return gravy to skillet, incorporating with it the juices from the chicken in the roaster. Turn flame very low and add 2 additional ounces of sherry. Stir in one pint of heavy sour cream. Rectify the seasoning. (Salt, paprika and white pepper may be needed.) Add one dessertspoon Worcestershire sauce, 2 dashes Tabasco and one tablespoon C and B mushroom sauce. Stir gently and let simmer, being careful not to boil.

Pour over chicken and serve with boiled white rice or wild rice.

The sauce will stand reheating if you are careful not to let it boil. If you wish to prepare the dish an hour or two in advance be very careful that your chicken does not dry out.

CHICKEN PIE
Mrs. J. T. Grace

1 large chicken, 4 to 5 lbs.
Sauce:
  3 tablespoons butter
  4 tablespoons flour
  3 cups of chicken stock
  1 cup cream
  ½ teaspoon salt, ¼ teaspoon pepper
Crust:
  2 cups flour
  4 teaspoons baking powder
  1 teaspoon salt
  2 tablespoons melted butter
  1 egg, 1 cup milk

Cut up the chicken and boil until the meat can be easily removed from the bones. Arrange in a baking dish.

Sauce: Blend together the butter and flour in a double-boiler, and add very gradually the warm chicken stock, the cream, then the salt and pepper. Cook to a creamy consistency and pour over the chicken in the baking dish, reserving enough sauce for a gravy bowl.

The Crust: Sift together the flour, baking powder and salt, then add the melted butter, the egg well-beaten and the milk. This mixture should be thick enough to drop from the spoon over the chicken and sauce in the baking dish.

Bake 15 to 20 minutes, and serve with the reserved sauce.

CHICKEN À LA PIERRE
Mrs. Paul Selley

  8 large pieces of meaty chicken, use
      only breast and second joint
  4 tablespoons butter
  6 chicken livers
 20 mushrooms, sliced
  4 tablespoons salted pistachio
      nuts, chopped
1½ cups sherry
  2 minced onions
  1 cup shredded ham
  4 apples, sliced
  ¼ cup blanched almonds
  2 egg yolks
      salt, pepper to taste
      bouquet of herbs

Sauté chicken pieces in butter, lightly, then remove and sprinkle with 1 tablespoonful hot sherry. When cool, remove chicken from bones and cut into small pieces. Pour off and reserve all but 1 tablespoonful butter. Into but-ter put minced onions, salt and pepper, cook for 1 minute. Add livers, cook 3 minutes with lid on. Remove livers and cut into thin strips. Now add a little more butter to the pan, sauté mushrooms and apples. Add the pistachio nuts, sliced liver and shredded ham, cook 5 minutes, add bouquet of herbs. Remove from fire and add the beaten egg yolks carefully. Set the pan aside. In another pan heat ½ tablespoon butter, sauté the almonds 2 minutes, add the cut up chicken pieces, and pour the rest of the hot sherry over it. Add to this and mix the contents of the other pan, put in a casserole and bake 30 minutes in medium 350° oven. Serve with hot buttered noodles. This dish can be prepared ahead of time and baked at serving time.

POULET À LA RAPHAEL
Mrs. Odette J. Hemenway

  2 large fryers
1½ sticks butter
  2 onions, clove garlic, bay leaves
  2 cans consommé, 2 cups white wine
  1 can mushrooms
  2 tablespoons flour
  1 pt. cream
      salt, pepper, to taste

Melt butter in a large pot. Put chicken in, cut as for frying. Brown well with the onions and garlic, sliced fine. Cover with boiling water, drop in the bay leaves, salt, pepper, consommé, boil 15 minutes, add white wine. Simmer 20 minutes. Fifteen minutes before serving add the can of mushrooms with the juice. Remove chicken to the serving platter and add to the sauce two tablespoons of flour, one pint of cream, and cook. Just before serving add two egg yolks that have been well beaten. Delicious.

ROASTED CHICKEN
Mrs. Alfred T. Pattison

  1 tender large roasting chicken
  1 lb. thinly sliced bacon
  ½ onion, chopped fine
  1 cup very stale white bread crumbs
  1 lb. small sausages
  1 lump butter
  1 cup milk
      parsley, caramel

Roast chicken as usual. Take giblets and boil in a pint of water with a small piece of onion and parsley. When gizzard is tender remove giblets and pour this stock to which you have added a little coloring matter—say a drop or two of caramel—in the pan in which chicken has been roasted, first removing the bacon and sausages. In the meantime boil the milk with chopped onion, then add bread crumbs until whole is a thick mass. Season to taste. Make curls of bacon cooking them with the sausages in the same pan as the chicken. Place chicken on platter, garnish with sausages and bacon, strain sauce in pan into sauce bowl. Then into another sauce bowl, put bread sauce to which you add a small lump of butter stirring all the while, before removing from fire. Serve piping hot.

POULET SAUTÉ
A LA BORDELAISE

Mr. Francis J. Selman

1 small fryer, quartered
8 - 10 pods of garlic, chopped finely
¼ - ½ cup oil, enough to brown the
   chicken quarters

Brown chicken in oil thoroughly, being sure that chicken is done through and through. Remove to a warm serving plate. In the pan in which the chicken was fried, saute the chopped garlic. Stir constantly so that it will not brown, you want only the suggestion of brownness. Sprinkle over the chicken. It is delicious!! Note: Chicken and garlic readily marry and therefore this does not produce any ill effects.

SCALLOPED CHICKEN

3 lb. hen
2 tablespoons each butter, flour
1 pt. rich milk
1 can mushrooms
2 eggs
1 tablespoon Worcestershire sauce
   salt, white pepper to taste

Boil the chicken, and cut up in pieces of desired size. Melt butter and flour together, and add the milk very gradually, stirring constantly until the mixture thickens. Add the chicken, mushrooms, salt and pepper to taste and last of all, the egg yolks, stirring constantly. This is best done in a double boiler. When the eggs have thickened the sauce, add the Worcestershire and fold in the beaten whites. Stir for another moment o' two and serve at once.

SMOTHERED CHICKEN

Mrs. David A. Hopkins

1 small chicken, cut in quarters
   milk, to cover
1/3 cup butter
1 pt. light cream
½ cup flour
1 teaspoon salt
¼ teaspoon pepper
½ teaspoon ginger

Soak chicken in milk at room temperature for one hour. Mix all dry ingredients in a paper bag. Drain chicken, put in bag and shake, fry quickly to a light brown in the butter. Drain and place pieces in a casserole. Sauté mushrooms in butter, slowly stir in cream, season to taste and pour over the chicken. Bake, covered at 350 degrees for forty-five minutes. Serve on rice.

CHICKEN SOUFFLÉ

Mrs. W. P. Bentley

2 tablespoons flour
2 tablespoons butter
1 wine glass sherry
1 pt. milk
½ cup stale bread crumbs, grated
3 eggs
2 cups chicken meat, chopped
   parsley, chopped; salt, pepper to
   taste
   mushroom sauce

Melt the butter, add the flour, then the milk gradually, add the bread crumbs and cook 2 minutes. Salt, and pepper. Then add the chicken meat, allow to cool. Now add the yolks, beaten light, the chopped parsley, and fold in the well-beaten whites. Bake in a buttered dish 35 minutes. Serve with mushroom sauce.

CHICKEN IN SOUR CREAM
Mrs. George Villeré

3½ lb. chicken
2 tablespoons hot sherry
1 teaspoon tomato paste
1 tablespoon flour
¾ cup chicken stock
1 to 1½ cups sour cream
salt, cayenne pepper, dry mustard
butter
1 tablespoon Parmesan cheese, grated

Disjoint the chicken, brown all over in the hot butter. Pour the hot sherry over it. Take the chicken from the pan, and add the tomato paste, the flour, and the chicken broth, and stir until it boils. Add bit by bit the sour cream, add the salt, pepper, mustard, then the grated cheese. Put the chicken back, and let it simmer gently for ½ hour. Arrange the chicken on the serving dish, pour the sauce over it, and sprinkle a little more cheese, and let it brown under the broiler.

CHICKEN TURENNE
Mrs. Yvonne Galatoire Wynne
Galatoire's Restaurant, Inc.

Take a spring chicken of 2 lbs., disjoint it, season with salt and pepper, fry it in butter until brown. Drain butter from pan then add 3 ounces of claret and 3 ounces of demi-glace or brown gravy. Slice 4 ounces of fresh mushrooms, 3 hearts of artichokes. Let chicken cook on a very slow fire for 30 minutes.

CHICKEN VALMONT
Mr. Claiborne Perrilliat

1. Clean three 3# fryers that have been quartered and allow to dry.
2. Make stock with necks, livers, gizzards, flippers of wings, 2 onions, 1 bunch shallots, 6 carrots, parsley, celery, 1 pod garlic, thyme, bay leaf, Worcestershire sauce, one shake Tabasco, pepper corn, and salt to taste. Allow to boil slowly for three hours.
3. Place one cup of sifted flour in copper or cast iron frying pan and brown very slowly, stirring constantly. Flour will be browned sufficiently when it becomes same color as cigarette tobacco.

4. Add liquid stock to brown flour slowly and stir vigorously in order to avoid separation and lumps. Add 1 jar currant jelly and 1 cup good French claret. Simmer until sauce thickens and, if necessary, add more claret. Mix in 2½ cups fresh green seedless grapes.
5. Oven broil, salt and pepper chickens in olive oil, only enough oil to keep chickens from sticking. When chickens are lightly brown on both sides, pour gravy over and baste in moderate oven for 45 minutes. Add more claret while basting, if needed.

SAUTÉED DUCK BREASTS
Mr. Shaun Viguerie

6 duck breasts, any kind
1 stick butter
2 onions, finely chopped
2 lemons
4 tablespoons Lea & Perrins
½ cup red wine, optional

Sauté onions and breasts together in butter, turning once until almost cooked. (Cooking time depends on size of ducks.) Add to pan lemon juice and Lea & Perrins. Sauté quickly until done. Add wine for last few minutes of cooking. Serve immediately. Simple but delicious.

HALVED DUCKS
Mrs. Eli W. Tullis

3 ducks, cleaned and halved
3 apples
3 oranges
3 onions
3 stalks celery
½ cup Lea & Perrins
½ cup honey
salt and pepper

Salt and pepper the duck halves. Put seasoned ducks in baking pan, placing under each duck half equally divided pieces of apples, oranges, celery and onions. Cook as is with the vegetables for 20 minutes in a 350° oven.
Mix Lea & Perrins and honey and pour over halves. Put back in oven. Cook teal or other small duck for another 10 minutes; cook larger ones for 20 more minutes, basting all the while. Serves 6.

ROASTED WILD MALLARDS OR FRENCH DUCKS

Mrs. Lester Lautenschlager

5 ducks (½ duck per person)
2 cups beef stock or consommé
5 medium onions, whole
    celery tops
½ cup bacon grease
2 bay leaves
¼ cup flour
    salt and pepper to taste

Stuff greased cavity of ducks with onion, celery tops, salt and pepper. Sew up cavity and tie legs together. Brown in a Dutch oven, using ¼ cup bacon grease. Turn to brown evenly. When browned, remove and place in another Dutch oven with beef stock, bay leaves, salt and pepper. Cover securely and bake in 250° - 300° oven for about 2 hours. Baste every 15 minutes and add water if necessary.

In the meantime, brown flour slowly in ¼ cup of bacon grease. Make this roux very dark. Set aside. When ducks are tender pour duck drippings into hot roux. Sample and correct seasoning of this gravy to your taste preference.

Arrange ducks on platter. Place parsley where legs are tied and decorate platter with fresh mint and glaceed green grapes. Serve with Paradise Sauce (see index), wild rice and duck gravy. Serves 10.

NOTE: To glace grapes, choose ripe grapes and refrigerate until ready to make an arrangement. Wash grapes and drain well. Beat 1 teaspoon to 1 tablespoon water into an egg white to break it up. Roll grape clusters in white; drain slightly. Working with granulated sugar in a shallow baking pan, spoon sugar over each cluster of moist grapes. Set clusters on a rack to crust over.

MALLARD DUCK

Mrs. Alfred T. Pattison

1 mallard duck
2 lbs. ground artichokes
2 tablespoons butter
1 teaspoon salt
1 tablespoon chopped shallots
    parsley, dash of pepper

Season duck as for roasting. Scrape ground artichokes thoroughly and leave whole. Put butter in large pot with tight cover. When butter is hot add whole duck. Let brown lightly. Then add ground artichokes, salt, pepper, and perhaps a little more butter if the quantity used seems to have been absorbed by the duck, then chopped shallots and the parsley. Cover tightly. Stir every few minutes, cooking on a slow fire. When duck is very tender to the prick of a fork and ground artichokes are very soft and brownish in color, the dish is done. It takes about an hour. Remove duck, cut it into 4 quarters. Pile in center of dish and put ground artichokes around it. This is also excellent with chicken.

POT ROAST DUCK AU COON ASS

Mr. George Douglass

Purchase:
1 shot gun
    shot gun shells
    duck blind
    pirogue
1 hunting license
one duck
    yellow mustard
    Worcestershire sauce
2 small red peppers or 1 Jalapeno
    pepper
    oil
    onion
    Kitchen Bouquet

Make up a mixture of yellow mustard and Worcestershire sauce (light on the Worcestershire sauce). Rub duck inside and out with mixture. Cut a hole about 3/4" long in thickest part of breast on each side of duck all the way to the bone. Take a black iron pot, put in a little bit of grease, throw in a dash or two of Kitchen bouquet. Put the lid on and cook slowly for about 3½ hours. Turn the duck over after cooking for about 2 hours.

SMOKED DUCKS

John R. Peters, Jr.

8 ducks
    salt and pepper

Sauce:

2 sticks butter
1 tablespoon Worcestershire sauce

Dry ducks. Salt and pepper well inside and out. Melt butter for sauce. Add Worcestershire sauce. Using a smoker or large barbeque pit with cover, build a fire away from the ducks, and that will maintain about 210° temperature. Add water soaked hickory chips to the fire to maintain smoke. Baste about every ½ hour. (Be sure that smoke travels over ducks and fire is not underneath.)

Teal takes 3 hours, and large ducks take 4-5 hours. Serve with horseradish sauce.

Horseradish Sauce:

1 pint whipping cream
3 tablespoons horseradish
1 teaspoon salt

Whip cream until stiff. Fold in salt and horseradish. May be made several hours before serving.
Serves 8.

WILD DUCK A LA FELL

Mrs. Frederick D. King

Clean a wild duck thoroughly; singe the fowl and be careful not to burn the skin. Rub well with salt, pepper, and olive oil inside and out. Place half an orange (do not remove the peel), several sprigs each of bay leaf, thyme, and parsley inside the duck.

Place three strips of bacon across the breast of the duck and bake in an uncovered pan in a moderate oven about twenty minutes to the pound. Baste with drippings and a small amount of water.

When done, turn off heat and pour a glass of orange wine over the duck. Do not remove from oven until ready to serve.

Garnish with currant jelly and thin slices of orange.

WILD DUCK

Mrs. E. V. Benjamin III

Ground sage, oregano, thyme, marjoram, parsley flakes sprinkled on outside of duck. Put ¼ onion and ¼ orange in each duck. Sprinkle Wesson oil and flour over the duck.

Start oven at 500 degrees for fifteen minutes then lower to 350 degrees.

Cook until done using two cans consommé while cooking, basting frequently the whole time. Follow directions carefully for perfect result.

GALANTINE OF GOOSE

An Old Frontier Recipe

10 lb. goose
5 lbs. ground lean pork
1 lb. dripped pork fat
1 small hog's head
5 lbs. skinned pork, without fat
10 or 12 hogs' feet, cut at first joint
lots of seasoning
allspice, cloves
salt, red pepper to taste

Take a dressed goose, cut the wings and feet at the first joint, cut the neck high. Slit the goose down the back and bone it, removing the carcass and entrails with a small sharp knife. Sew the neck, wings, and feet at ends. Season highly.

Stuff the goose putting seasoned ground meat—1 layer, then strips of fat 2 ins. apart, and continue stuffing the goose. Sew up the back and place the stuffed goose in cheesecloth and sew it up. Then put it in well-seasoned water, enough to cover. Let boil until tender, testing with a fork. Remove from the water, take the cloth off, and place a heavy weight for 12 hours on the goose.

Make a jelly using 5 gallons of highly seasoned water, with the hogs' feet, skin, and head, and boil until very thick. Add water when it boils down. Strain through cheesecloth. Set the goose in a mold and pour the jelly over it. (This makes a gallon, and there will be some left over to put in another mold to serve on the side.) A gala dish for the holidays, and it lasts for weeks in the refrigerator.

BREAST OF GUINEA

Allow one guinea for each couple. An entire half breast is served for each portion. Roast the guinea until they are quite tender using exact method as in roasting chickens. When thoroughly done detach each breast from the breast bone and lay each half on thin slivers of broiled ham which you should have ready. Pour over the gravy and serve with any tart jelly. The unused portions may be reserved to make croquettes or stew the next day.

TURKEY HASH
Mrs. Walter Cook Keenan III

  3 cups cooked turkey cut in large
      cubes
  4 tablespoons butter
  1 cup cooked celery, cut in bite
      size pieces (including ¼ cup
      minced tops and leaves)
  2 tablespoons flour
  1 medium onion, minced
  ¼ cup minced bell peppers
  1 can Swanson's chicken broth
      season with at least 1 teaspoon
      salt, pepper and Worcestershire

Melt butter in large skillet, remove from heat, and slowly stir in flour. Return to heat and stir constantly until brown. Add onion, bell pepper and celery tops. Saute until onions are transparent. Add chicken broth; continue stirring. Then add turkey and cooked celery pieces. Season to taste. Simmer until thoroughly heated. Serve with baked grits.

ROAST PHEASANT WITH CRESS
Mrs. Rachel Bunting Wilmot

Let the birds be hung by the under part of the beak, separately on hooks, and sufficiently long to develop their flavor; for this purpose a cold, dry and above all a thoroughly airy place should be chosen. About four days hanging in such a place will generally meet the requirements; but when a higher stale is wished for, let the birds hang until the feathers from the under part at the tail end are easily detached. When the bird has reached the required degree of flavor, pluck it, remove the crop by making an incision in the back of the neck, taking care not to break the skin of the crop. Remove the entrails by cutting the vent a little, singe and truss it for roasting, but in no case wash it.

Tie a piece of fat bacon over the breast and roast it for fifteen or twenty minutes under a quick fire, the exact time of course, depending on whether the bird has to be well done or rare. It is an essential point, and one which must be insisted on, that the bird must be well basted during the roasting, especially during the beginning, for, if it once becomes dry in any part, no amount of after attention can rectify it. If the bird is baked instead of roasted, basting is even more important. Serve on toast, garnish with water cress and serve with it, browned bread crumbs, bread sauce and gravy prepared from game bones.

In no case should the gravy be sent to table on the same dish as the bird.

Bread Sauce

Put ½ pint of milk to boil with a small shallot into which a clove is stuck; when the milk comes to the boil, mix with it two ounces of freshly made bread crumbs and one ounce of butter, let boil slowly 15 minutes, remove the shallot, then add half a gill of cream, boil again for five minutes, add a tiny pinch of salt and white pepper, mix well. Serve. Good on any game or fowl.

QUAIL IN SHERRY

Take six birds, clean and put aside. Put in a deep pot one heaping tablespoon butter, one teaspoon chopped parsley and one teaspoon chopped onions. Fry until the onions are a light brown. Add one tablespoon flour, let brown lightly and add one can mushrooms, including the liquor, then one cup sherry wine, ½ teaspoon salt, pepper and Tabasco to taste. Now drop in the quail, breasts down and simmer until done.

QUAIL WITH TRUFFLES

  8 quail
  8 truffles
  2 tablespoons butter
  ½ cup olive oil
  ½ coffeespoon cayenne pepper
  1 teaspoon salt

Dress quail, salt and pepper inside and out.

Slice truffles and dry in butter and put into quail and let stand 24 hours. Heat olive oil in baking pan, put in the quail, cook ¾ hour, basting frequently.

This recipe can be used with pigeons by larding birds with ½ lb. fresh pork fat and leaving in refrigerator 12 hours instead of 24.

RABBIT AUX FINES HERBES
Cmtsse. Gilberte de Charentenay

1 rabbit, cut in pieces
1 cup of breakfast cream
garlic, salt, pepper, dry mustard
butter, lard, olive oil, fine herbs

The pieces of rabbit are rubbed thoroughly with olive oil, and let stand overnight. The next day the pieces are rubbed first lightly with garlic, then thoroughly with the mustard and fine herbs (the commercial moutard au fines herbes serves perfectly well) and set to cook in half lard, half butter.

BAKED TURKEY
Julie Bowes, Sue Baker

After the bird has been thoroughly cleaned and dried, follow these simple steps for best results:
1. Rub the cavity lightly with salt.
2. Fill neck cavity with sufficient stuffing to make it plump, then fasten neck skin to back with skewer.
3. Stuff abdominal cavity well, but do not pack tightly as it will expand when roasting. Lace or sew together opening to retain dressing.
4. Truss bird and grease skin thoroughly with melted fat.
5. Place on rack in a shallow pan, breast down.
6. Cover with a fat-moistened cloth, such as clean, white cheesecloth.
7. Place in a preheated oven, 300 to 325 degrees F.
8. Do not sear, cover pan, or add salt.
9. Moisten cloth with drippings from bottom of pan if it becomes dry during cooking.
10. Remove cloth and trussings, turn, breast up, when about three-quarters done, to allow breast to brown.

8- to 12-pound turkey will require about 4 to 4½ hours cooking; a 16- to 20-pound one about 5 to 5½ hours. The bird is done when the leg joints give readily as the drumsticks are moved up and down, and if the meat feels soft to the touch. Be sure to protect your finger, of course, with a piece of paper or cloth. Do not prick with a fork as this causes a loss of juices. Remove skewers and any stitching threads. Allow about 20 minutes before carving. The job will be easier and the meat will have a chance to absorb the juices. Serve with simple garnishes so as not to handicap the carver.

WILD TURKEY
Mrs. Dora Harris Jackson

Melt 2 sticks Mazola margarine and rub on turkey inside and out. Do this on roasting pan so that the excess goes into the pan.

Salt and pepper turkey inside and out. Stuff cavities with small chucks of celery and onion.

Place bird breast down on pan. Cover with foil. Bake in 325° oven. Roughly 2½ hours for a 12-15 lb. bird, or 3½ hours for 15 lb. or more.

The last 45-50 minutes remove the foil -- baste every 15 minutes or so to brown.

Add ½ cup of water to juices in the pan and heat for a minute or two -- makes a delicious natural gravy.

VENISON EN CASSEROLE
Mr. Albin Provosty, Pointe Coupée

3 lbs. venison, loin
2 tablespoons olive oil
2 tablespoons sherry
2 tablespoons butter
2 tablespoons flour
1 small can of mushrooms
1 teaspoon salt
1 teaspoon sliced onion
1 coffeespoon of black pepper
1 tablespoon parsley, minced
1 to 1½ pts. stock
a pinch of cayenne

Brown the venison loin in olive oil or butter. Add stock, mix flour in some of the stock, also a small can of chopped mushrooms, onion and seasoning. Let simmer an hour. Before serving, add butter and sherry. A small can of truffles will improve the flavor.

VENISON STEAK

2 venison steaks
2 tablespoons butter
1 tablespoon water
1 tablespoon olive oil
1 tablespoon salt, scant
  pinch of cayenne and black pepper
  garnish with parsley

Wipe steak off, brush with olive oil, brown quickly first on one side and then the other. Place in oven and cook as you do beef steak. Have platter very hot. Put butter and water in it, salt and pepper steak on both sides, put it into platter and turn it several times, mashing it into the butter. Serve with plum or tart jelly or, best, sugared oranges.

GERMAN TURKEY DRESSING

Mrs. Victor G. Nunes

1 lb. lean ground meat
1 lb. mild bulk pork dressing or
  sausage
1 cup diced bell pepper
1 cup diced celery
1 whole bunch diced green onions
1 or 2 large yellow onions, diced
1 loaf long poor boy French
  bread (cut bread in pieces,
  wet in large bowl of water
  until soft, squeeze out excess
  water
½ cup chopped parsley
  salt, pepper and poultry seasoning
  to taste

Brown pork sausage and ground meat in large Dutch oven. Add diced vegetables and saute a few minutes longer. Add seasonings to taste and wet bread. Cook on medium fire for about 30 minutes or until browned, stirring often to prevent sticking. Dressing may be stored in zip lock bag in refrigerator until next day for ease in handling and stuffing turkey.
Serves 6 to 8.

OYSTER DRESSING

Mrs. James Selman

(This can also be used as an hors d'oeuvre.)

2 pints oysters, chopped
  oyster water
3 medium cloves garlic, chopped
2 whole bunches shallots, chopped
2 medium onions, chopped
1 bunch parsley, chopped
  day old French Bread, 2 or 3 cups
  (if using as an hors d'oeuvre, use
  less bread)
  salt and pepper
½ cup butter
½ cup bacon grease
  bread crumbs, plain
  buttered casserole

Remove oysters from their water and dry well on towel; chop finely. Soak 2-3 cups torn up French Bread in oyster water and then squeeze dry. Saute all vegetables (chopped) in butter and grease until transparent. Add oysters and cook 5 minutes longer. Place in buttered casserole. Sprinkle top with bread crumbs and dot with butter. Bake at 350° till bubbly.
This makes a wonderful hors d'oeuvre when served with homemade Melba toast!!

RICE DRESSING

Mrs. Joseph Simon Brown, Jr., New Iberia, La.

3 cups uncooked rice
1½ lbs. chicken livers
1½ lbs. ground meat (can be chuck
  or pork-lean)
2 large onions
3 tablespoons cooking oil
4 cloves garlic (optional)
  (cook with onions)
1 green pepper
2 cans mushrooms (optional)
4 pieces celery—also green onion
  tops and parsley
  salt, red and black pepper
  liquid pepper sauce

Cook the rice in the usual way. Put oil in large iron skillet to heat. Add chopped onions, celery and green pepper and allow to wilt. Add all the meat and giblets (parboiled gizzards which have been ground up with the livers can be used) and cook until brown. Lower the fire. Add a little water occasionally and season highly. When done (about one hour) add the cooked rice. Just before serving sprinkle and mix in the chopped parsley and green onion tops.
Serves twelve.

CHESTNUT STUFFING

3 lbs. peeled chestnuts
1 qt. stale bread

¾ cup butter
1 lemon, juice and grated rind
1 tablespoon chopped parsley
   salt and pepper to taste
   a dash of nutmeg

Boil nuts in salted water, mash. Fry bread crumbs in butter which has first been slightly browned, mix with nuts. Add seasoning and enough stock until it is of the desired consistency. This is excellent for turkey, chicken or duck.

OYSTER STUFFING FOR TURKEY

Mrs. Albin Provosty

This dressing will stuff a ten pound turkey.

   liver and gizzard of the fowl
3 doz. oysters
½ loaf stale bread
2 tablespoons butter
1 tablespoon bacon drippings or lard
3 large onions, chopped fine
1 tablespoon each chopped parsley,
   thyme, bay leaf
1 pinch salt, pepper to taste

Drain oysters of their liquor and use it to moisten the stale bread, which should be squeezed afterwards until quite dry. Chop oysters, liver and gizzard of fowl. Put a tablespoon of bacon drippings or other fat in a frying pan with the onions. Fry these to a golden brown, add the liver and gizzard which have been boiled and chopped. When they begin to brown add the seasonings and mix well. Then add the butter, blending all thoroughly and last of all the oysters. Stir and cook for five minutes, remove from the fire and stuff the fowl.

OLD FASHIONED OYSTER STUFFING

Mrs. George Douglass, Sr.

4 toes garlic, chopped
4 branches celery, with leaves,
   chopped
2 onions, chopped
6 shallots, chopped
½ lb. bacon, cut in small pieces
1 small loaf French bread
¼ cup parsley
1 bay leaf
2 dozen oysters

Cook bacon until done but not crispy. Remove from pan and set aside. Saute all vegetables except parsley. Add a little oil if necessary. When limp, add oysters cut in half and the bacon. Cook until the oyster edges curl. Add the French bread that has been soaked in water and squeezed dry. Add parsley and then stuff in the cavity of the bird.

SAUSAGE STUFFING
(for 2 12-lb. turkeys or
1 24-lb. turkey)

Mrs. James Selman

1 large loaf French bread (8-9
   ozs.)
1 cup each, chopped: parsley, green
   onions, regular onions
½ cup celery, chopped
1 lb. sausage
   the liver from the turkey,
   chopped finely
1 big apple, or 2 small ones
½ cup bacon grease
1 cup butter
½ teaspoon thyme
1 teaspoon salt
¼ teaspoon pepper, if using hot
   sausage, if not, use more
   pepper
1 teaspoon paprika

Saute in the melted bacon grease and butter the chopped parsley, green onions, and regular onions, and the celery. In another skillet, saute the sausage and the turkey liver, which has been chopped finely or mashed. Combine with the sauteed vegetables. Add the French bread which has been soaked and then squeezed out and combine well. Add seasonings, and if you desire, a little paprika for added taste and coloring.

TURKEY STUFFING

Miss Charlotte Mitchell

2 onions, chopped fine
1 green pepper, chopped fine
4 stalks celery
1 sprig each of parsley and thyme
4 bay leaves (remove after cooking)
½ lb. fat
2 lbs. ground meat
2 lbs. Tennessee sausage
3 loaves French bread (made into
   bread crumbs)
   salt, Tabasco to taste

Cook onions, peppers, celery, bay leaves, parsley and thyme in fat until well browned, stir constantly. Add meat, sausage and bread crumbs. Fry until well cooked and quite dry. Season with salt and Tabasco. This is sufficient for a 20-lb. turkey.

PECAN STUFFING

Agnes Thompson
Through Mrs. T. S. Behre

12 lb. turkey
1½ loaves stale French bread

Soak in water, squeeze as dry as possible. Chop medium sized onion and some shallots (including some of green part), about one tablespoon in all. Fry these with chopped giblets in 4 tablespoons butter until a light brown. Add the prepared bread and cook all together until thoroughly blended. Add salt and pepper to taste. Then add one tablespoon chopped parsley. Break up about 2 cups of pecans and add to mixture. Do not cook after adding nuts. Rice may be used instead of bread.

meats

BAKED CANADIAN BACON

Mrs. Charles L. Seemann

6 to 7 lb. piece of Canadian bacon
1 cup brown sugar
½ teaspoon dry mustard
1 teaspoon commercial "Creole Mustard"
1 teaspoon flour
  whole cloves
  vinegar, cognac

Moisten dry ingredients with the vinegar or cognac to paste consistency. Cut diamond pattern in fat side of bacon and insert a clove in each diamond. Bake about one and a half hours in a 300 degree oven. Remove and pat one half of paste mixture over the top surface. Return to the oven for fifteen minutes then remove and add the remainder of the paste. Bake for fifteen minutes more. Slice and serve hot or cold. This is very nice with rye bread.

BEEF BURGUNDY

Pete Finney

¼ cup butter
¼ cup salad oil
1¼ lb. small white onions
4 lb. chuck, trimmed, cut into 2" cubes
¼ cup unsifted flour, all purpose
1 teaspoon meat extract paste
1 tablespoon tomato paste
3 cups Burgundy
¼ teaspoon pepper
2 bay leaves
½ teaspoon dried thyme leaves
½ teaspoon dried marjoram leaves
3/4 lb. fresh mushrooms
  chopped parsley

Preheat oven to 325°. In 4 qt. Dutch oven heat butter and oil. In fat saute onions 5 minutes; remove. Add beef, a third at a time to fat; brown well on all sides; remove. Remove Dutch oven from heat, discard all but 1 tablespoon fat.

Stir in the flour and meat extract paste until smooth. Gradually add Burgundy, stirring until smooth. Then add beef, pepper, herbs, parsley sprigs and mushrooms, stirring until well mixed. Bake, covered 1½ hours. Add onions, bake 1 hour longer, or until meat is tender. Sprinkle with chopped parsley. Can be served with mashed potatoes. Makes 8 servings.

BEEF BUSCHELONE

Mrs. Robert Ruppel

1 beef round steak, ½-1" thick, salted and peppered

Stuffing:

3 tablespoons parsley, finely chopped
6 toes garlic, minced
3 tablespoons Parmesan or Italian cheese, freshly grated
2 hard-boiled eggs, chopped
  salt and pepper to taste

Sauce:

1 large onion, finely chopped
½ bell pepper, chopped (optional)
6 toes garlic, minced
1 can tomato paste
1 1-lb. can tomatoes (mashed to reduce pulp)
  pinch of oregano, basil, crushed hot pepper (each)
3 tablespoons Italian cheese, freshly grated
2 tablespoons sugar
  salt and pepper to taste
  olive oil

Mix together stuffing ingredients and smooth over round steak. Carefully roll round steak and secure with cord or heavy string. Brown in olive oil and set aside.

Prepare sauce by sauteing onions and garlic in olive oil until transparent. Add bell pepper and cook 2 minutes.

Add tomato paste and cook over fairly high flame stirring constantly until a reddish brown color is achieved. Add mashed canned tomatoes. Cook five minutes. Fill tomato can and paste can with water and add. Add other ingredients and seasonings and cook slowly for ½ hour.

Prepare pasta (spaghetti, shell noodles or fettucini). Slice Buscheleone and arrange over pasta on platter, removing strings. Pour over sauce. Serve immediately. Serves 4.

FLEMISH BEEF CARBONADES

Mrs. Paul Selley

3 lbs. beef—top shoulder, neck, thin flank, eye of round
¼ lb. smoked ham
3 teaspoons salt
¾ teaspoon pepper
1 clove garlic—pressed
1 lb. onions
¾ cup lard
3 tablespoons flour
2½ teaspoons sugar
2½ tablespoons vinegar
1½ bottles of beer, or more
bouquet of herbs

Cut meat for stew. Cut ham into ½ inch cubes. Heat lard in skillet and brown meat and ham. Lift out with slotted spoon, let drip a minute, place on a dish and sprinkle with 1 teaspoon salt. Slice thin onions and brown in the same lard, lift out, let drip a minute, and place in another dish. Drain off fat, except 3 tablespoonfuls. Stir flour into this and make a light brown roux. Add all seasoning and sugar, but **not** vinegar. Thin roux with the beer, adding gradually and stirring all the time. Bring to a boil for 2 minutes, until a good smooth gravy is made. In a 2-quart casserole arrange the meat and onions in alternate layers; pour on the gravy, which should cover the meat completely. Cover the pot tightly and cook in slow oven at 300° for 2½ hours. After the first hour look into pot from time to time, and if the gravy level is going down, add more beer—never water. When stew is ready, just before serving, add the vinegar. Serve with plain boiled potatoes.

BEEF AND PORK BARBEQUE

Mrs. D. Blair Favrot

2½ lbs. lean beef
1½ lbs. lean pork (have butcher cut into pieces with no fat)
1 onion, chopped fine
2 stems celery, chopped fine
1 button garlic, put through garlic press
1 regular size bottle catsup
3 tablespoons Worcestershire sauce
½ bottle barbeque sauce (large bottle)
½ cup vinegar
½ cup lemon juice
1 sprig rosemary
salt and red pepper to taste

Cover meat with cold water and put in all ingredients. (Cook in heavy pot.) Bring to a boil and cook for about 6 hours on a low heat. Keep lid on pot. If barbeque is not real thick, take off lid the last hour of cooking. Serve on toasted buns.

This is better made a day before serving. Serves 6-8.

BEEF STUFFED PORK

Mr. Jack Parker

3 lb. boned pork loin
1 recipe Barbeque Sauce
½ lb. ground beef
¼ cup chopped onion
1 small clove garlic, minced
¼ teaspoon salt
dash pepper
1 6-oz. can sliced mushrooms, drained (about 1 cup)
¼ cup fine dry bread crumbs
¼ cup grated Parmesan cheese

To butterfly loin, split meat lengthwise almost all the way to opposite side, then spread open flat. Pound out to 15 x 10 inch rectangle, about 3/4" thick. Brush top with ¼ cup of the Barbeque sauce. Combine ground beef, onion, garlic, salt, pepper, and ¼ cup of the Barbeque sauce, spread evenly over the roast. Press mushrooms into the ground beef. Sprinkle bread crumbs and Parmesan cheese over the meat. Starting from 10" side, roll up and tie. Place on rack in shallow roasting pan. Roast, uncovered, in 325° oven for about 2½ hours. Baste with additional Barbeque sauce during last 15-20 minutes of roasting. Pass remaining Barbeque sauce.

Barbeque Sauce:

In medium saucepan, combine 1 fourteen-oz. bottle catsup, ½ cup chili sauce, 1/3 cup wine vinegar, ¼ cup mustard, 2 tablespoons lemon juice, 2 tablespoons Worcestershire sauce, 2 tablespoons cooking oil, 2 tablespoons steak sauce, 1 teaspoon dry mustard, ¼ teaspoon salt, ¼ teaspoon pepper, and 1 clove garlic, minced. Simmer 30 minutes. Makes 2-2/3 cups.

BEEF STEAK AND KIDNEY PIE

Mrs. Frank H. Lawton

    2 lbs. rump steak, free from fat
    6 or 8 lamb kidneys cut in halves
    4 large onions
    1 bay leaf
    2 teaspoons Worcestershire sauce
      parsley, salt, pepper, butter

Cut steak into thick squares. Thoroughly cover each piece of meat and each piece of kidney with flour.

Put a layer of meat in bottom of a good sized casserole.

Add salt, pepper, chopped parsley, dot with bits of butter and add drops of Worcestershire sauce. Then add a thick layer of onions sliced thin. Follow same procedure with floured sliced kidney, salt, pepper, parsley, butter, Worcestershire sauce and onions to top of casserole, onions last. Now cover completely with freshly boiling water, not merely hot. Put on cover of casserole and let stand 3 or 4 hours. Now remove kidneys. Re-cover pot and cook slowly 4 hours on low heat. Do not hurry it. Just before wanted, replace kidneys, take cover off and cover with rich pastry rolled very thin so it will cook and brown quickly. The onions should be entirely cooked away if heat is kept low for 4 hours.

BEEF STEW BOURGUIGNONNE

Mrs. H. Stanley Butterworth

    ½ lb. salt pork, cut into small cubes
    2 lbs. beef (round steak, cut into 2-
      inch pieces)
    1 tablespoon flour
    1 teaspoon salt
    ¾ teaspoon black pepper
    1 clove garlic, 1 big onion, chopped
    1 cup bouillon
    ½ bay leaf, marjoram

   12 or more potato balls, small
    ½ lb. sliced mushrooms
    6 carrots, cubed
   1½ cups Burgundy wine

Brown salt pork in a hot skillet, sauté the beef in the drippings. Sprinkle beef with flour, add seasoning. Cook until boiling, the garlic, onion, bouillon and bay leaf; combine the above with meat in a Dutch oven and cook slowly for 4 hours. After it has been cooking for about 3 hours add wine, potatoes, mushrooms and carrots. Just before serving more wine may be added.

This dish has a better flavor if cooked the day before. It serves six people and is obviously a one-dish meal, needing only a good green salad as an accompaniment.

BEEF STROGANOFF

Pam Hayne

    2 cloves garlic
    ¼ lb. butter
    2 lbs. fillet of beef
    3 tablespoons flour
   1½ cups bouillon
    2 onions, chopped
    1 pt. sour cream
    1 pt. mushrooms
    1 bay leaf
    2 tablespoons Worcestershire sauce
    ½ to 1 cup white wine
      salt, pepper, cayenne and paprika

Rub skillet with garlic. Dredge meat in flour and saute in butter. Add bouillon, onions, wine and seasonings. Cook several hours. Add sour cream and mushrooms before serving. Serve over rice or noodles.

FILET DE BOEUF AU MADÉRE

Mrs. Louis Perrilliat

    8 lbs. of filet
    1 onion, 1 garlic clove
    1 tablespoon allspice, thyme, parsley
    1 tablespoon black pepper
    ½ pt. Madeira wine
    1 small can truffles
    1 large can mushrooms
    ½ lb. suet

Have your butcher insert strips of suet all through your filet.

Put filet in a mixing bowl. Pour over it ½ pint Madeira wine. Cover it with the chopped garlic, onion, thyme and parsley, pepper and allspice. Allow it to marinate 12 hours. Baste it now and then with this juice of Madeira wine while in box.

When ready for roasting, cut your truffles, make gashes in roast and insert as many pieces of truffles as are in small can. Baste it frequently so as to use the wine drained from onion, garlic and spice.

ESTOUFFADE DE BOEUF PROVENCALE

M. Raymond Sauget
Executive Chef De Cuisine
Royal Orleans Hotel

Ingredients:

    3 lbs. lean beef shoulder
    3 lbs. chuck meat with fat layer
    ¾ lbs. salt pork, blanched and diced
    ½ lb. sweet butter
    4 med. size onions
    1 oz. salt
    1/6 oz. pepper
    6 tablespoons flour
    2 peeled garlic cloves
    24 pearl onions sautéd in butter with
        pinch salt and pinch sugar
    1½ lbs. fresh quartered mushrooms
    2 lbs. peeled, seeded and crushed
        tomatoes
    1 lb. blanched and pitted olives
    1½ bottles Rosé wine
    1 bouquet garni:
        green leek
        parsley branches
        ½ celery stem
        1 bay leaf
        1 fresh thyme stem

For 12 portions.

Procedure:

1. Sauté in butter ¾ lb. of salt pork, previously diced and blanched. Drain. In the same grease that has been drained off put all the pieces of beef, 2 ozs. each of the fresh medium size onions, cut in quarters. Add 2 peeled garlic cloves, 6 tablespoons of flour, and stir ingredients lightly; then pour in 1½ bottles of Rosé wine and 2½ qts. of beef bouillon. Add the bouquet garni and cook covered in a 300 degree oven for 2½-3 hours.

2. After this period of time, retrieve the meat and the salt pork and place in a casserole. To this add the fresh mushrooms that have been previously sautéd in butter, the olives, and the

tomato material. Allow this sauce to stand for approximately 15 minutes in order that the fat rise to the surface. Remove grease completely. Rectify the flavor by adding seasoning to taste (salt and pepper). Allow to reduce. If the sauce is too clear do not degrease to any great degree. If the sauce is too thick, add some more beef bouillon. Pass the sauce through a strainer and add meat to the sauce and allow to stand 20 minutes before serving.

Garnitures that accompany Estouffade de Boeuf Provencale:

    A. Buttered noodles with Parmesan
        cheese
        Fresh buttered boiled fennel
    B. Gnocchi a la Romaine
        Buttered spinach

    C. Boiled potato
        Braised hearts of celery

Gnocchi a la Romaine:

Procedure: In 1 qt. of boiling milk pour 9 ozs. of cream of wheat, season with salt, pepper and nutmeg and cook slowly for 20 min. Reduce the fire. Place 2 egg yolks to thicken substance and place on a shallow baking dish. After this composition has become cooled cut rondelles or rectangles of approximately 1½″ each and arrange these pieces in a buttered shallow baking dish, powdered with grated Gruyere and Parmesan cheese. Butter this substance and gratinee in a hot oven.

BRAINS AU FROMAGE
Mrs. William Westerfield

    2 calves' brains
    4 tablespoons flour
    2 teaspoons dry mustard
    1 cup milk
    4 tablespoons Parmesan cheese
    lard, or oil
    cream sauce

Put the brains in cold water and skin them. Mix the mustard with the flour and dredge the brains in the mixture.

Fry them until they are light brown, then add the milk, and let cook until done. Put the brains on toast. Add to the cream sauce 2 tablespoons of Parmesan cheese, and pour this over brains, then sprinkle with the rest of the cheese. Run this under the broiler until light brown.

CALF'S FEET RAVIGOTE
Count Arnaud

The calf's feet are thoroughly cleaned, then boil with bay leaf, chopped onion, one or two carrots, thyme, and hot seasoning -- a red pepper or two, and salt.

"When ready to serve, over them goes a sauce; mayonnaise, with cream stirred into it, finely minced shallots, and bay leaf."

This dish was offered by Arnaud, known as the "Count" in the gourmets' rendezvous over which he presided. He presented it first in New Orleans some years ago apologetically. "It has been known for centuries along the Normandy coast," said he, "but perhaps it appeals not to your Anglo-Saxon consciousness."

CHILE CON CARNE
Mrs. Petrie Hamilton

5 good sized onions, cut fine
1 lb. ground round steak, fried
1 2-lb. can tomatoes
1 2-lb. can red kidney beans or
1 cup red kidney beans soaked over
   night and boiled until done
1 chopped green pepper
2 tablespoons chili powder, salt

Mix all together and let simmer for at least an hour, adding a little water from time to time if necessary. Cook in a covered iron skillet.

CUTLETS de VILLENEUVE
Miss Eleanor LeBlanc

1 lb. top quality ground beef
1 egg
2 or 3 slices white bread
   salt, pepper, to taste
1 cup milk
1 medium sized can mushrooms
1 pt. sour cream, butter

Soak the bread in the milk and squeeze out some of the moisture. Add it to the meat in a bowl with salt and pepper and the yolk of the egg. Mix all thoroughly. Shape into flat oblong patties, brush with the white of the egg which has been beaten slightly. Roll in bread crumbs. It is preferable to allow them to set in the refrigerator for at least two hours. Fry in an iron skillet in melted butter.

When brown on both sides set aside but keep hot.

In another pan heat the cut mushrooms in a little butter, add the sour cream. Cook slowly till thick. Arrange the meat patties on a hot platter and pour over the sauce.

DAUBE GLACÉ
Mrs. Caroline Merrick

3 lbs. lean beef
2 large knuckle bones, or
2 or 3 calf's feet
2 large onions, 2 carrots
2 pods of red pepper, or
½ teaspoon red pepper
   celery tops, bay leaves
10 cloves
   small pod garlic
1 tablespoon salt (scant)
1 teaspoon whole black pepper

Cover bones with water and boil for about 3 hrs., with the herbs, celery tops, etc., tied in bag; then add meat and cook 2 hrs. more. Lift out seasoning, place meat in a mold.

Strain the stock and color it with caramel, adding more salt and pepper if necessary. Pour it around the meat and when it is cold, place on ice for 24 hours.

All the grease will rise up on top of mold, scrape it off when you are ready to serve your daube. Invert it on the serving dish. Serve with mayonnaise if desired.

This is one of the best and simplest Daube Glacé.

CHILI CON CORNIE
Mrs. Cornie Gundlach

1 lb. ground meat
1 large onion, chopped
½ teaspoon garlic salt
1 can tomatoes (No. 2 size)
1 can tomato sauce, small
½ teaspoon paprika
¼ teaspoon cayenne
1½ tablespoons chili powder
1 teaspoon salt
½ teaspoon ground cumin
1 bay leaf
1 bell pepper, chopped

Brown meat, onions, and bell pepper. Add seasonings, then remaining ingredients. Cover and cook slowly for

1 hour, adding water as necessary to keep the proper chili consistency.

DAUBE GLACÉ

Mr. Valerian Allain
Through Mrs. Felix J. Puig

3 lbs. beef round with bone
4 calf's feet
3 or 4 onions
3 or 4 pieces of garlic
3 or 4 sprigs of thyme
1 tablespoon salt
½ stalk of celery
1 tablespoon parsley
2 whole carrots, cooked
8 ozs. claret wine
  the tip of a teaspoon of red pepper

Soak daube over night in refrigerator with all seasonings and wine. Next morning, place all in a large pot filled with cold water, let come to a quick boil for a short time then reduce heat and let simmer three or four hours, until bones can be removed from calf's feet and beef. Skim the grease from time to time. Take from the fire. Skin meat, cut carrots in fancy slices, place around sides and bottom mold, put beef in whole or chopped. Strain juice, taste to see if sufficiently seasoned. Add a few drops of lemon juice. Pour over meat in mold and set aside to congeal.

DAUBE GLACÉ

Mrs. Walter Torian

1 large thick round steak
1 lb. fresh pork
1 pt. olive oil
2 pods garlic
2 pig's feet, 2 calf's feet
4 shallots chopped, green peppers,
   parsley, celery, bay leaf
   sliced lemon
   red pepper, salt

Lard steak with pork.

Into olive oil put the garlic, sage, green peppers (seeded and veined) bay leaf, and celery.

Put the steak to soak in this overnight, adding a large quantity of red pepper and salt.

Next morning, fry it a little in the same olive oil.

Pour all together in a pot, adding the pig's feet and the calf's feet,

cover plentifully with water, cover the pot and let it cook three hours or more, till thoroughly tender.

Take out the bones of the pig's feet and the calf's feet, strain the liquid and put it over the meat. Add parsley and shallots, let the pot come to a boil, then remove.

Fold daube into a deep rectangular pan preferably, or into a bowl, and pour the liquid over it. Set in the icebox for 24 hours. Put several thin slices of lemon on the top.

Instead of leaving the meat in one large piece, as above, some prefer cutting it into small chunks to facilitate slicing after it has jelled.

DAUBE GLACÉ

Mrs. Milian H. Hughes

In a large pot put 1 gallon of water. Add knee and shank bones and any others you can beg or buy, to water. Add three or more large onions, celery, garlic, lemon, carrots, salt and pepper. Let this cook down, not too fast, till about half of liquid remains. Prepare the meat by salting and stuffing with fresh peppers and brown thoroughly in oil of your choice. Add to liquid and cook slowly for 2 hours till meat is very tender. Remove meat. Add cloves to stock and thyme plus a small bay leaf.

To make a very clear jelly beat up a couple of egg whites and crush the shells. Add to liquid then strain through a cheese cloth. Soak gelatine in a ½ cup of water. Add to hot liquid. Rinse mold. Place meat in it and pour liquid over it. Allow to chill over night.

4 to 5 lb. beef or veal chuck roast
3-4 large onions
   knee and shank bones cracked
2 pods (the whole root) garlic
3 carrots cut up
2-3 sprigs of thyme, 1 bay leaf
   red pepper—fresh—or cayenne
4 cloves
   bunch of celery
   salt to taste
2-3 packs of gelatine

If fresh pig's or calf's feet are available they may be used in place of some of the gelatine.

More expensive cuts of meat may be used but this serves the purpose.

DAUBE GLACE
Mrs. William H. McCandless, Jr.

    2 tablespoons gelatin
    2 cans consomme
    2 cans Libby's beef
    4 shallots
    2 garlic cloves
    1 tablespoon minced parsley
    2 bay leaves (broken large, to strain
      out later)
    2 teaspoons salt
      pinch red pepper
      lemon juice
    3 ounces claret wine (add last)
    ½ stalk celery (chopped large to strain
      out later)

Dissolve gelatin in 1 cup cold consomme; than stir mixture into rest of hot consomme. Heat seasonings, beef and consomme for 15 minutes. Slice carrots around side and bottom of loaf pan. Arrange meat. Pour in liquid. Mold. (Serves 10.)

DAUBE GLACÉ CLEMENCEAU
Mrs. Pierre B. Clemenceau

    2½ lbs. beef, chuck or round
    1½ lbs. pork, shoulder or neck
    2 veal knuckles (broken in three
      pieces)
    2 calf's feet

Arrange over the bones, alternating layers of beef and pork. Salt and pepper each layer generously. Add:

    2 onions
    3 carrots (sliced)
    2 cloves of garlic
    8 or 9 sprigs of parsley
    3 or 4 bay leaves
    1 teaspoon thyme
    6 cloves

Cover with a few pieces of bacon. Pour into pot one quart dry white wine, French if possible, and ½ cup of brandy. Cover pot closely and simmer for three or four hours, until tender. Take out meat and carrots, chop, put into pyrex dishes. Carrots can be used at bottom as a decoration. Throw away bones. Let stock cool to remove grease. Put through a sieve, add 1 or 2 cans of White Rose Consommé (Artique) to stock and 1 envelope of Knox Gelatine, several tablespoons of brandy. Stir and season to taste. Then pour over meat in pyrex dishes. Cool before placing in refrig-

erator. When set, turn out on a platter and serve. This recipe can be doubled or tripled as it can be kept in the deep freeze. Gelatine need not be used in cold weather.

DAUBE POT ROAST
Mr. Francis J. Selman

    boneless chuck roast, about 2 lbs.
    Del Monte stewed tomatoes, 3-4 cups
    *Chef Seasonings, to taste

Brown meat thoroughly in a heavy Dutch oven. Add tomatoes and simmer covered until the meat is tender when pierced with a fork. Add Chef Seasonings* to taste. Do not salt or pepper. Amount of seasonings in recipe is ample; salt and pepper may be added later according to individual taste.

*Chef's Seasonings is a frozen package of minced onion, parsley, celery, and garlic. If this is not available, use minced vegetables to taste. (Suggested: ¼ cup minced parsley, ¼ cup minced celery, ¼ cup minced onion, and 1 to 2 cloves garlic, minced.)

This freezes well.
For converting above recipe to Daube Glace:
Dissolve 1 or 2 envelopes of gelatin in ¼ cup cold water, then mix with the hot pureed gravy from the daube. Pour gravy in a flat oblong pyrex dish to the depth of 1/8 inch. Slice meat ¼" thick and arrange slices neatly on top of the congealed gelatin. Cover with the balance of the pureed gravy and gelatin mixture, and refrigerate until thoroughly congealed.

ROASTED BEEF DAUBE
Mrs. Lester Lautenschlager, Jr.

    3 lbs. short ribs of beef
    3 lbs. beef bones
    1 lb. veal knuckles
    5 carrots
    5 stalks celery
    ½ bunch parsley
    4 large onions
    6 shallots
    seasonings: (1 tablespoon each) salt,
      pepper, garlic salt
    Tabasco, Lea & Perrins to taste

Let cook all day and refrigerate with vegetables still in broth. Next day, cook a 4 lb. sirloin tip roast until meat thermometer registers 140° rare. Slice the meat thin and into bite sized pieces. Sprinkle 2 packs plain gelatine on top of ½ cup water. Reheat stock and strain. Dissolve gelatine with 1½ cups stock. Coat 2 quart ring mold with ½ cup gelatine mixture. When congealed, decorate with pimento, cut outs and capers. Cover well with gelatine. Add remainder of the stock to the gelatine and let it cool. Pack the mold with layers of roast beef and chopped parsley and fill with the cooled beef stock. Turn out onto a large platter and garnish with parsley and radishes and watercress. Serve with horseradish sauce.

VIEUX CARRÉ DAUBE

Rémy Moran
Through Mrs. Helen Pitkin Schertz

    3 lbs. heavy veal or beef
    2 tablespoons lard
    4 onions, minced
    1 pod red pepper or cayenne to taste
    1 clove garlic, sweet pepper, minced
    ½ can tomatoes, at least ½ lb.
    1 teaspoon flour
    ½ cup of hot water
      salt, green onions, and parsley

Put lard in a deep iron pot and, when hot, put in the meat and brown well on both sides. Then add onions, garlic, red pepper cut fine or cayenne to taste, and bell pepper. Put onions, garlic and pepper in with the daube and fry until brown. Add tomatoes to which has been added the flour. Cover the pot well and cook 15 minutes on a slow fire, then add ½ cup of water and cook until daube is tender. Add green onions and parsley, salt and pepper to taste. Serve hot with rice.

STUFFED FILET SUPREME

Mr. David D. Duggins
Café Brulot Restaurant

    5 to 6 lb. filet mignon (whole
      strip)
    ½ stick butter
    1 bunch green onions, chopped fine
    1 box fresh mushrooms, chopped fine
    1 pint fresh oysters, each cut in
      4 pieces
    ½ to 1 cup French bread crumbs
    ½ cup finely chopped fresh parsley
    1 egg
      salt, pepper
      string and/or small skewers

Basting Sauce:

    1 stick butter or margarine, melted
    ¼ cup hot Coleman's English style
      Dijon prepared mustard
    ½ cup domestic brandy or cognac

Saute chopped green onions and mushrooms about 5 minutes in ½ stick butter, add cut oysters, cook another 5 minutes or until oysters curl, remove from heat and add sufficient bread crumbs to make a moist dressing, add beaten egg and salt and pepper to taste.
Cut a deep slit the length of the filet -- stuff with dressing and tie securely with a string. (If you have short skewers they can be used to lace the filet closed as you would the opening in a turkey.)
Broil steak over charcoal or roast in a very hot (500°) oven. Cooking time about 25 minutes. Serves 8.

GRILLADES

Mrs. J. Mort Walker, Jr.

    2 thin veal rounds
    1 large onion
    ½ sweet pepper
    1 clove garlic
    2 tomatoes
    1 level tablespoon of finely chopped
      parsley
    1 large can B & B sliced mushrooms
    ½ cup red wine
      salt and pepper

Cut veal rounds into 4-inch square pieces; salt, pepper and flour meat. Fry in bacon drippings until brown and remove from skillet. Add to skillet the chopped onions, sweet pepper and garlic and simmer until cooked. Add chopped tomatoes and cook until well done and dark brown, stirring constantly. Return meat to skillet with one cup of water, mushrooms with liquid, parsley, and ½ cup of red wine. Cook covered, slowly, for at least one hour until gravy thickens. Add salt and pepper to taste.

GRILLADES

Ethel Rose
Through Mrs. Carl E. Woodward

    2 veal rounds cut in pieces
    1 large cut up onion

Salt and pepper the veal rounds

and dip in flour. Fry in shortening until golden brown. Take out and then brown onion. After onion is browned, add veal and about one and a half cups of water. Simmer slowly for about 1½ hours. When done, sprinkle cut up parsley and shallots over platter.

GRILLADES PANNÉES
Mrs. C. H. Bailey

2 veal rounds
1 egg
  salt and pepper
  toasted bread crumbs

Cut rounds into pieces about 4 inches square. Make some bread crumbs which you have toasted a light color in a slow oven. Run these through the sifter to avoid lumps. Break egg, dip each piece of meat in the egg, then in the bread crumbs, seeing that both sides are covered. Fry each piece in deep hot fat, turning gently from side to side until a rich golden color. Then salt and pepper. The Creoles always serve pickles with this dish, and place the meat on a platter with mashed potatoes in the center.

GRILLADES POINTE COUPÉ

2 large veal rounds
½ bell pepper, veins, seeds removed
1 large tomato, fresh or tinned
1 large onion, sliced
1 clove garlic
4 shallots (including green stalk) minced
3 tablespoons flour
2 tablespoons lard
4 cups hot water
  salt, pepper, to taste

Cut the rounds for individual servings. Fry them about five minutes in hot fat in iron skillet. Remove and set aside.

Lower the fire and cook onion until transparent; then the bell pepper, minced, and the flour go in, to brown. Then add other ingredients, including the meat. Cover and let cook very slowly for an hour and a half for thin sauce, two hours for thicker, as preferred.

HAM AU MARQUIS
Mrs. Walter Torian

4 slices ham, ¼" thick
2 teaspoons Coleman's mustard
2 tablespoons brown sugar
2 tablespoons vinegar (maybe less, enough to make paste)

Mix the brown sugar and vinegar, and mustard to make a paste. Spread this over the ham; broil.
An aristocratic legacy. Serves 4.

BAKED HAM
Miss Margot Samuel

12 to 14 lb. southern ham
1½ cups each vinegar, sherry
6 apples
  Seasonings: 1 bunch carrots, 1 large stalk celery (with the green leaves), 6 onions, 1 small bunch thyme, 1 small bunch bay leaves, a handful each of black peppercorns, cloves, allspice, 2 long hot peppers, 2 large sweet peppers, and the peelings of the apples

Soak the ham overnight and in the morning discard the water and cover with fresh cold water. Add all the seasonings, bring to a boil. Allow it to cook slowly about twenty minutes to each pound of ham. When done remove from the fire and allow the ham to stand in the liquor all night. Skin the ham, score and rub brown sugar well into the fat. Place in a baking pan and pour sherry over it. Surround with the apples and bake for about a half an hour until piping hot all through. Then run under the flames to brown. Serve with the baked apples.

BAKED STUFFED HAM PONTALBA

14 lb. ham.

If a dry smoked ham is used it must be soaked 12 hours, but with the modern cured hams this is unnecessary.

Remove the bone. This is difficult to do, and small, very sharp knives are necessary. Your butcher will, however, perform this feat for you.

Take out about half a pound of meat from the cavity and grind it. Add it to the following stuffing:
3 lbs. pecans, shelled and ground,

1 onion, chopped fine, 1 small can truffles, cut up, 2 bay leaves, 2 sprigs thyme, 2 teaspoons sage, 1 teaspoon powdered cloves, ½ coffeespoon cayenne. 1 glass Madeira wine.

These are all mixed well with the ground ham and the whole stuffed firmly into the cavity of the ham and sewed in tightly. Then get a large cloth. Place the following seasonings in it:

1 onion, chopped, 2 bay leaves, 1 tablespoon sage, 1 teaspoon powdered cloves.

Sew the cloth firmly around the ham and put on to boil with about three gallons of water. Put all the same seasonings in the water that you put inside the cloth. Add also:

1 apple
1 cup cane syrup

Allow the ham to boil for six hours and then to cool in the same water in which it boiled. Remove the skin, dress with sugar and bread crumbs, bake until thoroughly heated through and browned.

While these directions are given for a large ham a picnic ham may be substituted which will serve for the ordinary family meal. One pound of pecans will be sufficient and seasonings reduced.

JAMBON AU CHAMPAGNE
Mrs. William P. Burke

A pre-cooked 10-12 lb. ham
1 cup French Champagne
4 tablespoons yellow mustard
1 tablespoon Tarragon vinegar
¾ cup dark brown sugar
2 tablespoons cinnamon

Pour the Champagne over the ham, after removing all the skin, and bake one hour at 300 degrees, basting frequently.

Make a paste of the remaining ingredients and spread it over the ham.

Glaze in a 500 degree oven for 15 or 20 minutes. It's delicious.

HAM MOUSSE
Mrs. Stephen Voelker

2 lbs. ham
1 cup bread crumbs
4 egg whites
½ cup milk
salt and pepper to taste

Put the ham through a meat chopper four times. Smooth even with spoon. Cook one cup bread crumbs and one cup milk together. Let cool and add to ham. Season and add the four egg whites well beaten. Pour into a greased mold, place in a pan of hot water and bake for ½ hour or more. Serve with mushroom sauce.

MOUSSE AU JAMBON
Mrs. Olivier A. Billion

2 cups fresh white bread
2 cups milk, scalded
2/3 cup sharp cheddar cheese, grated
½ teaspoon garlic or onion salt
dash of pepper
½ teaspoon dry mustard
2 teaspoons Worcestershire sauce
½ cup finely ground cooked ham
1 tablespoon butter, melted
4 eggs, separated

Tear the bread apart lightly, to make crumbs roughly the size of peas. Scald the milk; take it from the fire and add grated cheese, crumbs, garlic, salt, pepper, mustard and Worcestershire sauce. Stir gently. Then add the ham. Fold in the beaten egg yolks, then the butter. Beat the egg whites until stiff but not dry, fold them lightly into the Mousse. Pour into a buttered baking dish and set in a pan of hot water in a 350° oven. Bake until the Mousse is set and well browned, about one hour. It should, of course be served as soon as possible after taking from the oven, but even with standing it will not fall as a soufflé, and is delicious.

STUFFED HAM
Hermann Deutsch

Ingredients:

One cup each finely chopped celery, shallots (white and green parts both), bell pepper; half a cup each pecans, mushrooms, minced parsley; a cup of coarsely chopped mixed dried fruits; bird's eye peppers (or Tabasco sauce) to taste; salt and herbs (marjoram, cumin, etc., to taste; one package of frozen spinach; two or three cans of beer; blackberry jelly, brown sugar, cloves; one cup of cooked rice.

Get the butcher to bone a ham of approximately the proper size for your table, and take off the rind. (Bone and rind make wonderful seasoning for red beans, hence should not be discarded.)

In three tablespoons of shortening (peanut oil, cottonseed oil, lard, Crisco, etc.) smother shallots, celery, bell peppers, coarsely chopped pecans, parsley and seasonings. When the mixture is soft, but not brown, add the spinach and blend well, stirring constantly. As the final step add cooked rice, mushrooms and chopped fruits, again stirring until the mixture is blended but not cutting up the mushrooms; taste to correct seasoning, set aside and reserve.

Take the boned ham, wipe well inside and out, then stuff the cavity left by removal of the bone with the herb-rice- and seasoning mixture, in which the spinach should predominate. If the ham has been cut in removing the bone, tie it firmly into its original shape with kitchen string at several points.

Place it in the oven uncovered, fat side up, pour a can of beer over it, and baste the ham from time to time with the mixture of beer and drippings as it roasts in a 375-degree oven 20 minutes to the pound. Add more beer from time to time to the drippings to make up for evaporation. Forty minutes before the ham is done take the pan from the oven, stud the fat side with cloves, brush with blackberry jelly and hand-pack dark brown sugar over the top, to glaze the ham, basting with the beer-jelly-fat drippings as before.

Serve hot or cold, removing fat from the pan sauce before serving with the meat either as a sauce (hot) or as an aspic (cold).

These are two of my favorites; and they are served each New Year's afternoon, following the Sugar Bowl game, at my house.

VIRGINIA HAM
Mrs. Walter J. Barnes

Soak overnight in cold water. Scrub well with brush. Boil in plain water until bone in end becomes loose. Remove skin. Cool. Remove excess fat.

Put cloves in and cover with brown sugar and sprinkle with Worcestershire sauce. For a pretty glaze, bake in oven. Do not cut for 48 hours.

BAKED HASH

2 lbs. brisket
1 onion
2 tablespoons butter
3 large potatoes
salt, pepper

Use brisket which has made a pot of rich soup. Grind this brisket through a meat grinder. Chop onion and fry lightly in butter. Mix with the ground meat, season highly with salt and pepper, put in a baking dish, covering with mashed potatoes. Dot with butter and bake until the potatoes are well browned.

JERKY
Mrs. E. V. Benjamin

This is great for snacks, with cocktails, for children, for dieters, for travelers, etc.

venison or beef (hindquarters and forequarters, parts of the animal which have large muscles make excellent prospects for jerky).

Trim off all fat and slice your meat into thin strips, about ½ to 1 inch wide and 3 - 5 inches long. Always cut with the grain or the meat will crumble after it is dried. Prepare a mixture of one part black pepper and two parts salt. If you like your jerky hot add a little red pepper to the mixture, or if you like garlic salt, add some.

After the meat is cut, roll the strips in the seasoning mixture and put it in a crock for 3 - 4 days, covered and refrigerated.

Boil a large pot of water and dip the meat in it (a little at a time) until it turns white. Drain it in a colander, then place strips on a cookie sheet in a single layer. Dry the meat in the oven, as low as the fire will go. The time will vary depending on the thickness of each piece, but it will take anywhere from 10 - 15 hours. It is not necessary to turn it, and when it is thoroughly dehydrated, remove it from the oven and let it cool. Store in a cool place in brown paper bags -- not plastic -- or, you may put it in jars in the freezer.

CURRIED KIDNEYS

Mrs. Stanley Arthur

3 sets kidneys, veal preferred
1½ tablespoons butter
1 tablespoon flour
1 large onion, chopped
½ clove garlic, minced
2 teaspoons curry powder
salt and pepper

Wash and slice kidneys, removing gristle and hard parts. Season well with salt and pepper. Put butter in saucepan; when very hot add flour and stir constantly to prevent burning, then the onion and garlic and stir until brown. Put in sliced kidneys, cover and let cook not longer than five minutes. Longer cooking makes kidneys tough and indigestible. No water is necessary, as the kidneys make their own gravy which is rich and delicious. Stir in curry powder and serve with boiled rice.

This recipe can be used with pie crust dough for covered kidney pie.

LAMB KIDNEYS FLAMBÉS

1 doz. kidneys
4 tablespoons butter
1 glass Madeira wine
1 glass brandy
salt, pepper, to taste

Slit the kidneys lengthwise and remove the thin skin. Season them.

Put the saucepan onto a brisk fire, and put in 3 tablespoons of butter, then toss the kidneys quickly in, and let them cook three or four minutes. Remove them, drain them, and let them stand in a warm place, so that any blood remaining in them may ooze out.

The saucepan again—pour the Madeira into it, then, slowly, add the brandy, and as it heats, set it alight. Add a tablespoon of butter, then the kidneys. Toss the kidneys lightly, not allowing them to boil in the sauce (which would toughen them).

A dramatic touch is to perform the burning process at the table.

ALSATIAN LAMB

Mrs. Florence Martinson

leg of lamb
bottle of dry white wine
bacon
onion, garlic, carrots, bay leaf
fresh ground black pepper, salt

Have the butcher remove every bit of fat from the lamb. Let it marinate at least overnight in the wine with the onion, garlic, carrots, bay leaf, pepper.

Next day, wrap it completely in bacon, tying it securely about the meat; sear for a few minutes in a very hot oven (about 500 degrees) then cook for an hour in a moderate oven basting faithfully and frequently with the wine sauce.

BOILED LAMB À L'ANGLAISE

Mrs. Walter Torian

1 small leg lamb
4 cups stock (water in which lamb boiled)
4 hard-boiled eggs
2 raw eggs
1 clove garlic, minced
1 tablespoon minced parsley
2 tablespoons melted butter
2 tablespoons flour, heaping
1 cup capers
red pepper, salt, to taste

Place the leg of lamb in tepid water enough to cover it, and let boil until done.

Mash up the yolks of hard-boiled eggs with 2 raw yolks to paste, rub in garlic, parsley, red pepper, salt, then add the melted butter. Add the flour, stirring it into the stock slowly. When cool, add the hard-boiled egg mixture.

Cook until thick, then add the capers, and cook only one minute after that. Pour over the lamb and garnish with chopped white of hard-boiled eggs and minced parsley.

GIGOT DE MOUTON

Mrs. Vera Revailler von Meysenbug

6 to 7 lb. leg of lamb
1 pt. red wine
1 teaspoon black pepper
2 teaspoons salt
1 whole onion, 1 clove garlic
parsley, thyme, bay leaf

Make incisions in the meat with a sharp knife and insert slivers of garlic. The amount may be modified to taste. Rub surface of meat well with salt and pepper.

Melt a tablespoon of butter in an iron skillet and brown the meat well.

Then remove and place in a roasting pan. The whole onion is placed beside it.

Pour the wine in the hot skillet with a few bay leaves and a sprig of thyme. Bring to a boil and stir well to take up all the flavor of the broiled meat and butter. Pour over the lamb leg and place in the oven which has been pre-heated to 300 degrees. Bake until tender allowing 22 minutes per pound. Baste frequently with the wine in the pan.

PARSLIED LEG OF LAMB

Mrs. George Douglass

5 pound leg of lamb
 corn oil
 salt
 pepper
1 cup fine bread crumbs
4 tablespoons chopped parsley
2 lemons

Rub leg of lamb with corn oil, salt and pepper. Put lamb in 350° oven and baste with pan juices every 15 minutes. About one-half hour before lamb is done, sprinkle lamb with the juice of one lemon, bread crumbs and parsley mixture. Slice one lemon paper thin, and place the slices on the lamb. The lemon and parsley impart a marvelous flavor and the aroma is irresistible.

LIVER AUX VINGT-CINQ PIASTRES

1½ lbs. calf's liver
1 tablespoon each onions, green pepper, minced
1 clove minced garlic
4 tomatoes, or 1 small can
1 tablespoon lard, heaping
1 tablespoon flour
1½ cups water
 thyme, bay leaf, salt, pepper

This is worth twelve hours expectancy at least. Buy a chunk of the finest calf's liver. Place on ice the night before serving, in a deep bowl, with a large piece of ice on top. Before cooking, remove all skin and fibres.

Have ready a large pot of boiling water, and at the same time, a roux, made of the flour stirred evenly into the lard; brown the onions slightly, and add the other seasonings and to-matoes.

Plunge the liver into the boiling water, remove at once, plunge it in again, and then put it immediately into the roux. Add the water, cover, and let simmer till tender, basting at intervals.

When done, and the sauce nicely thickened, slash the liver (not cutting completely through) in several places, baste well with the sauce, and serve piping hot.

This recipe was given as a token of great regard by the famous Mme. Begué to one of her most favored clients with the injunction that he must never give it away, but that he might sell it for twenty-five dollars. The gracious gentlewoman, his wife, parts with it now for the first time.

LIVER WITH SWEETBREADS

Mr. A. Ferrer

2 lbs. fine calf's liver
1 lb. sweetbreads
½ lb. chicken livers
1 can mushrooms
¼ lb. butter
 garlic, parsley, salt, pepper
 Worcestershire sauce

Parboil the sweetbreads, cut in small pieces, set aside.

Cook the liver in a very hot skillet with olive oil, 5 minutes. (Turn liver with spatula: it should never be pricked with a fork.) Place on a platter and set in a warm oven.

Now put the chicken livers in the hot skillet, then the sweetbreads, then the mushrooms, a dash of Worcestershire sauce, minced parsley, a tiny speck of minced garlic and butter.

Turn all of this out onto the liver and serve piping hot.

GLORIFIED MEAT BALLS A LA RUSSE

Grace Thompson Seton

This recipe feeds four people economically and as it is both delicious and attractive looking, it need not be confined to the family.

Buy 1½ lbs. of beef, chuck or round, and have it ground very fine by the butcher. Put the meat in a large bowl and add to it four slices of white bread (without crusts) crumbled up, 1 cup of milk, one beaten egg, salt and pepper. Mix this all together very thoroughly, so that the bread disappears. The mixture should be just stiff enough to hold its shape, then it should be formed into balls no bigger than a plum. These balls may be fried or broiled.

Serve them with the following sauce: Fry a small, minced onion and half a chopped green pepper in butter or beef fat. If you have mushrooms, slice a quarter pound of them thin and fry them too at the same time. When all is cooked add flour to thicken and then the liquid which is made as follows: beat a tablespoonful of mayonnaise into a cup of canned consommé, add a few drops of Worcestershire sauce and a tablespoonful of ketchup, salt and pepper to taste.

Combine this liquid slowly with the mixture in the frying pan, stirring all the while until the sauce is of the proper consistency. Pour it over the meat balls, decorate with parsley or pimento and serve.

MEAT LOAF A LA VON FRONK

Mrs. Frank Harbison

4 lbs. beef
2 lbs. veal
2 lbs. pork
1 cup corn flakes
½ small bottle catsup
4 Bermuda onions
2 raw eggs
2 tablespoons Pick-a-Pepper sauce
  Lea & Perrins, salt, pepper, to taste

Mix all ingredients together and shape into 1 large or 2 small loaves. Cook, uncovered in 350° oven until brown and done. Time depends on size of loaves desired.

CRANBERRY MEAT LOAF

Mrs. Karl M. Zander, Jr.

2 lbs. ground meat, lean
1 lb. pork sausage
1 finely chopped onion
1 finely chopped green pepper
1 can whole cranberry sauce
¾ cup dark brown sugar
1 cup moistened bread (4 slices)

1 beaten egg
  salt and pepper to taste
4 potatoes

Combine all ingredients except cranberry sauce and brown sugar. Mold into loaf. In large roasting pan spread sugar and half of cranberry sauce. Place loaf on the mixture. Poke three deep holes into top of loaf. Add water to fill the half empty can of cranberries. Pour over loaf. Cover and cook at 350° for 45 minutes. Uncover and add 4 peeled and quartered potatoes. Cook for another 45 minutes.

MUTTON WITH CABBAGE

Mrs. Neils F. Johnsen

2 to 4 lbs. lamb or mutton (breast or shoulder) cut in serving pieces
4 to 8 lbs. cabbage (about twice the weight of meat used)
1 oz. butter, a little flour
1 tablespoon peppercorns
  salt and pepper to taste

Melt the butter in a large thick bottomed pot. Sprinkle with a little flour and place in the meat and cabbage in alternate layers each sprinkled with a little flour and salt. Pour on boiling water till the pot is one-third full. Cover and simmer slowly for two to three hours stirring occasionally to prevent burning. This dish may be reheated and used a second time. Many hold that the second serving is the better.

MUTTON CHOPS AU DIABLE

6 mutton chops
1 egg
½ cup butter, 1 tablespoon flour
½ cup water, ½ teaspoon salt
1 tablespoon Worcestershire sauce
½ cup capers
7 tablespoons mushroom sauce
  toasted bread crumbs

Take off the outer skin as this is the part of the mutton that gives the strong taste. Grate crackers or crust of bread, break an egg, stir and dip the chops in this, then in the crumbs and broil them. Use ½ cup of butter, brown a tablespoon of flour in the heated butter, add ½ cup of water, Worcestershire sauce, capers and mushrooms to pour over chops.

ROAST PORK

1 8-lb. pork leg
1 tablespoon olive oil
2 tablespoons vinegar, flour
2 teaspoons ground sage
2 teaspoons cayenne pepper
2 teaspoons salt

Rub meat with vinegar and seasoning, wrap in a linen cloth that has been dipped in vinegar, repeating this when dry. Let stand 24 hours. When ready to cook, rub with olive oil and flour. Roast 25 minutes to the pound.

SAUERBRATEN

Mrs. William F. Cook

5 lbs. beef chuck (or equivalent)
2 cups vinegar
1 cup water
10 whole cloves
2 teaspoons sugar
2 medium sized onions, grated
10 ginger snaps
4 tablespoons sour cream
2 tablespoons horseradish

Mix the vinegar, water, sugar, cloves, and onions in a bowl to make a marinade. Soak the beef in the marinade for thirty-six hours turning several times. Brown the meat as for a pot roast than add one and a half cups of the marinade. Cook slowly for about two hours or until tender, adding more of the marinade from time to time as it cooks away. Remove the meat, skim off fat and add the ginger snaps to thicken the gravy. Just before serving add the sour cream and horseradish.

HOMEMADE SAUSAGE
(CROQUETTES DE SAUCISSE)

Mrs. Walter Torian

3 lbs. pork sausage
  spices to taste (suggested: rosemary, thyme, sage)
  crushed garlic to taste
½ cup sherry
1 to 2 tablespoons vinegar

The sausage meat is left overnight with the vinegar, spices and garlic. The next morning, season it highly with salt, pepper and cayenne pepper to taste. Add the sherry and mix well.
After that pleasant touch, it is shaped in croquette form, and fried in sizzling hot lard.

HOMEMADE PORK SAUSAGE
Mrs. David Merrick
Bel-Air Plantation

8 lbs. pork, the lean
8 lbs. pork, the fat
3 tablespoons salt
1 tablespoon each red pepper, black pepper, sage

Grind the pork very fine. Add the seasonings. Either shape into patties or put into sausage casings, which can be obtained from your butcher. Put into saucepan with a small amount of water. When water evaporates, let sausage fry slowly in their own juice, turning constantly. Excellent.

BARBEQUED STEAK
À LA GENERAL TROUSDALE
Mrs. L. K. Burton

Purchase first cut of loin, without sirloin tip, preferably from prime Black Angus, four inches thick. Trim off all surplus fat. Sear the steak on all sides after charcoal is down to a glow and there is no flame. Should be cooked in a barbeque apparatus with a cover and the steak should be turned frequently. After the steak has cooked about 30 minutes, apply salt and pepper. In another 5 minutes apply salt and pepper again, and 5 minutes later baste with barbeque sauce prepared as follows:

1 large bottle Worcestershire sauce
1 small bottle A-1 sauce
  juice of a large lemon
1/3 of a grated onion
1 clove of garlic, chopped
1 stick butter
  small amount of celery tops or onion tops, chopped fine

After cooking for 1 hour, the steak should be ready to serve, medium rare. Serves 4 - 6.

CHARCOAL BROILED STEAK
À LA EARL
Mrs. Allard Kaufmann

1 3½ to 4 lb. sirloin steak (best cut)

1 stick of butter
2 whole cloves of garlic

Broil steak on hot charcoal fire out-of-doors for about 15 to 20 minutes for medium rare. Turn every 3 or 4 minutes in order not to burn. Melt butter in saucepan with garlic. Slice steak crosswise in strips and arrange on long, deep silver platter garnished with watercress. Season to taste after cooking. Remove garlic from melted butter and pour butter over steak. Serve at once. New, small boiled potatoes, green or vegetable salad go well with this steak.

GENTLEMAN'S STEAK

Mr. George Persons

thick steak
2 cloves garlic, minced
2 onions, 4 shallots, minced
Worcestershire sauce
butter
salt, pepper, minced parsley
button mushrooms

Rub the steak well with salt and pepper on both sides. Rub the garlic also well into both sides of the steak. Sprinkle the Worcestershire sauce lightly on both sides, then rub it in. Have the oven red hot, and put the steak in on the broiler, covering it immediately with dots of butter liberally, and then with the chopped onions. The steak should be about 2 inches below the broiler flame.

Cook until the steak begins to brown, then turn it over, dotting the other side freshly with butter and onions and shallot tops, and as it cooks, baste it at intervals with the melted butter. Turn it frequently, continuing to baste it, until it is cooked to taste.

Remove it to a hot platter, and add the minced mushrooms, sprinkling the whole lightly with parsley.

HOW TO COOK A STEAK

By Roark Bradford

"If you are one of these people who are impatient, go to any good restaurant and order your steak. On the other hand, if you realize that it took time to build up civilization, and that even Cleopatra was not made in a

day, it will be worth your while to undertake broiling your own steak in the following fashion:

THE STEAK

Go to a good butcher-shop, make him trot out that prime loin of corn-fed steer, and cut off your meat from the big end of the loin. The meat should be not less than two, nor more than four inches thick. Insist upon the cut being of uniform thickness; for no reason, a butcher will thin it down toward the tail of the steak if you don't watch him.

Once in possession of your prime cut of meat, you had, just for the sake of unexpected emergencies, better buy half a dozen, or even a dozen more such cuts. It will cost you money, but you said you wanted a steak, didn't you?

Take your cut steaks to a cold storage house and hang them separately, so that air can circulate all around them. Then forget about them for at least six months. A year will be better; longer than a year will do little, if any good. Some claim they are better after two years, but I doubt it. It sounds like intellectualism instead of ordinary healthy lust.

PREPARATION FOR BROILING

Get one of your steaks out of storage—one ought to be enough for half a dozen hungry people—and trim off the leathery outside edge. Also trim out and save about half the suet. Rub one teacup of powdered sugar to each side of steak. This sounds pretty bad, I know, but it really is what makes your steak worth waiting for. Be certain that all the sugar has dissolved, and that the surface of the meat has a sticky glisten to it. Imbed one clove of garlic into the steak, next to the bone. Do not attempt other flavoring, such as salt, pepper and the like. This will come later.

BROILING

Your charcoal furnace should be fired well in advance of the time for cooking, so that only a bed of live embers are in the hod when actual cooking begins. Put your steak in a wire broiling rack and sear each side by holding it about six inches above your fire, allowing about one minute for each side. (This quick heat draws together and burns all the sugar into a thick black crust, which holds all the juices in the meat.)

After both sides are seared, hold your broiling rack about a foot above the coals so the cooking process will be slower than the searing, and turn frequently so the heat will be applied evenly to both sides. For blood-rare steak, ten minutes usually is long enough for the cooking. For well-done steak, 20 to 25 minutes will be needed.

SAUCE—IF YOU LIKE SAUCE

Take the suet from the steak, and render slowly in a deep iron skillet. As soon as the fat begins to run, put in two finely chopped cloves of garlic and one finely chopped small onion. As the garlic and onion begin to burn black, remove the burned bits, and at the same time, add an occasional tablespoon of red wine and a dash of Tabasco sauce until a teacup of wine and approximately a teaspoon of Tabasco has been slowly worked into the sauce. Add salt to taste.

SERVING

After steak is done, scrape burnt sugar from surface, carve into suitable portions, arrange on platter and pour sauce over it."

BRUNSWICK STEW
Mr. James L. Crump

3 lbs. pig jowl or pork
3 lbs. beef
2 lbs. pig liver, ground

"Also a nice fat hen will do no harm."

Place in water about 4 or 5 times the above volume and boil vigorously for 1 hour. Then slow down and let remain at boiling point or just simmering for 3 hours or more. Now add the following vegetables.

2 lb. can each peas, corn, tomatoes
pint bottle catsup
quart mashed potatoes
1 lb. chopped onions

Add the following seasoning 1 hour before serving:

4 tablespoons vinegar
2 tablespoons Worcestershire sauce
½ lemon rind, grated

salt and pepper, to taste

Always keep the stew simmering. This quantity is for a large crowd.

ARTICHOKES AND SWEETBREADS
Mrs. Felix J. Puig

6 artichokes
1 lb. sweetbreads
1 cup cream sauce
1 tablespoon chopped green onion
1 tablespoon parsley
1 small can truffles, sliced thin
2 tablespoons butter
a sprig of thyme
bread or cracker crumbs
salt, pepper

Boil artichokes, remove center choke, scoop out heart, scrape tender part of leaves. Brown green onions, parsley, and thyme in a little butter, season, add to artichokes. Cream boiled sweetbreads with artichokes and truffles. Fill center of artichokes with this mixture, sprinkle with bread or cracker crumbs, dot with butter and heat very hot. Mushrooms add to this delicious dish.

SWEETBREADS AND FRESH MUSHROOMS
Mrs. A. T. Pattison

1½ lbs. sweetbreads
6 small shallots
1 sprig parsley
2 teaspoons butter
1 tablespoon flour
½ lb. fresh mushrooms
½ cup thick cream
1 egg yolk
salt, pepper

Soak sweetbreads in cold water to blanch, then boil until tender. Remove all skins from them. Keep the stock.

Make a roux with the butter and flour and cook until golden brown. Then add sweetbreads, the shallots chopped very fine, and the parsley. Add the stock, season and let simmer very slowly until the sauce is quite thick. The mushrooms must meanwhile be smothered in butter. When ready to serve, add them, with the cream in which the yolk of the egg is beaten. Be careful not to let the mixture boil, once the cream and yolk of egg have been put in.

SWEETBREADS AND HAM
Lt. Comdr. and
Mrs. S. W. Wallace

1 lb. sweetbreads
6 slices of ham, boiled
6 slices toast, sandwich bread
1 can Campbell's mushroom soup
2 tablespoons butter
flour, milk, salt, pepper

Parboil sweetbreads according to directions in Sweetbreads Supreme. Fry ham slightly on each side and place on toast, then cut sweetbreads into ½ inch slices, flour well and brown in butter, salt and pepper, then place on the slices of toast and ham. This can be kept in a warm oven until ready to serve. Heat the mushroom soup and thin with milk to desired consistency and pour over all.

TONGUE
Mrs. J. L. Onorato

Boil tongue until tender. Chop fine. Melt a glass of currant jelly and pour over it, and let simmer about two hours. Serve with it, red cabbage, cooked with raisins, and ground artichokes.

TOURNEDOS ROYAL
Ella Brennan Martin
Brennan's French Restaurant

¼ cup butter
½ cup chopped onion
¼ cup bread crumbs
1 teaspoon each paprika, capers
1 teaspoon chopped truffles
pinch powdered thyme
1 cup sweetbreads, par-boiled and
chopped fine
4 artichoke cups
¼ cup Bearnaise sauce
4 filet mignons (12 to 14 ounces each)

In a small skillet melt butter and sauté onion, bread crumbs, paprika, capers, truffles and thyme until done. Add sweetbreads and heat through. Remove pan from heat. Divide mixture in 4 portions and roll into balls.

Place each ball in an artichoke heart. While this is cooking, season filets and grill to taste. Place each filet on a serving plate. Pour about 1 tablespoon Bearnaise sauce over filet and place stuffed artichoke heart on top. 4 Servings.

BLANQUETTE OF VEAL, LAMB OR CHICKEN
Mrs. Renée Gavinet Bowie

½ lb. butter or margarine
4 lbs. veal or lamb or 7½ lbs. chicken
1/3 cup flour
1 twelve oz. can mushrooms
3 tablespoons parsley, finely minced
4 tablespoons shallots, finely minced
3 pints hot water
3 eggs, the yolks only
4 tablespoons cream
1 tablespoon vinegar
salt, pepper to taste

Melt butter without browning in a heavy gallon saucepan. Cube veal or lamb and stir very thoroughly in butter. (If chicken is used instead of lamb or veal, take the wings, legs, neck and giblets for this, adding the choice pieces after the addition of the water.) Sift flour into the meat and butter and stir until well rubbed in. Do not allow to brown. Add the hot water a little at a time stirring until smooth between each addition, then the mushrooms with their stock. Add the parsley and shallots, the salt and pepper. Cover tightly and simmer slowly for at least two hours and a half. Great care must be taken that it does not burn. Best use a plate of some kind beneath the pot. (Up to this point the dish may be prepared in advance and set aside to be reheated before finishing.) When meat is very tender drain from the sauce and dress on a hot platter. Surround with individual molds of boiled rice which may also be prepared in advance and reheated by placing the molds in boiling water. Now take the sauce from the fire and quickly stir in the egg yolks which have been beaten well with the cream and vinegar. Pour the foamy sauce over the meat and serve at once. The ideal accompaniment is Grapefruit Aspic.

BLANQUETTE DE VEAU

Mrs. Oliver A. Billion

2 or 3 lbs. of veal from the shoulder
2 onions, 1 carrot
1 each tablespoon of butter, flour
2 egg yolks
2 wine glasses of white wine
½ gal. of water
  salt and pepper to taste

Cut veal in small regular pieces (about 2 inches). Put in casserole and cover with water (cold). Add wine, carrot and onions cut in rondelles, bouquet garni, seasoning.

Bring to boil, skim, let simmer 2 hours. Drain the meat, strain the bouillon and use to make roux with flour and butter. Cook roux about 10 minutes stirring constantly.

Add veal to sauce, heat and at time of serving add yolks of eggs.

One-half can of mushrooms may be added to this if desired.

Before the war this was served as an entrée in France.

VEAL CUTLETS MAINTENON

6 veal cutlets
1 each cup consommé, milk
½ clove garlic, 1 teaspoon salt
1 egg yolk
1 wine glass Madeira
½ tablespoon mushrooms
2 tablespoons butter

Trim your boned cutlets, fry very quickly so that they are browned but not fully cooked. Put them in the flat dish in which they are to be served, leaving plenty of room for the sauce. Make this sauce of equal quantities of rich clear consommé and milk, with seasoning and a mere suggestion of garlic.

Let the sauce reduce until it begins to thicken.

Take it from the fire and stir in beaten yolk of egg so that it will be thick enough to cover the cutlets well. Put the dish into a quick oven. The cutlets should be cooked by the time the sauce begins to brown. Pour over them Madeira that has been slowly cooked with chopped mushrooms, and serve more of this in a sauce boat.

MARINATED VEAL

Mrs. Richard Adler

1 to 2 cloves mashed garlic
1/3 cup salad oil
2 tablespoons ketchup
¼ teaspoon pepper
3 tablespoons soy sauce
1 tablespoon vinegar
2 lbs. veal cutlets

Mix all ingredients together. Turn veal pieces over in sauce and refrigerate overnight.

About 30 minutes before serving, pour off marinade. Saute veal in 2 tablespoons butter or oil over medium heat for about 25 minutes.

VEAL PANNE À LA "BOO BIRD"

Bob Roesler

2 veal rounds, thinly sliced
4 beaten eggs
1½ cups Italian bread crumbs
½ cup minced parsley
½ cup chopped shallots
2 garlic cloves, crushed
  salt and pepper (about 2 teaspoon each)
½ cup oil, ½ cup butter

Cut rounds in serving pieces. Beat eggs and put in shallow bowl. Mix rest of ingredients in separate bowl.

Melt butter and oil in frying pan. Dip veal pieces in egg and then dip in the crumb mixture, pressing crumbs into meat. Saute over medium heat until crispy brown on both sides. Sprinkle with additional parsley if desired and serve.

ROAST VEAL WITH ORANGE SAUCE

Mrs. Killian L. Huger, Jr.

4 teaspoons salt
1 teaspoon pepper
1 teaspoon mace
1 teaspoon paprika
2 6-lb. rolled boneless veal roasts
¾ cups butter
1½ cups shallots, chopped
3 navel oranges
1 cup sugar
1½ cups water
1½ cups white wine

3 cups beef bouillon
½ cup currant jelly

Mix salt, pepper, mace, and paprika, and rub into roasts. Spread each roast with 4 tablespoons butter. Butter the roasting pans with the remainder of the butter. Surround roasts with the chopped shallots. Put in oven preheated to 450° and roast 30 minutes, basting twice. Turn meat and roast 10 minutes longer. Turn again and lower heat to 375° and roast 2½ hours. (Turn even lower is cooking too fast.)

Pare orange rinds; cut into julienne strips and poach 5 minutes in syrup made from sugar and water. Strain. Remove pith and skin of oranges and reserve sections.

Remove roast when done to platter; cover with foil. Place roasting pan on top of stove, and de-glaze with wine over medium heat. Add bouillon and simmer for 5 minutes.

Strain into saucepan and add currant jelly. As jelly melts, add orange strips. Slice roast and arrange orange sections around the meat. Spoon a little sauce over the meat and serve the remaining sauce in a gravy boat.
Serves 16.

STUFFED VEAL POCKET
Miss Ethel Forman

8 slices bread, toasted hard and crumbled
2 onions, chopped
1 green pepper, chopped
1 tablespoon flour
1 tablespoon lard
1 teaspoon salt
2 teaspoons parsley
1 veal pocket

Make roux with the flour and the lard. Add rest of ingredients and cook for five minutes. Stuff the pocket well as you do chicken, and sew up. Put in

a 350° oven for 1 to 1½ hours, basting all the while.
Serves 6 to 8.

VEAL WITH WINE
Mrs. Richard Adler

2 tablespoons butter
6 tablespoons wine
4 slices veal steak, or 6-8 slices veal cutlets
2 tablespoons flour
juice of 3 lemons
½ cup white wine

Melt 2 sticks of butter with 6 tablespoons olive oil. Brown veal in oil-butter mixture. Remove meat to platter. To oil and butter add flour and juice of lemons. Add ½ cup white wine. Stir well. Put meat back, and cook for five minutes. Serve over cooked noodles.

WIENER SCHNITZEL
Mr. Conrad Kolb

2½ lbs. of veal from the leg
2 eggs
⅛ lb. butter
½ lemon, the juice
6 eggs, fried
flour, salt, pepper

The veal is cut into six ¾ inch slices, pounded, salted, peppered. Beat the egg well, dip the meat into it and then into the flour. Heat the butter and fry the slices light brown on both sides. While they fry drip the lemon juice on.

When well done put them on a hot platter. Make the gravy with ½ cup of water poured into frying butter. Add salt if necessary, cook and pour over the cutlets. The eggs are fried and placed on each cutlet.

vegetables, pastas, jambalayas
and casseroles

FRIED APPLES

One of the nicest of all dishes is fried apples, cooked in plenty of butter, with a few drops of water and a sprinkling of sugar added. Slice the apples thinly, leaving the skins on; lay them in the hot butter in the open frying pan and turn occasionally until perfectly tender and somewhat candied around the edges. Serve with French toast and bacon; fried oatmeal or mush; or plain buttered toast and on an omelet for breakfast.

APPLES DOROTHY DIX

6 red apples
6 slices bacon
1 cup sugar

Core apples but do not pare. Cut in quarters or in eighths if apples are large. Fry out bacon, remove from pan, and cook apple pieces in the bacon fat until delicately browned. Only bacon fat gives the delicious flavor that distinguishes this dish. Arrange in flat, ovenproof dish, cover with sugar, and bake for about ten or fifteen minutes.

ARTICHOKE BOTTOMS STUFFED WITH GROUND ARTICHOKES

Mrs. John R. Peters, Jr.

2 lbs. ground artichokes
1 cup water
1 teaspoon salt
½ teaspoon pepper
8 cooked artichoke bottoms brushed
   with butter and sprinkled with salt
   and pepper
1 cup Hollandaise sauce
2 tablespoons butter

Peel and cook ground artichokes in salted water until tender. Drain, mash and season with butter, salt and pepper. Place artichoke bottoms in a baking dish and fill with mashed artichokes. Bake in 350° oven for 15 minutes until warm. Top each serving with Hollandaise sauce.

ARTICHOKE CASSEROLE

Mrs. Carl E. Woodward

2 packages frozen artichoke hearts
½ cup chopped celery
   several chopped shallots
1 can mushroom soup
1 can sliced B & B mushrooms
¾ stick of butter

Cook artichoke hearts as directed on package. Sauté sliced celery and shallots in butter. Add mushrooms, then soup. Last of all drained artichoke hearts. Stir gently, then put all in buttered casserole and cover with fresh bread crumbs. Bake in 350° oven until very hot—about 15 or 20 minutes.

FRENCH ARTICHOKES

1 artichoke for each serving
1 tablespoon each vinegar, salt
   Hollandaise sauce or drawn butter

Trim the sharp points of the leaves with scissors.

Wash well, place in cold water, adding vinegar to destroy possible insects.

Put the artichokes in a pot of boiling water seasoned with a teaspoon of salt. Let them boil gently, until you can draw out the leaves easily 'or until the outer leaves are tender.

Remove from the fire and drain placing them upside down, so that the water will run off. Serve hot, with drawn butter or with Hollandaise sauce. The time for boiling an artichoke varies with the vegetable, from 25 to 30 minutes.

Note: Before cooking artichokes, it is well always to soak them in cold water some two or three hours; it makes them more tender.

149

ARTICHOKE HEARTS AND ASPARAGUS
Flora M. Brill

1 can artichoke hearts
1 can asparagus tips
1 medium can sliced mushrooms, drained
1 cup grated sharp cheese
½ cup bread crumbs
cayenne and Lea & Perrins to taste

Butter 1 quart casserole. Put hearts in bottom in layer. Using a small cocktail fork, fan hearts out. Top with asparagus spears. Season soup with cayenne and Lea & Perrins, and pour over hearts and asparagus. Sprinkle over this ½ cup of the sharp cheese.
Now sprinkle over the sliced mushrooms. Sprinkle over this the bread crumbs and the remaining cheese. Bake at 350° until bubbly.

ARTICHOKE AND HAM CASSEROLE
Mrs. George Douglass, Sr.

4 tablespoons butter
4 tablespoons flour (all purpose)
2 cups warm milk
½ teaspoon seasoned salt
¼ teaspoon cayenne
¼ teaspoon white pepper
½ cup shredded Swiss cheese
½ cup Parmesan cheese
4 tablespoons dry sherry
2 - 1 lb. cans artichoke hearts
12 slices ham

Melt butter in saucepan over medium heat; blend in flour gradually. Stir in warm milk until smooth. Stir constantly until thick. Add seasoning, then cheese. Stir over low heat until melted. Remove from heat and add sherry. Cut hearts in half, and wrap 2 halves in a slice of ham. Arrange in a buttered casserole with sides touching. Pour sauce over all, and sprinkle with bread crumbs. Bake at 350° for about 30 minutes.

ARTICHOKE MOUSSE
Mrs. Lester Lautenschlager, Jr.

8 artichokes
4 packs gelatine
2/3 cup water

1½ cups consomme
1 cup mayonnaise
12 ozs. Philadelphia cream cheese (1 large and 1 small pack)
½ cup chopped chives
½ cup chopped white onions
1 cup whipping cream, whipped
1 tablespoon Worcestershire sauce
2 teaspoons Tabasco
3 drops green vegetable coloring
salt and white pepper to taste
Seasonings for cooking artichokes:
bay leaves, celery, onions, parsley lemons, 2 tablespoons salad oil, salt and pepper to taste.

To cook artichokes, place upright in 2" of boiling water seasoned with bay leaves, etc., listed. Cook covered for 1 hour or until leaves pull easily. Drain, scrape leaves and mash hearts. Put this through meat grinder if one is available.
Soften gelatine in cold water. Dissolve with hot consomme, then pour a small amount in bottom of a 12 cup ring mold. Let set in refrigerator until firm. Cut out decorative designs with carrots, green peppers and pimentoes and arrange in a pattern. Capers, tiny pickled onions and olives may also be used. Design is made directly on already firm gelatine in mold. Cover design with gelatine and chill until firm.
To mashed artichokes add remaining ingredients (also remaining dissolved gelatine which has been colored with green vegetable coloring). Mix well and pour on top of firm decorative layer and chill overnight. Unmold on serving dish and garnish with a bit of lettuce, chicory, cherry tomatoes and radish flowers. Place bowl of homemade mayonnaise in center.

ARTICHOKE RING
Mrs. Frank H. Lawton

4 artichokes, boil 15 to 25 minutes. Scrape off tender part including the hearts.
Put through meat grinder with small clove of garlic.

add ½ pt. cream
½ cup bread crumbs
4 eggs (whites beaten very stiff and folded in last)
salt and pepper to taste

Bake ¾ hour in moderate oven with mold in pan of water.

Creamed sweetbreads and mushrooms go well with this, also crabs or oysters.

STUFFED ARTICHOKES
Mrs. Gilbert Green
Through Mrs. Charles Green

6 artichokes
⅛ lb. butter
salt, pepper, red pepper
1 tablespoon cream
cracker crumbs

Use method for cooking artichokes from above recipe "French Artichokes." Let them cool, pull off all the leaves and scrape off the tender part at the bottom of the leaves. Mash well, add seasonings, butter and cream. Remove the hairy part in the heart of the artichoke and fill these hearts with the above which is shaped in a rounded form. Sprinkle with rolled cracker crumbs. Dot with butter. Brown in a hot oven with a medium white sauce poured over the hearts.

STUFFED ARTICHOKES
Mrs. Victor Nunes

4 artichokes (wash, cut off tip of stem and leaves and drain)
2 cups Italian style bread crumbs
1 cup grated Parmesan cheese
1 whole head garlic, minced (mash cloves through garlic press)
8 teaspoons olive oil
salt and pepper to taste
1 lemon sliced

Mix salt, pepper, bread crumbs, Italian cheese and garlic together. With teaspoon, stuff each leaf starting at bottom till filled. Saturate each artichoke with two teaspoons of olive oil. Top each artichoke with lemon slice and place on rack of pressure cooker. In bottom of pressure cooker add one cup of water, ¼ cup olive oil and left over lemon pieces. Pressure cook 15 minutes. Cool pot under water. Serve artichokes fingertip cool. Serves 4.

ARTICHOKES STUFFED WITH SWEETBREADS
Mrs. Hugh C. St. Paul

3 lbs. sweetbreads
6 large artichokes

Clean sweetbreads, removing skin, wash well, place in pot of salt water with the following seasoning: onion, sweet pepper, celery and black pepper. Boil until tender, drain and cut in small pieces.
Cut up more seasoning: onion, sweet pepper, celery—place in pot to brown. Add one can tomato paste, cook well. Add salt and pepper to taste, allow to cook together with sweetbreads until well done.
Boil artichokes—cool, trim stickers on leaves, hull out—trim bottom to set flat on plate.
When sweetbreads are done, fill artichokes, tie a string around each, place in colander over boiling water until ready to serve—remove string.

ASPARAGUS AMANDINE
Mrs. Killian L. Huger

Tie asparagus into bunches and place upright in tall container so that water will come up to 1 inch below tips. The water should be salted 1½ teaspoons to a quart of water. Time to cook depends on the size, usually 15 to 20 minutes. Serve with Amandine sauce or Bechamel sauce with toasted almonds added.

ASPARAGUS CASSEROLE
Mrs. Clifford Stem

1 large can asparagus
½ cup almonds blanched and chopped
1 can cream of mushroom soup
2 tablespoons grated cheese
buttered bread crumbs
salt and pepper to taste
a dash cayenne pepper

Heat mushroom soup—add cheese, seasoning and chopped almonds. Pour over layer of asparagus and cover with buttered bread crumbs, continue until all is used. Dust top with buttered bread crumbs. Place in oven and cook.
Baked ham and this dish followed by a light salad will make a delicious, satisfying meal.
(Use recipe for buttered bread crumbs.)

FRENCH FRIED ASPARAGUS
Mrs. Grace Stevenson

1 can of asparagus (or equivalent
  amount of fresh cooked)
2 tablespoons flour
2 tablespoons cream
1 egg
  salt, white pepper

Drain asparagus well, season with salt and pepper, and roll in batter made from rest of ingredients. Fry in oil at 380° until golden brown.

ASPARAGUS MOUSSE
Mrs. Harry A. Thompson

2 large cans asparagus
4 eggs
1 tablespoon flour
⅛ lb. butter, ½ cup milk
  salt, white pepper, to taste

Beat yolks and whites of eggs separately. Make custard in double boiler with flour, butter, milk and yolks of eggs with added juice of asparagus. When cooled, add whites of eggs and asparagus tips, put in greased mold and bake slowly with mold set in water.

BANANAS IN JACKETS
Mrs. J. N. Roussel

large, ripe bananas
biscuit dough, sugar

Peel the bananas. Roll dough thin. Cut off the ends of each banana, slantwise, and follow the slant in cutting each banana in two.
Roll each one in sugar, then cover with dough, as in a jacket. Bake in a moderate oven, and serve as a vegetable.

BANANAS, ORLÉANS CLUB
Mrs. Royal Bastian

six medium size bananas
3 tablespoons melted butter
1 tablespoon lemon juice
¼ teaspoon grated lemon rind
½ cup sugar syrup
¼ cup maraschino cherry juice
1/3 cup rum

Remove peel and place bananas in shallow baking dish. Mix sugar syrup, cherry juice, lemon juice, and rind and melted butter.

Pour over bananas and cook at 375° until fruit is tender. Remove from oven and pour rum over dish and serve. Makes 6 servings.

BAKED BEANS
Mrs. James Mulvaney

1 qt. marrow fat beans
1 lb. fat salt pork
3 medium sized onions, sliced thin
1 tablespoon molasses
3 tablespoons sugar
¼ tablespoon dry mustard
  pinch of ginger, salt

Soak the beans overnight in cold water to cover. In the morning drain, cover with fresh water and cook very slowly, adding the mustard, ginger, onions, salt and about ¼ of the pork. Cook very slowly testing from time to time by removing a few beans in a spoon and blowing on them. When the skins burst they are done. Scald the rind of the remaining pork and cut a ¼ inch slice from it. Lay it in the bottom of a "Boston Bean" pot. A deep earthenware casserole will do. Cut through rind of remaining pork every half inch making the cuts about one inch deep. Drain off any remaining water in which the beans have boiled and pour them in the pot. Bury the pork in the pot, leaving the rind exposed. Mix, in a cup or bowl, the molasses, sugar, and 1 tablespoon of salt, with a cup of boiling water. Stir well and pour over the beans.
Cover the pot and allow to cook very slowly for six to eight hours adding more water from time to time as needed. Uncover for the last hour to brown and crisp the pork rind. The secret of success with baked beans is in the long slow cooking, which is most easily attained by using the very heavy earthenware pots which are made for this purpose.

BAKED BARLEY & MUSHROOMS
Mrs. Fleur Hampton

½ cup chopped onion
6 tablespoons butter
½ cup uncooked barley
3 cups chicken broth
½ lb. sliced mushrooms
½ cup slivered almonds

Fry onions in 6 tablespoons of butter. Add uncooked barley and brown lightly. Pour in casserole with 1½ cups chicken broth (canned or homemade). Bake 30 minutes at 350°.

Add mushrooms which have been sauteed in butter. Add 1½ cups more chicken broth (will look runny).

Top with slivered almonds and cook about an hour or until liquid is absorbed. Serves 8.

This is nice instead of rice with chicken or turkey. It will also serve large crowds well. (3 cups barley to 7 cups of liquid will feed 50 people.)

BARBEQUED BEANS

Mr. Louis Perrilliat

2 large onions
2 stalks celery
½ medium size bell pepper
1 30-oz. can pork and beans
2 medium cloves garlic
3 pieces thick sliced bacon

Saute bacon, cut into 1 inch strips in deep iron pot. Add finely chopped vegetables and minced garlic. Saute until tender. Add beans, ½ cup barbeque sauce (Blue Plate), ¼ cup salad dressing (Wishbone, Italian), ¼ cup yellow mustard, ¼ cup honey or cane syrup. Then add dash thyme, bay leaf, oregano, cayenne, Lea & Perrins, Tabasco and chili powder. Simmer ½ hour, stirring regularly. Add liquid if necessary.

RED BEANS LOUISIANA STYLE

Mittie Williams

1 lb. of red beans
½ to 1 lb. salt meat, lean and fat
1½ qts. of water
3 onions, chopped
3 cloves of garlic, chopped
salt and pepper to taste

Wash the beans and soak them in cold water overnight.

Put the beans, onion, and garlic, in cold water, and cook them until the beans are tender; then add the meat that has been cooked (either fried or boiled) and cook it all slowly, stirring until throughly done. Do not add the salt until toward the end, as it may have the disastrous effect of toughening the beans. The beans must be tender. Some hot water may be added, if the beans have cooked down too much.

Serve this with "Boiled Rice, Créole Style," and everyone from the "field hand" who calls it "Raid bean'en Raice" to the lord of the plantation will be happy.

Sweet pickled meat or a slab of bacon may be used.

STRING BEANS WITH CORN

Mrs. Edwin T. Merrick III

1½ lbs. green or wax string beans
6 to 8 ears of fresh corn

Cook the beans until tender with a small piece of bacon or ham. Cut off the corn and add to the beans for the last ten minutes of cooking. Add butter.

ITALIAN STRING BEANS

Mrs. Robert Ruppel

3 1 lb. cans cut or whole string beans, drained
1 lb. can Progresso hearts of artichokes, drained
1 cup freshly grated Parmesan cheese
Italian style bread crumbs
salt and pepper to taste
1 cup olive oil

Gently fold string beans and artichoke hearts together with fork. Add Parmesan cheese gently lifting with fork as to not bruise vegetables. Sprinkle generously with bread crumbs. Evenly pour olive oil over mixture and bake at 350° - 400° for 20 minutes.

STRING BEANS WITH MUSHROOM SAUCE

Mrs. LaVergne Thomas, Jr.

1½ lbs. string beans (or two boxes, frozen)
1½ cans mushroom soup
1 can French fried onions

Boil the beans until tender. Drain and add them to the mushroom soup which has been heated but not diluted. Turn into a serving dish when very hot and sprinkle the French fried onions over the top.

PIQUANTE BEETS
Mrs. Mabel Goetter Godchaux

3 tablespoons minced onion
6 tablespoons butter or margarine
1½ teaspoons salt
1 tablespoon granulated sugar
¼ teaspoon powdered cloves
3 tablespoons vinegar
4 cups hot, sliced or diced beets

Sauté onion in butter in skillet until tender. Add next 4 ingredients; cook 5 minutes. Add beets, heat well. Serves six.

STUFFED BELL PEPPERS
Mrs. W. Elliott Laudeman III

6 bell peppers, large
1 lb. ground beef
1 lb. shrimp, peeled and deveined
½ lb. ham, diced
1 large onion, chopped
2 cloves garlic, minced
1 stalk celery, chopped
¼ bunch fresh parsley, finely chopped
½ teaspoon oregano flakes
½ teaspoon rosemary leaves
    pinch of thyme
3/4 cup sharp grated cheese
¼ cup fresh grated Parmesan
2 slightly beaten eggs
    bread crumbs
1 large can tomato sauce
    olive oil

Wash and cut bell peppers in half. Carefully remove seeds and membranes so as not to make any holes in outer shell. Parboil bell peppers for five minutes. Drain and set aside to cool.

Coat heavy iron skillet with olive oil and saute onions, garlic, celery, and parsley till onions are transparent. Add ground beef and shrimp and cook until beef is browned. Add ham, seasonings and salt and pepper to taste. Turn off heat.

Add cheeses and eggs, mix. Add bread crumbs until good stuffing consistency is obtained. Stuff mixture into bell pepper shells and sprinkle with bread crumbs.

Dilute one can of tomato sauce with 1½ cans of water. Salt and pepper tomato mixture. Place stuffed peppers into shallow baking container and pour tomato mixture on and around peppers. Bake in 350° oven for 30 - 35 minutes.

CRAYFISH STUFFED BELL PEPPER
Mrs. Gene Jefferson

1 lb. peeled crayfish tails
5 medium bell peppers (halved) with seeds and pulp removed
1 medium bell pepper, chopped
1 large onion, chopped
2 slices of dried bread, crumbled
1 container of crayfish fat (4 ozs.)
    salt and red pepper to taste

In saucepan, cover crayfish tails with water, season with salt and red pepper, cover and boil gently for 20 minutes. Drain, reserving stock. Parboil bell pepper shells for 5 minutes or less just to remove crispness for stuffing purposes.

Meanwhile, saute onions and chopped bell pepper in butter until onions are transparent. Add bread crumbs and container of crayfish fat. Slightly chop crayfish tails and add to mixture. Add crayfish stock until good stuffing consistency is obtained. Taste and season with additions 1 salt and red pepper as needed. Fill pepper shells with mixture and bake in preheated 350° oven for 30 - 45 minutes.

STUFFED CABBAGE
Mrs. J. N. Roussel

1 green cabbage
½ lb. boiled ham
2 tablespoons butter
1 onion
1 tablespoon salt

Select a loose leafed green cabbage. For stuffing used boiled ham chopped. Lightly broil ham in butter with chopped onion, salt and pepper. Carefully pull open the outer leaves of the cabbage and insert the stuffing. Tie in a clean cloth and boil.

CARROTS AU SUCRE
Mrs. Alfred Pattison

4 bunches young carrots
1½ to 2 tablespoons butter
1 cup sugar or to taste
1 saltspoon salt

Scrape carrots, cut into thin rounds. Put butter, carrots, sugar, and salt in heavy iron frying pan. Cover tightly and cook over slow fire until carrots are very tender, shaking pan every three or four minutes to prevent sticking to bottom. Serve hot. The time for cooking varies. It should take at least ¾ of an hour. Try to uncover pan as little as possible as the carrots are cooked by steam only. This is excellent.

CARROT RING
Mrs. Edward Rightor

2 cups boiled carrots
6 eggs, beaten separately
1 cup grated bread crumbs
1 teaspoon each onion juice, mustard
½ teaspoon paprika
1 pt. thin cream or top milk

Mash the carrots, add bread crumbs and seasoning, beat in the egg yolks and then fold in the stiffly beaten whites. Turn into a buttered ring mold, place in a pan of hot water. Cook thirty minutes.
Serve as a vegetable, or fill with crab or shrimp with mushroom sauce. The lowly carrot is glorified.

BAKED CAULIFLOWER
(HUNGARIAN KARJOL)
Mrs. Gerald Derks

1 large cauliflower
½ cup buttered bread crumbs
2 eggs, separated
2 cups sour cream
½ cup grated Parmesan cheese
1 cup ham, cubed

Lightly grease a 1½ qt. casserole. Remove leaves and cut off all the woody base of cauliflower. Trim off blemishes. Break into florets and soak in cold, salted water for 30 minutes.
Rinse cauliflower and cook until tender but still firm, about 20 minutes.
Mix together and set aside: bread crumbs, parmesan and 2 slightly beaten egg yolks. Beat two egg whites until peaks form. Salt sour cream to taste. Fold egg whites into sour cream.
Drain cauliflower. Arrange ½ on bottom of casserole. Spread cubed ham on top. Pour ½ sour cream sauce over ham. Arrange remaining cauliflower and add remaining sauce. Sprinkle crumb mixture over top and bake in 350° oven for 20 - 30 minutes,

or until top is lightly browned. Serves 6 to 8.

CAULIFLOWER
WITH SHRIMP SAUCE

1 cauliflower
1½ cups cream sauce
1 cup chopped shrimp
1 teaspoon Lea & Perrins Sauce
salt and pepper to taste

Remove outer leaves from cauliflower. Boil in salted water until tender. Drain. Prepare cream sauce, add chopped shrimp, Lea & Perrins, salt and pepper. Pour over cauliflower and serve.

CORN PUDDING

6 ears corn, grated
3 eggs, 1 cup milk
2 tablespoons butter
1 teaspoon each salt, flour
½ green pepper
¼ teaspoon baking powder

Cream butter well, then add the beaten yolks of eggs, the corn and the other ingredients, lastly the whites of eggs, beaten stiff. Bake slowly for thirty minutes. Green pepper may be omitted.
Grated American cheese may be added.

CORN PUDDING
Mrs. J. C. Greenoe
Vicksburg, Mississippi

1 stick butter
2 cans cream style corn
1 cup milk
½ cup flour
salt and pepper to taste

Melt butter in a pyrex baking dish. Combine all other ingredients in a mixing bowl and blend well. Pour in melted butter. Then pour mixture into the pyrex dish. Bake at 325° until firm.

QUICK CORN PUDDING
Mrs. Frank C. Moran, Jr.

2 cups cooked corn
    (canned white or yellow is fine)
2 eggs beaten

1 teaspoon sugar, salt, and pepper
2 cups scalded breakfast cream
1½ tablespoons melted butter

Heat oven to 325°. Combine all ingredients. Pour into greased 1½ quart casserole and bake for 1½ hours in a pan of water.

CORN SOUFFLÉ

Jimmy Plauché
Dunbar's Restaurant

Although not a true soufflé in the sense of the extremely light cheese soufflé, Dunbar's recipe for fresh corn makes a delightful summer vegetable as delicious as simple corn on the cob. This dish provides a new way to add a variety to hot weather meals.

4 large ears white corn
1/3 cup evaporated milk
¼ lb. butter, 1/3 cup sugar
2 tablespoons flour
2 teaspoons baking powder
1 egg, well beaten
cinnamon, red cherries

Clean corn and grate on coarse grater. Melt butter and sugar, add flour slowly, then cream. Now add egg and baking powder. Stir thoroughly. Pour in large buttered pyrex dish. Bake in 235° oven until brown. Glaze with butter, sprinkle with sugar and cinnamon. Garnish with red cherries. Serves 8.

CUCUMBER RING

2 cups grated cucumber
3 eggs
1 teaspoon each sugar, baking powder
1½ tablespoons flour
1½ cups milk
½ teaspoon black pepper
¾ teaspoon salt

Beat egg yolks until light. Add milk, cucumber and seasoning. Sift in flour and baking powder. Add stiffly beaten whites. Turn into a well buttered baking dish and place in moderate oven and cook until firm. Serve hot.

CUSHAW

Mrs. Guy Bruce Scoggin

Cushaw is in the pumpkin family. It is an old Louisiana dish. It is not terribly accessible, but delicious. Very good with fowl or game. It is sweet and served hot.

4 cups cubed cushaw
½ stick oleo, or vegetable shortening
2 cups sugar
½ teaspoon nutmeg
½ teaspoon cinnamon
pinch of salt

Cut a sizeable piece of cushaw, peel and remove seeds. Dice in 2 inch cubes; enough to make four cups.

Melt oleo in iron skillet. Put in cubes of cushaw; add a touch of water if necessary. Cover and steam cook until cushaw pieces will mash and mix into a semi-soft mush. Add sugar, nutmeg and cinnamon. Continue cooking over a LOW fire, or mixture will scorch. Cook about 1 hour, or until honey colored. (not too soft.)

CANDIED CUSHAW

Mrs. Leonard M. Levy

1 cushaw
¼ lb. butter
1½ cups sugar

Cut the neck of the cushaw into small rounds about ¼ inch thick (about eight rounds). Peel off the rind, place in a large long biscuit pan, cover with water, add butter and sugar, cook on top of the stove, carefully turning once with the pancake turner, until the syrup has thickened and they look crystallized. Serve as you would candied yams.

EGGPLANT À L'OLIN

Mr. and Mrs. Olin Downes

8 1-inch slices eggplant
2 cups finely chopped leftover steak or roast beef with gravy
1 cup grated Parmesan or sharp cheddar cheese
mustard, flour, lard and butter
salt and pepper to taste

Peel eggplant and slice in one inch thick slices. Press eggplant slices under weight for 2 hours to remove the bitter juices. Dredge in flour and fry in mixture of ½ lard and ½ butter until brown and tender.

Heat chopped roast beef or steak in

its own gravy.

Arrange eggplant slices in shallow baking dish. Cover slices of eggplant with meat and gravy mixture. Spread thin layer of mustard over meat and then cover with thick layer of grated cheese. Season with salt and pepper. Place under low flame of broiler until cheese melts. Serve hot.

EGGPLANT CASSEROLE

Mrs. W. Elliott Laudeman III

1 large eggplant
½ lb. ground or finely diced ham
1 pt. fresh mushrooms, sliced
1 small bell pepper
2 ribs celery
1 large onion, chopped
1 toe garlic, minced
1 tablespoon grated Parmesan cheese
½ stick butter
2 small cans of chopped black
    olives (about 4 ozs.)
1 cup sharp cheese, grated
2 teaspoons Lea & Perrins sauce
½ teaspoon Tabasco
  salt and pepper to taste
  cracker crumbs

Peel and cut up eggplant. Steam in salted water over low heat until tender and mashable. Saute celery, onions, garlic and bell pepper in butter till onions are transparent. Add ham and cook five minutes more. Add mushrooms and coat with butter. Add seasonings, cheeses and olives. Mix well.

Pour into oven-proof casserole bowl. Cover with cracker crumbs, and dot with butter. Bake in 350° oven for 35 minutes until crumbs are lightly browned.

EGGPLANT WITH CRABMEAT
CHEESE TOPPING

Mrs. Joseph Merrick Jones, Jr.

8 one-inch peeled slices eggplant
½ cup oil
1 stick butter
1 cup chopped onions
2 cloves garlic, minced
1 teaspoon thyme
1 teaspoon crushed bay leaf
2 tablespoons chopped parsley
½ - 1 cup bread crumbs
1 lb. lump crabmeat
1 cup grated Parmesan cheese

Lightly sprinkle eggplant slices with salt and pepper. Pour over oil and broil about 10 minutes.

Put butter in saucepan, add onions and simmer 5 minutes. Add garlic and tomatoes and simmer 5 minutes more. Add thyme, bay leaf, parsley and salt and pepper to taste. Simmer 2 minutes. Add bread crumbs and crab meat, fold in gently. Divide mixture evenly on top of eggplant slices. Top with cheese. Broil 2 minutes.

EGGPLANT FARCIS

Mrs. M. C. Maury-Lyons

2 very large eggplants
4 onions, medium sized
1 can tomatoes
3 dozen oysters, 2 tablespoons butter
  bread crumbs
  cooked spaghetti
  salt, pepper

Cut off the stem part of each eggplant so that they may stand lengthwise. Cut off the other end more deeply and carefully scoop out the inside.

Brown the onions in butter, add the tomatoes and sauté the scraped out eggplant with seasonings.

Mix in the boiled spaghetti, then the oysters, and let it cook a few minutes more. Stuff the eggplants with this, sprinkle the bread crumbs thickly on top. Dot with butter, and run them in the oven until the bread crumbs brown.

It is a pretty sight for the table, and a savory taste for the palate. With a salad, and this, a luncheon or a Sunday night supper is complete.

EGGPLANT SOUFFLÉ

Mrs. S. A. Fortier

1 eggplant
2 tablespoons butter
2 teaspoons flour
1 cup milk
½ cup grated cheese
¾ cup soft bread crumbs
2 teaspoons onion, grated
1 tablespoon tomato catsup
2 eggs, 1 teaspoon salt

Peel the eggplant, dice and cook until tender, then mash well. Melt the butter, in a saucepan, stir in the flour slowly till smooth, then add the milk, stirring till smooth and thick. Add the mashed eggplant, cheese, bread crumbs, onion, catsup, salt and the lightly beaten egg yolks. Lastly fold in the stiffly beaten whites. Bake in a greased baking-pan set in a pan of hot water in a moderate oven, about 30 minutes.

Here you have an old New Orleans standby.

EGGPLANT SOUFFLÉ

Mrs. Furman B. Pearce

    1 medium sized eggplant
    1 or 2 onions
    2 eggs
    ¾ cup cracker crumbs
    1/3 cup milk
    1 teaspoon sugar (optional)
    1 tablespoon butter

Peel and slice eggplant, cut onion. Put eggplant, onion, salt, and pepper in boiler. Add ½ cup water and boil until tender; about 30 min. Pour off excess water, mash vegetables, and then add eggs (which have been beaten slightly), melted butter and add other ingredients. Put in buttered casserole, sprinkle top with bread crumbs and place in oven at 350° temperature. After soufflé rises, place two strips of bacon over top, and return to oven. Cooking time about 20-25 minutes.

EGGPLANT-TOMATO WITH CHEESE SAUCE

Mrs. V. L. Gaston

Peel an eggplant and cut in half inch slices; soak in salt water for half hour then dry, dip in egg and bread crumbs and fry until done. Have tomatoes sliced, sprinkle with salt, pepper and a little sugar; dip in flour and fry in butter. When both are done serve eggplant with a slice of tomato on top and pour over cheese sauce.

Cheese sauce:
    2 tablespoons each butter, flour
    1 cup milk
    ½ cup grated sharp cheese
    salt and pepper to taste

Melt butter and add flour, gradually, add milk and stir until mixture boils and thickens; cook about three minutes and then add grated sharp cheese, cook, add salt and pepper to taste.

This may be served on a slice of ham or topped with a slice of broiled bacon.

MIRLITON FARCI

(Stuffed Mirliton)

Jimmy Plauche
Dunbar's Restaurant

The mirliton is a variety of summer squash found almost exclusively in Louisiana. The vine grows easily in back yards. Although a small portion of stuffed mirliton is used as one of several vegetables at a Dunbar dinner, the old-time Creoles made stuffed mirliton the main dish.

    4 mirlitons
    ½ lb. ham finely ground
    1 lb. shrimp boiled and ground
    1 small onion (ground)
    2 sprigs thyme, 2 bay leaves
    1 tablespoon chopped parsley
    salt and pepper to taste
    ½ loaf stale French bread
    ¼ lb. butter
    garnish: pimento strip, parsley sprig

Wash mirlitons well, parboil till tender, halve, scoop out center and save shells. Mash pulp, place in skillet with melted butter. Add ham, shrimp and seasonings. Simmer 20 minutes. Soak bread and press dry. Add to mixture. Add salt and pepper. Cook 10 minutes over low flame, stirring constantly. Fill shells with stuffing, sprinkle with bread crumbs, dot with butter. Bake at 375° in oven. Garnish and serve.

STUFFED MIRLITONS

Mrs. W. Elliott Laudeman III

    6 mirlitons
    ½ lb. ham, finely chopped
    1½ lbs. shrimp (peel and devein)
    1 large onion chopped
    2 cloves garlic, minced
    1 rib celery, finely chopped
    2 tablespoons parsley flakes
    3 shallots, finely chopped
    1 cup grated sharp cheese
    ½ teaspoon thyme
    salt and pepper to taste
    bread crumbs
    1 stick butter
    dash of Lea & Perrins and Tabasco

Select smooth skinned mirlitons, not ones with tough and prickly skins.

Wash mirlitons well and cook in boiling water till tender. Cut in halves and carefully scoop out pulp so as not to tear outer surface. Mash pulp and set aside.

Saute onions, parsley, celery, garlic and shallots in butter. Add peeled shrimp and ham and cook till shrimp turn pink. Add mashed mirliton pulp, cheese and seasonings. Stuff mirlitons with mixture, top with bread crumbs. Dot with butter and bake in 375° oven till crumbs brown.

MIRLITON, STUFFED

Olga Petit

3 mirlitons
1 large green pepper, chopped
1 large onion, chopped
½ cup chopped parsley
½ cup shallots, chopped
1 clove garlic, minced
1 lb. chopped raw shrimp
3 or 4 slices bread
1 cup bread crumbs
    salt, pepper, fat

Boil mirliton. Scoop out inside. Fry onion, green pepper on slow fire. Add shrimp. Fry 5 minutes. Add scooped out mirliton. Wet 3 or 4 slices of bread and squeeze out. Add this to mirliton, onions, pepper. Add parsley, garlic and green onion, salt and pepper. Fry on slow fire and stir frequently for 25 minutes. Put mixture in shells of mirliton. Put bread crumbs on top. Dot with butter. Bake in 400 degree oven for 10 minutes until brown.

STUFFED MUSHROOMS

Mrs. E. B. Ludwig

1 lb. ground sirloin steak
2 tablespoons minced onion
1 large can large mushroom buttons
    dash of thyme and marjoram
    butter

Mix meat, onions, and seasonings. Fill mushroom buttons and dab each with a piece of butter. Broil under low heat until brown.

STUFFED MUSHROOMS

Mrs. James Selman

8 huge mushrooms, stems removed and reserved

1 stick butter (another ½ stick also
    for sauteeing the stuffing)
juice of ½ lemon
salt and pepper

In large skillet melt butter and add juice of ½ lemon. Swish salted and peppered mushroom caps in this and place in buttered casserole.

Add the other ½ stick butter to the same pan that the mushrooms have been slightly cooked in, and saute in this the finely chopped stems of the mushrooms. Add ½ cup of Italian style bread crumbs. Combine well and cook 5 minutes longer, adding salt, pepper and Tabasco to taste. Pack stuffing in the caps and squeeze some lemon juice over them. When ready to serve, bake in 325° oven until caps are cooked and the stuffing is golden. (around ½ hour.)

MUSHROOMS STUFFED WITH BRAZIL NUTS

Mrs. Paul B. Lansing

1½ lbs. large mushrooms
¼ cup butter
1 onion, chopped
1 cup soft bread crumbs
1 cup chopped or ground brazil nuts
1 teaspoon salt, pepper to taste
1 tablespoon tomato ketchup
1 tablespoon lemon juice
½ cup cream

Wash mushrooms and remove stems. Chop stems fine. Melt butter and saute onions and mushroom stems for five minutes. Stir in bread crumbs and brazil nuts. Cook two minutes and stir in seasonings. Stuff mushrooms and put into oven-proof platter, garnishing with narrow strips of bacon (1/3" wide) by criss-crossing strips over mushrooms. Pour cream around and bake in hot oven (400°) for 25 minutes.

Serves 6. Great as a side dish to a main course.

OKRA, CORN AND TOMATOES

Mrs. Joseph Merrick Jones, Jr.

4 packs of frozen okra or 3 lbs.
    fresh sliced
1 lb. bacon
2 packs frozen shoe peg corn

8 - 10 tomatoes fresh
2 onions, chopped
4 toes garlic, minced
2 bay leaves
1 teaspoon thyme
1 teaspoon basil
   salt and pepper to taste

Cook bacon. Remove from pan and chop coarsely. In bacon grease, saute okra and onions until okra loses ropiness. Chop tomatoes and reserve juices. Add remaining ingredients to pan, including chopped bacon and tomatoes plus juices. Simmer 30 minutes. If too thick, add a little water.

FRENCH FRIED ONIONS
Mrs. Hunter Leake

1 large Bermuda onion
1 pt. milk
   thin batter

Slice onion, soak an hour in milk. Drain and dry. Dip in thin batter as for batter cakes and fry a light brown. Very delicious with steaks or any kind of meat. This will serve 5 or 6 people.

ONION PIE
Mrs. Charles H. Behre, Sr.

2 cups white onions, chopped
4 tablespoons vegetable oil
1 or 1½ cups sour cream
4 eggs, beaten
   salt, pastry, bacon

Make a plain pastry for a bottom crust only. Bake. Cook onions until soft with vegetable oil. Do not brown. Add salt. Remove from fire. When cool add sour cream and eggs and fill pie shell. Bake in moderate oven. When firm remove. Sprinkle top with bits of bacon. Replace in oven until bacon crisps and pie is a light brown.

NEW PEAS
Mrs. Alfred T. Pattison

1 tablespoon sugar
1 qt. shelled peas
1 cup diced raw ham, with fat
10 hearts of shallots
1 cup cold water

Put all the ingredients together in a pot and allow them to simmer very slowly three quarters of an hour or an hour. Shake from time to time to prevent burning.

FRIED PLANTAINS

2 plantains, ripe
4 to 6 tablespoons sugar
1 stick butter

Select very ripe plantains, peel and slice lengthwise. Fry them slowly in butter or other fat until nicely browned. Remove them to a hot platter and dust with sugar. Add a few tablespoons of sugar to the fat left in the pan and just a little water, about half a cup. Pour the remaining syrup over the plantains. (Brown sugar is preferred by some.) Serves 4 - 6.

FRIEND PLANTAINS
Terry Flettrich

Let plantains ripen fully (skin black). Cut in half crosswise, then slice lengthwise in pieces ¼" to ½" thick. Melt in skillet enough shortening to cover bottom of pan about ¼" deep. Brown plantain slices slowly so as to cook all the way through. Sprinkle granulated sugar on plate, place plantain slices on plate and sprinkle lightly with sugar. Cover with another plate and allow to set over mild heat at back of stove to steam slightly for about ½ hour. As a dessert, served warm. Good with a meat course, too!

DUCHESSE POTATOES
Mrs. J. N. Roussel

3 cups mashed potatoes
1 egg
1 teaspoon baking powder
1 tablespoon butter
   lard

The potatoes should be well seasoned with salt and pepper. Add to them the beaten egg, the butter and the baking powder. Drop a heaping teaspoonful at a time, in deep boiling fat. A small, crisp, fluffy bouché results.

RAW POTATO PANCAKES
Mr. Philip Holland

Peel and soak for several hours in cold water 6 large potatoes. Dry them with a cloth. Grate or put through a grinder. Put the potato pulp into a piece of cheesecloth and press out the excess water. Place the pulp in a mixing bowl and add:

    3 beaten eggs
    1 teaspoon each sugar, salt
    2 tablespoons flour or fine bread
        crumbs
    ⅛ teaspoon baking powder
    2 tablespoons milk

Sauté the batter in hot fat; turn cakes when brown to the other side. Serve hot with apple sauce, brown sauce or gravy.

POTATO PUFF
Mrs. William Perry Craddock

    2 cups hot mashed potatoes
    ½ cup hot milk
    2 eggs, 2 tablespoons butter
        salt, pepper to taste

Add the beaten egg yolks to the potatoes, milk, butter and seasonings. Mix well, then fold in the egg whites beaten stiff.
Place in buttered baking dish and bake until light brown.

SWEET POTATO SOUFFLÉ
Mrs. Joseph Merrick Jones, Jr.

    1 large can Trappey's Yams, with
        juice (30 ozs.)
    1 bag chopped pecans, 2½ ozs.
    1 stick butter
    1 tablespoon bourbon
    3 eggs, well beaten
    1½ cups miniature marshmallows
    ¼ teaspoon each cinnamon, nutmeg

Melt butter. Remove from heat and add yams and juice. Mash by hand with a potato masher. Stir in beaten eggs, pecans, bourbon. Top with marshmallows and bake in 350° oven for 45 minutes or until set. (If you add the marshmallows in the beginning of the cooking period, they melt down into the casserole, which I like best. It does look prettier if you add them during the last 15 minutes of cooking, then they puff and brown.)

SOUFFLÉES POTATOES AU CORDON BLEU DE PARIS
Mrs. J. N. Roussel

Take large firm potatoes. Wipe them off and peel them. Wipe them again,

to keep them dry. Slice them evenly, about ⅛ inch thick. Dry each slice in a towel. Have two large pots of kidney beef lard, the deeper pot very hot, but not boiling. Drop one slice in this; if the lard does not bubble, it is not hot enough. When it is hotter, put in potatoes, moving them about constantly for about four minutes. Then drop a cupful at a time into boiling fat in the second pot. Leave them in till they are puffed (soufflées), which occurs very soon. Remove from the fire and set aside, to keep warm while others cook. Add salt.

POTATOES STRATA
(Ground potatoes and cheese)
Mrs. Julius L. Perlt

    6 medium Irish potatoes, ground
        grated cheddar cheese
        cream
        salt and pepper to taste

In a buttered baking dish layer potatoes, grated cheese, salt and pepper. Repeat layers ending with cheese. Pour enough cream over layers to almost reach top of casserole. Do not fill too full or it will boil over. Bake in 350° oven until the casserole is hot, then lower heat to 250° and bake 3 hours.

SWEET POTATO BALLS
Mrs. Anne Harbison

Mash sweet potatoes as you would white potatoes. Mold around marshmallows. Fry in deep Crisco the same as fritters.

SWEET POTATOES EN CASSEROLE

    3 large sweet potatoes
    24 marshmallows
        brown sugar
        sliced canned pineapple
        salt

Select large sweet potatoes of uniform size, the diameters of which correspond to that of pineapple. Wash potatoes thoroughly and boil until tender in boiling salted water (½ teaspoon salt to 1 pint of water). Remove, cool and peel potatoes. Slice in half-inch slices and place a layer in a buttered casserole. Then place over them alternate layers of pineapple, brown sugar and potato until all ingredients are used up. Add ½ cup of pineapple juice. Bake in a moderate oven until the whole is flavored throughout and candied. Top with marshmallows and run in the oven to brown.

PLANTATION SWEET POTATO PUDDING

6 medium sweet potatoes
1 teaspoon each of nutmeg and cinnamon
1 tablespoon butter
1 cup dark molasses
1 cup sugar
3 eggs, well beaten

Pare sweet potatoes and grate them. Mix in remaining ingredients and bake in a buttered dish for an hour in a slow oven.
This is delicious with roast pork.

BOILED RICE, CRÉOLE STYLE

Boiled rice makes its daily appearance on southern tables with as great regularity as the boiled Irish potato appears in other parts of the country. Perfectly dry, every grain separate and thoroughly cooked with its delicious nutty flavor, it is entirely different from the sticky glutinous mass which horrifies the wanderer north of the Mason and Dixon line. The proper preparation is very simple and two methods are here described:

1½ cups whole grain rice
½ teaspoon salt

Have a large pot full of briskly boiling water. Add the rice slowly so as not to arrest the boiling. Stir as little as possible. When the water begins to thicken and the grains to soften remove from the fire, drain water off through a colander and pour cold water over it, then place the colander over another pot containing boiling water. Allow to steam thus for an hour or so.

OR

1 cup rice to each cup cold water
½ teaspoon salt
1 level teaspoon lard

Put all on to cook in a double boiler for an hour or longer. Every bit of water will be absorbed and the lard has the magical effect of keeping each grain separate.

CAJUN RICE
Mrs. Victor H. Schiro

The following recipe is the more virile Cajun cousin from Louisiana, often called "Dirty Rice" due to the dark giblet addition.

2 cups of rice, cooked
2 lbs. raw chicken giblets
2 cups chopped onions
2 cups chopped celery
1 quart water
⅓ cup cooking oil
3 tablespoons flour
½ cup chopped green onion tops and parsley
salt, black pepper and cayenne (red) pepper

Season giblets generously with salt, black pepper and red pepper. Boil slowly in water until tender (about ½ hour).
Make roux by browning the flour in the oil until very brown. Add onions and celery and cook in uncovered heavy iron pot over medium heat until onions are wilted.
Remove giblets from broth and chop fine or grind. Pour minced giblets and broth into roux. Cook until mixture is consistency of thick gravy. Add cooked rice, green onions and parsley.
Serves 8.

CAROLINA CURRIED RICE
Mrs. Victor H. Schiro

Rice dishes have long been favorites in my family; perhaps because a South Carolina ancestor, Dr. Henry Woodward, in 1685 planted the first rice in America at Charles Towne.

2 cups rice
2 tablespoons curry powder
1 teaspoon salt
2 cups chicken stock

Make stock by boiling 1 pound of chicken odds and ends, minced celery, onions and a bay leaf in enough water to make two cups strained stock. To stock add rice, curry and salt. Cook until dry and fluffy. Add bits of chicken meat and serve.

DIRTY RICE
Terry Flettrich

It's not really dirty at all. It's very rich and could easily be a meal in itself when combined with a crisp green salad. Up and down Bayou Lafourche you'll get modifications of this basic Cajun recipe which was given to me by the cook at the Cafeteria of the Thibodaux High School.

2 tablespoons fat
4 tablespoons flour (level)
2 medium chopped onions
1 large pod pressed garlic
1 cup chopped celery
  cooked rice
½ lb. ground beef
½ lb. ground pork (lean)
1 lb. raw chicken giblets
  few dashes of Tabasco and
  Worcestershire
  salt, black and red pepper to taste

Cook fat and flour over medium heat until flour is well browned, stirring constantly. Add onion, green pepper and celery and cook until slightly wilted. Add ground meat and giblets, cook over medium-high heat until meat is cooked through and slightly browned. Add enough water, in which a bouillon cube has been dissolved, to make the mixture the consistency of a thick gravy. Add the garlic (by squeezing through a garlic press) and a few dashes of Worcestershire and Tabasco and season to taste with salt and red and black pepper. Let this cook slowly for about 30 minutes, to let the seasonings blend but do not allow the mixture to become too thick or "dehydrated." Mix this with cooked rice, this amount should be just about enough for 2 cups of raw rice which has been cooked. Individual tastes will vary, so make the mixture to suit your own taste.

LAS VEGAS RICE
Mrs. Edwin W. Edwards

1 stick margarine
2 cups raw rice
1 medium onion, chopped
1 teaspoon salt
4 cups water
1 can ripe olives, chopped

Melt margarine. Add rice, cook over medium heat until rice begins to brown. Add chopped onions. Continue to cook until rice is very brown, about 20 minutes after onions have been added. Add water and salt, boil until water has almost evaporated and is just bubbling on top of rice. Cover and reduce heat. Simmer about one hour, or until thoroughly cooked.

When ready to serve, add chopped ripe olives. Serve immediately.

LOU'S DIRTY RICE
Mrs. Lou Leathem

1½ cups rice
1½ lbs. ground meat (1 lb. chuck; ½ lb.
  ground round)
3 tablespoons shortening
4 sets giblets (livers, hearts and
  gizzards)
4 cups water
1 large onion
2 toes garlic
2 cups celery
3 tablespoons parsley
3 tablespoons green onions
  dash cayenne pepper

Cook rice in usual manner. Set aside. Boil giblets in 4 cups water until tender, approximately 30 minutes. Chop giblets fine; reserve broth they were cooked in.

Saute in shortening the ground meat and ground chuck. When partially done, add the onions, garlic, celery and green onions. Cook this mixture until done, then add the reserved broth, parsley and cayenne.

Mix in chopped giblets and cooked rice. Keep warm over low heat.

RICE OCTAVIE
Mr. Claiborne Perrilliat

1. 2 cups rice boiled in salted water to taste.
2. Steam in colander covered with paper napkins until grains are separated.
3. Sauté one cup finely chopped shallots, ½ cup parsley and ½ cup water cress in stick of butter.

When seasoning begins to wilt, add ½ crumpled bay leaf and 2 cups coarsely chopped celery; allow to simmer and stir in rice.

Do not overcook celery as it should remain crisp.

SPOON BREAD RICE
Mrs. L. P. Le Bourgeois

Combine in the order given, then stir until well blended.

1 cup boiled rice
¼ cup corn meal
2 cups sour milk
½ teaspoon soda
1 teaspoon salt
2 eggs, beaten
2 tablespoons melted fat or butter

Place the batter in a greased ovenproof dish. Bake in a 325° oven for about 1 hour, until it has a light brown crust on top.

WILD RICE
Mrs. Dora Harris Jackson

Boil 1 lb. box of rice according to the directions -- set aside. Cook 1 lb. bacon, crumple, set aside.
In Dutch oven saute until soft:

1 stick of butter
2 cups finely chopped shallots
  (lot of green ends)
2 cups finely chopped celery
Add:

2 teaspoons of salt
3 tablespoons Lea & Perrins
2 tablespoons bacon drippings
1 cup minced fresh parsley
  Tabasco to taste
8 tablespoons grated onion juice

Combine the seasonings, rice, and crumbled bacon in the Dutch oven -- mix well -- heat.
Always make this a day or two ahead of using. It freezes beautifully. Same recipe may be used with Uncle Ben's long grain and wild rice -- delicious.

SPINACH "AU BAIN MARIE"

3 bunches spinach
1 teaspoon salt
1 kitchen spoon butter
½ lemon
2 egg yolks
½ lb. mushrooms

Mash boiled spinach in an earthenware bowl with melted butter and lemon juice. When cool add well beaten egg yolks and pour into a buttered mold. Place in another pan containing water and cook for thirty minutes in a moderate oven. Turn out on a hot platter and fill the center with broiled mushrooms.

SPINACH AU GRATIN
Miss Hélène Villeré

6 bunches spinach, cream sauce
½ lb. cheese
  hard-boiled eggs
  bread crumbs, salt

Pluck the veins and stems thoroughly from the spinach, boil it in a minimum of water, then press it through a colander and whip it well.
Dissolve the cheese in the cream sauce. In a baking dish, put a layer of spinach, then a layer of the sliced hard-boiled eggs, then a layer of sauce. Repeat until the dish is filled. Top with bread crumbs, dotted with butter, and bake.

SPINACH CASSEROLE

Make 1 to 1½ cups cheese sauce and add sauteed fresh mushrooms. Season well with Lea and Perrins and a couple of dashes of Tabasco and salt. Cook and drain well 2 or 3 packages of frozen chopped spinach or an equal amount of fresh spinach (chopped). Mix sauce with spinach and pour into well-buttered casserole dish. Sprinkle top with bread crumbs, Parmesan cheese and paprika. Bake at 350° for about 30 minutes or until bubbly and brown on top. This amount serves four to six people. Other vegetables such as broccoli or cauliflower may be used for this.

SPINACH CASSEROLE
Mrs. John V. Baus

2 packages frozen spinach, chopped
1 8-oz. package of Philadelphia cream cheese
1 stick butter divided in half
1 cup Pepperidge Farm Herb dressing
  salt and cayenne to taste

Cook spinach according to directions on package. Drain and add Philadelphia Cream Cheese and ½ stick of butter. Mix well and season with salt and pepper. Put spinach in casserole and cover with Herb dressing to form a top crust. Pour on the melted butter. Bake in moderate oven 20 to 30 minutes, until thoroughly hot.

CREOLE SPINACH
Mrs. William Westerfield

3 packages chopped frozen spinach, or
    equivalent in fresh
1½ cups heavy cream
½ teaspoon nutmeg
1 table spoon garlic salt
4 tablespoons butter

Have water boiling. Put in spinach;
cook only 2 - 4 minutes. Drain. Put
spinach in the frying pan with the
butter and cream. Cook slowly for five
minutes. Add garlic salt and nutmeg.
(If too thin, dust with a little flour,
and stir.)

SPINACH PUDDING
Mrs. Charles H. Behre

1 cup cooked spinach
2 cups cooked chopped pork
3 slices white bread, soaked in milk
    and squeezed dry
4 whole eggs
  salt and pepper

This is an excellent way to use left-
overs. Mix all ingredients together
thoroughly in a large bowl. Grease a
mold and pack, leaving about an inch
for expansion. Place in a large pot of
boiling water and keep boiling slowly
about an hour and a half. This can
also be cooked in a double boiler,
greasing it well before filling. Turn
out on a hot platter. Garnish with
small boiled new potatoes and slices
of broiled tomatoes.

SOUFFLÉ AUX EPINARDS
Mrs. Olivier P. Billion

2 cups cooked spinach (chopped fine)
1½ cups of milk
4 tablespoons butter
3 tablespoons flour
3 eggs, salt, pepper to taste

Make cream sauce with flour and
milk, add yolks of eggs, beaten. Season and add spinach. Fold in stiffly
beaten egg whites. Put in baking dish,
set in pan of hot water, bake in moderate oven about one hour. Serve with
Hollandaise sauce or cook in ring and
fill with creamed scallops or any kind
of fish.

SPINACH STUFFED SQUASH
Mrs. Matt G. Smith

3 pounds fresh spinach
    (or 3 packages frozen)
  head of lettuce
  tops from 3 bunches of
    green onions
1 pound butter
10 little summer squash
    (the orange gourd shaped ones)

Grind first three ingredients in
blender. Melt butter in Dutch oven,
add ground ingredients and bread
crumbs enough to make stuffing consistency. Season with Worcestershire
sauce, Tabasco (hot sauce), lemon
juice, salt and pepper, and a teaspoon
of Absinthe. Gently pile this mixture
into shells of squash, which have been
steamed or boiled and then halved
and scooped out. Heat in oven before
serving. Serves 8-10.

SPINACH WITH ARTICHOKES
Mrs. James Selman

3 boxes frozen chopped spinach
½ cup green onions, chopped
1 teaspoon salt
¼ cup bacon grease
1 cup cream sauce
8 freshly cooked artichoke hearts,
    cleaned
  all scrapings from the leaves
1½ cups Hollandaise sauce
½ stick melted butter

In heavy saucepan saute the onion
in the bacon grease. Add spinach and
salt and cover. Cook slowly over low
heat until spinach is tender. Drain
well, reserve spinach juice.
Make the cream sauce, using all of
the spinach juice; supplement enough
cream or milk to make 1 cup. Combine cooked spinach with the cream
sauce, set aside.
Saute artichoke scrapings with the ½
stick butter; add this to the spinach
mixture.
Arrange artichoke hearts in a buttered casserole. Cover with the spinach
mixture. Cover all of this with the
Hollandaise sauce. When ready to
serve, bake in moderate oven (350°)
until hot and bubbly. Serves 8.

SQUASH CASSEROLE
WITH SHRIMP
Mrs. Rosie Farvre

6 lbs. squash
¼ cup bacon grease
1 cup chopped onion
¾ cup chopped bell pepper
1 cup chopped celery
1 cup chopped green onions
3-4 garlic cloves
2 lbs. shrimp, boiled
1/3 cup bread crumbs
  butter

Wash squash and slice. Melt bacon grease in a Dutch oven and add squash, onion, bell pepper, celery, green onion and garlic. Cook over medium-hot fire until excess water evaporates, stirring occasionally. Season with salt, black pepper and cayenne. Add shrimp and put it all into a casserole. Top with bread crumbs, dot with butter, and bake until browned in a 400° oven.
Serves 8 - 10.

TOMATOES À LA CRÉOLE*
Mrs. W. J. Bentley

1 large green pepper, chopped
1 small onion, chopped
3 large tomatoes
  salt, pepper, butter

Sauce:

¼ cup each milk, cream
1 tablespoon each flour, butter
  rounds of toast
  salt, pepper

Pare the tomatoes and cut them in two. Put them in baking tin, covering each one with a layer of chopped onions and peppers. Dot liberally with bits of butter, salt, and pepper. Bake about ½ hour, in a hot oven. Remove from the fire and keep hot.
The sauce: To the liquor in the pan, add the milk and cream. Rub the flour and butter together, and stir them in with the other ingredients, and add the salt and pepper. When the mixture thickens, remove it from the fire. Put the tomatoes on the rounds of buttered toast, and pour the cream sauce over all.

* All tomatoes grown in New Orleans or vicinity are known as Créole tomatoes.

TOMATOES FELECIE
Mr. Claiborne Perrilliat

1. Slice tops and bottoms of 4 firm tomatoes and place in shallow terra cotta or pyrex baking dish which has been buttered.
2. Scrape leaves of 4 boiled artichokes and dice hearts, after removing chokes. Sauté hearts and parts of leaves in generous portion of olive oil, adding thyme, one half crumpled bay leaf, and one pod crushed garlic. Salt and pepper to taste.
3. Place generous portion of artichoke mix on tomatoes and cover with Parmesan cheese, freshly grated.
4. Add one cup imported vermouth to baking dish and place in 400° oven until cheese is lightly brown.
Bless and serve.

TOMATOES L'AIGRE-DOUCES
Mrs. William J. Nolan

4 large, ripe, firm tomatoes
1 teaspoon each sugar, lard
1 clove garlic, minced
1 teaspoon parsley, minced
1 tablespoon vinegar
2 tablespoons olive oil
½ teaspoon salt

Cut the tomatoes in half. Place the cut centers flat into a skillet in which the lard is already hot. Let fry a few minutes until light brown. Then turn them over to have the centers up. Add seasoning, and allow to simmer on the back of the stove until tender. If any are left over, they may be set away to reappear in a Spanish omelet the next day.

STUFFED TOMATOES
Mrs. Van Norman J. Bailey

6 large Créole tomatoes
12 strips bacon
1 loaf French bread (day old)
1 large yellow onion
2 or 3 stalks celery
2 cloves of garlic, through press
1 tablespoon finely cut parsley
1 pt. can tomatoes
½ stick oleo or butter
  bread crumbs
  salt and pepper to taste

Fry bacon crisp and drain. Remove centers of tomatoes cutting away hard parts and place in a mixing bowl. Add broken up pieces of French bread and the can of whole tomatoes. Tenderize onions celery, parsley, and garlic in a bit of left over bacon fat. Next all ingredients go into a heavy Dutch oven type pot, except 6 pieces of bacon. All bacon is to be crumbled. Cook entire mixture over slow fire about one hour or until dry enough to handle. Stuff into tomato shells. Sprinkle with bread crumbs and bacon, place in a shallow pan with a small amount of water and bake about 30 minutes at 350 degree oven and Voila! It's ready.

TOMATOES STUFFED WITH CHEESE

Mrs. Joseph Merrick Jones, Jr.

6 tomatoes
3 cups grated sharp cheddar cheese
4 shallots, chopped
½ - 1 teaspoon cayenne
    mayonnaise, enough to bind together

Cut tops from tomatoes and scoop out one tablespoon from inside. Let drain upside down.

Mix cheese with mayonnaise, shallots and cayenne. Mound on tomatoes. Bake in 350° oven until cheese melts.

TURNIP OR MUSTARD GREENS

2 to 3 bunches of turnip tops or
    mustard greens
½ lb. salt meat or bacon
4 to 5 tablespoons bacon drippings
1 cup of water
    salt and pepper to taste

Stem and pick the greens and wash several times in salt water.

Put bacon drippings or lard in the old reliable iron pot, then the greens and the water, and let them cook slowly.

Meanwhile, fry the salt meat a little, add it to the greens, and let them cook until the greens are tender. The old-fashioned southerner always has hot corn-bread and plenty of fresh butter to serve with this, and rates the combination as one of life's joys.

For the information of the uninitiated, the liquid in this dish of greens is the far famed "pot-likker", and in the intimacy of the family, the cornbread is often surreptitiously dunked therein.

YAMS WITH FRUIT

Mrs. Robert M. Monsted

2 or 3 large yams
¼ lb. butter
1 cup light brown sugar
1 cup unsweetened pineapple juice
1 orange, the grated rind
    sliced oranges

Slice raw yams in thin slices and arrange in a buttered baking dish with alternate layers of sliced oranges, until the dish is nearly full. Cream butter and sugar well together and dot liberally between each layer. Add the grated orange rind to the pineapple juice and pour all over the yams. Cover the dish, bake slowly for one hour and then uncover and continue baking for another hour or until the yams are tender and the juice is reduced to a thick syrup.

MACARONI PIE

Mrs. Charles A. Farwell

½ lb. spaghetti or macaroni
½ lb. boiled ham
    pepper, salt, pastry, butter

Line a baking dish with pastry. Boil the spaghetti until tender. Grind or chop the ham fine, and add the pepper. Fill the pastry shell with alternate layers of the macaroni and the ham. Dot the top with the butter. Cover with pie crust, slit top two or three times for steam to escape. Bake in a hot oven for a half an hour. This is good hot or cold.

NOODLE RING

Mrs. Edward Rightor

1 package noodles
1½ tablespoons butter
1½ tablespoons flour
1½ cups milk
½ teaspoon salt
2 eggs beaten separately
    dash of pepper and of mace

Let the noodles cook in boiling salted water, then drain them. Heat the butter in a double-boiler, adding the flour and milk very gradually to make a cream sauce. Add salt, pepper, and mace (or nutmeg), then the eggs well-beaten. Combine all this with the noodles.

Bake in ring mold which has previously been well buttered and placed in refrigerator. This makes it much easier to remove.

Turn out on a hot platter and fill the center as desired: with creamed fish, with a filling made after the recipe for Crabs St. Jacques; with meat, creamed shrimp or crab, what you will. Hot asparagus tips placed about the edges make a pretty and savory touch.

NOODLE RING

Mrs. Clifford Stem

1 medium sized package of egg
  noodles
½ lb. sharp cheese grated
4 eggs
  buttered bread crumbs
  salt and pepper to taste

Boil noodles about twenty minutes, pour into colander—drain, pour cold water over noodles—drain again. Now add well beaten egg yolks to noodles, cheese and seasoning and lastly the well beaten whites—not too dry. Turn into a well buttered ring that has buttered bread crumbs dusted in bottom and around sides of mold.

Place in water in oven—325° and cook about forty-five minutes—test with a paring knife before removing from oven. Creamed oyster, crab meat, shrimp or chicken are delicious served in this.

SPAGHETTI À LA AIMÉE

Mrs. Aimée G. Howard
Charlotte Farms

1 lb. ground beef
1 onion, diced
1 green pepper, diced
1 cup celery (mostly leaves), diced
  flour
1 28-oz. can "Progresso Fancy Free
  all-purpose Peeled, Ground Pear
  Tomatoes"
1 can beer
1½ tablespoons sugar
  salt and pepper to taste

Form meatballs from ground beef. Salt and pepper the balls, and roll in flour; then brown in an iron pot. Remove meatballs from oil and saute onions, pepper and celery until tender.

Add tomatoes, beer, sugar, salt and pepper. Let sauce come to a boil, add browned meatballs and reduce heat to a simmer. Cook about 2 hours, stirring occasionally, and, as necessary, skim off the surface grease. Sauce will be thick. Do not add water. If more liquid is needed, add more beer.

Serve over cooked spaghetti. This makes two generous servings.

SPAGHETTI MICHELE

Mrs. Edward Stauss, Jr.

4 large Bermuda onions
3 large green peppers
1 lb. of fresh mushrooms
2 cans of tomato soup
1½ lbs. of raw ham
1/3 cup of olive oil
1 package of spaghetti
  salt to taste

Cut up onions, peppers and mushrooms in small pieces. Sauté the mushrooms in the olive oil first, and remove. Using the same oil cook the onions and peppers until tender. Boil spaghetti about twelve minutes. Mix all ingredients together and add tomato soup. Season to taste. This dish should be made the day before if possible and left in the refrigerator until ready to bake. Bake in a 325° oven for about 30 minutes. Mushroom soup may be substituted for fresh mushrooms. Serves eight.

SPAGHETTI AND OYSTERS

Mrs. James Selman

¾ pack thin spaghetti
2 - 12 oz. jars oysters and their
  water
½ stick butter
2 tablespoons olive oil
2 cloves garlic
¼ cup flour
3 shallots (whole), chopped
  same amount chopped parsley as
  shallots
1 small stalk celery (whole), chopped
  (optional)
  salt, pepper, Tabasco
  Parmesan cheese

Chop vegetables finely and cook until clear in the oil and butter. Add flour and cook over low heat for 5 minutes. Add oysters and their water and cook, stirring for about 15 or 20 minutes. Cover and uncover from time to time. Take heart!! What first looks like a mess shapes up to be a fine sauce! Add your salt, pepper and Tabasco to taste, and serve over cooked spaghetti. Sprinkle with Parmesan cheese.

Serves 4 generously.

SPAGHETTI ROLLINO

Mrs. Stanley Arthur

1 large onion, 1 clove garlic
½ cup olive oil
1 qt. can Italian tomatoes
1 small can tomato paste
2 teaspoons salt, pepper, thyme,
    cayenne pepper
1 cup dried mushrooms
1 cup boiling water
1 lb. each Parmesan cheese, spaghetti

Boil the spaghetti in 2 quarts of salt water. Drain, and put back in same boiler until ready to use.

Soak the mushrooms for a minute in a cup of boiling water or stock. (If you can not get the dried mushrooms, a small can of button mushrooms may be used.) Drain and chop them fine.

Chop the onions, cook five minutes in the olive oil, add the tomatoes and tomato paste, salt, pepper and other seasoning. This is the sauce. Add mushrooms 10 minutes before serving.

To the drained spaghetti, add one-third of the cheese, then pour over it one-third of the sauce, mix thoroughly and heat piping hot, pour on hot platter or round dish, then pour over it the rest of the sauce.

The rest of the grated cheese serve on the side.

The sauce may be made in the morning, and heated again at night.

SPAGHETTI SUPRÊME

Mrs. Stephen Seyburn

1 lb. spaghetti
2 lbs. ground meat
2 large cans tomatoes, 2 cans water
4 large onions
1 clove garlic
1 lemon, sliced
1 can mushrooms
1 can tomato paste
1 teaspoon each allspice, cloves
3 bay leaves
1 tablespoon shortening
    pinch of soda, salt, pepper

Fry onions in shortening, add tomatoes, water, ground meat, and let come to a boil. Now add pinch of soda and let simmer 1½ to 2 hours, and add garlic, salt and pepper to taste, and other seasoning, and boil for 1 hour, then add tomato paste and mushrooms and cook ten to fifteen minutes longer.

WHITE HOUSE SPAGHETTI

President and
Mrs. Woodrow Wilson

1½ cups spaghetti
¾ lb. Swiss cheese
1 tablespoon each white pepper, salt
1 pt. milk
2 tablespoons butter
1 tablespoon flour

Boil the spaghetti in salted water, then drain it, and make a white sauce, by creaming the butter and flour in the double boiler and adding milk in the usual way.

Butter a pyrex dish, and put in a layer of spaghetti, then a layer of cream sauce, then a layer of grated cheese, and continue until all of the spaghetti, sauce, and cheese have been used, having sauce and cheese on top. Run in the oven and bake until creamy. A dish fit for kings—and a president's favorite!

JAMBALAYA

Miss Virginia Fassmann

1 lb. rice
2 cups left over chicken or turkey
1 slice ham
2 doz. oysters or 1 lb. shrimp
2 tablespoons lard
    salt, pepper to taste

Wash rice, soak in cold water two hours. Dry and fry rice until it is slightly straw color. Cut up the cold roast chicken or turkey, and a slice of ham; fry in a tablespoon of lard.

Now stir rice into the meat slowly and at the same time add a pint of hot water. Cover your pot and set where it can cook slowly; should you add oysters, cook them in their own liquor for a few minutes on a slow fire until they curl, then add to the Jambalaya and serve. If desired, add a dash of saffron.

CREOLE JAMBALAYA

Roy L. Alciatore—Antoine's

1½ cups rice
1½ qts. of water
½ lb. uncooked ham (or cooked) cut in
    small pieces
1 clove garlic
2 teaspoons salt
2 tablespoons butter
½ lb. sliced cooked spicy sausage
2 onions chopped
4 tomatoes chopped
2 green peppers chopped
2 cups beef stock
2 cups cooked shrimp
1 cup cooked chicken, cut Julienne

Wash rice carefully and place in large saucepan with the water and salt. Cover and cook over low heat until boiling point is reached. Cook 5 minutes longer. Drain and rinse with cold water. Drain once more.

In separate saucepan melt the butter and add the ham, garlic, sausage, onions and green peppers. Cook over medium heat for 10 minutes, stirring frequently. Reduce to low heat and add the tomatoes and beef stock. Add the sliced chicken and shrimp.

If the Jambalaya is intended for a fast day, leave out the chicken, sausage and ham. Use only the shrimp, but increase quantity of shrimp to 3 cups instead of 2.

JAMBALAYA EN FAMILLE

12 shallots, with tops, minced
1 large onion, 1 clove garlic, minced
1 large green pepper, minced
½ cup tomato paste
2 tablespoons bacon fat
4 cups of cooked rice
    sausage, chopped (or shrimp, boiled,
    or oysters and shrimp)
    salt, pepper to taste

Cook the minced shallots, onions, garlic, and green pepper quite gently in the hot fat until they are completely softened, to a pulp-like consistency. The quantities given are conservative —one may well use more. In fact, it is a case of the more the merrier for the dish.

Add the seasoning, and then the tomato paste; then the sausage (or other chosen ingredient) to cook a few moments only. Last of all add the rice.

This recipe can be varied infinitely. A very popular version much used in country districts of Louisiana is known as "Dirty Rice." This version requires the chopped and browned giblets of a fowl as the basis of the gravy with the addition of such other seasonings as are preferred. The gravy is mixed with boiled rice and the whole placed in a baking dish and run in the oven to brown. Any Jambalaya makes an excellent dish for a buffet supper.

LOUISIANA JAMBALAYA A LA KOLB'S

Courtesy of

Mr. W. W. Martin, Manager

¼ lb. butter or oleo, melted
1 lb. raw, long grain rice
½ teaspoon paprika
1 lb. small, peeled, deveined shrimp
2 ozs. claw crabmeat
1 cup tomatoes
¼ cup tomato paste
1 small onion, finely chopped
1 small green pepper, finely
    chopped
1 cup celery, finely chopped
2 green onions, finely chopped
1 tablespoon chopped parsley
1 teaspoon Lea & Perrins
    dash Tabasco, or to taste

Melt butter; add raw rice and paprika, cooking over low fire until rice is lightly browned.

In separate pot combine shrimp, crabmeat, tomatoes, tomato paste, chopped onions, peppers and celery. Cook 20 minutes. Combine with brown rice and simmer, covered for 20 - 30 minutes. (Until rice is tender.)

Stir in chopped green onions, parsley and seasoning.

CHICKEN AND HAM CASSEROLE

Mrs. Richard Gallman

2 cups chicken
1 to 2 cups ham
1 5-oz. can water chestnuts, sliced
1 3-oz. can mushrooms and juice
1 cup light cream
3 tablespoons sherry
1 cup chopped onion sauteed in 3
    tablespoons butter
½ cup grated Swiss cheese
½ cup buttered bread crumbs
3 tablespoons flour

salt and pepper to taste
2 teaspoons A-1 Sauce

Cut chicken and ham into bite size pieces. Spread in casserole. Mix other ingredients (except bread crumbs) and pour over chicken and ham. Sprinkle bread crumbs over top. Bake in 350° oven for 35 - 45 minutes.

CHICKEN SPAGHETTI DINNER
Mrs. J. I. Hebert

3½-4 lb. chicken
2 qts. water
1 package spaghetti
1 large can tomatoes
1 can tomato paste
2 cups chopped celery
2 onions, chopped
1 teaspoon chili powder
1 clove garlic, chopped
2 bell peppers, chopped
2 cups grated Parmesan cheese
1 can mushrooms
2¼ tablespoons butter
celery leaves and one onion

Put chicken in water, add a teaspoon salt. Boil slowly until tender with celery leaves and one onion. Pour off broth; when cold skim off fat. Now saute celery, garlic, bell peppers and onion in butter, but do not allow to brown. Add tomatoes and tomato paste. Add two cups of broth, simmer an hour or more; add mushrooms. Season to taste with salt, pepper, a dash of cayenne pepper. Cook spaghetti until tender about twenty-five minutes. Drain and keep hot.
Put chicken in sauce for a few minutes to heat; pour it over spaghetti. Serve with Parmesan cheese. A green salad and compote of fruit will make an excellent meal.

CHICKEN OR TURKEY CASSEROLE
Mrs. Wm. Scoggins

3 cups cooked chopped fowl
1 cup gravy
1 small can mushroom pieces
1 small package egg noodles
Romano and Parmesan cheese, grated

Boil the noodles about fifteen minutes in salted water and drain. Combine meat and mushrooms with the gravy and the noodles. Sprinkle generously with cheese. Turn into a Pyrex pie plate and bake in 325° oven. An inexpensive dish and very delicious.

CHOU-CROUTE GARNIE
Compliments
J & B Stables

½ lb. bacon, about 10-12 slices
2 large cans (1 lb. 11 oz. size) sauerkraut
6 thick pork loin chops
6 sausages or franks (knockwurst and/or bratwurst)
½ lb. salt pork
3 cloves garlic, minced
1 medium onion, chopped fine
1 8-oz. can stewed tomatoes
12 new potatoes
6 carrots
¼ bunch finely chopped parsley
1½ teaspoons cracked pepper
salt to taste
curly parsley garnish

Line a Dutch oven with strips of bacon. Drain sauerkraut and pour around sides of pot leaving a hole in center of kraut for seasonings. Meanwhile brown pork chops in butter and remove from pan. Saute briefly chopped onions and garlic in remaining butter and meat juices and spoon into center of k raut. Now add to center the hunk of salt pork (which has been soaked in water to remove excess salt). Pour stewed tomatoes over sauerkraut and sprinkle with pepper. Arrange browned pork chops over kraut so that it is now completely surrounded by meats for cooking. Bring to boil, cover and cook over low heat for 2 hours.
Meanwhile boil new potatoes and carrots till tender. Drain water and pour over a stick of melted butter and chopped parsley.
To serve, arrange kraut in center of platter with meats and vegetables around periphery. Serves 6.

CHOU-CROUTE GARNIS
Mr. Robert Dunham

12 thin slices ham
2½ lbs. sauerkraut
1½ - 2 lbs. andouille (or any hot link sausage)
1 cup fresh carrots, sliced

2 cloves garlic, minced
¼ cup fresh parsley, chopped
1 cup dry white wine
2 medium onions, whole
2 whole cloves

Line a 2 quart casserole with 6 browned ham slices. Wash sauerkraut and squeeze it well by hand. Place half of it in the casserole. Place 1" pieces of sausage and place on top of sauerkraut. Then add the rest of the sauerkraut and top with carrots. Sprinkle over all the garlic, parsley and wine. Place the onions studded with cloves into mixture. Salt should not be added, and the sausage will make it peppery. Add a layer of the remaining browned ham slices, cover tightly, and cook in a 325° oven 1½ hours. Serves 6.

FISH CASSEROLE
Mrs. Paul Selley

3 lb. fish
½ cup flour, 1/3 stick butter
2 potatoes, raw
½ cup cream
1 teaspoon paprika
salt and pepper

Clean and filet fish. Score the edges every 2 inches, then rub with salt and pepper. Mix flour and paprika in a plate, roll the fish pieces in it. Grease the casserole very well and line the bottom with 2 rows of thinly sliced raw potatoes; bottom should not show at all. Place fish on top, dot with butter, pour on the cream and bake in 350° oven about 35 minutes, or until light brown. Serve hot from casserole.

HAM AND POTATOES AU GRATIN
Mrs. James M. Batchelor

1 large slice raw ham, ¾ inch thick
3 large Irish potatoes, sliced thin
½ cup plain flour
¾ stick butter or oleo
½ teaspoonful black pepper
enough milk to cover

Place ham, cut into 4 pieces or whole, in bottom of deep baking dish. Cover with half of sliced potatoes. Sprinkle ½ of flour over potatoes and one-half of butter cut into slices, then sprinkle one-half of black pepper. Re-

peat procedure with balance of potatoes, flour, butter and pepper. Over this, pour enough milk to completely cover. Do not fill dish above 2 inches from top to prevent boiling over. Cover loosely with silver foil and bake in preheated oven 325° for one hour.

MEAT CASSEROLE WITH NOODLES
Mrs. Henry H. Vatter

1 lb. ground beef
1 package wide noodles
1 can corn, cream style
1 can tomato sauce
1 can mushrooms
½ lb. sharp cheese
1 tablespoon chili powder
1 each large onion, green pepper
1 large clove garlic
salt to taste

Boil noodles in salted water until soft. Brown onion, pepper and garlic in a little bacon fat, add the ground meat and chili powder. Simmer a few minutes. Then mix with the boiled noodles, add the corn and tomato sauce. Fill a baking dish with the mixture adding cheese, sprinkled throughout and saving most for the top. Sprinkle a little chopped parsley on top of the cheese and bake in a slow oven about forty minutes. Will serve eight.

MOTHER GOOSE CASSEROLE
Mrs. Richard Gallmann

2-3 lbs. ground meat (or more)
½ cup chopped green onions
1 large onion, chopped
1 large can tomatoes
3 small cans tomato paste (cut with water if desired)
Suggest: 1 can paste with remaining chili catsup sauce
1 large can whole kernel corn
1 large can mushrooms (stems and pieces)
½ cup sliced ripe olives
1 lime (juice of)
½ lb. grated American cheese
1 cup slivered almonds (roasted)
1 10-oz. package elbo macaroni
½ teaspoon pepper
½ teaspoon salt
1 teaspoon Worcestershire sauce
2 garlic cloves minced

Saute onions, pepper and meat. Add seasonings, tomatoes, corn and mushrooms. Cook few minutes. Add olives, cheese, and almonds. Pour in casserole dish and warm in oven when ready to serve.

PORK CHOP
CASSEROLE
Mrs. Victor G. Nunes

4 - 8 pork chops
1 cup rice
1 bell pepper, sliced
1 tomato, sliced
1 onion, sliced
1 can beef bouillon plus water to
    make 3 cups liquid, OR
3 beef bouillon cubes and 3 cups
    water
salt and pepper to taste

Place raw rice in bottom of casserole dish. Salt and pepper pork chops and brown in skillet. Arrange pork chops on top of rice. Place a slice of onion, bell pepper and tomato on each chop. Add bouillon liquid. Cover and bake at 375° for one hour.

SHRIMP AND CHEESE
CASSEROLE
Mrs. Charles L. Brown

3 cans shrimp
2 cans mushroom soup
1 can mushrooms
¼ lb. Old English cheese
salt, pepper, Worcestershire sauce

Mix shrimp, soup and seasoning. Add grated cheese. Place in a buttered casserole, top with cheese and bread crumbs, bake until very hot.

CASSOULET TOULOUSAIN
Mrs. Robert Cutting

3 cups dried white beans, soaked
    overnight
1 tablespoon salt
¼ teaspoon pepper
¼ teaspoon thyme
1 bay leaf
½ pound sausage (garlic or Polish
    preferred)
½ pound lean salt pork, diced
4 tablespoons butter or oleo
2 pounds shoulder of lamb, cut
    for stew
2 large onions, chopped
¼ cup tomato paste
2 cloves garlic, crushed
3 tablespoons fresh bread crumbs

Drain beans and place in large kettle. Cover with water. Add salt, thyme, bay leaf and sausage. Bring to boil and simmer slowly for ½ hour. Remove sausage and continue simmering for 1 hour. Cook salt pork in boiling water for 5 minutes. Drain and set aside. Heat butter in large sauce pan. Add lamb and cook until lightly browned on all sides. Pour off excess fat, add onions until well-browned. Cover with water, add tomato paste, garlic, pepper and boiled salt pork cut in pieces. Simmer gently. Add drained beans and sausage to pan. Simmer for 1 hour. Rub inside of large casserole with garlic. Remove lamb and sausage from pan, turn contents of pan into casserole. Arrange lamb, sausage and bread crumbs on top of beans. Dot with butter. Broil under broiling flame until well-browned. Serve hot.

sauces for meats, poultry, fish

and vegetables

ACCOMPANIMENTS TO SERVE WITH CURRY DISHES
(SAMBALS, OR "BOYS")
Editors

TAKE YOUR PICK!!!
These are best served with any fowl curry, i.e., duck, chicken, or turkey. Just serve your favorites alongside.

chopped peanuts
crumbled bacon
chopped hard boiled eggs
chopped green peppers
capers
toasted grated coconut
small pieces of lemon
Major Grey's Chutney
picalilli
chopped fresh pineapple
chopped shrimp

HOT MUSTARD
Mrs. Guy Bruce Scoggin

1 cup Coleman's dry mustard
1 cup vinegar
1 cup brown sugar
2 eggs

Mix mustard and vinegar and smooth out the lumps. Add sugar and do the same. Beat 2 eggs and add to the mixture. Cook over low fire, stirring constantly. Makes large batch of hot, delicious mustard!!!

ANCHOVY SAUCE

To one pint of drawn butter add one heaping tablespoon of anchovy essence, stir well together and serve.

ARNAUD SAUCE
Mrs. James Selman

½ cup green onions, chopped
¼ cup parsley, chopped
¼ cup celery, chopped
1 small jar Creole mustard (2/3 cup)
¾ cup olive oil
¼ cup cider vinegar
1 small box paprika
1 teaspoon salt
1 teaspoon cayenne pepper

Chop vegetables finely and whirl in blender with vinegar, oil, and salt. Add rest to ingredients by hand. This, after much experimenting, is the real McCoy. The amount of cayenne may vary according to individual taste.

SAUCE ARNAUD

1 cup French dressing
  (proportions: 1/3 cup
  vinegar to 2/3 cup olive
  oil)
1 bunch shallots, minced
5 tablespoons Creole mustard
2 tablespoons paprika
1 heaping tablespoon horseradish
  salt and pepper to taste
  boiled shrimp

Peel boiled shrimp and set them aside in bowl. In another bowl, mix sauce ingredients. Pour mixture over shrimp and turn them about in it repeatedly. Refrigerate for an hour before serving. Serves 6.

AVOCADO SAUCE

2 avocados, peeled
1 tablespoon mayonnaise
1 teaspoon grated onion
1 cup French dressing
2 limes or one lemon, juice of
  salt and pepper to taste

175

Mash avocados to smooth paste. Add lemon or lime juice, onion, mayonnaise, French dressing, and salt and pepper to taste. Mix well. This is delicious served on lettuce and/or tomatoes. If tomatoes cut in small pieces are added to sauce, it is an excellent relish to use with meat or pancakes filled with creamed chicken.

BAR-B-QUE SAUCE

1 lb. oleo
6 lemons (juice)
1 bottle horseradish (5 oz.)
1 tablespoon Tabasco
½ cup vinegar
½ bottle catsup
2 tablespoons Lea and Perrins
2 or 3 tablespoons salt (be very careful here)

This makes enough sauce for 4 or 5 chickens.

BARBEQUE SAUCE

Mrs. Richard Adler

2 small cans tomato paste
1½ cups cider vinegar
4 cups water
2 tablespoons flour
2 teaspoons sugar, Coleman's mustard and ground cloves
2 tablespoons Lea & Perrins salt and Tabasco to taste
2 large onions

Mix sauce ingredients and stir until smooth. Bring to boil and add 2 large whole onions. Simmer mixture until it thickens. Remove onions and refrigerate sauce. This is a taut but yummy sauce.

BARBECUE SAUCE

Mr. James L. Crump
Holly-Bluff—on the Jordan River

1 qt. each water, vinegar
1 pt. catsup
1 bottle Worcestershire sauce
½ lb. butter
1 cup each black pepper, red pepper
¼ cup flour dissolved in cold water to thicken

Put on stove and bring to a boil. This will make three quarts of sauce.

BARBECUE SAUCE

Dorothy Dix

2 tablespoons each butter, vinegar
1 teaspoon mustard
1 teaspoon Worcestershire sauce
1 teaspoon sugar, ½ teaspoon salt
    dash Tabasco and black pepper

Blend all together, heat to a boil, and pour over broiled chicken or any other meat desired. Let stand a few minutes before serving.

BARBEQUE SAUCE FOR FRESH PORK

Mr. Francis Selman

1 pint white vinegar
1 pint water
juice 2 lemons
4 large Bermuda or Spanish red onions
1/3 cup salt, approximately
1 large can Hunt's Tomato Sauce
½ teaspoon Italian Seasoning
¼ small bottle Worcestershire Sauce
a bit of Tabasco for seasoning (not hotness)
(BY ALL THAT'S HOLY, NO SUGAR)

In proper size pot, slice onions thin as possible. Then add all other ingredients. Stir well, and let sit awhile before tasting. As an old friend said, "The flavor will strike through." Should you have to add anything, it would be salt or Worcestershire.

This sauce is not to be cooked. It can be stored under refrigeration indefinitely. Use for basting on barbeque pit after salting meat.

If used on a pork ham and ready to serve, slice ham to fit small bun. Then heat in sauce, with lots of onions, in double boiler or chafing dish. Onions are pickled at this point and become an important part of the sandwich. Great for cocktail parties or football gatherings.

HEAVY'S SUPER BARBEQUE SAUCE

Mr. Harry Merritt Lane, Jr.

2 sticks butter (not margarine)
1 pint catsup
1 pint vinegar

1 tablespoon Tabasco
1 small bottle Worcestershire
  sauce
½ cup maple syrup
1 tablespoon brown sugar
1 tablespoon onion juice
2 garlic cloves, crushed
¼ teaspoon black and red pepper
2 tablespoons salt

Simply bring all ingredients to a
simmer. Use as needed; refrigeration is
not necessary. Makes about 2 quarts.
Especially good on spare ribs.

BÉCHAMEL SAUCE

2 cups thick white sauce
1½ cups white stock (veal or chicken)
  carrot, celery, onion, thyme, salt
    and pepper

Cook seasonings in stock until reduced to 1 cup. Strain. Add slowly
to white sauce, stirring to prevent
lumping. If a golden color is desired,
two egg yolks may be stirred in after
removing from the fire. Use a double
boiler for this sauce.

BÉARNAISE SAUCE

Ella Brennan Martin
Brennan's French Restaurant

yolks of 4 eggs
juice of 1 lemon
1 lb. melted butter
  minced capers, chopped parsley
  dash of vinegar

Beat the egg yolks add lemon juice.
Cook in double boiler on low fire, adding melted butter to above slowly.
Cook until thick. Add salt to taste,
the capers and parsley, and the dash
of vinegar.

BÉARNAISE SAUCE

Mr. Fred B. Otell

GROUP A
2 tablespoons chicken broth
2 tablespoons Tarragon vinegar
1 tablespoon lemon juice
3 tablespoons chopped onions or
    scallions
GROUP B
3 egg yolks
½ cup butter
2 sprays celery leaves, 2 sprigs parsley
½ teaspoon salt
  dash pepper and Tabasco

Bring ingredients in Group A to a
boil. Place all ingredients in Group B
in Waring blender. Put cover on and
start blender. Remove cover and with
blender running gradually pour in hot
mixture. Run until well mixed, about
one minute. Cook over hot water,
stirring constantly to a consistency of
soft custard.
Good over hot fish or meat.

BÉARNAISE SAUCE

Justin Galatoire
Galatoire's Restaurant, Inc.

To a Hollandaise sauce, add a little
of Tarragon vinegar and chopped very
fine parsley. Serve over chops and
steaks.

SAUCE BÉARNAISE CRÉOLE

Mrs. M. C. Maury-Lyons

4 eggs, the yolks
2 tablespoons grated onion
2 tablespoons Tarragon vinegar
½ teaspoon each salt, pepper
1 stick butter
½ cup water
½ teaspoon beef extract

Beat yolks carefully, put into a
double-boiler and add the other ingredients, stirring gently but steadily.
This sauce you will find has more
character than its pure French prototype.

BLACK BUTTER SAUCE

Warm an oz. of butter in a small
frying pan until it turns brown. Add
a little finely chopped parsley and
cook for one minute more controlling
the heat carefully to prevent its turning too dark. Add five drops of vinegar. This is delicious poured over a
raw egg in a small individual casserole
and run into the oven till the egg sets.

HOT SAUCE FOR BROCCOLI

Mr. Fred B. Otell

¼ lb. butter
1½ cups mayonnaise
2 tablespoons of fresh ground horse-
    radish
1 onion, grated

½ teaspoon prepared mustard
¼ teaspoon each cayenne pepper, salt
½ tablespoon pepper, vinegar

Place all ingredients in a china bowl over steam and stir until thoroughly blended. This sauce is also delicious with fresh salmon steaks.

CHILI SAUCE

Mrs. W. J. Bentley

24 large red tomatoes
6 green peppers, chopped
4 large onions, chopped
1 cup sugar, 1 tablespoon salt
1 teaspoon each whit e mustard
    seed, allspice and cloves
4 cups vinegar

Peel the tomatoes, peppers and onions. Chop. Mix all the ingredients and boil for two hours until the mixture is done. Bottle and seal.

COCKTAIL SAUCE

Mrs. Lucien E. Lyons, Sr.

1 cup stiff, unsalted mayonnaise
1 tablespoon chili sauce
2 tablespoons Crosse and Blackwell
    Tarragon vinegar, a must
2 tablespoons, anchovy sauce, or more
4 tablespoons tomato catsup
1 tablespoon olive oil

Mix anchovy sauce in olive oil, add other ingredients and stir until creamy. Lemon juice and more pepper may be added if mayonnaise does not carry sufficient seasoning.
This is to be used with lobster, crab meat or shrimp.

COCKTAIL SAUCE BONFOUCA

Mrs. Homer Dupuy

1 cup chili sauce
1 lemon, juice
1 tablespoon vinegar
1 onion, chopped fine
1 teaspoon Worcestershire sauce
    few drops Tabasco

Strain, let stand for several hours in refrigerator before serving.

CREAM SAUCE

1 tablespoon each butter, flour
1 cup milk (or milk and cream)
    salt, pepper, paprika to taste

Melt the butter in a double-boiler, stir in the flour slowly, and add the seasonings. Cook about a minute, stirring constantly, and not allowing the flour to brown. Then add the milk very slowly, stirring continually, and bring to the boiling point. Let boil two or three minutes, never cease stirring.
Keep warm over hot water until ready for use. If a medium thick sauce is desired, use 2 tablespoons of butter and 3 of flour. If a thick sauce is the object, then use 4 tablespoons of butter and 4 of flour.

CURRY SAUCE

Lt. Comdr. and Mrs. S. W. Wallace

2 tablespoons shortening
2 tablespoons flour
½ teaspoon salt
1 lemon, juice
2 teaspoons curry powder
1 can apricots, small, chopped

Use small size can apricots. Blend shortening, flour, curry and salt. Add syrup from apricots and enough water to make desired consistency. Add lemon juice to suit taste. Add any meat, fish or eggs as may be desired. Serve with chutney and sambals.

ENGLISH HORSE-RADISH SAUCE

1 teaspoon dry mustard
1 tablespoon vinegar
1 good sized root horse-radish, grated
½ pt. cream, salt to taste

Mix the mustard and vinegar and add the horse-radish; let stand for an hour, then add the cream. Excellent with roast beef.

EPICUREAN SAUCE

Lt. Comdr. and Mrs. S. W. Wallace

3 tablespoons mayonnaise
½ cup cream, whipped
1 teaspoon Worcestershire sauce
1 tablespoon prepared mustard
3 tablespoons horseradish

Mix all ingredients well.

FISH SAUCE

Mrs. Reuben E. Tipton

½ cup sour cream
½ cup A-1 sauce

Blend well. This sauce can be made in any quantity and kept on hand in the refrigerator. It is unusual and perfect! Good with any kind of fish.

SAUCE FOR BOILED FISH

1 small jar sour gherkins
1 small jar capers
¼ bunch each parsley and shallots
¾ cup olive oil, ½ cup salad oil
  salt, pepper, to taste

Chop the gherkins, capers, parsley and shallots fine. Heat the oils, add the chopped ingredients, salt and pepper. Continue to heat for a few minutes. Serve with boiled fish.

FISH SAUCE MÈRE

Mrs. Jeanne Castellanos

6 hard-boiled eggs
1½ teaspoons dry mustard
1½ cups mayonnaise
6 shallots, minced
¼ small jar capers, or more, to taste
1½ teaspoons garlic oil (use garlic press)
7 drops Tabasco sauce
1 teaspoon horseradish

Mix the yolks of the eggs with the mustard. Stir this into the mayonnaise. Add the shallots, the garlic oil, Tabasco, and a teaspoon of horseradish. Last add the capers and chopped egg whites. Serve. This is excellent with any cold fish or with shrimp.

SAUCE FOR FISH OR SHRIMP

1 cup mayonnaise
1 small onion, grated
½ cucumber, grated
1 teaspoon horseradish
½ teaspoon celery salt
  cayenne pepper or Tabasco

Combine all ingredients thoroughly. If it becomes too thin in mixing, place in the icebox to become firm.

HAM SAUCE

Mrs. Frank Harbison

1 pint apple jelly
1 pint pineapple preserves

½ jar horseradish (Kraft's)
½ can Coleman's dry mustard

Heat all ingredients until blended in double boiler. Serve warm over ham.

SAUCE FOR BAKED HAM

Mrs. John May

2 tablespoons tomato catsup
2 tablespoons sherry
2 tablespoons Tarragon vinegar
2 tablespoons butter
1 tablespoon Worcestershire sauce
1 teaspoon mustard

Mix vinegar with mustard, add other ingredients. Heat.

HOLLANDAISE SAUCE

Mr. Fred B. Otell

3 egg yolks
2 tablespoons lemon juice
1 sprig parsley
  dash of pepper, dash of Tabasco
½ cup butter
½ cup boiling water

Place all ingredients, except boiling water, in the Waring blender. Have butter at room temperature. Put cover on blender and turn on switch. Remove cover and, with blender running, gradually pour in boiling water. Run blender until thoroughly blended, about one minute. Remove and cook over hot water, stirring constantly, to consistency of a soft custard. Makes about 1 pint.
Will keep well in refrigerator.

HOLLANDAISE SAUCE

Mrs. James Selman

1 egg yolk
½ lemon, the juice
1 stick butter, or oleo, cut
  into 6-8 chunks
Have on hand a saucepan, with
  a bowl to fit, and an
  eggbeater.

Bring water to boil in the saucepan, then turn down the heat as far as possible so that the water is hot, but not boiling. Place bowl, (stainless steel is excellent) to fit over the pot. Now place lightly beaten egg yolk and lemon juice in bowl. Begin to add butter or oleo a chunk at a time. Mash down with the egg beater and blend all the time. When all is added and melted beat and scrape with the beater until fluffy. (Take care to maintain low heat of water.) Lift bowl every now and then during process, as this will prevent overheating. When sauce is nice and fluffy, remove from heat. If you want a thicker sauce, use 2 egg yolks to 1 stick of butter.

HOLLANDAISE SAUCE
Justin Galatoire
Galatoire's Restaurant, Inc.

½ lb. of melted butter
3 egg yolks
salt, pepper and cayenne to taste
juice of strained lemon

Place the egg yolks in a double boiler, then gradually pour in the melted butter, lemon juice and seasonings. Stir very slowly until thick.

EASY HOLLANDAISE SAUCE

½ cup butter or oleomargarine
4 egg yolks, salt
¼ cup each lemon juice and light
   cream

Melt butter in top of double-boiler. Mix well, but do not beat the egg-yolks. Add salt, and lemon. Stir all this into the butter. Beat with rotary egg-beater until it thickens. Add light cream, continue beating and cook in double-boiler two minutes longer.

WHITE "HOLLANDAISE"

1 cup mayonnaise
½ cup melted butter
⅜ cup lemon juice
   dry mustard to taste

Stir together thoroughly. The consistency is thin. Very good for broccoli, cauliflower, as well as for green salads.

For cole slaw, add ½ teaspoon sugar (or to taste).

MOCK HOLLANDAISE SAUCE

1 pt. milk
2 tablespoons flour
½ stick butter
2 eggs, the yolks
½ lemon, the juice, salt, pepper

Put the milk, the flour, and the butter in a double-boiler to simmer gent-

ly until thick. Turn off the fire, but leave over the boiling water until the beaten eggs are beaten in. Remove from fire and squeeze in the lemon juice and seasonings.

SAUCE FOR LAMB
OR GAME
Mrs. C. Peck Hayne

¾ cup currant jelly
¼ cup mint leaves
¼ cup catsup
¼ cup burgundy
1 tablespoon orange peel
¼ lb. butter

Mix all together, simmer 10 minutes after butter melts. Glaze meat with sauce and serve remainder.

MINT SAUCE FOR LAMB
Mrs. Walter Torian

1 cup vinegar
2 tablespoons water
4 tablespoons minced mint leaves
2 tablespoons sugar

Soak 3 hours and serve with lamb.

SAUCE MARCHAND DE VIN

6 green onions, chopped fine
3 tablespoons olive oil
1 tablespoon flour
1 cup mushrooms, cut fine
3 cloves garlic, minced
1 glass red or white wine
   marrow from a large beef bone

Cook the onions in the olive oil until lightly browned, rub in the flour until smooth. Add the mushrooms and garlic and continue cooking for ten minutes. Remove the marrow from the bone, cut in slices and add to the sauce, then the wine. Cook five minutes or more and serve hot on steak or chops. If sauce is too thick add a little stock or juice from the meat.

MARGUERITE SAUCE
FOR POACHED
RED FISH
Lucius K. Burton

4 tablespoons butter
2 tablespoons flour

2 cups fish stock, strained
2 egg yolks
¾ cup dry sherry
2 tablespoons chopped parsley
1 teaspoon lemon juice
  salt and pepper to taste

Blend butter with flour in top of double boiler; then add the fish stock slowly and blend until smooth. Lower flame and add slightly beaten egg yolks, constantly stirring slowly. Add lemon juice.

When sauce becomes quite thick, remove from fire. Add salt, pepper, sherry and parsley. Pour over the poached fish and serve at once.

HOT MEAT SAUCE

1 large can mushrooms
1 small can truffles
1 teaspoon tomato paste
¼ glass Madeira wine
½ cup "juice" from cooking roast

Take out the "juice" from the roasting pan about half an hour before the roast is done. Stew the mushrooms and truffles gently in this juice. Add the tomato paste for color. When ready to serve, add the crowning touch, the Madeira wine.

ITALIAN MEAT SAUCE

Mrs. Michael James Ruppel

1 lb. pork, ground
2 lbs. beef, ground
1 lb. can tomatoes, mashed
1 can tomato paste, small
3 onions, finely chopped
1 garlic, minced
1 tablespoon sugar
2 - 3 bell peppers, chopped
  salt, pepper and sweet basil
  (fresh if possible) to taste

In a small amount of olive oil, cook meat just until redness is gone. Season. Remove to another container. In meat juices, brown tomato paste and add onions, garlic and bell peppers. Cook 7 - 10 minutes. Add sugar, mashed tomatoes, and water (1 tomato paste can and 1 tomato can full). Cook ½ hour over low heat. Add meat and cook 45 - 60 minutes.

Serve over spaghetti or macaroni with freshly grated Parmesan cheese.

MUSTARD SAUCE

2 tablespoons butter
½ small white onion, chopped
2 tablespoons flour
1 cup milk
2 tablespoons prepared mustard,
  thinned with ¼ cup milk
½ teaspoon salt, dash pepper
3 tablespoons sherry

Heat until slightly cooked and serve hot or cold.

CREOLE MUSTARD
Miss Louise Hill

½ cup powdered English mustard
  olive oil, vinegar
½ teaspoon sugar, salt to taste

Put the mustard in a bowl. Add the olive oil drop by drop beating vigorously as you would for mayonnaise until you have a stiff paste. Thin out by adding vinegar until the mixture has the consistency of mayonnaise. Add the sugar—a little more if you like. This has authority!

SAUCE FOR CRAYFISH NEWBURG
(Or Shrimp, Crab Meat or Oysters)
Mrs. John P. Labouisse

½ lb. butter
1 heaping cup flour, unsifted
¾ qt. milk
1½ pts. heavy cream
1 can small white mushrooms
1 can Jacobs B&B mushrooms
  black pepper, salt, Tabasco, Worcestershire sauce, dash of mace
  All seasoning to taste

Melt butter in double boiler. Sift flour and stir in slowly. Add milk stirring constantly. When very thick add ½ cup B&B mushroom juice. Add cream, then crayfish and seasonings. Mince both kinds of mushrooms and serve.

This sauce is sufficient for 4 lbs. of shrimp, 2 lbs. of crab meat or 4 doz. oysters.

NEWBURG SAUCE FOR SHRIMP

½ lb. butter
1 tablespoon flour
4 eggs
½ pt. cream, or rich milk

1 glass sherry
    salt, pepper, to taste

Melt the butter in a double boiler. Add the flour gradually, blending well together. Beat the yolks of eggs with the cream or milk and add slowly, stirring constantly. Cook in double boiler until thick. Add salt and pepper. Just before serving add the sherry.

PARADISE SAUCE
FOR DUCKS

Mrs. Lester Lautenschlager, Jr.

3 tablespoons butter
¼ cup flour
4 stalks celery
1 cup beef stock
6 slices bacon, cut into
    pieces
4 shallots
1 can seedless grapes
    (drained)
1½ jars red currant jelly
2/3 cup Madeira Sherry

Fry bacon, remove from pan and drain. Make a light roux with the bacon grease and flour. In another skillet, saute celery and shallots (sliced into 3" strips) in butter. Add this to the roux. Slowly work in red currant jelly, then the hot beef stock and Madeira Sherry. When thick, add the drained seedless grapes. This may be garnished with crisp, chopped bacon. One tablespoon of B. V. extract may be added to darken.

PINHEAD'S
BARBEQUE SAUCE
FOR POULTRY

Mr. W. Elliott Laudeman III

6 sticks margarine
3 tablespoons Lea & Perrins
1-2 teaspoons Tabasco, or to taste
½ cup French's yellow mustard
½ cup white vinegar
2 tablespoons rosemary leaves
2½ medium lemons, juice of

Salt and pepper one 10-12 lb. turkey, or three chickens, either whole or cut into pieces for barbequeing. If cooking whole birds, they can be placed on spit, or if you prefer, simply place on the grill over hot coals. Intensity of heat depends on size of bird, and whether you are cooking it whole or in pieces. Use your own judgment and baste constantly until done. This is delicious!!!

RÉMOULADE SAUCE

Miss Charlotte Mitchell

4 egg yolks, hard boiled
4 tablespoons each oil, vinegar
2 tablespoons prepared mustard
4 stalks celery, chopped
    parsley (a little), chopped
5 shallots, chopped
2 tablespoons Tarragon vinegar
    salt, and Tabasco, horse-radish

Put egg yolks through a sieve and make a paste with the rest of the ingredients. If too thick add a little mayonnaise. When ready to use chop some egg whites and some tops of shallots, using only tender shoots. Will serve 8 people and may be kept in refrigerator for 2 or 3 days. To be used as an appetizer for cocktails, shrimp or crabs. Fried oysters are delicious dunked in this sauce.

OYSTERS ROCKEFELLER
SAUCE

Mr. Francis J. Selman

3 boxes frozen chopped spinach
2 tablespoons dried parsley
3 bunches shallots, tops only
1 heaping kitchen spoon (about
    2 - 2½ tablespoons)
    finest imported Romano or
    Parmesan cheese, freshly
    grated. More if desired.
    (To be cooked with
    greens.)
2 stalks finely chopped celery
    (use a few of the tender
    leaves, too)
6 pods of garlic
2 lbs. butter
1 cup thoroughly strained
    oyster water; vary as to
    need for proper consistency
1 box bread crumbs, to be used
    as needed for thickening
*3 tubes anchovy paste
*1 small bottle Worcestershire
    sauce
    Tabasco sauce to taste
    Absinthe
2 boxes Rock Salt, to be used
    for making beds for the
    oyster shells

*Anchovy paste is very salty; Worcestershire sauce, if cooked too long becomes very salty and can ruin the dish. I have left out any mention of salt itself, because whoever prepares this dish must taste as they go along, and if more salt is desired for the individual taste, simply add it. Again, be very careful, for the salt can ruin this dish!!

Battle Procedure:

All greens that need chopping, and the garlic must be chopped very finely. Melt butter in a suitable pot and blend all ingredients thoroughly. Simmer until ingredients are cooked.

When buying oysters, it is best to buy by the dozen at some oyster house, such as the Magazine oyster house. Purchase 48-50 deep half shells. (Oysters are served on the half shell on the bed of rock salt.)

After purchasing the oysters, pour them into a bowl with their juice, and with your hands remove any shell particles from the oysters; this stirring around will remove all excess grit, too. Drain oysters, reserving the juice and strain the juice at least three times. Next, clean shells thoroughly.

Put about 1 inch of rock salt in shallow baking pans, and imbed the cleaned oyster shells in the salt. Put one oyster in each shell, and place pan in pre-heated 350° - 450° oven. Remove when oysters curl. Cover with spinach mixture. Sprinkle generously with more of the above mentioned cheese. Put into broiler until the cheese is browned. Remove. With a demi-tasse spoon, crack the cheese crust lengthwise and insert ½ of a demi-tasse spoonful of the Absinthe. Serve immediately.

OYSTERS ROCKEFELLER SAUCE

Mrs. Joseph Merrick Jones, Jr.

12 packs frozen chopped spinach,
   completely thawed
3 lbs. butter, not margarine
3 pints oysters, with juice
6 bunches shallots, coarsely
   chopped
1 whole bunch celery, coarsely
   chopped
1 half bunch parsely, coarsely
   chopped
1 tablespoon Mei Yen seasoning

1 tablespoon fine grind black
   pepper
1 tablespoon garlic salt
1½ - 2 teaspoons cayenne pepper
1½ - 2 teaspoons anise seed
4 ozs. Lea & Perrins
½ lemon, sliced and seeded
   Tabasco to taste
   salt to taste
4 jiggers absinthe (at least)
1 - 2 cups bread crumbs (enough
   to thicken to right
   consistency, which should be
   a heavy mush

Melt the butter in a large pot. Add the thawed spinach. Do not cook, set aside.

Put rest of ingredients (except for the absinthe and the bread crumbs) through the blender. Add blended ingredients to the pot of butter and spinach. Cook this mixture over a medium flame for about 20 minutes, stirring all the time.

Remove from fire, cook, and put through blender again, a little at a time. Return to pot. Add absinthe and bread crumbs. (Bread crumbs for proper consistency.) Cook over low heat for 5 minutes.

This freezes beautifully, and can be kept on hand fresh for at least 2 weeks in the refrigerator.

To serve:

Remove oysters from the half shell. Reserve shells. Heat oysters in their own juice until the edges curl slightly. Drain in colander. Place partially cooked oysters back in shells, which have been placed on a bed of rock salt in a shallow baking pan. Cover oysters with the sauce. Put in a hot, pre-heated oven (450°) until sauce bubbles.

For future use of sauce in freezer:

To make life easy, put used oyster shells in the dishwasher to sterilize. Store in plastic bags. Next time, just buy your oysters and you are home free. (You can even rinse the rock salt if you are thrifty and store it in a plastic bag, too.)

WHITE BUTTER SAUCE FOR SHRIMP

Mrs. Joseph Merrick Jones, Jr.

¼ cup vinegar
2 tablespoons white wine
2 tablespoons lemon juice

1 tablespoons shallot.
1 stick of butter

Mix first four ingredients and cook on medium flame until mixture is reduced to about 4 tablespoons. Add cold butter and beat with whisk until creamy, over very low flame. Do not put on high heat.

SPAGHETTI SAUCE de LUXE
Mr. Fred B. Otell

3 No. 2 cans tomatoes
2 cans consommé
6 bouillon cubes
5 onions, 3 green peppers (chopped)
¼ lb. oleomargarine
3 tablespoons salt, 1 teaspoon black pepper
½ bunch celery

Cook all of above until green peppers are soft (about 30 minutes), then run through blender. Put back in pot and add:

4 cans tomato paste
2 cans tomato sauce
hot pepper sauce to taste

Cook slowly down to a thick gravy and add:

10 large cloves garlic, pressed
2 teaspoons each marjoram, basil
1 teaspoon each oregano, savory

Simmer for short time, then remove from stove and cool. Will keep frozen for months.
TO USE: Place desired amount in saucepan; melt—add enough dry wine (red) to thin to proper consistency. For each person to be served, add one small clove garlic pressed and a pinch of each of the herbs named above.

SPANISH SAUCE

Spanish sauce is made exactly like the Tomato sauce for Spaghetti but every bit of grease is removed and it is served after being strained. A glass of Madeira wine added to a pint of this sauce transforms it to **Madeira sauce**.

STEAK SAUCE
Dorothy Dix

½ cup vinegar
4 ozs. butter

1 cup tomato catsup
½ tablespoon each salt, white pepper
½ lemon, sliced
1 small clove garlic, minced
1 medium size onion, chopped
½ cup olive oil
1 tablespoon prepared mustard
few drops Tabasco

Mix all ingredients together, boil for fifteen minutes on a slow fire and strain. The advantage of this sauce is not only in its tang, but in the fact that it will keep indefinitely in the refrigerator.

TARTAR SAUCE
Mrs. D. D. Curran

2 eggs
½ cup olive oil
3 tablespoons vinegar
1 tablespoon mild mustard
1 teaspoon sugar
¼ teaspoon pepper
1 teaspoon each salt, onion juice
1 tablespoon chopped capers
1 cucumber pickle, chopped

The first step is the same as for making mayonnaise using first of ingredients. Then the other ingredients chopped fine, are added.

SOUR CREAM TARTAR SAUCE

1 cup (½ pt.) commercial sour cream
2 tablespoons chopped pickles (any kind you like)
½ teaspoon salt
dash or two of Tabasco
1 teaspoon grated onion

TOMATO CATSUP
Mrs. Burton Dawkins

½ bushel ripe tomatoes
1 qt. good cider vinegar
1 doz. small red Creole onions
½ cup sugar
2 tablespoons cayenne pepper or six small hot red peppers to taste
2 tablespoons black pepper
1 teaspoons allspice, ground
¼ teaspoon allspice, ground
¼ teaspoon cloves, ground
2 tablespoons powdered mustard
4 tablespoons salt, 4 cloves garlic
1 cup horseradish, grated
4 tablespoons each black and white mustard seed
1 package celery seed

Tie in a bag the following: black and white mustard seed, and celery seed.

Clean tomatoes well, do not peel. Quarter them, sprinkle lightly with salt and allow to stand three hours. This will give water enough time in which to boil them. Place on a slow fire and boil until they fall to pieces. There should be one gallon of the tomato pulp. Add finely chopped onions and garlic to this, and cook until soft enough to pass through a colander. Add remaining ingredients except the horseradish. Cook down on a very slow fire for three or four hours until it thickens (It burns easily!). Add horseradish. Bottle while hot.

SAUCE TOURAINE

½ cup butter
1 egg yolk
1 tablespoon vinegar
½ teaspoon paprika, salt to taste

Cream butter, beat in egg yolks, and then remaining ingredients. Consistency, very stiff.

Excellent, and so quick. May be used for hot broccoli, cauliflower, for green salads, and also for cold meats—in last named, a little dry mustard (to taste) may be added.

desserts, candy and ice cream

BANANAS FLAMBEAUX
Terry Flettrich

Skin bananas. Coat with sugar. Then coat with flour. Coat with sugar again. Cook until done in melted butter. Then pour a generous amount of rum over cooked bananas. Ignite. Serve immediately. Use chafing dish.

BANANAS FOSTER
Mrs. Ella Brennan Martin
Brennan's Restaurant

This recipe is adapted from one used by Brennan's restaurant. It is typical of the flaming dishes popular in New Orleans restaurants.

    1 tablespoon butter
    2 teaspoons brown sugar
    1 banana, halved lengthwise and
      crosswise
      cinnamon, 1 oz. rum
    1 teaspoon banana liqueur

(1) Melt the butter; add the sugar. Cook the banana in this mixture over medium heat till lightly browned. Turn pieces once. Sprinkle with cinnamon.
(2) Heat liqueur and rum. Ignite and pour flaming over banana.
Yield: two servings.

BIG SINK
SPECIALTY
Mrs. E. V. Benjamin, Jr.
Big Sink Farm,
Versailles, Kentucky

    4 cups whipping cream
      crystalized ginger chunks
      salted pecans, chopped
      cognac
      Major Grey's Chutney
      Meringues, either 8 individual
      ones, or one large one

Soak crystalized ginger chunks in cognac to soften them. Whip cream and season to taste with ginger, pecans, chutney, and cognac. Spoon over meringues and serve with a crisp sugar cookie.

BLACKBERRY BREAD
Mrs. Catherine Howell Laycock

This dessert was made for generations at Oak Hill Plantation in East Feliciana Parish, and given to me.

Bring fresh blackberries to a boil with a little water to start juice. Simmer ten minutes and add sugar to taste. Trim and butter slices of bread. Place a layer of buttered bread in a pudding mold, cover with the hot berries and continue alternating bread and berries until mold is filled. Cool and chill. Serve with cream.

BLACKBERRY ROLY-POLY

    2 cups flour
    2 teaspoons baking powder
    ½ teaspoon salt
    4 tablespoons butter
    ¾ cup milk
    1½ cups fresh blackberries
    6 tablespoons sugar

Sift flour once, measure, add baking powder and salt, and sift again. Cut in shortening, add milk gradually until soft dough is formed, turn out immediately on slightly floured board and roll ¼ inch thick. Brush with melted butter, cover with blackberries and sprinkle with sugar. Roll as for jelly rolls. Place in greased loaf pan with edge of roll on under side. Brush with melted butter, bake in hot oven (400 degrees F) twenty to twenty-five minutes. Serve hot with cream or Blackberry Sauce.

BRÛLOT BREAD PUDDING

Mr. David Duggins
Cafe Brûlot Restaurant

1 loaf stale French bread
  (large)
1 quart milk
4 eggs, beaten
2 cups sugar
1 cup raisins
1 tablespoon vanilla
1 tablespoon nutmeg
1 tablespoon cinnamon
½ stick or 4 tablespoons
  butter

Break bread into small pieces and mix all ingredients together. Bake in greased shallow 2 quart baking dish for one hour at 350°.

BUTTERSCOTCH BROWN

Mrs. E. K. Thomas
Paris, Kentucky

1 stick butter (melted)
1 cup graham cracker crumbs
1 cup Eagle Brand condensed milk
1 cup coconut
1 cup chopped pecans
1 pkg. butterscotch morsels or
  chips

Put all ingredients into a 9" square pan and bake at 350° for about 20 minutes or until done. Leave in pan 2 hours to cool before cutting into squares. May be frozen if desired.

CARMEL MOUSSE
AU ST. AUBIN

Mrs. David T. Merrick

1 tablespoon cornstarch or flour
1 cup sugar, caramelized
2 eggs, 1 qt. milk
1 teaspoon vanilla
2 cups heavy cream

Put the sugar in a saucepan and brown it. Make a custard with milk, eggs, and cornstarch and add sugar. Stir until melted. Freeze.

Line a melon mold with this caramel mixture, fill the center with whipped cream flavored with whiskey, sherry, or vanilla. Cover with greased waxed paper before putting on the lid. Pack with two parts of ice to one of salt and let freeze 3 hours.

CHARLOTTE RUSSE

Mrs. David T. Merrick

1 qt. whipping cream
5 tablespoons sugar
1 package gelatine
1 cup cold water or milk
1 cup hot milk
¾ cup sherry wine, ½ cup whiskey
2 teaspoons vanilla

Soak the gelatine in cold milk, or water and add it to the hot milk. When melted, allow it to cool. Whip the cream, add sugar, wine, whiskey and vanilla. Now pour in the gelatine mixture and whip until it begins to jell. Place in the refrigerator until ready to serve.

CHERRIES IN THE SNOW

Mrs. Jerry Derks

Meringue:

6 egg whites
½ teaspoon cream of tartar
¼ teaspoon salt
1½ cups sugar

Beat whites till stiff, slowly adding other ingredients. Put in 9" x 13" pan, greased. Bake at 270° for 1 hour. Turn oven off and leave 1 hour minimum.

Filling:

2 3-oz. packages Philadelphia cream
  cheese
1 cup sugar
1 teaspoon vanilla
1 pint whipping cream
2 cups miniature marshmallows
½ teaspoon almond flavoring
1 can cherry pie filling

Cream together cream cheese, sugar and vanilla. Then whip 1 pint cream and fold in the marshmallows. Add cream cheese mixture to this. Spread on top of meringue. Refrigerate 12 hours.

To serve: cut in squares. Add ½ teaspoon almond flavoring to 1 can cherry pie filling and spoon on top. Serves 12.

CHERRIES JUBILEE

2 large cans of black seeded cherries
  the juice of 1 can
1 cup of sugar
3 cups of brandy

Heat the sugar and the juice until a heavier syrup is formed, and then add the cherries. While it is still all quite warm, pour it into the brûlot bowl, pour in your brandy and proceed as for Café Brûlot. Serve generously over vanilla ice cream.

CHOCOLATE DESSERT

Mrs. William Kearney

2 bars German sweet chocolate
½ cup finely slivered blanched
  almonds
8 eggs, separated
¼ teaspoon salt
  whipped cream for topping
  few drops almond extract

Put chocolate and almonds in double boiler until chocolate is melted. Separate eggs, beat whites with salt until stiff but not dry. Beat egg yolks until thick and lemon colored. Add chocolate and almonds to egg yolks and mix well. Fold all into egg whites until well blended. Pour in shallow serving dish and chill thoroughly. Top with whipped cream which has been flavored with a few drops of almond extract.

CHOCOLATE
ICE BOX DESSERT

Mrs. Harry Merritt Lane, Sr.

12 marshmallows, cut up
1 bar German sweet chocolate
4 egg yolks
1 cup sifted powdered sugar
4 egg whites, beaten stiffly
1 cup chopped pecans
  graham cracker crumbs
  whipped cream for topping

Place chocolate in top of double boiler. When melted, stir in the egg yolks, beaten slightly. Then add the powdered sugar. Stir well, mix in the egg whites and the nuts. Cook ten minutes more, stirring often. Then mix in the marshmallows, and stir again.

Pour into a rectangular shaped pyrex dish or pan that has been lined with the crushed graham cracker crumbs. Then sprinkle crumbs over the top. Chill and cut into squares and serve topped with whipped cream.

FROZEN CHOCOLATE ROLL

Mrs. David T. Merrick

1 qt. milk, 1 cup sugar
2 squares Baker's chocolate
1½ teaspoons vanilla
1 pt. whipping cream
1½ tablespoons sugar
  salt

Melt the chocolate. Add the sugar and the milk, and let come to a boil. When cool, add vanilla and a tiny pinch of salt. Freeze.

When hard, take out the dasher, spread the cream around the sides of the freezer, leaving a hole in the center, into which pour the whipped cream, which has been sweetened and flavored. Cover freezer and pack to stand for two to three hours. Turn out on a platter by holding a hot cloth around the freezer. Cut in rounds.

Any flavor of ice cream may be used to make this roll and the whipped cream center may be flavored to make a good combination. Commercial ice cream can be utilized for the outer part, the center filled with whipped cream and packed in ice and salt for two hours.

CHOCOLATE
TART PUDDING

Mrs. Richard Adler

1½ cups sugar
8 tablespoons cocoa
6 tablespoons flour
2 cups milk
4 egg yolks
1 stick butter
  whipping cream

In top of double boiler: Mix dry ingredients, add hot water gradually; add beaten egg yolks. Add milk. Cook over hot water, stirring occasionally, until thickened. Add butter and stir until melted. Put in ramekins and top with sweetened whipped cream.

COFFEE CREAM

1 qt. sweet cream
2 cups black coffee
2 envelopes gelatine
  sugar to taste

Pour ½ pint of cream on the gelatine and let it stand long enough to soften. Then add to the hot coffee, cream and sugar, which are mixed together. Pour through a fine sieve into a bowl and stir occasionally until cold. Put in glasses or mold, before it begins to set. Place in refrigerator.

COFFEE DELIGHT

Mrs. Fleur Hampton

½ lb. small marshmallows
½ pint whipped cream
1 cup hot coffee

Pour hot coffee over marshmallows and dissolve. Let cool and start to congeal; add whipped cream and pour into molds. Place in refrigerator of set. Shave chocolate over top.

COFFEE FRAPPÉ

Mrs. Frank Harbison

3 cups very strong black coffee
3 lightly beaten eggs
1 cup milk
¼ cup sugar
1 teaspoon flour
½ teaspoon cinnamon

After making black coffee, add sugar, flour, eggs and milk. Cook in double boiler stirring constantly until mixture will coat the spoon. Remove from fire and add cinnamon. Chill for four hours in the refrigerator tray. Stir once or twice to prevent hard freezing. Consistency should be semi-frozen. Before serving add whipped cream.

FROZEN FRUIT COMPOTE

Mrs. James Selman

1 box frozen blueberries,
  (unsweetened)
1 box frozen raspberries
1 box frozen dark cherries, pitted
2 boxes frozen sliced peaches
½ cup cassis (black currant liquer)
silver bowl and mint leaves

Remove fruit from freezer a few hours before serving time, and put in silver bowl. When partially thawed, add cassis and keep in refrigerator. At serving time stir carefully and garnish with sprigs of fresh mint.

(You may also add strawberries, but most brands get so soggy and discolored that I don't recommend it. Fresh are delicious.)

CORN FLAKE RING

Mrs. Bessie Behan Lewis

2 cups of brown sugar
1 cup of cream, ¼ lb. butter
1 cup crisp corn flakes
1 cup pecan halves, vanilla ice cream
  caramel or chocolate sauce

Chill a buttered ring-mold in the refrigerator 2 hours.

Put the brown sugar, cream and butter into a double boiler to bubble gently until it will make a soft ball in iced water. Stir in the corn flakes and pecan halves.

Now, take out the chilled mold and pour in the corn flake mixture. Let the filled mold stand two more hours, outside the refrigerator.

Now turn on platter and fill the center with vanilla ice cream. Pour a sauce over all.

COUER À LA CREME

(French Heart of Cream with Peach Sauce)

Mrs. C. Nolte DeRussy, Jr.

1½ cups heavy or whipping cream
6 egg yolks
½ cup sugar
1 teaspoon vanilla extract

Peach Sauce:

2 10-oz. packages frozen peaches
½ teaspoon almond extract
¼ teaspoon nutmeg

Early in the day or the day before; in small bowl with electric mixer at high speed, whip cream until soft peaks form. Wash beaters.

In large bowl with electric mixer at high speed, beat egg yolks and sugar until thick and lemon colored. Beat in vanilla extract. Fold in whipped cream. Pour into 6-cup heart shaped mold; freeze until firm. Unmold; serve with peach sauce.

Peach Sauce: In covered electric blender container at low speed, blend peaches, thawed, almond extract and nutmeg.

FROZEN CREAM CHEESE

Mrs. Walter Torian

4 cream cheese with their cream
1 pt. sweet cream
1 can condensed milk, pinch soda
   vanilla, sugar to taste
2 egg whites, beaten

Mash the cream cheese alternately with the pint of cream, through a wire sieve. Add a pinch of soda and condensed milk and sweeten to taste. Add vanilla and the stiffly beaten whites of eggs. Pack and freeze.

CRÈME BRULÉE

4 egg yolks, well beaten
1 pt. cream
   brown or maple sugar

Beat the egg yolks very stiff. Heat the cream to the boiling point and pour it over the beaten egg yolks. Return to the fire in a double boiler. Cook five minutes stirring constantly. Remove and pour it into a buttered baking dish. Chill it well. Cover the top with sugar, then run in the oven, leaving door open and let it remain until a crust is formed. Take out and allow to cool. Refrigerate until time to serve. Excellent with baked pears or any other cooked fruit.

CRÈME BRULÈE

4 egg yolks, well beaten
1 pint cream
   brown sugar

Beat the egg yolks very stiff. Heat the cream to the boiling point and pour it over the beaten egg yolks. Return to the fire in a double boiler. Cook five minutes stirring constantly. Remove and pour it into a buttered baking dish. Chill it well. Cover the top entirely with sugar so that no custard shows. Place the dish on a bowl of crushed ice and place the custard under the flame of the broiler until the

sugar caramelizes. Watch it very carefully or the sugar will burn. Take out and allow to cool. Refrigerate until time to serve. Excellent with baked pears or any other cooked fruit. The secret of this is always make it the day before.

CRÉOLE PUFFS

1 pt. water
1 tablespoon each butter, sugar
1 lemon, the rind peeled thin
4 eggs, flour

Boil sugar, water, and lemon rind, five minutes. Remove rind. Take flour a handful at a time and sprinkle into the boiling syrup which has been kept on the fire. Stir vigorously every minute until it is so thick it is difficult to stir. Continue stirring and cooking until it leaves the side of the pan (the longer the better). Remove from fire. Beat in four eggs, one at a time, stirring vigorously between each egg. Success depends on the vigor of the stirring. Drop bits of the paste the size of an egg into deep hot fat. Fry to a beautiful brown. Sprinkle with sugar.

CRÊPES

Mr. John Devlin

Basic Recipe:
   ½ cup all-purpose flour
   1 cup light cream
   2 eggs
   ¼ teaspoon salt

Sift flour, measure and resift into mixing bowl. Add cream and beat with wire whisk or portable beater until perfectly smooth.

Add eggs and salt and beat again until well-blended. Batter should have the consistency of light cream.

Let stand at room temperature for at least one hour—preferably two, before using. Beat again before cooking.

COOKING CRÊPES

Necessary Equipment:
   treated six-inch skillet
   a two-tablespoon measure
   spatula
   fork

Preparation of Crêpe Pan:
   Get a five- or six-inch cast alumi-

num, tin, iron, steel or copper skillet.

Using lard or vegetable shortening, grease it with a paper towel. Rub it hard until thoroughly clean. The paper towel will tell you when the skillet is completely clean.

Fill the pan seven-eighths full with olive oil or a commercial salad oil. Let it stand for one full day.

The next day preheat oven to 500°F. Place pan, filled with oil, in oven for five minutes.

Remove the pan and let cool before emptying oil.

Wipe clean with paper towel.

The pan must never be washed with soap or water. After using, wipe it clean with a paper towel. When not in use, place the pan in a paper bag and put it away. The secret of good crêpes is in the pan. It must be treated first, respected forever, and used only for omelettes and crêpes.

Place pan over medium heat until hot.

Drop in 1 teaspoon of sweet butter.

When butter bubbles, pour in 2 tablespoons of batter. (Note—under no circumstances pour any additional batter on top of the original amount, even if there are holes in the crêpes.)

Quickly tilt and rotate pan to cover the entire bottom thinly and evenly.

Cook the crêpe about one minute on one side. The top side will start to bubble slowly when bottom side is cooked.

Turn gently using a spatula and fork.

Cook for one more minute on the other side. The edges will begin to curl when done.

Remove to platter in 200°F. oven. They may be stacked or placed overlapping each other.

Repeat operation until enough crêpes are made. The amount will depend on how they are to be used.

This recipe yields 14 to 16 crêpes.

For 8 people—take two crêpes and place on silver serving platter—fold into 2 crêpes 2 tablespoons vanilla ice-cream. Repeat until all crêpes have been used. Pour Cointreau over entire silver platter holding crêpes and light the Cointreau. Serve immediately. (Cointreau should be heated until it bubbles before pouring over crêpes.) Use about 2 tablespoons of Cointreau for each 2 crêpes—folded over ice-cream—or 16 tablespoons of Cointreau for 16 crêpes.

CRÊPES BRULÉES

¼ lb. flour
4 eggs
½ pt. cold milk
4 ozs. powdered sugar
1 teaspoon orange flower water

Sift flour into pan or bowl. Break the eggs, beat well, and add 1 oz. of powdered sugar. Mix thoroughly with the flour and then add the cold milk, pouring it in gradually. Mix well, add the orange flower water.

Have ready a pan, buttered slightly and when hot, drop 1 large tablespoon of batter in it. Turn pan around to spread the batter as thin as possible.

Cook until brown and turn cake to cook other side. Lay the pan cake on a dish, butter well, sprinkle with powdered sugar and roll.

Place in baking dish: peeling of 3 oranges grated, 12 lumps of sugar, 4 ozs. of good brandy, 4 ozs. of Kirschwasser.

Light brandy. When burning well dip pan cakes in one by one for 1 minute and serve.

CRÊPES FITZGERALD
Ella Brennan Martin
Brennan's French Restaurant
Pan Cake Crêpes

¾ cup sifted flour
   pinch salt
1 teaspoon sugar
2 eggs, milk

Mix eggs with flour, sugar and salt. Add milk until batter is consistency of condensed milk. Beat until smooth. Heat a 6 inch skillet oiled with pastry brush dipped in vegetable oil. Pour batter (2 tablespoons) into pan, tilting quickly to distribute batter evenly. Cook 1 minute or so, until brown, then turn and brown other side. Repeat until all batter is used. Keep cooked cakes warm in a towel.

Filling:

2 heaping teaspoons Philadelphia
   cream cheese
2 tablespoons sour cream
½ cup strawberries

sugar, butter
strawberry liqueur, kirsch

Roll cream cheese and sour cream in crepes and put on plate. In a chafing dish, cook strawberries in sugar and butter. Flame in strawberry liqueur and kirsch and pour over crepes.

CRÊPES SUZETTE

1 cup powdered sugar
1 coffeespoon absinthe
1 egg yolk
2 cups each flour, milk
4 tablespoons melted butter
3 eggs, beaten together

Mash the powdered sugar well into the absinthe, then add to it the well-beaten egg yolk to make a paste, beating it until it is like mayonnaise or thicker. Set aside. To make the crêpes, stir the milk into the flour, with melted butter, and add the eggs beaten together. Mix all this and beat again. Add sugar mixture.

Put a generous spoonful of the mixture just off the center of each and fold the crêpes over it at the sides and ends, pocketbook shaped. Run these into a brisk oven until brown. They puff up like an omelet soufflé and melt exquisitely in the mouth. To serve this style crêpes, sprinkle them with a little powdered sugar, pour curacao over them, and let the alcohol burn a few moments.

CRÊPES SUZETTE GAULOISES

2 cups flour
¾ cup powdered sugar
5 eggs, 2 cups milk
salt, flavoring

Sauce:

2 oranges
6 tablespoons butter
1 cup powdered sugar

Mix together the flour, salt, and sugar. Add the milk slowly, forming a thick paste. Add the well-beaten eggs, and mix thoroughly. Add flavoring, such as grated lemon or orange peel. Fry on a hot buttered griddle. (The cakes should be paper thin.) Fry them until they are almost crisp, but just soft enough to roll.

Sauce: Cream the butter and add the sugar, grated rind of the orange and the juice drop by drop, stirring while it is added, so that the sauce does not curdle. A little curacao helps a lot. Spread a spoonful of the sauce over each pancake, before it is rolled (or folded) to be served.

CUP CUSTARD

1 qt. milk
5 ozs. granulated sugar, 6 eggs
2 teaspoons vanilla

Heat milk. Break eggs into sugar, beat and add milk gradually, not too hot, stir until the sugar is melted. Put a spoonful of caramel sauce in each cup, fill with the custard and cook in a pan of water in slow oven. Test with paring knife.

To serve turn cups over on a plate and caramel will be on top.

PEACH DUMPLINGS

½ cup milk
6 large soft peaches, dusted with sugar
1 cup flour, ½ teaspoon salt
2 teaspoons baking powder
butter size of an egg

Sift together dry ingredients, with the fingers mix in butter thoroughly and add milk. Roll out and cut in pieces to cover fruit. Have dough just moist enough to be able to handle it.

Sauce: 1 cup sugar, butter, the size of a large egg, 2 cups water. Boil, and while boiling, drop in dumplings.

Then place in oven about ½ hour, or longer, if necessary.

Serve hot, with cream—or, they are also good cold.

EGGNOG RING

8 eggs, beaten separately
1 cup granulated sugar
1 envelope gelatine soaked in ½ cup
of cold water
½ cup boiling water
¾ cup whiskey
whipped cream
macaroons, lady fingers, almonds

To the yolks add whiskey, to the whites add a cup of sifted sugar. Then mix. Dissolve the gelatine in boiling water and fold it into the mixture.

Line a ring mold with lady fingers

and pour in the above mixture.

When ready to serve, turn on a platter and fill the center with stiffly whipped cream, in which are mixed the almonds and macaroons, rolled and sifted.

This beautiful and delicious dish may be garnished with strawberries, cherries or raspberries.

GRAPEFRUIT ASPIC

Mrs. Renée Gavinet Bowie

6 fine grapefruit
1 pt. orange juice, freshly squeezed
1 envelope unflavored gelatine
¼ cup cold water, ½ cup boiling water

Peel the grapefruit and separate in sections carefully to avoid breaking. Free from all white pulp. Moisten the gelatine in cold water and dissolve in the hot water in the usual manner. Add it to the orange juice. Place the grapefruit sections in a mold, fill with orange gelatine and set in the icebox until firm. Turn out on crisp lettuce leaves and serve with mayonnaise. This is either a salad or a dessert.

GREEN GRAPES

Mrs. H. Chotard Eustis

seedless green grapes
brown sugar
sour cream

A very simple but delectable dessert is prepared in the following manner. Pick, wash and drain seedless grapes —the amount depending on the number to be served. Half fill a serving bowl, sprinkle with brown sugar and cover with sour cream. Repeat, having an entire covering of the cream on top. Place in refrigerator several hours before serving. Other fruit, such as Damson plums or peaches may be substituted. A pleasant variation is to cover fruit with brandy, whiskey or cointreaux. Dust with powdered sugar and cover with sour cream. At table serve brown sugar to cover cream.

HOT WEATHER SPECIAL

Mrs. Charles L. Seemann

1 watermelon
½ gal. orange sherbet

1 qt. assorted fruit (plums, peaches, figs, pears, strawberries and cantaloupe in balls)
4 small bunches of grapes or cherries

Cut watermelon in half (lengthwise). Remove seeds from one half. Lightly scoop out center. Wedge the edge and drain. Keep cool.

With other half make a quart of watermelon balls. Prepare fruit and sugar lightly. Keep very cold until ready for use. Mash remaining pulp of melon and add to sherbet and re-freeze.

When ready to serve place sherbet in center of melon shell. Pour fruit and melon balls on top. Run slender stick from end to end of melon shell, suspending at each end a decorative bunch of grapes. As good to the eye as to the palate.

ICE CREAM CRUNCH

Mrs. Wallace E. Sturgis
Ocala, Florida

1 package Pillsbury's Butter Pecan Ice Box Cookies
½ gallon vanilla ice cream
¾ jar Kraft's caramel sauce

Slice cookies thin and cook according to directions. Line sides and bottom of pyrex dish with cookies, saving some for top.

In a bowl soften ice cream slightly. Add caramel sauce and mix well. Spread this over cookies in pyrex dish. Top with remainder of cookies (crumbled). Freeze. Cut into squares to serve.

THE PONTCHARTRAIN'S FAMOUS ICE CREAM PIE

Mr. Albert Aschaffenburg

1 qt. egg whites
1 lb. sugar

Put egg white and sugar in rotary mixer and beat at a low speed for about 3 minutes so that sugar can mix well with egg white and then beat at high speed for another 2 to 3 minutes until the meringue stiffens.

Place two layers different flavors of ice cream, each about 1½ inch thick, in a 10 inch pie pastry shell and cover with meringue to a thickness of about 2½ to 3 inches.

Place under broiler for about 30 seconds to brown meringue and then put pie in deep freeze for several hours before serving. Just before serving pour chocolate sauce or fruit sauce, such as Melba, over each slice.

Pie Shell: To make two ice cream pie shells use ingredients as follows:

1 cup shortening
3 tablespoons ice water
2½ cups flour, ⅛ teaspoon salt

Bake in moderate oven (about 400°).

LEMON AND CHOCOLATE FROZEN PIE

Mrs. V. L. Gaston

2 eggs
1/3 cup lemon juice
½ cup vanilla wafers, crumbed
½ cup sugar
1 cup evaporated milk

Beat egg yolks in top of double boiler, add sugar and lemon juice and a thin slice of rind. Cook until it thickens, stirring all the time. Remove the rind and let mixture cool. Beat egg whites stiff and add to cooled custard. Have milk in freezing tray and let it just begin to freeze, pour out in bowl and whip until stiff then mix all together. Butter refrigerator tray and sprinkle well with crumbs in bottom, pour in mixture and cover with crumbs; when frozen cut in pie shape.

For chocolate add water instead of lemon juice and add 1½ ounces chocolate and a teaspoon vanilla.

FROZEN LEMON SPONGE

Mrs. Lewis Puller

1 large lemon and rind
4 egg yolks, beaten
½ cup sugar
1 cup whipping cream

Cook above until consistency of custard.

3½ tablespoons lemon Jello dissolved in
1 cup hot water

Cool above mixture, add the whipped cream, and stiffly beaten egg whites. Pour into melon mold and freeze.

LUCINDA'S SURPRISE

Mrs. Lester Lautenschlager, Jr.

½ watermelon
½ gallon vanilla ice cream
1 medium pack M & M candies
(use only chocolate candies)
½ gallon raspberry sherbet
1 pound cake
3 jiggers rum, 1 jigger Falerium

Scoop out all the watermelon leaving the half watermelon shell. Dry cavity well. Fill bottom with vanilla ice cream. Place in freezer. One hour later add ½ of sliced pound cake over which ½ of rum and Falerium has been sprinkled. Add ½ of the raspberry sherbet. Place in freezer. One hour later add the rest of the vanilla ice cream and the remainder of the pound cake and liquors. Return to freezer. The a.m. of the day you plan to serve this dessert, add the rest of the raspberry sherbet and line up the chocolate M & M's to look like watermelon seeds.

This dessert can be served sliced (slicing the rind and all) or served scooped out.

MOCHA CREME

Mrs. William H. McCandless, Jr.

32 regular-sized marshmallows
1 cup strong coffee
1 pint whipping cream

Dissolve marshmallows in coffee. Allow to set in refrigerator. Whip and fold ½ pint of whipping cream into marshmallow mixture. Spoon into compotes. Top with the other ½ pint of whipping cream, whipped. Garnish each compote with 1 maraschino cherry and 1 teaspoon of Creme de Cacao (Serves 6 to 8.)

OMELET SOUFFLÉ

Mrs. Curran Perkins

3 eggs
3 tablespoons powdered sugar
½ lemon, juice and grated peel

Beat the yolks and whites of the eggs separately, the whites until they are stiff enough to cut with a knife. Add the sugar gradually to the yolks, beating until the mixture is thick and smooth. Add lemon juice and peel. Fold the yolks and whites lightly together, pour into a warmed and buttered dish and bake in a quick oven a few minutes.

ORANGE MOUSSE
Mrs. David T. Merrick

1 pt. whipping cream
½ cup sugar
1 teaspoon gelatine, ¼ cup water
¾ cup orange juice, 1½ oranges
2 egg whites, stiffly beaten

Whip cream, add sugar, flavor with orange juice. Melt gelatine that has soaked in water. When cool add to cream. Add the egg whites well beaten. Line mold with oranges that have been separated into sections. Pour in cream. Pack in ice and salt for 3 hours. Serve with orange sauce.

PEACHES AGLOW
Mrs. William J. Bentley

6 large luscious peaches
simple syrup
champagne, very cold

Peel and remove the seeds from the peaches. They may be sliced or left in halves. Cover with simple syrup and chill in the refrigerator. When ready to serve put them in a large sherbet glass and fill glass with very cold champagne.

This can be served before a meal or it serves as a delicious finish to a dinner.

FROZEN PEACHES
Mrs. Walter Scott Merrill

8 or 9 ripe, soft peaches
1 lemon, the juice
1½ cups sugar

Peel peaches and mash thoroughly. Pour the lemon juice over them. Dissolve the sugar over the fire in about a half a cup of water. Do not boil. Add the syrup to the peaches, cool, and freeze. This is simple but delicious.

PEACHES IN BRANDY
Mrs. Burton Dawkins

1 can (1 lb. 11 ozs.) peaches, drained
  (reserve syrup)
brandy

ice cream or whipped cream

Drain peaches. Measure reserve syrup and add an equal amount of brandy to it. Pour over peaches and let stand for two hours. Serve with whipped cream or with ice cream.

PEACHES AU CHATEAU BLANC

4 large freestone peaches
6 macaroons, rolled fine
2 eggs
2 crushed peaches
1 peach kernel, crushed to a paste
  sugar to taste

Cut the peaches round and remove the stones. Add to the crushed peaches the powdered macaroons, mix well with the stiffly beaten yolks and sweeten to taste. Add the peach kernel and blend with the mixture.

Stuff the peaches with this, place them in a pan, and bake until done. Remove from the oven, and top with meringue made with the sweetened beaten whites of the eggs. Run into the oven and brown slowly. A delicious sweet after a heavy dinner, or luncheon.

SUPER MELBA

4 scoops of vanilla ice cream
4-8 peach halves, brandied, fresh
  or tinned
4 tablespoons apple jelly
4 tablespoons currant jelly

The jellies are melted. Over each serving of ice cream one or two peach halves are placed, cut side down, and the melted jellies are poured over all.

PEARS AU COINTREAU
Mrs. Richard Adler

1 lb. 13 ozs. can pears
1 tablespoon sugar
½ cup orange juice
1 lemon (juice of)
¼ cup Cointreau

Drain pears well. Pour over them the sugar, orange juice and the lemon, and the Cointreau. Chill. Serves 4.

POTS DE CRÈMES
Mrs. Samuel P. Schwing

1 cup (6 oz. pack) semi-sweet choco-
    late bits
2 whole eggs
2 tablespoons of sugar
1 tablespoon whipping cream
1 teaspoon vanilla
    pinch of salt

Place all ingredients except chocolate in the blender. Gradually add the
chocolate bits. Blend until smooth.
Heat to a simmer ¾ cup of milk.
Blend in milk with other ingredients.
When well blended, pour in cups and
chill. Top with whipped cream. Makes
about six cups.

BUTTERSCOTCH PUDDING
Mrs. William J. Mitchell

1 lb. brown sugar, ¼ lb. butter
1 qt. milk, 2 eggs
1 package gelatine

Melt the butter and sugar slowly
in an iron skillet. Have ready the
milk, scalded. Pour part of it into the
melted butter and sugar, the remainder over gelatine which has been
soaked in cold water. Mix with the
beaten yolks and add to the first mixture, which has been left over a very
slow fire. Mix well. Remove from the
fire and add the beaten whites of eggs.
Put into a melon mold. When ready
to serve, surround it on the platter
with whipped cream.

CARROT PUDDING
Mrs. David T. Merrick

2 cups raw grated carrots
2 cups bread pulled in small pieces
¼ lb. butter, slightly soft
3 eggs beaten together
1 cup each currants, raisins
¼ lb. citron shaved fine
1 teaspoon each cinnamon, cloves, all-
    spice
1 tablespoon orange juice
1 tablespoon flour (to dust fruit)
1 orange (grated rind)
1 tablespoon crystallized orange peel
1 tablespoon crystallized lemon peel
1 teaspoon soda, scant, in a little water

Mix the ingredients in the order
given, then steam for three hours in

a double boiler. This dish, served hot
with eggnog sauce or hard sauce will
give you a memorable dessert.

CHAMBLISS PUDDING
Mrs. Amédée Bringier

1 light cup chopped butter
1 cup pulverized sugar
2 cups flour, measured after sifting
3 eggs beaten separately
1 teaspoon baking powder, heaping
3 tablespoons cream

Cream the butter and the sugar together. Add the well beaten yolks,
fold in the whites, the flour with the
baking powder sifted in, and lastly the
cream. Beat well, and flavor to taste.
Bake. Serve with liquid sauce. Currants will add further grace to this delicious pudding, an old-time favorite
that has not lost its prestige.

COCONUT PUDDING
Mrs. Odette J. Hemenway

4 cups of sugar
2 **fresh** coconuts well grated
4 whole eggs, 4 egg yolks
2 slices of bread, ½ cup milk
1 cup of water
1 tablespoon of butter
1 teaspoon each salt, vanilla

Melt 1 cup of sugar in pot until
light brown. As it begins to boil pour
immediately into ring mold being sure
that it is evenly distributed at the
bottom. Let cool. In a bowl mix well
the grated coconut and two slices of
bread that have been well soaked in
the milk. Place 3 cups of sugar, 1 cup
of water and teaspoon of vanilla in a
pot and let it come to a boil. Do not
stir. Turn off heat and add 1 tablespoon of butter. Mix it all in the coconut bowl adding 1 teaspoon of salt.
Now mix in 4 eggs and then 4 yolks.
The mixture is now ready to be poured
in the ring mold, over the browned
sugar which should be cool. Put mold
in a pan containing water. Consign to
oven that has been preheated at 250
for thirty minutes. Raise heat to 300
and leave pudding in oven for 1 hour.

Cool before turning into serving
platter. Do not put in refrigerator
but just in cool place.

MARSHMALLOW PUDDING

24 to 30 marshmallows
1 egg, ¾ cup sugar
2 cups sweet milk
  cracker crumbs, sherry or almond

Butter a baking dish and cover the bottom with a layer of cracker crumbs, broken fine. Cut marshmallows in half and spread over cracker crumbs. Continue with a layer of cracker crumbs and a layer of marshmallows until the dish is full. Beat the egg until very light and combine with the sugar and milk. Flavor with sherry, or almond, if preferred. Bake. The substitution of crumbled macaroons for the plain cracker crumbs makes a very delicious pudding. In this case the sugar is omitted.

NO NAME PUDDING

6 egg whites
6 tablespoons sugar, sifted
½ cup raisins (large)
½ glass sherry
1 cup pecans (chopped)
  whipped cream

Seed the raisins and soak them in sherry overnight. Beat the whites of eggs stiff, add sugar, beat vigorously, add raisins and nuts. Turn into a pyrex bowl and bake slowly until done. Serve with whipped cream.

This delicious pudding remains nameless for no name has yet been found that does justice to its worth.

ENGLISH PLUM PUDDING

½ lb. crumbled suet or
½ lb. butter
2 lbs. raisins, 1 lb. currants
½ lb. brown sugar, 1 lb. flour
1 cup milk, 8 eggs
1 cup black molasses
2 cups pecans, ½ lb. citron
2 teaspoons baking powder
1 teaspoon salt
1 tablespoon each allspice, nutmeg, cinnamon

Mix as you would for fruit cake. Dredge fruit and pecans well with flour and add to cake mixture. Pour into a well floured cloth, tie tight but allow room for pudding to expand. Drop into a kettle of boiling water and cook three hours. Serve with

hard sauce. This recipe makes two large puddings.

CREAMY RICE PUDDING

1 qt. milk, 2 tablespoons rice
6¼ tablespoons sugar
¼ teaspoon salt, ⅛ teaspoon nutmeg
½ cup seedless raisins
2 teaspoons butter

Turn into a buttered baking dish. Dot top with butter. Place into a slow oven (300°F). Stir occasionally, the first hour to keep rice from sticking. Bake another hour without stirring. Then mix ½ cup seedless raisins. Bake another hour (three hours in all); extra milk may be added if necessary, stir. Serve hot or cold with cream.

FROZEN RICE PUDDING
Mrs. David T. Merrick

½ cup rice
1 qt. each water, milk
2 small cups sugar
1 pt. whipping cream
1 teaspoon each rum, vanilla

Bring the rice to a boil in the quart of cold water, pour off the water, add the milk and let cook one hour in a double boiler, add the sugar and cook half an hour longer, then add a pinch of salt, and cool. When cool add flavoring, add the whipped cream and freeze. Serve with melted currant jelly or any fruit sauce.

RUM PUDDING
Mrs. George Frierson

2 eggs, ½ cup sugar
4 tablespoons whiskey or rum
1 pt. cream, lady fingers

Beat the yolks and whites separately. To the yolks, add the sugar, then the whiskey or rum, then the whipped cream. Lastly, the well beaten whites. Line a mold with lady fingers, and fill it with the above mixture. Pack in ice for 3 hours, and turn out on a platter, and decorate it with whipped cream.

This recipe is delicious if you soak a package of gelatine in ¼ cup cold milk and add to ¼ cup hot milk. When dissolved and cool, beat in mixture and proceed as above. This can be made the day before.

RUM CHESTNUT PUDDING

Mrs. James Selman

4 egg yolks
2 cups heavy cream
¼ cup rum
*½ can chestnut paste

Make rich custard in double boiler of 4 egg yolks and the 2 cups of cream. Let cool, and add ¼ cup of rum and ½ cup of chestnut paste. Put in pot de creme cups. Chill and serve with whipped cream. Serves 6.

*Chestnut paste is available in New Orleans at Langensteins Market; elsewhere, probably at a delicatessan or a store that specializes in gourmet products. If you are fortunate to have fresh chestnuts available, roast, mash, and use equivalent.

RUM CHESTNUT PUDDING

For custard beat eggs together lightly, add the sugar, beat well and pour over scalded milk. Pour into a double boiler to cook until the mixture thickens. Then set to cool. Boil the chestnuts until they pop open, mash them and let them cook. Then mix into them thoroughly the whipped cream.

Now a mold: Line it with lady fingers dipped in rum. Pour in first the custard and then the cream chestnut mixture. Pack to freeze—and to delight your gourmet guests.

SPONGE PUDDING

Mrs. Petrie Hamilton

½ cup flour, measured before sifting
1 pt. milk, 1 cup sugar
¼ cup butter, 5 eggs
1 teaspoon vanilla

Mix the sugar, milk, and flour together, and cook in a double boiler until it becomes a clear, smooth paste. Then add the butter. When well mixed, stir in well beaten egg yolks, the flavoring, and fold in beaten egg whites. Pour into a baking pan, set in a pan of hot water, and bake 50 or 60

minutes in very slow oven. Serve at once with Cabinet Sauce.

Mrs. H. Waller Fowler blends two and one-half squares of Baker's unsweetened chocolate to the above mixture and presto!—a delicious chocolate souffle. Serve with whipped cream.

WALDORF STEAMED PUDDING

Mrs. J. B. Barnard

1 cup molasses
1 cup suet, chopped
1 cup milk
2½ cups flour, 1 teaspoon soda
1 cup large raisins
1 lb. English walnuts, chopped
¼ lb. figs, chopped

Mix well and steam two to three hours.

SAUCE

½ cup butter, 1 cup powdered sugar
1 cup whipped cream
brandy if desired

Cream butter and sugar as for hard sauce, add whipped cream and heat to scalding over hot water. Add brandy.

WALNUT DATE PUDDING

2 cups stoned dates, cut or chopped
1 cup English walnuts, or pecans
3 tablespoons flour, heaping
½ cup sugar, 2 eggs
1 teaspoon baking powder, heaping
1 cup whipped cream

Break up the nuts. Sprinkle the dates with flour. Beat the eggs together. Mix well all the ingredients except the cream, pour into a baking dish and set in a pan of hot water. Bake half an hour.

When done, cut in squares while the pudding is still warm. Chill and serve with whipped cream.

SABAYON

Mrs. J. Mort Walker, Jr.

6 eggs
1 cup sugar
2 heaping teaspoons sugar
½ level teaspoon salt
½ pt. whipping cream
4 tablespoons rum
4 tablespoons bourbon whiskey

Beat yolks of eggs well, adding sugar until well mixed and cook in double boiler, stirring constantly until mixture thickens. Remove and allow to cool in refrigerator, add whiskey and rum, beat whites of eggs with ½ teaspoon salt and add 2 heaping teaspoons of sugar to egg whites and beat until firm but not dry. Beat ½ pint of whipping cream, fold egg whites and whipping cream in custard, place in ramekins, sprinkle shaved chocolate on top and chill for at least 4 hours.

SAVARIN
Mrs. Russell Clark

4½ ozs. flour, yeast cake
1 coffee cup lukewarm milk
1¾ ozs. creamed butter, 2 eggs
1 dessertspoon sugar, pinch salt

Syrup:

1 cup sugar, ½ cup syrup
¾ cup water, brandy

Put the flour in a warm bowl, and add to it the yeast cake which has been dissolved in the warm milk. Add the eggs, and beat lightly with your hand until it is well mixed—stir with the tips of your fingers. Add sugar, butter, salt. After mixing well, set the bowl in a warm place for 1½ hours.

After it has risen, butter a ring mold well, half fill it with the mixture and allow it to rise against the top of the mold. Bake this in a very hot oven, 450 degrees, for 12 to 20 minutes. Turn out at once and serve with the following syrup:

Mix the ingredients indicated above, place in a pan and cook to a light syrup, flavoring it with brandy. Now put your cake on a rack over bowl and baste with this syrup until the cake is well soaked. In the center, put anything you like—whipped cream, pastry cream, ice-cream. Decorate with cherries and your guests will classify you as worthy of the Cordon Bleu.

CHOCOLATE SPONGE VIENNOIS
Mrs. David T. Merrick

4 eggs, beaten separately
½ cup sugar

¾ tablespoon gelatine
¼ cup cold water, ½ cup boiling water
⅛ lb. unsweetened chocolate
1½ teaspoons vanilla

Beat sugar into yolks. Add gelatine to chocolate that has been melted over hot water and stir all into yolks. Fold mixture into whites, flavor. Turn into mold and place in the refrigerator. Serve with ice cream. A cold chocolate sauce poured over the pudding before decorating with ice cream adds to the deliciousness of this dessert.

STRAWBERRY CASSEROLES
Mrs. Olivier A. Billion

1 pint strawberries
2 tablespoons sugar
1 tablespoon of rum, brandy or Cointreau
3 egg whites
6 tablespoons confectioners sugar

Cut ripe strawberries in quarters, sugar them and flavor with a few drops of brandy, rum, or Cointreau Put generous spoonfuls in the bottoms of individual ramekins or casseroles. Top with a meringue made by beating 2 tablespoons of confectioners sugar with each egg white used. Brown quickly under broiler and serve at once. Easy to make and delicious.

STRAWBERRY CELESTE

1 qt. strawberries, dusted with powdered sugar
1 pt. cream
brandy

Have berries very cold, put powdered sugar over them, add brandy and then have cream stiffly beaten and pour over them, dipping up and down to mix well.

STRAWBERRY CREAM
Mrs. Pauline Curran Perkins

1 qt. berries, 1 cup sugar
2 envelopes gelatine, ½ cup cold water
½ cup boiling water
1 pt. whipping cream

Mash the berries with sugar and let them stand until the sugar is well dissolved. Strain them through a sieve fine enough to keep back the seeds. Soak the gelatine in the cold water. Then dissolve in boiling water. Strain it into the berry juice. Cool and beat until slightly thickened, add the whipped cream and place in a plain mold.

STRAWBERRY MOUSSE

1 pt. strawberries, 1 cup sugar
2 tablespoons gelatine
½ cup water
1 qt. cream, whipped

Let the berries stand with the sugar about an hour. Crush the berries through a sieve. Soak the gelatine in the water, then dissolve over hot water, and mix with the strained berries. Put into the refrigerator until it becomes slightly hard, then fold in the whipped cream. Pack in salt and ice for several hours.

STRAWBERRY SHORTBREAD

A short biscuit dough is rolled very thin and circles cut the exact size of the bottom of the pan to be used. The unbaked layers are placed one on top of the other with a generous spreading of softened butter between each one and baked in a slow oven until nicely browned. In the meantime the strawberries have been mashed and sweetened. On removal of the shortbread from the oven the layers are separated and the berries spread between. The whole is topped with whipped cream and served at once. If a crisper torte is desired each layer is baked separately, whereas, for the New England Strawberry Shortbread only one thick cake is baked. It is split and buttered while hot and the strawberries added as before.

TART ANGÉLIQUE

8 egg whites
2 cups sugar
1 teaspoon each vinegar, vanilla
1 cup whipping cream
sherry or whiskey

Flavor whipped cream highly with sherry or whiskey, add 2 tablespoons

of sugar.

Beat whites of eggs for ten minutes, then add the rest of the sugar gradually by sifting a little in at a time, beating it for ten minutes. Add vinegar and vanilla. Put in a large deep cake pan with loose bottom lightly buttered. Bake in a slow oven for one hour. When cold, pile flavored whipped cream on top. Before serving sprinkle with nuts and cherries.

TIPSY TRIFLE
Mrs. Hu B. Stephens

2 doz. lady fingers
2 doz. almond macaroons and sherry enough to saturate them
¼ lb. blanched almonds, sliced
1 qt. custard as above
1 cup preserves, cherry or strawberry
1 cup whipping cream

Line the bottom of a large serving bowl with the lady fingers and macaroons saturated in the sherry. Stick them with some of the almonds and pour over some of the custard. Dot with the preserves. Continue this process ending with the custard. Chill for several hours, top with whipped cream and serve.

QUEEN OF TRIFLES
Mrs. Joseph P. Burton

Make a thick custard of 6 eggs, 1 cup of sugar, 1 quart of milk, 1 teaspoon cornstarch, cook until thick. Have ready:

1 doz. each macaroons, lady fingers
¼ lb. blanched almonds, cut fine
¼ lb. crystallized cherries
sherry

Line a deep dish with macaroons that have been dipped in sherry. Then make a layer of nuts, cherries and lady fingers dipped in sherry until all are used. Pour custard over all, put in refrigerator when cool. Before serving top with whipped cream.

"ZABAYON"
Mrs. Wm. T. Nolan

8 egg yolks, 6 tablespoons sugar
9 tablespoons Marsala wine

Cream yolks with sugar until very light, stir in wine slowly. Put in a double boiler and cook to the consistency of a thick cream, stirring all the time to prevent curdling. When cool, pour into parfait glasses and put in the refrigerator until ready to serve. Plain rice wafers or sponge cakes are a happy combination.

This is an old Creole derivative of Italian Zabaglione, which begins in the same way, but goes on to add half of the stiffly beaten whites to the original mixture. And it is served hot as often as cold.

CANDIED APPLES

2 cups sugar
1½ cups water
apples

Wash, pare, and core the apples. Put parings on to boil in the water. Cut the apples in balls with the potato cutter. Take the water from parings and make a syrup with the sugar. Cook the apple balls in syrup until candied. A drop and a half of vegetable coloring enhances their appearance.

APRICOT GLAZE

One pound dried apricots soaked over night in one quart of water. In another pan soak ¼ ounce agar-agar in one pint of water. The next day, press apricots through sieve, place on fire and bring to a good boil. Bring the agar-agar mixture to a boil, stirring constantly until all agar-agar is dissolved. To this hot mixture add two pounds sugar, stir until melted, and let it come to the boiling point again. Now add the sieved apricots, and when this has boiled again for a moment, strain the entire mixture. It keeps indefinitely.

This sets like a gelatine mixture to use as a glaze over baked ham or fowl, tarts or pastry. Simply melt over low heat and do not stir or it becomes cloudy.

HONEY CARAMELS
Dean Albert K. Heckel, Univ. Mo.

2 cups granulated sugar
1 cup honey (orange, clover)
¼ lb. butter

1½ cups milk
1 small can evaporated milk
⅛ teaspoon salt
1 tablespoon of vanilla
1 cup pecans or walnuts

Cook sugar, honey, butter, milk and salt together, stirring constantly until boiling point is reached, then add evaporated milk, slowly to prevent curdling. Stir constantly and cook mixture until it forms a firm ball in cold water (246 degrees if candy thermometer is used). Remove from fire and add one tablespoonful of vanilla. Pour into buttered pan. When cooled cut into strips, then into squares and wrap in waxed paper.

CRYSTALLIZED PUMPKIN
Mrs. E. M. Choppin

1 large yellow pumpkin
1 cup lime
6 to 8 lbs. sugar
2 tablespoons vanilla

Cut the pumpkin in pieces 1 to 2 inches in size. Mix the lime in a large pan of water. When it settles, pour over the pumpkin. Soak over night. Mix the sugar in just enough water to make a thick syrup.

Wash the pumpkin in several waters and let it drain in colander. When the syrup begins to cook, put in the pumpkin, stirring and basting it. When the sugar begins to crystallize, put in the vanilla. Take off the fire and stir until cool and crystallized.

A most marvelous candy, one which defies the taste of pumpkin in a "guess-what?" contest.

Note: Be sure to let water run in your drain pipe after you have poured off the lime water.

DATE LOAF
Miss Ethel Forman

2 cups pecans
3 cups sugar, 1 cup milk
1 lb. dates

Mix all ingredients except pecans and cook until it leaves the side of the pot. When you take it off the fire stir in pecans. Put in wet napkin and roll. Cut in slices when cold.

CHOCOLATE FUDGE

Mrs. Harry C. Kammer

2 tablespoons cocoa
2 cups sugar
1 small can evaporated milk
3 tablespoons marshmallow cream
2 cups pecans

Mix cocoa and sugar, add evaporated milk, place over low fire for ten minutes stirring constantly—remove from fire, add marshmallow cream and pecans and then beat until mixture thickens, place on buttered pan.

EASY FUDGE

2 packages chocolate chips
1 can sweetened condensed milk
1 cup of pecans or walnuts, chopped

Melt chips in top of double boiler. When melted stir in condensed milk, then add chopped nuts. Leave in double boiler and dip out with a spoon on waxed paper. Makes two dozen pieces of candy.

GRAPEFRUIT GLACÉ

Mrs. James Amedée Puech

1 grapefruit, the skin
1½ cups granulated sugar

Quarter skin of fruit and cut in long slices. Boil skins seven times. When water boils, pour it off, each time using cold water for subsequent boiling. In 7th water, put in sugar, letting it come to a syrup. When cooked, take each strip with fork and roll piece by piece in granulated sugar. Sprinkle sugar on a large platter for convenience.

MARRONS GLACÉS

Roast one lb. chestnuts. Peel and remove inner skins. Cool. Make a syrup in the proportion of ½ cup water to 1 cup sugar and boil to the cracking point. Place pan containing syrup in another pan of hot water. String the chestnuts onto a fine wire and make a ring. Hang the rings on the handle of a wooden spoon and place across the syrup pan so the chestnuts are immersed in the syrup. When they are thoroughly coated hang up to dry.

MARZIPAN

½ lb. sugar
½ lb. shelled almonds
rum (or water)
powdered cocoa

Grind the sugar and almonds to a powder, pulverizing them thoroughly. Then work them together with either rum or water. Make into balls and dredge in uncooked cocoa. The balls should be in the shape and size of small new potatoes.

FRENCH NOUGAT

Mrs. James Selman

1¼ cups sugar
1 cup ground pecans
1 buttered pie sheet or baking
pan

Caramelize sugar in- this fashion: place in skillet over low heat and stir with spoon until it turns to liquid and begins to brown. Be careful not to burn. Quickly add nuts and combine well. Transfer as quickly as possible to buttered sheet or pan, smoothing down with back of buttered spoon or spatula. Let cool and break into pieces.

Makes nice gift if done in disposable pie tin and covered with Saran Wrap.

SPICED NUTS

Mrs. Fleur Hampton

1 cup sugar
¾ teaspoon salt
¼ teaspoon nutmeg
¼ teaspoon cloves
2 teaspoons cinnamon
¼ cup water
½ lb. walnuts or pecans
(2¼ cups)

Mix all ingredients but nuts and boil to soft ball stage. Add nuts. Remove from heat; stir until sugary. Spread on waxed paper. Cool. Break apart. Nice for Christmas.

CARAMEL PECANS

Mrs. Hunter Leake

3 cups granulated sugar
1 cup milk
2 tablespoons butter

2 cups pecans
1½ cups sugar

Boil sugar with the milk. Melt the 1½ cups of sugar in an iron skillet to caramel. When the sugar and milk mixture makes a soft ball on being dropped into cold water, pour in the caramel, nuts and butter. Take off the fire and beat until creamy. Pour out and cut in squares.

ORANGE SUGARED PECANS

Use the above recipe substituting brown sugar for white, and as you remove from the fire, add two tablespoons of grated orange rind. If a stronger flavor of orange is desired, add more of the grated rind.

SALTED PECANS
Mrs. Wm. J. De Treville

½ lb. shelled pecans
1 teaspoon butter
1 teaspoon salt

Break butter in bits over pecans, run in a quick oven and stir until brown. Turn out on brown paper, sprinkle salt over them and let cool.

SPICED PECANS
Pauline Griggs

1 cup sugar
½ cup water
1 or 2 tablespoons cinnamon
2½ cups pecans

Make a syrup of the sugar, water and cinnamon, and boil until it begins to thread from the spoon. Drop in the pecans and cook until the syrup almost crystallizes in the pot. Pour out on a platter and separate the nuts with a fork.

TEZCUCO PLANTATION NOUGAT
Mrs. Trist Bringier

1½ cups sugar
1 cup chopped pecans
　small lump butter

Put the sugar into a saucepan with the butter, and stir until it is melted

to a syrup. Then throw in the pecans. Stir and then remove at once, pouring the candy into a buttered tin or marble slab. Cut quickly, before it hardens.

PRALINES
Mrs. Hughes P. Walmsley

3 cups granulated sugar
1 cup cream, or top of the milk
1 tablespoon butter
1 or 2 teaspoons vanilla
1 cup pecans or 1 can coconut

Cook first four ingredients until ball forms. Add pecans or coconut, and drop by tablespoons on marble slab, if you have one; if not, on waxed paper.

PRALINES
Mrs. Wm. H. Rhodes

1 cup open kettle cane syrup
1 tablespoon Karo syrup
½ cup each Lá Cuite, brown sugar
1½ cups white sugar
1 heaping tablespoon butter
½ teaspoon salt
1½ cups water
2 cups pecans

To syrup add sugar, salt and water. Cook until it forms a very soft ball, add butter and cook one minute, then add nuts and beat until creamy and until mixture gradually changes color to a lighter brown. Drop on wax paper to harden. The cane syrup must be thin.

DEBORAH'S PRALINES
Miss Debbie Huger

2 cups sugar
½ cup milk
1 teaspoon Karo syrup
½ teaspoon baking soda

Boil ingredients to softball stage, stirring slowly. Add 1 teaspoon vanilla and 2 cups chopped pecans. Beat for 2 minutes. Drop on waxed paper and let cool.

PECAN PRALINES
Miss Ethel Forman

3 cups pecans
2 cups brown sugar, 1 cup cream
1 cup white sugar, 1 cup water

Cook brown sugar with cream, and white sugar with water, separately, till each is thick. Combine. Add 3 cups of pecans cut extra fine. Stir well. Drop by spoonfuls on buttered sheet.

PECAN PRALINES
Great Grammaw Flettrich
(Through Terry Flettrich)

There are more stories about the origin of the praline. And there are just as many recipes, but absolutely the very best recipe I ever tried is Grandma Flettrich's recipe. When Grandpa was alive, he would crack and peel pecans for weeks before Christmas. Then Grandma would get her ingredients, her marble slab and go to town. Relatives and friends could always depend on a box of her pralines for Christmas, and at her house the pralines would always lie in state in a lacquered wood box Grandpa made for her.

1 cup buttermilk
2 cups sugar
  large pinch salt
1 teaspoon baking soda
2 teaspoons vanilla
1/8 lb. of butter
2 cups pecans

Stir buttermilk and sugar together plus soda and salt, and cook in deep pot, stirring all the time until mahogany brown in color. Add vanilla, butter and beat till almost thick. Add nuts, and drop by spoonful on marble slab.

PRALINES TOURNÉS
Mrs. Wm. J. De Treville

2 cups granulated sugar
2 cups shelled pecans
½ cup hot water
1 tablespoon vanilla

Boil sugar mixed with water until it threads. Add pecans and stir until

sugar creams. Then add vanilla. Do not boil after pecans are added.

STUFFED PRUNES OR DATES

2 doz. large prunes or dates
2 doz. pecans
1 doz. marshmallows
1 small orange, the peel, cut into
  tiny slivers
  granulated sugar
  brandy

Pit the prunes or dates and cover with the brandy, allow to stand for 2 hours. Stuff each one with a half marshmallow, a half pecan, and a sliver of orange peel. Roll in granulated sugar.

ICE CREAM AU CARAMEL

8 egg yolks
1½ cups sugar, 1/3 cup hot water
2 cups milk
¼ teaspoon salt
2¾ cups light cream

Heat the sugar in a saucepan until it is melted and amber colored. Now add the hot water and cook until the mixture is blended thoroughly.

Put the milk in a double boiler, scald, add it slowly to the well beaten egg yolks. Add the caramel syrup, sugar and salt, and cook over hot water until the mixture thickens, stirring constantly to avoid lumps. When done, it should be the consistency of custard.

Cool, add the cream, strain and freeze. Toasted pecan bits sprinkled over it are good, or a chocolate sauce; but it is delicious per se and reminiscent of the famous old Mannassier's, where it was a choice offering.

CARAMEL ICE CREAM
Mrs. Charles Crawford

1 pt. whipping cream
2 cups milk
1 cup sugar, caramelized
2 tablespoons plain sugar
1 tablespoon gelatine
1 teaspoon vanilla

Dissolve gelatine in one cup of milk. Caramelize 1 cup sugar and dissolve in the rest of the milk after it has been scalded. Add milk with the dissolved gelatine and the plain sugar. When ready to freeze add pint of cream whipped stiff and vanilla. This makes about 1½ quarts of ice cream when frozen.

GINGER ICE CREAM
Mrs. Charles N. Monsted

1 cup sugar, 4 eggs
1 qt. milk
1 pt. whipping cream
2 level tablespoons imported ginger

Boil milk, beat sugar and egg yolks together, add to milk and cook slowly over hot water stirring constantly until thick. Beat egg whites and add to the custard after you have removed it from the fire and allowed to cool a little. Cool further and add the cream which has been whipped until stiff, and the chopped ginger. Freeze.

PISTACHIO ICE CREAM

½ cup chopped pistachio nuts
½ cup chopped almonds
1 tablespoon almond extract
¼ teaspoon salt
1 cup sugar, 4 cups cream
   few drops green coloring

Mix all the ingredients and freeze.
For a yet more stupendous effect, press the cream around the sides of the freezer, and fill with grated French chocolate. Pack for 2 hours.

PRALINE ICE CREAM

1 cup sugar
2/3 cup chopped pecan meats
2 cups milk, 3 egg yolks
1 cup cream, whipped
1 teaspoon vanilla
½ teaspoon salt

Caramelize ½ cup sugar and add to it the pecan meats. Turn into a slightly buttered pan. Cool and pound, then sift, or commercial pralines may be used.
Scald the milk, add the egg yolks, rest of sugar, and the salt, and cook in a double boiler, stirring constantly until thick. Add to this the sifted caramel and nut mixture. Cool. Add the whipped cream and the vanilla, and freeze.

FROZEN BUTTERMILK
Mrs. David T. Merrick

1 qt. buttermilk, pinch soda
1 can condensed milk
1 pt. cream
2 teaspoons vanilla
3 egg whites, well beaten

Add soda to buttermilk, then milk, cream and vanilla. Mix well. Fold in whites and freeze. A healthful refreshing summer dessert.

APRICOT ICE
Mrs. Dora Harris Jackson

Boil together:

1½ cups of water
½ cup of sugar

Add juice of 2 or more fresh oranges, and the juice of 2 or more fresh lemons.
Puree 2 cans of apricots with the juice of 1 of the cans of apricots in the blender.
Mix all together (should be slightly tart) and pour into meatloaf type pan and freeze.
May be topped with whipped cream. Unmold, slice, and serve.

LEMON ICE
Mrs. William J. Mitchell

1 cup sugar, 2 cups water
3 lemons (grated rind of 1)
4 egg whites

Put the sugar and water into a saucepan and allow to boil for 8 minutes. Remove the saucepan from the fire and beat the contents until cold. Add the stiffly beaten whites of eggs, the strained juice of lemon and the grated rind. Freeze. Refreshing, cooling and delicious.

WATERMELON ICE
Mrs. Philip Steegman

½ large watermelon
4 oranges, 3 lemons, the juice
1 cup sugar
1 egg, the white

Scoop meat from melon, extract juice. Add lemon and orange juice and sugar. Stir thoroughly and freeze. When slightly frozen add stiffly beaten white of egg and finish freezing. Serve in melon rind that has been neatly trimmed at top edge. Scoop out holes with potato scoop, one or two inches all around the top and fill with large cherries or grapes. Decorate generously with fresh mint.

BANANA SHERBET
Mrs. Rachel Bunting Wilmot

3 cups water
3 bananas run through potato ricer
3 each, lemons, oranges, the juice
1 cup sugar, or to taste

Combine and freeze. Delicious!

ORANGE SHERBET

1½ qts. orange juice
½ cup lemon juice
1 cup sugar, 1 cup water
  grated rind of one orange

Boil sugar and water, add grated rind. Strain into fruit juice and freeze. Serve in candied orange cups.

BLACKBERRY SAUCE

1 cup fresh blackberries
1 cup water
1 tablespoon flour
½ cup sugar
2 teaspoons butter
¼ teaspoon salt, dash of cloves
2 tablespoons lemon juice

Heat together blackberries and water. Let boil three minutes, strain. Combine flour and sugar. Add to hot fruit and cook until thickened, stirring frequently. Add butter, cloves, salt and lemon juice.

BRANDY SAUCE
Mrs. H. Waller Fowler

½ cup butter
1 teaspoon flour, heaping
2 cups powdered sugar
1 cup top milk
4 egg yolks
2 glasses wine or brandy, or to taste

Put the butter and flour in a saucepan and blend. Beat the egg yolks and combine with the milk, then add slowly to the flour stirring constantly to a smooth consistency. Cook in double boiler five minutes until thick as custard. Do not boil. Just before serving add the wine or brandy. This sauce is to be used hot on puddings.

CABINET SAUCE
Mrs. Petrie Hamilton

¼ cup each butter, sugar
¼ cup each whipping cream, whiskey
  nutmeg

Cream butter and sugar together, and slowly add the cream and whiskey. Place in a pan of hot water until hot and well blended. Then add nutmeg if desired.

CHOCOLATE SAUCE

2 squares Baker's chocolate
2/3 cup sugar
2 tablespoons butter
1 cup milk, ½ cup Karo syrup
1 teaspoon vanilla

Melt the butter and chocolate well together. Add the milk, stirring constantly, add sugar, bring to a boiling point and let boil ten minutes. Flavor.

CHOCOLATE SAUCE
Mrs. Chapman Marshall

3 squares unsweetened chocolate
¼ cup (½ stick) butter or margarine
1½ cups confectioners sugar
1 small can evaporated milk
  pinch salt, 1 teaspoon vanilla

Put all ingredients in a double boiler, cover and heat over boiling water. Stir together well when chocolate has melted. Cook 30 minutes stirring occasionally. Add vanilla. Makes about 1 pint. Easy and excellent.

SHERRY'S CHOCOLATE SAUCE

1½ cups powdered sugar
¼ lb. Baker's chocolate
1 tablespoon butter
¼ cup sherry
1 teaspoon vanilla
½ cup cream, ¼ cup Karo

Beat the butter and sugar, add the chocolate, grated and melted, then the cream and Karo.
Boil for seven minutes, add sherry and vanilla.

YUM YUM CHOCOLATE SAUCE
Mrs. Irving Lyons

2 cups sugar, ¼ cup cocoa
¾ cup cornstarch
¾ cup milk
2 tablespoons butter

Boil all the ingredients except the butter together for four to five minutes. Add the butter and continue boiling until a soft ball forms when dropped into cold water. Serve warm with ice cream or over a simple hot cake.

DEVONSHIRE CREAM
Mrs. David T. Merrick

1 qt. raw certified milk
1 pt. double cream

Put one quart of raw certified milk and one pint of double cream in a shallow enamel pan. Set in a cool place for twelve hours. When this time is up, the cream should have risen to the surface. Now set the milk and cream in a pan of water and place it either on top of the oven part of a gas stove or on the very back of a wood or coal stove. Let the milk gradually warm, but not get too hot. Leave it on the stove until the cream crinkles and puffs away from the edge of the pan. When this happens, set the pan of milk in the refrigerator for at least twelve hours. Then carefully skim off the cream and place in a glass dish. It should be thick, slightly lumpy or clotted and have a peculiarly delicate, sweet taste.

This is delicious with strawberries or any other fruit.

EGGNOG SAUCE
Mrs. David T. Merrick

3 egg yolks, well beaten
1 cup powdered sugar (sifted)
1 cup brandy
½ pt. cream (whipped)

Mix ingredients in the order given.

This sauce is good on plum, carrot, sponge pudding, in fact gives zest to almost any pudding.

HARD SAUCE

½ cup butter
1 cup powdered sugar
1 egg, the white
  sherry, brandy or vanilla

Cream butter and sugar thoroughly, add unbeaten white and beat again. Flavor with brandy, sherry or vanilla. The egg white can be omitted.

PRALINE SAUCE, VIEUX CARRÉ
Mrs. Wm. H. Rhodes

1 cup open kettle cane syrup
1 tablespoon Karo syrup
½ cup La Cuite
½ cup brown sugar
1½ cups white sugar
1 heaping tablespoon of butter
½ teaspoon salt
1½ cups water
2 cups pecans

To syrup add sugar, salt and water. Cook until it forms a very soft ball, then add butter. Do not beat. It is better to add nuts just before serving.

ORANGE SAUCE
Mrs. David T. Merrick

6 oranges and grated rind of 4
¾ lb. sugar
3 cups boiling water

Wash oranges, grate rind. Take out pulp and juice of the six and set aside. Take the remainder of oranges, pour the boiling water over this and cook until tender, then press through ricer or sieve, now add sugar and grated rind and cook until thick. Serve with orange mousse. The juice and pulp are saved for the mousse.

cakes, small cakes, cookies, frostings, pies and pastries

BANANA CAKE
Mrs. Albin Provosty

½ cup butter, 1½ cups sugar
2 eggs
1¾ cups flour
4 tablespoons buttermilk with 1 teaspoon soda or 4 tablespoons sweet milk with 1 teaspoon baking powder
1 cup bananas, mashed and run through a sieve
1 teaspoon vanilla, salt to taste

Mix like any batter cake and add the banana pulp to the batter. Cook in layer pans and put together with sliced ripe bananas and with whipped cream on top.

CHEESECAKE
Mrs. Richard Adler

Filling:

36 ozs. Philadelphia cream cheese
1 cup sugar
4 whole eggs
½ teaspoon salt
1 tablespoon lemon juice

Crumb mixture:

1 package unsweetened Zwieback (or Holland Rusk), crumbled
1 teaspoon cinnamon
¼ cup sugar
½ cup melted butter

Topping:

1 pint sour cream
3 tablespoons sugar
1 teaspoon vanilla

Mix filling ingredients with mixmaster until smooth.
Meanwhile, make crumbs from Zwieback and add to this melted butter, cinnamon, and ¼ cup of sugar. Mix well and take a little more than half of this mixture and spread, patting gently, in the bottom of a spring-form pan. Add cream cheese filling mixture and bake in a preheated 374° oven for 20 minutes.
Over baked cake, spoon and smooth the topping mixture. Sprinkle evenly the remaining crumb mixture. Bake 10 minutes at 450°. Cool and refrigerate. Never serve the day cheese cake is made.

CHOCOLATE ALMOND CAKE
Mrs. M. C. Maury-Lyons

4 eggs
1 stick butter
1 cup sweet powdered or grated chocolate
1 cup sugar
1 cup pounded almonds

Beat eggs separately. Cream the butter and sugar, add beaten yolks, then the chocolate and almonds.
Beat well, then fold in the beaten whites. Pour in a buttered mold and bake in a slow oven for half an hour. Remove to cool, and put in the ice-box for an hour. Serve with whipped cream.
Note that it requires no flour and that it is easy to make.

EASY CHOCOLATE CAKE

2 squares Baker's chocolate
½ cup water
1 cup sugar
1 cup sour cream
2 eggs, slightly beaten
1½ cups cake flour
1 level teaspoon soda, pinch salt

Melt the chocolate in the water, over hot water. Remove from the fire and add sugar, sour cream and eggs. Sift flour once before measuring and twice afterwards with soda and salt. Beat hard for ten minutes and bake in a medium oven.

CHOCOLATE FUDGE CAKE

Mrs. Robert L. Morris

2 cups sugar
2 cups flour
2 sticks butter
½ cup shortening
4 tablespoons cocoa
1 cup water
½ cup buttermilk
2 eggs, beaten
1 teaspoon soda
1 teaspoon vanilla

Icing:

1 stick butter
4 tablespoons cocoa
6 tablespoons milk
1 box powdered sugar
1 teaspoon vanilla extract
1 cup pecans, chopped

Sift sugar and flour into large bowl. Mix in a saucepan; butter, shortening, cocoa and water and bring to rapid boil. Pour it over dry ingredients and stir well. Add buttermilk, eggs, soda and vanilla, mix well. Pour into greased 11"x6" pan and bake at 400° for 20 minutes. Five minutes before cake is done make icing. It is important to do this step correctly so the hot icing will be poured over the hot cake and it will seep into the air holes.

To make icing, melt butter, then add cocoa, milk and sugar. Bring to boil. Remove from fire and add pecans and vanilla, blend and pour over HOT cake as soon as you take it out of the oven.

CHOCOLATE ICE BOX CAKE

Mrs. Morrell Trimble

1 cup powdered sugar
¼ lb. butter
3 eggs
1 square unsweetened chocolate
1 doz. macaroons
1 doz. lady fingers
1 teaspoon vanilla

Cream sugar and butter. Drop egg yolks into mixture, one at a time, beating after each addition. Add melted chocolate, crushed macaroons, and vanilla. Fold in stiffly beaten egg whites. Cover bottom of a deep dish with lady fingers, pour in half the mixture, then add another layer of lady fingers and pour in the rest of the mixture, covering with lady fingers. Put in ice box for several hours. Serve garnished with whipped cream.

LAYER CAKE À LA CAJOU

Mrs. David T. Merrick

1½ cups sugar, ½ cup butter
3 eggs beaten separately
2 cups flour, sifted
1 teaspoon soda, scant
1 cup milk
8 ozs. Baker's chocolate
3 tablespoons hot water

Dissolve chocolate in hot water. Add half the milk to the chocolate.

Cream butter and sugar, and add the yolks. Beat in the cooled chocolate and milk. Sift the flour and soda into the batter, then add the rest of the milk and vanilla. Mix well. Fold in whites.

Bake in two or three layers, and put the layers together with cooked white icing, or caramel. This cake is dark in color but light in consistency.

CHOCOLATE NUT CAKE

Mrs. Arthur Newell

Have prepared two cups of nuts. Grease three 8-inch cake pans, line with wax paper, grease again. Set oven at 375 degrees.

2 cups sugar, 1 stick butter
2 eggs separated·
4 ozs. unsweetened chocolate
2 cups cake flour, lightly packed
2 teaspoons baking powder
1½ cups milk
2 teaspoons vanilla, ½ teaspoon salt
1 cup rolled pecans

Have chocolate melted and slightly cooled.

Sift flour, salt, baking powder three times together. Cream butter and sugar well, add beaten yolks, melted chocolate. Add some flour mixture and pecans. Alternate with milk. Continue alternating until all used. Add vanilla and fold in stiffly beaten whites.

Bake 30 to 35 minutes, or till done.

Frosting:

1 lb. powdered sugar

1 whole egg
1 heaping tablespoon butter
2 ozs. unsweetened chocolate, melted
2 teaspoons vanilla, 2 tablespoons rum
1 cup pecans

Mix well. Put between layers and heap on top.

FRUIT CAKE
Mrs. E. G. Simmons

12 eggs
¾ lb. butter, 1 lb. sugar
1 glass tart jelly
2 glasses Bourbon whiskey, or brandy
1 lb. flour
2 level teaspoons baking powder
½ teaspoon soda
1 teaspoon each cinnamon, cloves, all-
    spice
4 lbs. raisins
1 lb. each crystallized pineapple,
    pecans
½ lb. each orange peel, lemon peel
1 lb. each dried figs, dates, citron

Cut up all the fruits and nuts but not fine, and dredge well with flour using one half of the pound. Set aside. Beat the eggs, yolks and whites separately. Cream the butter and sugar together well and add the yolks. Beat thoroughly. Then add the jelly and the brandy or whiskey. Mix thoroughly. Sift the remaining flour with the soda and baking powder and powdered spices. Now mix in the floured fruits and nuts and last of all fold in the beaten egg whites. This will make about ten pounds of cake and may be cooked in several pans of whatever size desired. The oven must be very slow and they should bake from three to five hours according to the size of the cake.

WHITE FRUIT CAKE
Mrs. Petrie Hamilton

16 egg whites
¾ lb. butter
1 lb. each sugar, flour
1 wine glass brandy
2 teaspoons baking powder
2 lbs. blanched almonds
2 grated cocoanuts
½ lb. each crystallized cherries, crys-
    tallized pineapple, 1 lb. citron,
    cut fine
1 nutmeg, grated
2 teaspoons cinnamon
1 teaspoon vanilla

Use the directions for mixing in preceding recipe.

BRAZIL NUT FRUIT CAKE
Mrs. William H. Carter

2 cups Brazil nuts (whole or coarsely
    chopped)
½ cup pecans
¾ lb. dates (cut in half)
1¾ cups whole candied cherries
1¾ cups diced candied pineapple
1 cup each flour, sugar
½ teaspoon each baking powder, salt
4 eggs
1 teaspoon vanilla

Put nuts and fruit into large bowl. Sift together flour, sugar, baking powder, salt over fruits and nuts. Mix until well coated. Beat eggs until foamy, add vanilla and mix with fruit mixture. Grease and paper line 9 x 5 x 3 pan. Bake 300° one hour and forty-five minutes.

FRUIT CAKE HERMIONE
Mrs. Florence Phares Kells

1 lb. each butter, sugar, flour
12 eggs
2 lbs. seeded raisins
1 lb. each citron, currants
1 pt. brandy or rum
1 tablespoon powdered cinnamon
1 teaspoon each ground allspice, cloves
1 nutmeg, grated
1 teaspoon soda in ½ cup warm water
1 cup crushed nuts
1 qt. fig preserves

Soak all the spices in the brandy, chop fruit and add with nuts. Flour all your fruit well. Mix everything together, stirring conscientiously till well mixed. Reserve the fig preserve till the last, draining off most of the syrup, and mix it in.

Bake about 3 hours at 300 degrees, and you will have two large-sized delectable cakes.

FRUIT CAKE
Mrs. J. Pettegrew Wright

1 lb. each butter, sugar
10 eggs
2 lbs. puffed raisins
1 lb. each pecans, blanched almonds
1 lb. each crystallized cherries, crys-
    tallized pineapple, ½ lb. citron
1 teaspoon each allspice, cinnamon

½ teaspoon cloves
1 lb. flour
1 glass brandy, wine or whiskey

Use directions for mixing above. Put in pecan meats whole and also cherries and almonds. For two five pound cakes steam for 2 hours and then bake thirty minutes in a slow oven.

FUDGE PIE CAKE
Mrs. Frank C. Moran, Jr.

1 stick butter
2 squares unsweetened chocolate
3 eggs
1¼ cups sugar
⅓ cup flour
1 teaspoon vanilla

Melt chocolate and butter in saucepan. Add sugar, eggs (one at a time and beating after each), flour, and vanilla. Mix well and pour into a 9-inch pie pan. Bake for 35 minutes in a moderate oven. Serves 8. Serve with ice-cream or whipped cream.

GINGERBREAD AU VIEUX TEMPS

2 cups molasses, ½ cup butter
3 eggs, 1 cup sugar
1 teaspoon each cloves, allspice
1 tablespoon each ginger, cinnamon
3 cups flour
1 cup hot water
2 teaspoons soda, scant, in warm water

Warm the molasses with the butter. Beat the eggs and sugar together, and pour into the warm molasses. Add spices sifted with flour and soda. Bake in a very slow oven.

A hard sauce served with this makes a welcomed combination.

EMPANADAS
Mrs. Thomas Lind

1 cup all purpose flour, sifted
¼ teaspoon salt
½ cup margarine
1½ large packages Philadelphia Cream Cheese, softened
½ cup sugar
preserves of your taste
powdered sugar

Cream together margarine and cream cheese. Mix with flour, add ½

cup sugar. Roll out 1/8 inch thick. Cut out small rounds with glass or cookie cutter. Spread rounds with preserves, fold over to make crescents, and seal edges. (Crimp with a fork.) Bake in 350° oven until browned. Remove from oven and while still warm, roll in sifted powdered sugar.

JAM CAKE
Mrs. Albin Provosty

1 cup butter, 2 cups sugar
1 cup buttermilk, 1 teaspoon soda
2 cups flour
4 eggs
1 cup blackberry jam
1 teaspoon each cinnamon, cloves, nutmeg

Cream the butter and sugar together. Add the yolks of the eggs which have been beaten separately until thick and lemon colored. Add the blackberry jam and beat well. Stir the soda into the buttermilk and add to the above mixture, a little at a time alternately with the flour, into which you have already sifted the spices. Bake in layer cake pans and put together with the following filling:

½ cup milk, 2 cups sugar
1 medium sized can of grated pineapple
pinch of cream of tartar

Cook the milk, sugar and cream of tartar together until thick and creamy. Remove from the fire and beat thoroughly. When of the proper consistency to spread add the grated pineapple which has been drained and squeezed dry. Spread between layers.

OLD FASHIONED JAM CAKE
Mrs. Preston S. Herring

4 cups flour
2 teaspoons ground allspice
2 teaspoons ground nutmeg
2 teaspoons ground cinnamon
2 cups sugar
3 sticks butter
6 whole eggs
1 teaspoon baking soda
6 tablespoons buttermilk
2 cups blackberry preserves
pinch of salt

Sift dry ingredients together and set aside. Cream butter and sugar. Add whole eggs one at a time. Mix baking soda with buttermilk. Stir dry ingredients and buttermilk mixture into egg, butter and sugar mixture, alternating a little of each while stirring. Fold in preserves and a pinch of salt.

Bake in four 8-inch cake pans which have been greased with butter for 25 - 30 minutes in a 350° oven. Remove from oven when cakes are done and allow to cool on cake racks. When they are thoroughly cool, ice them with the following Butter Icing between layers and on top and sides.

Butter Icing:

1 stick butter
1 box powdered sugar, sifted
3 tablespoons Pet Milk
1 teaspoon vanilla extract
1 cup chopped pecans

Cream butter and sugar. Mix a little Pet Milk as needed. Then add vanilla and last of all fold in pecans.

JELLY ROLL

2 eggs
¼ cup milk
1 cup each sifted sugar, sifted flour
1 teaspoon baking powder
½ teaspoon salt
powdered sugar, jelly

Beat the yolks until they are lemon color. Add gradually the sifted sugar and the milk. Sift the baking powder, flour and salt together into the eggs and sugar, folding in, but not beating. Add the stiffly beaten whites.

Turn into a well greased shallow pan dusted with flour and bake ten minutes in a moderate oven. Turn out immediately on a slightly damp cloth sprinkled with powdered sugar. Spread with jelly and roll quickly.

LEMON BUNKUCHEN

Mrs. J. W. Stierman, Jr.

1 package Duncan Hines Lemon
   Supreme cake mix
1 package instant Jello lemon
   pudding mix
4 eggs
¾ cups Mazola oil
2/3 cup water

Marble mixture: take 2 tablespoons

sugar, one teaspoon cocoa, and one teaspoon cinnamon and hand mix for marble mixture.

Combine cake mix and pudding mix. Add eggs, water, and oil; beat at medium speed of electric mixer for 10 minutes. Add marble mixture and swirl by hand.

Pour into a thoroughly greased bundt or mold pan (butter) and cook for 50 minutes at 350°.

LEMON CAKE
(in Bundt Pan)
Mrs. Charles L. Seemann

1 package of Duncan Hines DeLuxe
   Yellow Cake Mix
¾ cups Wesson or Mazola oil
4 eggs
1 package of Lemon Jello
1½ cups sifted powdered sugar
   lemon juice

Pour the package of cake mix into the bowl of an electric mixer. To this add the oil. Next add the eggs, one at a time, beating after each one. Into a measuring cup pour the package of Lemon Jello and then fill the cup to the one-cup mark with boiling water. Stir until dissolved and add to the cake mixture. Add two teaspoons of lemon juice. Pour into greased cake pan and bake @ 350° for 40 to 45 minutes. Turn cake out of pan while still warm. Brush on immediately, or pour over, mixture of 4 tablespoons of lemon juice and the sifted powdered sugar.

NUT CAKE
Mrs. William Pipes

6 eggs, separated and beaten
½ lb. butter, well creamed
1 lb. each flour, sugar
1 teaspoon baking powder
1½ lbs. seeded raisins
1 qt. pecans
1 wine glass sherry or madeira
1 grated nutmeg
   extra flour to roll raisins and pecans

Cream butter, and ½ lb. of sugar. The remainder of sugar divide between egg yolks and whites. Add egg yolks, flour and baking powder, then mix in other ingredients in order given. Cook in slow oven and test with straw as you would a fruit cake.

This recipe is delicious and is preferred by many to fruit cake.

ORANGE CAKE À LA EVELYN

¼ lb. butter
1 orange, the juice and grated rind
1½ cups sugar
2 cups flour, 1 teaspoon salt
3 eggs
2 teaspoons baking powder, heaping

Filling:

1 cup sugar, 1 orange, the juice
1 egg
2 tablespoons flour, heaping
½ cup water

Cream the butter and sugar together. Add one egg at a time until all have been well beaten. Add the juice of one orange, then the grated rind, and finally the flour with the baking powder. Bake in layers. For the filling, cook the orange juice and the sugar on a slow fire. Mix the flour and water till smooth and add it to the cooking sugar and orange juice, and let all cook until thick. Remove from fire and add the egg yolk. Beat well and place on the fire again for a few seconds.

PECAN AND RAISIN CAKE

Mrs. Charles L. Brown

1 stick of butter, 1 cup sugar
2 cups of flour
4 eggs
2 teaspoons baking powder
½ cup of brandy
2 cups of pecans, broken in pieces
1 lb. seedless raisins

Line a round or loaf cake pan with brown paper and grease. Preheat oven for 15 minutes at 325°.
Sift flour 3 times before measuring. Sprinkle ¼ cup of flour over pecans and raisins, mix well. To rest of flour add baking powder. With electric mixer cream butter and sugar well, add eggs, one at a time. Then by hand fold in flour and baking powder mixture alternately with brandy, then add pecans and raisins. Pour into lined cake pan and bake 45 minutes to 60 minutes.
This is an old family recipe that we make every Thanksgiving and Christmas. Quite frequently we double or triple the recipe when baking before

Thanksgiving and store the other cakes for use at Christmas. Before storing, cool cakes thoroughly, wrap in aluminum foil and put in air-tight tins.

POUND CAKE

Mrs. Harry Jordan

6 eggs
½ lb. each butter, sugar
¼ teaspoon baking powder
½ lb. flour
vanilla or lemon flavoring

Cream the butter and sugar well. Beat the whites and yolks of the eggs separately. Sift the salt and baking powder with the flour. To the creamed butter and sugar add, alternately, the beaten egg yolks and the flour mixture. Beat very well between each addition. Last of all fold in the whites. Flavor. Bake in a loaf about 1 hour and 15 minutes.

SOUR CREAM CAKE

Mrs. Harry Merritt Lane, Jr.

2 sticks of butter
3 cups each sugar, cake flour
1 cup of sour cream
6 egg yolks, 6 egg whites
¼ teaspoon each salt, soda
1 teaspoon each vanilla, mace

Cream butter and sugar, add egg yolks, flour, sour cream, beat egg whites and fold in. Grease and flour cake pan well, pour in batter, sprinkle mace on top. Cook at 325° for 30 minutes—turn to 350° for 45 minutes or until cake leaves the side of the pan.

SPICE CAKE

Mrs. Thomas Jordan

¼ cup butter, ½ cup sugar
1 egg
½ cup milk
1½ cups flour
2½ teaspoons baking powder
½ teaspoon each, nutmeg, cloves, allspice, 1 teaspoon cinnamon
½ cup currants

Cream the butter, add sugar gradually, and egg well beaten. Mix and sift flour and baking powder, and add alternately with milk to first mixture. Then stir in spices and currants. Bake thirty minutes in a buttered shallow pan, or twenty minutes in muffin pans. Serve warm.

EMILIA'S SPICE CAKE
Mrs. Leopoldo Rodriguez

½ cup butter, 1 cup brown sugar
2 eggs, separated
1 cup milk
2 cups flour, sifted with
1 teaspoon soda, salt and cinnamon, and
½ teaspoon each nutmeg, and cloves
1 cup seeded raisins, ½ cup nuts, chopped

Make like any batter cake. Add the nuts and raisins last, slightly floured. Bake in a gingerbread pan and cut into squares when cooled.

SPONGE CAKE

¾ lb. sugar, 1/3 cup water
7 eggs, setting aside 2 whites for icing
1 lemon, the juice and grated rind
½ lb. sifted flour

Boil sugar and water. Beat yolks very light, then add the whites, stiffly beaten. Now pour the boiling sugar on the eggs, slowly beating all the while until cool. Add the lemon juice and grated rind. Have flour sifted 3 times and fold gently into the eggs and sugar. Place in a moderate oven as quickly as possible. The success of the cake lies in the mixing. Everything should be prepared before one beats the eggs. It is even better to have another beat the whites, so that the yolks need not stand one moment.

SPONGE CAKE
Mrs. Wilson Jones

4 eggs, 3 tablespoons water
1 cup sugar
1½ tablespoons cornstarch, flour
1 teaspoon flavoring
½ teaspoon baking powder
¼ teaspoon salt

Separate eggs. Add water to yolks and beat with Dover beater until light. Add sugar and mix well. Put cornstarch in cup, add sifted flour to fill, then baking powder and salt. Dump into cake, mix well, add flavoring, then stiffly beaten egg whites.

Bake in round pan with hole in center for 45 to 60 minutes, at 350°.

The secret of success of this cake is "dumping" in the ingredients.

SPONGE CAKE
Mrs. Thomas J. Walshe

6 eggs
1½ cups each sugar, flour
1½ level teaspoons baking powder

Cream the yolks very lightly. Beat one-half of the sugar with them. Then add half of the sugar to the well beaten whites. Sift baking powder and flour, alternately fold flour and beaten white mixture to the yolk mixture. This makes three layers. Cut recipe in half for jelly roll. Cook in long pan.

SPONGE CAKE
Mrs. William Hodding Carter, Sr.

6 eggs, 4 tablespoons cold water
2 tablespoons cornstarch
1½ cups sifted flour (less 2 tablespoons)
1½ cups sifted sugar
1½ teaspoons baking powder
½ teaspoon salt
1½ teaspoons vanilla

Beat egg yolks and water with electric mixer until lemon color. Add sugar gradually and continue beating until well mixed. Sift flour, cornstarch, baking powder and salt at least three times. Fold into egg mixture. Add vanilla. Beat egg whites until stiff. Fold into other mixture. Put into ungreased sponge cake pan and bake at 325° about forty or fifty minutes. Invert cake on cake rack and let stand until cold.

STRAWBERRY CAKE
Mrs. J. W. Stierman, Jr.

1 package yellow cake mix
1 package strawberry jello
3 tablespoons flour
½ cup water
1 cup water
1 cup Wesson oil
4 eggs, unseparated
½ 10-oz. package frozen strawberries (½ cup)

Bake in 3 8" pans at 350°.

Filling:

1 stick melted oleo
½ 10-oz. package frozen strawberries
1 package powdered sugar

UPSIDE DOWN CAKE

4 eggs, the whites
3 cups flour, 3 teaspoons baking powder
1¾ cups sugar
1 cup milk
½ cup butter
1 can sliced peaches
2 sliced bananas
4 slices canned pineapple
½ cup cherries
½ cup brown sugar
1 tablespoon butter, heaping

Cream the butter and the sugar. Add the beaten eggs, then the flour sifted with the baking powder, and the milk, gradually. Last of all, the vanilla. Put the butter in an iron skillet and add the brown sugar, letting it cook until it melts thoroughly. Then set the evenly cut fruits on the sugar, arranging them as close together as possible. Pour the cake batter over all. Bake in a medium hot oven. Serve with whipped cream.

WHITE CAKE
Miss Ethel Forman

6 egg whites
10 ozs. sugar, 5 ozs. butter
¾ lb. flour, 2 teaspoons baking powder
1 cup milk
1 teaspoon almond flavoring

Cream butter and sugar well, sift flour and baking powder together several times. Add to butter and sugar, alternating with milk. Add flavoring and stiffly beaten whites. Bake in moderate oven for loaf cake, or quick oven for layer cake.

ALMOND CAKES NO. 1

1 cup ground almonds
1 cup sugar
1 lemon, the grated rind
1 egg white

Put almonds, sugar and rind of lemon on board and mix with white of egg. Roll and cut in squares, and bake in slow oven. Watch carefully.

ALMOND CAKES NO. 2

1 lb. almonds
1 lb. sugar
1 doz. eggs

Cream sugar and yolks of eggs thoroughly. Grind almonds in meat chopper, without removing skins. Add them to the yolks, then fold in the whites of eggs beaten stiff. Bake in a moderate oven in small muffin tins.

BAISERS CRÉOLES
Miss Ethel Forman

½ lb. pulverized sugar
3 egg whites
½ cup chopped pecans
1 teaspoon vanilla

Sift sugar. Beat the whites of the eggs very stiff and add about a tablespoonful of the sugar at a time, beating very hard each time the sugar is added until it is all used. Stir in quickly pecans and vanilla. Drop on wrapping paper without greasing, by ½ teaspoons, 2 inches apart. Bake in moderate oven. Watch closely.

BATONS DES NOIX

1¾ sticks butter
5 tablespoons confectioners sugar
2 cups flour
2 teaspoons vanilla
1 tablespoon water
1 cup nuts, chopped fine

Cream the butter and sugar well, then add the sifted flour, vanilla, water, and nuts. Let chill in the ice box. Form with fingers into small rolls about the size of the thumb. Bake in oven at 450°. Sprinkle with powdered sugar.

BROWNIES
Mrs. John C. Calhoun

1 stick soft butter
1 cup sugar
5 tablespoons cocoa
½ cup sifted, self-rising flour
1 teaspoon vanilla
½ cup chopped pecans

Cream butter and sugar. Add cocoa. Mix until smooth. Add eggs and beat well. Blend in flour. Mix pecans into batter and pour into a greased 7 x 10½ pan. Bake in 325° oven for 35 minutes.

Icing:

    4 tablespoons butter
    ½ lb. confectioners sugar
    4 tablespoons cocoa
    ¼ cup milk
    1 teaspoon vanilla

Melt butter in a saucepan, add sugar, cocoa, milk, and vanilla. Heat about 1 minute. Remove from heat and beat with an electric mixer. Beat 1 minute or until smooth.

BROWNIES
Mrs. Thomas J. Walshe

    1 cup butter, 2 cups sugar
    2 large squares Baker's unsweetened
        chocolate
    3 cups pecans
    4 eggs, 1 cup flour

Cream butter and sugar slightly. Add melted chocolate which is cooled. Dredge pecans in flour and add to first mixture. Lastly, eggs beaten as for scrambling. After greasing pan, sprinkle sifted flour over it to keep cake from sticking.

BUTTERSCOTCH BROWNIES
Mrs. Norton Dickman

    1 cup brown sugar, ¼ cup butter
    1 egg
    ¾ cup flour
    1 teaspoon baking powder
    ½ teaspoon salt
    1 teaspoon vanilla
    1 cup nuts, ½ cup raisins

Cream butter, add ingredients in order listed, bake 30 minutes in slow oven.

BUTTER DOUGH
Mrs. Alma Malm

    1 lb. each flour, butter
    ½ jigger vinegar
    1 pt. water

Mix flour and butter together, using half the butter at a time and mixing with knives so as not to get your warm hands into the mixture. When it is uniformly crumbly make a hole in the center and add vinegar and cold water, working with the knives until it becomes a stiff dough. Handle lightly. Roll out thin and dab with butter. Fold over three times in one direction and then three more times at right angles. Place in the ice box for an hour. Take it out and roll out again on a floured board, butter and fold as before. Repeat this operation three or four times at intervals of a few minutes but not in a warm kitchen. Roll out and shape into pretzels, brush with egg, sprinkle with sugar and chopped almonds and bake.

Linse Macaroons. The same dough may be used to line small muffin tins and filled with the following mixture: ½ lb. almonds, chopped fine, 1½ lbs. sugar, 6 raw egg whites, 1 teaspoonful baking powder. Bake slowly in a moderate oven.

Apple Cookies. Cut apples in quarters and boil in a small quantity of water until quite soft. Sweeten and cool, sprinkle with cinnamon. Line a flat cookie pan with butter dough. Spread with the apples. Spread with another layer of dough, pressing the edges well together, brush with well beaten raw egg and bake ½ hour in a slow oven. Cut in squares, sprinkle with sugar and serve while still warm.

BUTTERSCOTCH BROWNIES
Mrs. Frank C. Moran, Jr.

    1 stick butter
    1 pound box dark brown sugar
        Melt above ingredients in a
        saucepan and then cool.
Add:
    2 eggs
    1 cup flour
    2 teaspoons baking powder
    1 teaspoon salt
    2 teaspoons vanilla
    1½ cups chopped pecans

Mix well. Bake in 2-eight inch square pans at 350° for 25 minutes. Pans may be greased and lined with wax paper. Cut into squares when cool. Makes 3 dozen chewey brownies.

CHOCOLATE CAKES
Mrs. Charles E. Fenner

    1 cup flour
    1 teaspoon baking powder

½ teaspoon salt
½ cup butter, 1 cup sugar
4 eggs, ½ cup milk
¾ cup nut meats
3 squares unsweetened chocolate
¾ cup raisins
½ teaspoon vanilla

Sift all dry ingredients three times. Cream butter and sugar until fluffy. Add melted chocolate, then egg yolks, nuts and raisins. Add flour, milk, vanilla. Fold in beaten whites. Bake in muffin rings or drop from a teaspoon. Bake in a rather slow oven.

CHOCOLATE NUT WAFERS

Mrs. E. C. Corliss

2 eggs, 2/3 cup butter
1½ cups sugar
1 cup flour (measured before sifting)
2 teaspoons vanilla
1 cup pecans broken
2 squares chocolate

Beat together the eggs, sugar, flour, vanilla and pecans. Stir thoroughly and mix with the butter and chocolate melted together. Drop by teaspoons on buttered cookie sheet, bake in a slow oven. These have no baking powder.

CHRISTIANA WAFERS

Mrs. Frank J. Tremont

3 eggs, 3 tablespoons sugar
3 tablespoons cream
flour, to make stiff dough
pinch salt
pinch cardamon seed or teaspoon vanilla

Roll out very thin, cut in diamond shapes and drop into hot lard until light brown. Excellent with cocktails or tea or coffee.

HELLO DOLLY COOKIES

Paul Renger III

½ stick oleo
1 cup Vanilla Wafers (crushed)
1 6-oz. package milk chocolate chips
1 cup pecans (broken)
1 can Eagle Brand Condensed Milk
1 cup coconut

Melt oleo in oblong cake pan. Sprinkle vanilla crumbs evenly in melted butter. Sprinkle coconut over crumbs, the sprinkle the chocolate chips and pecans over coconut. Drizzle can of condensed milk over all and bake in 325° oven for 30 minutes.

COCONUT KISSES

Mrs. Dave Hunter

1 can coconut
4 egg whites, beaten stiff
1 cup sugar
4 cups corn flakes
1 cup nut meats

Add sugar to egg and then add coconut, nuts, and corn flakes. Bake in a slow oven on greased paper until delicately brown.

BLANCHE'S COCOANUT KISSES

Mrs. Lucius M. Lamar

6 egg whites, 3 cups sugar
½ teaspoon salt
6 cups corn flakes
1½ cups pecans or walnuts, chopped
3 cups cocoanut, shredded
1 teaspoon vanilla

Beat egg whites until stiff; beat in sugar and salt until mixture is stiff. Fold in the corn flakes, nuts and cocoanut. Add vanilla.
Grease cookie sheet. Drop dollops (small teaspoon size) of the mixture on the cookie sheet leaving space between the dollops.
Bake in a moderate oven (350°) for 15 to 20″. Place on middle rack of oven to avoid burning.
When done place sheet on a damp towel, remove kisses with spatula.
Makes 2 doz. cookies.
Let cool off thoroughly before storing. Place in an air-tight container to prevent softening.

CORN FLAKE KISSES

Mrs. William Wall

2 cups corn flakes
¾ cup sugar
2 eggs, beaten separately
1 cup each chopped nuts, raisins

Mix the dry ingredients, then add the eggs and mix well. Drop by teaspoons, 2 inches apart on a greased baking sheet.

Bake in a moderate oven 15 to 20 minutes, until done.

CREAM PUFFS

Miss Ethel Forman

1 cup each butter, boiling water
4 eggs
½ teaspoon salt
1 cup flour

Pour butter and water in saucepan and place on stove. As soon as boiling point is reached, add flour all at once, and stir vigorously. Remove from fire as soon as mixed and add unbeaten eggs one at a time, beating until thoroughly mixed between the addition of eggs. Drop by spoonfuls on a buttered sheet 2 inches apart, having mixture slightly piled in center. Bake 30 minutes in moderate oven. With a sharp knife make a cut in each large enough to admit of cream filling. This recipe makes 20 cream cakes.

CROQUIGNOLES

Mrs. Walter Torian

3 eggs, ½ cup sugar
1 tablespoon butter
1 teaspoon baking powder
2 tablespoons ice water
1 tablespoon vanilla, nutmeg, a little flour (to make medium dough)

Beat the eggs together, mix in sugar, cream the butter into the mixture till light. Add flour (baking powder sifted with it), roll thin. Cut with cup and make 2 slashes in the centers of each piece and cook in deep fat. Sprinkle with powdered sugar and serve for tea.

DANISH COOKIES

Mrs. Geo. Villeré

1¾ sticks butter
4 tablespoons confectioners sugar
2 cups flour
2 teaspoons vanilla
1 teaspoon (or more) water
1 cup chopped nuts

Mix and shape with hand, break in small pieces and roll. Bake in moderate oven.

DROP NUT COOKIES

1 cup brown sugar
1 tablespoon butter, 1 egg
1 cup pecans
½ teaspoon vanilla
7 level tablespoons flour

Cream butter and egg together, add sugar, flour, vanilla and nuts. Drop on well greased sheet and cook in moderate oven.

EGGNOG CAKES

Mrs. Rachel Bunting Wilmot

Use small pieces of sponge cake or white cake. Roll in eggnog frosting:

2 cups powdered sugar
¼ lb. butter
enough Bourbon whiskey to make a paste

Then roll cakes in equal quantities of chopped pecans and macaroon crumbs.

FLUFF CAKES MERINGUES

6 egg whites
1 cup sugar
½ pt. cream
1 teaspoon vanilla

Beat the egg whites thirty minutes, add the sugar very gradually. Beat more. Drop the mixture from a spoon, about three inches apart, on well greased wax paper, placed on baking sheet. Light the oven as you place the cakes in. Bake very slowly, about 40 minutes. Serve with whipped cream or ice cream. Put the cream on top of cake, place another cake on top and put more cream on top of that or ice cream.

FUDGE CAKE SQUARES, AU PARISIEN

Mrs. Harry Merritt Lane

½ cup of butter
1 cup sugar
1 teaspoon vanilla
½ cup flour
2 eggs
1 cup pecans (broken)
2 tablespoons (heaping) cocoa

Cream butter and sugar and eggs, which have been beaten, together. Mix thoroughly. Sift flour and cocoa together and add to egg mixture. Then add nuts and vanilla. Cook in long fudge cake pan (6½ x 11) for 30 minutes in a moderate oven. Cut into squares and cover with Fudge Square Icing (look under Fillings and Frostings).

GINGER SNAPS
Miss Ethel Forman

1 egg
1 teaspoon salt
1 cup molasses
1 cup sugar
1 cup butter and lard mixed
1 teaspoon soda (dissolve in ½ cup water)
1 tablespoon ginger

Work in enough flour to mold out rather soft. Chill. Roll thin and bake in quick oven. Crisp and delicious.

ICE BOX COOKIES
Mrs. Chas. Crawford

1 cup each white sugar, brown sugar
1 cup butter
2 eggs, slightly beaten
1 teaspoon vanilla
½ teaspoon salt, 1 teaspoon soda
3½ cups flour
    (soda, flour, salt, sifted together)
1 cup nut meats

Make dough into smooth roll and divide into 3 parts. Put dough in covered dish and let stand at least over night in ice box before using. Cut thin across roll with very sharp knife and cook as needed. The dough will last indefinitely in ice box.

Cut very thin, bake in moderate oven. Take care not to burn.

KING'S COOKIES
Miss Nina Ansley King

1/3 cup butter, 2 cups sugar
3 cups flour, sifted
4 eggs
1½ cups seedless raisins
1 cup oatmeal
1/3 teaspoon each soda, cinnamon

Cream butter and sugar and add eggs, well beaten. Then stir in the flour a little at a time and last the oatmeal and raisins with the cinnamon. Drop by spoonfuls on a baking sheet and bake till a nice brown.

This recipe comes from the sister of Miss Grace King and has been handed down from plantation days.

KITTEN'S TONGUE

Take 2 eggs and not quite a cup of sugar. Whip them just a little, then add not quite a cupful of melted butter and a cup of flour. Stir the mixture, spread it on a tin in small quantities, bake them. Roll in nuts and sugar.

LEBKUCHEN

1 lb. brown sugar
1 teaspoon each cinnamon, cloves
½ nutmeg, grated
3 ozs. citron
4 eggs
¼ lb. unblanched almonds
1½ cups sifted flour

Frosting:
    powdered sugar, water
    white of egg, a little

Grind the almonds and the citron not too fine. Mix all the ingredients well together and spread very thin in a shallow pan. Bake in a moderate oven, taking care that it does not brown.

Remove from the oven and cut into squares with a sharp knife, leaving them in the pan while spreading on the frosting (use a pastry brush for this).

Set back in the oven only long enough to dry—a few minutes. Keep in a china jar or covered dish.

LOVE WREATHS
Mrs. Alma Malm

Take the yolks of four hard-boiled eggs and crumble them with ¼ lb. of flour. Mix with this ½ lb. of butter, ¼ lb. sugar and ½ teaspoon vanilla. Roll pieces of the dough into pencil size rolls, cut and form into rings. Dip these into raw egg and then into sugar. Place on a buttered pan, not too close together and bake.

Finnish Cookies are made in exactly the same way with the yolks of the hard boiled eggs omitted.

MERINGUE SHELLS
Mrs. Edwin T. Merrick III

4 egg whites
1 cup granulated sugar
½ teaspoon vanilla

Beat egg whites until stiff. Add very gradually 2/3 of sugar and continue beating until mixture will hold its shape. Add vanilla, then fold in remaining sugar. Shape with spoon on cookie sheet covered with letter paper. Bake 50 minutes in a very slow oven (250°F) until light, light brown. Remove from paper as soon as you take them from the oven. If desired put together in pairs. Serve with ice cream on top or between.

NUT-BUTTER COOKIES
Mrs. A. B. Dinwiddie

½ lb. butter at room temperature
¼ to ½ cup granulated sugar
½ teaspoon salt
2 cups all-purpose flour
½ teaspoon almond or vanilla flavoring
½ cup nuts, chopped fine

Cream butter well with the sugar. Add flour and salt sifted together, flavoring and nuts. Mix with the hands to a mass of rough looking dough. Clean hands and flour the palms. Pinch off bits of the dough and roll between the palms into balls about one inch in diameter. Flatten these and bake about 12 to 14 minutes at 350°. Take care not to bake beyond a light brown. When cold sprinkle with confectioners sugar.

THIN OATMEAL COOKIES
Mrs. J. B. Simmons

2 eggs, well beaten
2 cups sugar
1 cup melted butter
2 tablespoons sifted flour, heaping
½ teaspoon baking powder
1 teaspoon vanilla
2 cups rolled oats
pinch salt

Beat the sugar into the eggs, add the flour, with the baking powder sifted in it, then the vanilla extract, and finally the rolled oats. The beating process is continuous!

Drop the mixture by teaspoons 4 inches apart on a well greased pan. Bake in moderate oven until a pretty golden brown. But be on your guard constantly, they love to burn!

Removing from the pan is a difficult process and trying to the temper of the cook. While very hot they refuse to stick together and as soon as cold they become so crisp they are apt to break at a touch. Keep them near the stove and work quickly—pressing the broken bits together into little heaps with the fingers. The pan must be well greased. When the knack of handling them is mastered they are more than worth the pains.

LES OREILLES DE COCHON
Mrs. Walter Torian

2 teacups sifted flour
1 teaspoon baking powder
2 eggs, beaten together
1 tablespoon mixed lard and butter
1 teaspoon vinegar, pinch salt

Mix flour and baking powder, then rub in the butter, lard and vinegar. Add the eggs beaten together. Roll very thin, cover with saucer and cut round. Have a pot of deep fat very hot and drop the dough into it and give a twist with the fork. That forms the ear. When a golden brown, place on a dish and sprinkle with powdered sugar and cinnamon.

The secret of this famous, unique recipe is here released for the first time.

POINT COUPÉE COOKIES
Mrs. E. T. Merrick

½ cup butter, 2 cups sugar
3 eggs
½ cup sour heavy cream
1 teaspoon each lemon juice, vanilla
1 teaspoon nutmeg
3½ cups sifted flour
1 teaspoon soda, pinch of salt

Cream together butter and sugar and eggs (eggs beaten lightly together). Then add flour, then the cream to which soda has been added and well stirred. Add seasoning. Mix thoroughly and put in ice box until it stiffens (next day is better). Drop by half teaspoons on pan greased with butter, not too close together. Bake in moderate oven. You can sprinkle a few nuts on top.

"S"
Mrs. Chas. H. Behre, Sr.

1½ lbs. flour
1 scant cup sugar, 1 lb. butter
8 egg yolks

Wash the butter in two waters to remove the salt. Work into it the sugar, eggs, and flour, until you have a smooth paste. Take lumps of dough and roll out with the hand on a floured board into long rolls about the thickness of a finger. Cut rolls into three and a half inch pieces. Twist the pieces into S shapes. Brush with beaten egg white, sprinkle with sugar, and bake in a moderate oven to a delicate brown. Makes fifty to sixty cakes.

Editor's note -- Unsalted butter is now available in most stores.

SAND SHELLS

2 sticks butter (½ lb.)
2 cups flour
5 tablespoons powdered sugar
2 teaspoons vanilla
1½ cups chopped pecans

Cream the butter and the sugar, then add the flour, vanilla, and pecans. Work this and form it in crescents. Cook in a moderate oven ½ hour.
Roll the tarts in powdered sugar. Put them in paper lined tins and they will remain fresh and crisp a long time.

SESAME SEED COOKIES
Mrs. Joseph P. Burton

¾ cup butter
1½ cups brown sugar
2 eggs
1¼ cups flour
½ cup sesame seed toasted
1 teaspoon vanilla
¼ teaspoon baking powder

Lightly mix the ingredients. Then drop from teaspoon on waxed paper on baking sheet far enough apart for spreading. Bake at 325° 30 minutes. Makes seven dozen.

SPONGE CAKES
Mrs. David T. Merrick

4 to 6 eggs according to size
1 cup sugar

1 cup flour, sifted three times
½ lemon, juice and rind grated

Beat yolks very light, add sugar, lemon juice, part of flour, rind. Fold in whites well beaten and remainder of flour. Bake in buttered muffin tin in moderate oven just lighted.

SPRITZENKÜCHLEIN
Mrs. Helen Pitkin Schertz

1 cup each milk, water
½ stick butter
3 cups flour
3 teaspoons baking powder
½ teaspoon salt, 1 teaspoon sugar
4 or 5 eggs
1 tablespoon vanilla

Put the milk, water, salt and butter in a large pot and bring to a boil. Stir in the flour to which baking powder and sugar are added, about a cup at a time, and stir vigorously until it is a smooth stiff dough which leaves the sides of the pan. Remove from the fire and allow to cool a little. Then break the eggs one by one into the dough and stir between the addition of each egg until quite smooth. At the last add vanilla. Put dough into a pastry bag. Have a pot of oil ready at the proper temperature for frying doughnuts. Squeeze the dough into the oil in small bits and fry to a nice brown. Drain on paper, sprinkle generously with powdered sugar and cinnamon and serve hot. Delicious with afternoon tea.

TEA CAKES
Mrs. Gasquet de Zeriga

2 eggs
½ lb. butter, 1½ cups sugar
1 level teaspoon baking powder
1 coffeespoon salt
2 teaspoons vanilla
flour to make dough (use as little as possible)

Place in refrigerator. Roll dough very thin, dust with sugar and cinnamon. Cut cakes in any desired shape. Bake in a quick oven.

"'TI'S GATEAUX"
Mrs. James Amédée Puech

1 cup flour
2 eggs

¼ lb. butter, 1 cup sugar
1 teaspoon vanilla
1/3 cup milk
1 teaspoon baking powder

Cream sugar and butter. Add yolks of eggs, then put in flour sifted 3 times and beaten whites of eggs, alternately. Add milk, and then vanilla. Last add the baking powder. Drop batter in oblong cake pan with a small teaspoon. Do not allow to spread too much. Bake in a hot oven.

VANILLA TEA WAFERS
Mrs. Charles Henry Bailey

1 stick butter, 1 cup sugar, scant
1 large egg
1-1/3 cups Ballards self-rising flour, sifted
2 teaspoons vanilla
¼ cup water
    mixture of cinnamon and sugar
    to sprinkle on wafers

Cream butter and sugar add whole egg then vanilla. Alternate sifted flour with water. When batter is smooth drop from coffee spoon on aluminum foil lined cookie sheet leaving about two inches between wafers as they will spread. Sprinkle with cinnamon and sugar and bake for about 12' or until delicate brown in 350° oven.

CREAM FILLING

Beat together the yolks of 2 eggs, 1 cup sugar, powdered, 2 tablespoons of cream and 1 tablespoon of vanilla. Beat and mix to a thick cream.

LEMON FILLING
Mrs. Albin Provosty

2 eggs, the yolks only
1 cup sugar
1 lemon, the juice and rind
1 tablespoon cornstarch
1 cup water
2 tablespoons butter

Stir all ingredients, except butter, well together and cook in a double boiler until thick and smooth. Add the butter and when melted remove from the fire. Cool slightly and use between cake layers.

LEMON FILLING FOR CAKE
Mrs. Thomas. J. Walshe

¾ stick butter
1 cup sugar
2 egg yolks
2 whole lemons, juice and grated rind

Put all in skillet at one time, cook slowly about 10 minutes until thickened. It should be delightfully tasty and gummy when cold.

LEMON JELLY FILLING
Mrs. E. T. Merrick

2 eggs beaten thoroughly with 2/3 cup sugar, the rind and juice of 2 lemons

Mix together and let thicken in a vessel over hot water. It only needs to come to boiling point. Add a tiny piece of butter. Use between layers of cakes.

CHOCOLATE ICING

2 squares chocolate
1 cup sugar
1 tablespoon flour
1/3 cup milk
2 tablespoons butter
½ teaspoon vanilla

Melt the chocolate over hot water, add the sugar and flour mixed together. When smooth, add the milk slowly. Cook until it spins a thread 1 inch long. Add the butter and vanilla, cool, and beat until it is of such consistency that it will spread without running. If the frosting is too thick, set the pan over hot water and stir until it softens.

CHOCOLATE MARSHMALLOW PECAN ICING

3 squares bitter chocolate
1/3 stick butter
1 box confectioners sugar
6 teaspoons milk
12 marshmallows
½ cup pecans

Cream the butter and sugar together and beat until light. Melt chocolate in double boiler and add to the butter and sugar. Add the marshmallows, which have been cut and the chopped pecans. Spread quickly between layers and on top of cake.

CHOCOLATE NUT MINUTE FROSTING

When time is of the essence, a frosting for the cake may be saved by the simple process of sprinkling grated or finely shaved sweet chocolate mixed with coconut or broken nutmeats over the batter when it is in the pan, ready to go into the oven.

The cake emerges from the oven all ready to serve.

CHOCOLATE PECAN FROSTING

1 lb. powdered sugar
1 whole egg
1 stick butter
2 ozs. unsweetened chocolate (melted)
1 teaspoon vanilla, 2 tablespoons rum
1 cup chopped pecans

Mix well.

ICING FOR FUDGE SQUARES
Mrs. Harry Merritt Lane

2/3 package confectioners sugar
2 tablespoons cocoa
1 teaspoon vanilla
½ stick melted butter

Simply use sufficient cream or milk to mix ingredients so that frosting will be of right spreading consistency.

ICING À LA LUCIE

1½ cups milk
2 whole eggs
1 scant cup sugar
1 teaspoon cornstarch
1 cup grated chocolate

Heat the milk and add it to eggs and sugar. Dissolve cornstarch in a little water, and add chocolate. Boil all together until thick, then remove from stove, beat a little, and it is ready to spread on cake.

MARSHMALLOW FROSTING À LA MAMIE
Mamie Isadore

1 egg white
1 cup sugar
½ teaspoon salt
¼ cup water
½ cup chopped marshmallows
1 teaspoon almond extract

Mix sugar, salt, water, and egg white in top of double boiler. Beat for 1 minute. Set over hot water and beat for 10 minutes or until mixture stands in peaks. Add marshmallows and almond extract, and beat until spreading consistency.

SEVEN MINUTE FROSTING

2 egg whites, unbeaten
1½ cups sugar
5 tablespoons cold water
1½ teaspoons light corn syrup
1 teaspoon vanilla

Put egg whites, sugar, water and corn syrup in upper part of double boiler. Beat with rotary egg beater until thoroughly mixed. Place over rapidly boiling water, beat constantly and cook for 7 minutes, or until frosting will stand in peaks. Remove from fire, add vanilla, and beat until thick enough to spread. Makes enough frosting to cover two 9-inch layers.

MOCHA ICING AND FILLING

1 tablespoon butter
1 cup confectioners sugar
1 tablespoon cocoa
1 tablespoon strong coffee
½ teaspoon salt

Cream the butter and sugar together well. Add cocoa, coffee, and salt. Stir until smooth. If too dry, add coffee; if too moist, add sugar. This will cover one layer.

ORANGE GLAZE
Mrs. William Hodding Carter, Sr.

1 egg yolk
3 tablespoons melted butter
5 tablespoons orange juice
1 teaspoon grated orange rind
2 cups sifted powdered sugar

Mix and spread on top and sides of cake.

QUICK WHITE ICING

2 egg whites, pinch salt
1½ cups sugar, 5 tablespoons water
1 teaspoon vanilla or lemon juice

Beat whites with salt until stiff but not dry. Cook sugar and water until they form a soft ball in cold water. Add gradually to beaten whites until all is used and it stands in peaks. Add vanilla or lemon juice, mix well, do not beat.

CHESS PASTRY

Mrs. Fred Faust

Pastry:

HOT WATER PASTRY

¼ lb. butter
¾ lb. flour
1 gill hot water

Mix butter and flour in the usual manner. Moisten with the hot water, and roll.

½ cup butter
2 cups sugar
4 eggs
1 teaspoon vanilla

Icing:

1 lb. powdered sugar
¼ cup butter
4 teaspoons maple or other
 flavoring

Melt the butter and sugar in a double boiler. Separate the eggs and beat thoroughly. Add the yolks to the sugar and butter mixture and stir till mixed. They should hardly be cooked at all, simply well mixed over the fire. Then fold in the egg whites. Mix well and remove from the fire without further cooking. Add the vanilla. Have the pastry rolled out and fitted into a square pan. Pour in the egg mixture. Place in a very slow oven and cook for thirty minutes or more. It will be puffed up like a soufflé. On removal from the oven it will settle and come away from the pastry a little. Before it is cool cover with the following icing, which being somewhat thin, and the pie being still warm, will spread of itself over the surface of the pie.

Cool and cut in squares.

KIECHEN

Mrs. Julius Perlt

This dessert may be served hot or cold; may be kept refrigerated for several days, and loses none of its flavor or crispness in being re-heated.

Any fresh fruit may be used in the filling, such as apples, pears, plums, blueberries, huckleberries, et cetera.

Pastry: (about three shells)
2 cups sifted flour
½ teaspoon baking powder
⅔ cup butter
½ teaspoon salt
2 teaspoons sugar
2 egg yolks
⅓ cup cold water

Sift flour, salt, baking powder, and sugar together. Cut in butter, when well-mixed, add egg yolks and water. Mix well, turn out on floured bread and knead for a few minutes. Roll out and place in pans. Chill while fixing filling.

Fill pie shell with fruit.

Filling: (for one pie shell)
Mix together ½ cup sugar and 2 tablespoons flour.

Beat one egg and add a little more than ⅓ cup cream.

Add sugar and flour mixture.

Add one teaspoon vanilla.

Stir until smooth and pour over fruit.

Dot with butter and bake at 350° for about 30 minutes or until crust is golden brown.

(Cinnamon and nutmeg may be sprinkled over pie before baking.)

PIE CRUST INFALLIBLE

2 cups flour
8 tablespoons lard, 1 tablespoon butter
 teaspoon salt
 ice water

Sift flour 3 times, the third time with salt. Work lard into it with pastry mixer or silver knives, until mixture looks crumbly, like coarse meal. Mix in ice water gradually to make a stiff dough.

Roll it out and spread it with butter, fold over, butter again and continue until the butter has been used. A second tablespoon of butter will make it even richer.

Bake at 400°.

TART À L'APRICOT
Mrs. Donald Rafferty

2 cups milk
2 egg yolks, beaten
2 tablespoons sugar
2 tablespoons flour
1 teaspoon vanilla
1 can sliced apricots
1 tablespoon tapioca
    red coloring

Line a layer cake tin with pastry, bringing it well up the side and bake till a delicate brown. Make a custard of the milk, the egg yolks with the sugar and flour mixed together cooking until thick, add vanilla. Cool and pour into pastry.

Drain the apricots, saving the juice, remove the skins carefully, so as not to break the flesh. Lay them close together, round side up on the custard. Cook the tapioca in the apricot juice, add a little red color and pour it over the tart to glaze.

This recent importation by the inveterate traveler who gives it, is already taking a foremost place among our cherished French culinary inheritances.

PASTRY TARTS

1 stick butter
1 cup flour
1 Philadelphia cream cheese
    jam or jelly

Work the first three ingredients well together, and place in the refrigerator until ready to use. Roll out thin, cut in squares, put jam on each, fold the edges together, and prick each tart lightly with a fork. Bake in rather quick oven. This pastry can be used for appetizers like anchovies.

FRUIT TARTS
Mrs. Russell Clark

Pastry:

½ lb. flour
4 tablespoons butter
4 egg yolks
4 tablespoons sugar

Filling:

1 egg, separated, and another egg
    yolk

3 tablespoons flour
3 tablespoons sugar
¾ cup hot milk
1 tablespoon gelatine
1 tablespoon rum
1 egg white, stiffly beaten
2 tablespoons whipped cream
    fresh fruit
    apricot or currant jelly

Sift flour on marble slab and make well in center. Add butter (or other fat), egg yolks, and sugar. Work center ingredients to smooth paste, working flour quickly, roll out, not too thick. Line pan, cover with waxed paper, sprinkle rice to keep paper down. Bake in 350° oven for 35 minutes, remove from oven, cool, fill with cream filling.

To make cream filling: cream egg and egg yolk in bowl, add flour and sugar; beat well and pour over hot milk, stir over slow fire until same comes to a boil, add gelatine. Remove from fire and stir in rum, cool and add stiffly beaten egg white, and whipped cream.

Put fresh fruit over top then glaze with melted jelly (apricot for white fruit like grapes, peaches, or currant jelly for dark fruit like strawberries, cherries, etc.).

BLACK BOTTOM PIE
Mrs. W. P. Lipsey
Through Mrs. Charles de Douisquie

3 eggs separated
1½ cups milk
1 tablespoon cornstarch
1 tablespoon gelatine
1½ squares bitter chocolate
1½ cups sugar, butter
3 tablespoons whiskey
    dash of nutmeg, ginger snaps

Cook egg yolks, milk, sugar and cornstarch until mixture thickly coats a spoon. Add gelatine dissolved in 3 tablespoons cold water. Take one-third of custard and mix with melted chocolate. Flavor with vanilla and spread on pie pan that has been lined with rolled ginger snaps and butter. Cool remaining mixture; fold in beaten whites, whiskey and nutmeg. Pour over chocolate layer. Cool and top with whipped cream and grated bitter chocolate. Keep in refrigerator until ready to serve.

MOCK CHERRY PIE
Mrs. Stanley Arthur

1½ cups cranberries, seeded raisins
1 apple
1 scant teaspoon almond flavoring
¼ cup cold water, 1 cup sugar
2 tablespoons flour

Line a pie plate with pie crust and dot thickly with seeded raisins. Add cranberries that have been cut in quarters and rinsed thoroughly in cold water until all seeds are removed. Pare apple and slice in thin slices over the cranberries. Sprinkle almond flavoring over all. Add sugar and cold water. Dust top with flour. Cut crust for top in strips and lay it on in diamond fashion. Bake in moderate oven.

Tastes exactly like luscious cherry pie. This recipe has won first prize in a number of contests.

CHESS PIE
Mrs. Rachel Bunting Wilmot

10 egg yolks
3 cups sugar, 1 cup butter
½ cup sweet milk
1 tablespoon corn meal, pinch salt
1 teaspoon vanilla

Cream butter, add sugar, yolks and other ingredients. Pour in individual pie crust (cook crust first). Cook pie with filling at 300° until the filling is brown or nearly brown.

CHOCOLATE PIE
Mr. Buddy Diliberto

4 tablespoons cocoa
4 tablespoons flour
1 cup sugar
¼ teaspoon salt
2 cups scalded milk
3 slightly beaten egg yolks
2 tablespoons butter
½ teaspoon vanilla

Mix flour, sugar, salt and cocoa. Gradually add milk, stir until boils. Remove from heat, add egg yolks. Return to heat, boil 2-5 minutes until thick. Add butter and vanilla, pour in cooked pie shell. Top with meringue or whipped cream.

CHOCOLATE CHIFFON PIE
Mrs. Buell C. Buchtel

16 marshmallows
4 Almond Hershey bars
½ cup milk

Melt in a double boiler and let cool. Fold in one cup of whipped cream. Pour into a pie crust made of vanilla wafers and top with another cup of whipped cream.

CHOCOLATE MERINGUE PIE FILLING
Mrs. Harry Jordan

½ lb. of chocolate
¼ cup cornstarch
2 cups milk
3 egg yolks, ¾ cup sugar
1 teaspoon vanilla
1 teaspoon butter

Melt chocolate in double boiler. Add sugar, cornstarch, egg yolks, butter, and milk. Cook until thick, stirring constantly. Add flavoring. Pour into baked shell. Cover with meringue.
Meringue:
3 egg whites beaten until stiff
6 tablespoons sugar

CREAM CHEESE PIE

1 cream cheese, with its cream
1½ cups sugar
3 eggs
2 heaping tablespoons flour
vanilla
pinch of soda, butter, cinnamon

Beat the eggs, yolks and whites separately. Mash the cream cheese and soda into its cream, add the yolks, and heat in double boiler. Fold in the egg whites, stir in the flour, and add the vanilla. Place in a baking dish, sprinkle with sugar and cinnamon mixed, dot with butter, and bake in a hot oven 20 minutes or until done.

CREME DE MENTHE PIE
Mrs. James K. Wadick III

Filling:

4 egg yolks
¾ cup sugar

1 tablespoon unflavored gelatin (one
   envelope)
¼ cup cold water
¼ cup green creme de menthe
10 drops green food coloring
   (optional)
1½ cups whipping cream

Add sugar to the yolks and beat
until the mixture is very thick. Add
gelatin to 2 tablespoons cold water;
dissolve over heat. Stir into the egg
mixture along with the creme de
menthe and the food coloring. Set
aside while making crust.

Crust:

22 chocolate icebox cookies
¼ cup melted butter

Crush cookies fine and combine
with melted butter. Pat firmly into 8
inch pie shell and chill.
   Whip cream and fold into the egg
and gelatine mixture, which should be
beginning to set. Pour into the chilled
cookie crust and chill until firm. Shave
chocolate over top of the pie for
garnish before serving. Serves 6 - 8.

GRASSHOPPER PIE

Mrs. C. Nolte DeRussy, Jr.

Crust: (for 10" pie pan)

30 chocolate wafers, crushed
½ cup melted butter

Mix crushed wafers and melted butter in pan and shape to form of pan.

Filling:

¾ cup milk
42 large marshmallows

Cook in top of double boiler until
marshmallows are melted. Cool.
(Marshmallow mixture will jell if allowed to get too cold.)

1 pint whipping cream
2 ozs. green creme de menthe
2 ozs. white creme de cocoa

Whip cream. Fold in liquers, then
fold cooled marshmallow mixture into
whipped cream mixture.
   Fill pie shell with mixture and chill.

"JEFFERSON DAVIS" PIE

½ cup butter, 2 cups brown sugar
3 egg yolks
1 glass tart jelly
   pastry

Line a pie shell with a flaky pastry.
Cream the butter and sugar together,
add the well beaten eggs. Mix thoroughly and add the jelly. This is a
very rich pie and needs no meringue.

JOAN'S EASY PIE

Mrs. Walter Hagestad

1 graham cracker crust, baked and
   cooled

Mix:

1 can Borden's sweetened condensed
   milk
1 6-oz. can Lemonade Concentrate,
   defrosted
1 large container Cool Whip
¼ cup lemon juice, either bottled or
   fresh

Pour mixture into crust. Top with
grated lemon peel or finely grated
nuts. Refrigerate several hours or overnight.

LEMON PIE

Mrs. David T. Merrick

1 tablespoon flour
4 tablespoons sugar, 4 eggs
1½ large lemons, grated rind and juice
2 tablespoons boiling water

Cream egg yolks, sugar, and flour
until very light, add lemon juice and
grated rind. Put in a double boiler
and cook until the consistency of a
thick cream. Remove from fire, add
2 tablespoons of boiling water. Have
egg whites beaten very stiff with 2
tablespoons of sugar. Add half, folding in, to lemon cream, reserving the
other half for the meringue. Put into
a baked pie shell. Cover with meringue,
and place in a very slow oven and
brown.

LEMON PIE

Mrs. Henry Newton Pharr

4 eggs, 1 cup sugar
1 large lemon, juice and rind (grated)
1 teaspoon gelatine, ⅛ cup water

Cook sugar (½ cup), lemon juice, grated rind and egg yolks in a double boiler until rather thick, then add gelatine, and cook a little more. Do not let the boiling water touch the upper portion of double boiler. Take from stove and fold into stiffly beaten egg whites, to which remaining ½ cup of sugar has been gradually added while beating. Dip with spoon into pastry shell which has been baked and is cool. Let stand in refrigerator about 2½ hours.

Whipped cream may be added.

MINCE MEAT
RECIPE OVER 100 YEARS OLD
Mrs. D. D. Curran

4 lbs. apples pared and chopped
3 lbs. currants, washed and picked
3 lbs. raisins, seeded and chopped
¾ lb. citron, shredded fine
2 tablespoons cinnamon
1 tablespoon each nutmeg, cloves allspice
2 tablespoons powdered mace
2½ lbs. sugar
1 tablespoon salt
2 large glasses sherry
2 large glasses whiskey or brandy
2 cooked beef tongues, cold

Chop beef tongues fine and rub to a powder. Mix all ingredients in a crock. Cover closely and keep for at least three weeks before making into pies.

MOLASSES PIE
Mrs. Charles Farwell

½ cup butter, 1 cup sugar
4 eggs
1 cup New Orleans molasses
1 teaspoon nutmeg

Soften butter, add sugar, yolks of eggs, molasses, whites of eggs lightly beaten and nutmeg. Beat togther well. Bake in pastry. This makes two pies.

MYSTERY PIE
Mrs. Edwin Edwards

3 egg whites
1 cup sugar
1 cup chopped nuts

1 teaspoon vanilla
23 rolled Ritz crackers

Beat egg whites until stiff. Fold in remaining ingredients. Place mixture in buttered pie plate, shaping to sides and bottom of plate. Bake at 350° for 30 minutes. COOL.

Filling: ½ pt. whipping cream, whipped, to which you have added 2 tablespoons cocoa.

ORANGE PIE

2 tablespoons butter
1 cup powdered sugar
1 tablespoon cornstarch, cold water
1 cup boiling water
2 eggs
2 large oranges
2 tablespoons powdered sugar

Cream the butter and sugar. Mix the cornstarch with enough cold water to moisten it and stir it into the boiling water. Allow to cook only two minutes, stirring constantly. Add the butter and sugar and stir well. Remove from the fire and add the well beaten yolks of the eggs. Line the pie plate with pastry and bake. Add to the custard the juice of two oranges and the grated rind of one, place it in the baked crust and set back in the oven to brown slightly. Cover with meringue made of stiffly beaten whites, sweetened, set back in the oven to brown. Serve cold.

PECAN PIE
Mrs. James Selman

4 eggs, lightly beaten
1½ cups sugar
1 cup dark Karo syrup
1 cup light Karo syrup
1 stick butter, melted
½ teaspoon salt
1 tablespoon vanilla
7 or 8 ozs. pecans, halved or chopped
2 small uncooked pie shells

Combine all ingredients, mixing well and adding the pecans last. Pour into pie shells for 2 eight-inch pies. Bake on cookie sheet in 325° oven for 1 hour. Edges will be firmer than center. As it cools, the center will firm up.

If you like, brush on a layer of

melted chocolate when cool. Another option, is to serve each slice with a dollop of whipped cream.

PECAN PIE

Mrs. John Dent

3 whole eggs, well beaten
1 cup each brown sugar, light Karo
1 cup or more pecans
1 teaspoon vanilla

Mix in order given and bake in an uncooked pie crust, very, very slowly. That is the secret of success.

PECAN PIE

Mrs. Joseph Merrick Jones, Jr.

3 eggs, beaten lightly
½ cup sugar
½ cup dark Karo
2 tablespoons butter, softened
1 teaspoon vanilla
1 cup pecans

Beat eggs lightly. Add all rest of ingredients, and mix together thoroughly. Put in uncooked crust and bake at 350° for 30 - 35 minutes. Serve warm topped with Pecan Crunch Ice Cream or whipped cream.

PLANTATION PECAN PIE

Terry Flettrich

1 9-inch unbaked pie shell
3 eggs
2/3 cup white sugar
½ cup white corn syrup
½ cup dark corn syrup
½ cup melted butter
2 cups cut pecans
24 whole pecans (for top)
dash of salt

Beat eggs, add sugar, salt and mix well. Add syrup, butter and mix well. Add cut pecans. Pour into unbaked pie shell. Arrange whole pecans on top. Bake at 350° about 1 hour or until an inserted knife comes out clean.

PUMPKIN PIE

1½ cups pumpkin, fresh or canned
1 pt. water
½ teaspoon salt
butter, size of egg
2/3 cup brown sugar
1 teaspoon ground ginger
1½ cups milk, 1 cup cream

2 eggs, slightly beaten
pie crust

Cut the pumpkin into small slices peeling and scraping off all of the shreds which hold the seeds. Add the water and cook until tender and nearly dry. Strain through a colander. Add salt and butter.

Stir in other ingredients in order given.

Line a deep pie plate with pie crust, fill with the mixture, and bake in a moderately hot oven about ¾ of an hour, or until done.

PEACH SURPRISE PIE

Mrs. Morrell Trimble

1 No. 2 can of peach halves
2 eggs
1 cup sugar
2 tablespoons flour
1 stick of soft butter or oleo
pastry

Prepare pastry, then take peach halves and put on pastry, placing one in center. Combine and beat well the eggs, sugar, flour and butter and pour over peaches. Bake for one hour in slow oven, 325 to 375 degrees.

RHUBARB PIE

Mrs. Frank Harbison

2 cups rhubarb (skinned and chopped)
1¼ cup sugar
1 teaspoon melted butter
2 tablespoons flour
yolks of 2 eggs, slightly beaten

Line a pie plate with plain pastry and fill with rhubarb mixture. Bake until rhubarb is soft. Cover with a meringue made of the whites of 2 eggs, and beaten very stiff with 2 tablespoons powdered sugar. Put into a slow oven until set.

RUM PIE

Mrs. Clifford Stem

6 egg yolks
1 scant cup of sugar
1 pt. cream
½ cup Jamaica rum
gelatine

Soak one tablespoon plain gelatine in ½ cup cold water for 5 minutes. Then put over boiling water till dissolved and very hot. Then pour over eggs, well beaten mixture, stirring briskly. Whip cream. Fold in to egg mixture and flavor with rum. Cool, but do not let it set. Pour over Graham cracker crust. Sprinkle with shaved bitter sweet chocolate. This makes one very large pie or two small ones.

Graham cracker pie crust:

1½ cups graham cracker crumbs
½ cup sugar
½ cup melted butter

Mix well. Pat in pie shell very firm. Chill at least 20 minutes, before putting filling in shell. Can be made the day before using.

STRAWBERRY CREAM PIE
Mrs. Buell C. Buchtel

1 pint box strawberries
¾ cup sugar
½ cup water
2 tablespoons cornstarch

Put about ⅔ cup berries in saucepan with sugar and water over moderate flame. When they come to a boil simmer for fifteen minutes. Strain. Dissolve cornstarch in ¼ cup cold water. Add to the strained juice, cook slowly until a thick sauce is formed. Add the remaining uncooked berries, cut in fourths, stir and allow to cool.

Shortly before serving whip ½ pint of whipping cream, fill a baked pastry shell with the strawberry mixture, top with whipped cream and garnish with strawberries.

BRANDIED PEACHES

Mrs. David T. Merrick

9 lbs. peaches, 1 pt. water
5 lbs. sugar
1 qt. alcohol
1 pt. water

Skin peaches by plunging in boiling water. Then put them in cold water. Let the sugar cook with the water until it makes a thick syrup. Then put in peaches to float, cook until tender enough to be pierced with a straw. Next, put them in a colander to drain.

Continue in this way until all the peaches are cooked. Pour the syrup drained from the peaches back in with the other syrup and cook until thick. Put the peaches in jars, add 1 measure of syrup to ½ measure of alcohol, fill the jars and seal. Shake for several days.

These will keep indefinitely, if no one finds them!

CHOW-CHOW

From the late Margaret and Cora Walshe
(Through Mrs. John R. Peters)

1 quart (2 lbs.) sliced
  green tomatoes
1 quart (2 lbs.) cucumbers,
  peeled and cut lengthwise
3 quarts cauliflower
5 quarts (7 lbs.) small
  white onions, peeled
1 quart cabbage, finely cut
1 quart (2 bunches) celery,
  cut fine
6 green peppers, chopped
2 red peppers, chopped
1 quart (1½ lbs.) snap beans
5 long red peppers,
  cut in strips
2 2-oz. boxes dry mustard
1 box tumeric
1½ cups brown sugar
2 cups flour, or more

1½ tablespoons celery seed
1½ tablespoons mustard seed
3 quarts cider vinegar
1 pinch powdered alum
1 pinch soda

Prepare vegetables and soak in enamel pot for 24 hours in a weak salt water solution. Scald vegetables in the same pot, drain and add a pinch of powdered alum. Stir all dry materials together and make a smooth paste with cold cider vinegar. Put paste into 3 quarts of scalding hot vinegar and stir well until it thickens. Add a pinch of baking soda. Add cut up drained vegetables. Be sure liquid covers vegetables. If not add more vinegar. When liquid starts to bubble around edges, stir. Do not let it boil hard. Turn off heat and put into sterilized jars.

CHUTNEY

Lt. Comdr. and Mrs. S. W. Wallace

½ lb. onions, sliced, salt
2 lbs. each quince, hard apples, diced
2 lbs. seedless raisins
½ teaspoon each ground mace,
  cinnamon, cloves
1½ teaspoons each ground ginger,
  paprika
1¼ teaspoons ground cayenne
2 cloves garlic, chopped
3½ lbs. sugar
3 qts. cider vinegar
2 lbs. candied dry ginger

Combine all ingredients and boil slowly 3 hours. This makes 12 pts.

CRANBERRY CONSERVE

Wash two cups cranberries. Put into a small saucepan and cover with one cup of sugar. No water at all. Cover saucepan and set on moderate heat until cover gets hot to touch. Turn heat very low and cook 15 minutes. Remove cover and shake pan lightly to cool and glaze the surface. So easy, so quick, so good!

QUICK CRANBERRY JELLY

Miss Ethel Forman

To every quart of berries, put 1 pint of water. Let berries cook for about 20 minutes, then strain through sieve. While still boiling, stir in sugar, 1 pint to every quart of berries. Do not continue to boil. Cool and put in glasses.

CRANBERRY RELISH

Mrs. Carl E. Woodward

    2 qts. of cranberries
    3½ lbs. granulated sugar
    1 lb. seedless raisins
    2 large oranges—juice, slivers of peel
    1 cup of vinegar
    ½ teaspoon cloves, 2 teaspoons
        cinnamon

Mix all ingredients in large pot and cook over a slow fire until cranberries pop and mixture becomes transparent (about thirty minutes). This quantity makes five pints and keeps well.

CRANBERRY SAUCE

Mrs. Julie Bowles (Sue Baker) Food Expert

    4 cups fresh cranberries
    2 cups each water, sugar

Wash and pick over cranberries. Cook them in water until all the skins pop open. Strain through a coarse strainer or put through a food mill. Add sugar to juice and blend. Return to fire and allow to come to a rolling boil. When the temperature reaches 220 degrees, about 10 or 15 minutes, or a drop jells on a cold plate, remove from fire and pour into a mold, chill until firm.

ECONOMICAL MARMALADE

Mrs. Irving Lyons

    8 carrots
    5 lemons, 6 cups sugar
    1 teaspoon salt

Put carrots and lemon rinds through the food grinder. Cover with water, add salt, sugar, and lemon juice. Cook until thick. Place in sterilized jars and seal with paraffin.

FIG PRESERVES

Mrs. E. T. Merrick

Clip the end of the stem of each fig, weigh fruit. To each pound use 1 pound of sugar. Add enough water to the sugar to make a good syrup. Before boiling soak figs for 10 minutes in lime water, (1 ounce of lime to a gallon of water). Then wash fruit well. Strain syrup, pour over figs, cook until well done and syrup is thick. When half done, add lemon if desired, or ginger.

GINGER PEARS

Mrs. Irving Lyons

    4 lbs. cooking pears
    2 ozs. ginger root
    2 lemons
    2 to 2½ lbs. sugar

Scrape and cut ginger into tiny pieces and squeeze the juice of the lemon over it. Cover pears with sugar and allow to stand for several hours. Place over a slow fire with the ginger and the grated rind of the lemon. Continue cooking very slowly till the pears are tender and clear. Place in sterilized jars and seal while hot.

KUMQUAT CONSERVE

Mrs. Walter Stauffer

    1 lb. kumquats
    ¾ to 1 lb. sugar

Wash fruit well. Pierce each piece at stem end, using an ice pick. Boil the kumquats in about three cups of water till tender. Using about a cup of the same water make a simple syrup with the sugar and boil until thickened. Then put in the kumquats, a few at a time, and simmer slowly till each one becomes transparent. As each piece is done remove to a serving dish and when all are finished pour remaining syrup over them and cool. If desired a jigger of whiskey or rum may be added.

MARMALADE

Mrs. A. G. Johnston

Select one grapefruit, one orange, and one lemon. Wash thoroughly. Cut in halves and remove seeds and tough center membranes. Slice very, very thin.

Measure, and for every cup of fruit add three cups of cold water. Let stand twenty-four hours, place over a hot flame and boil for ten minutes. Remove cover, and let stand for another twenty-four hours.

Measure, and for each cup of fruit add one cup of granulated sugar. Mix until the sugar is melted, place over a hot fire, bring to a boil, and boil for an hour or longer. Then begin to test by a spoonful on a saucer. When it seems to jell it is done. Toward the latter part of the cooking place a stove lid or asbestos plate under the pot and use a low flame taking great care that it does not burn. You must use a large kettle to permit boiling.

Scouring the fruit rind prevents the necessity of skimming.

If you cannot get lemons, limes may be used in the same proportion.

Sour oranges are better than sweet, yellow skins than russet.

Quick cooking is better than slow. Boil for an hour or longer.

The principal danger is burning. Stir frequently with a wooden spoon, especially toward the end.

SPICED OLIVES

Editors

3½ cups green unpitted olives
4 toes garlic
1 can anchovy filets
1½ cups red wine vinegar
olive oil
rosemary, fennel, salt and dill

Drain olives and put in jar or bowl. Make a brine solution by bringing to boil enough water to cover olives to which is added 3 tablespoons of salt. Pour over olives after allowing to cool to room temperature. Soak in brine for 10 - 12 hours. Drain. Discard damaged (bruised or soft) olives.

Mix equal parts red wine vinegar and water (1½ cups). Cover olives with mixture and marinate 24 hours. Drain.

In one-quart jar place 2 peppercorns, one toe garlic, 2 anchovy filets, a sprig of rosemary, and a pinch of fennel. (Optional: a few sprigs dill.) Put ¼ olives on top in layer, repeat seasoning on top of olives. Continue in layers until olives are all used. Cover with olive oil, secure tightly, and let stand for three to four weeks.

ORANGES DE LUXE

Mrs. Seth Miller

Take six or more oranges and with a sharp knife, pare off the oily part of the skin, taking care to keep the oranges smooth. Then make a small opening in the blossom end.

Put the oranges on the fire in cold water in which has been dissolved a teaspoonful of salt. Bring to a boil, then place the oranges in more boiling water, without salt. Boil until soft enough for a toothpick to be passed through the oranges.

Use a pound of sugar to a pound of fruit and 1 cup of water and boil to the consistency of a thin syrup. Place the hot boiled fruit in the hot syrup and boil it until well done and the syrup thick and honey colored.

ORANGE AND PEACH MARMALADE

Mrs. Albert C. Grace

2 doz. oranges
4 doz. ripe peaches
6 lemons
3½ lbs. sugar

Wash oranges thoroughly, remove seeds and cut in quarters. Run through the meat grinder using smallest blade. Place ground-up pulp and rind in a large bowl.

Skin the peaches after immersing them in hot water for five minutes. Cut in pieces and run through the grinder. Add this to the orange and also the juice of the six lemons.

Measure cup for cup of sugar and juice, put all into preserving kettle and cook until thick. It must be stirred constantly to prevent burning. Fill sterilized jars, cover with paraffin and seal.

PEACH CONSERVE

Mrs. J. T. Grace

14 large peaches
4 oranges, 4 pts. sugar
½ lb. coarsely chopped pecans

2 slices crystallized pineapple
¼ lb. crystallized cherries, cut

Peel the peaches and cut into small pieces. Add the sugar, pulp of oranges, and about ¾ of the grated orange peel. Cook together for 45 minutes. Add the nuts and the crystallized fruits and cook ten minutes longer. This makes about 8 glasses.

PEACH AND PEAR PICKLE
Mrs. Carl Marshall

3 lbs. peaches, whole and peeled
3 lbs. pears, peeled, halved and cored
3 lbs. sugar
1 pt. vinegar
1 tablespoon each whole cloves, cinnamon
½ tablespoon allspice

Put all in pot and cook until fruit assumes a transparent look. Put in jars.

PEACH PRESERVES
Mrs. E. T. Merrick

Peel, and halve peaches, let soak in water to keep color. To each pound of peaches add 1 pound of sugar, drain fruit, cover with sugar and let stand over night. Next morning cook until syrup is thick. Seal in jars.

PEAR BUTTER
Terry Flettrich

1 cup pear pulp
1/3 to 2/3 cup sugar
2 teaspoonfuls cinnamon

Boil pears in a large pot until tender. Cool. Peel and remove cores from pears. Mash fruit thoroughly with potato masher. Measure pears into pot for stewing. Add 1/3 to 2/3 cup sugar for each cup of pulp and 2 teaspoonsful cinnamon per cup. Cook over very low heat for two or three hours, stirring often at the beginning and constantly as it thickens toward the end.

PEAR CONSERVE
Mrs. Walter Scott Merrill

6 lbs. pears
3 lbs. sugar

2 each lemons, oranges
1 large can grated pineapple

Peel pears, halve, and remove seeds. Place in water with lemon juice added so they will not turn dark, until all are prepared. Put them through the grinder. Remove seeds from the oranges and lemons and grind these also using the entire fruit. Add sugar and pineapple with its juice. Boil slowly about two hours till thick and clear. Stir to prevent burning. Makes six pints.

GREEN TOMATO PICKLE
Mrs. E. V. Benjamin III

2 qts. chopped green tomatoes
1 qt. chopped onions
½ cup salt
1 cauliflower, broken into small flowerets
2 qts. chopped cabbage
1 qt. chopped bell peppers
2 minced hot peppers
2 qts. cider vinegar
3 cups sugar, 1 cup flour
¼ cup dry mustard
¼ cup tumeric
1 tablespoon celery salt

Mix tomatoes and onions, sprinkle with salt and stir well. Cover and let stand overnight. Drain, put in large pot and add cauliflower, cabbage, bell peppers, and hot peppers.
Make dressing of vinegar, sugar, flour, dry mustard, tumeric and celery seed. Pour it over vegetables and cook until it begins to thicken, stirring constantly. Spoon into sterilized jars and seal.

PUMPKIN PRESERVES
Eleanor E. Riggs

1 medium sized ripe pumpkin
¼ lb. ginger root
1 oz. cinnamon
1 lb. brown sugar

Cut the pumpkin into pieces ½ inch thick. Wash in clear water removing the seeds and inner network that holds the seeds. Place the cubes of pumpkin in a large bowl of lime water, two tablespoons of lime to a gallon. Let the pumpkin remain in the lime water for sixteen hours. Wash in clear water and boil until the cubes can be pierced with a fork. Wash carefully and boil the ginger for one hour and a half. Use the water from the ginger and add the brown sugar and enough water to make enough syrup to cover the pumpkin and cook until it is almost ready to candy. Then move and place in jars for general use. These preserves are fine substitutes for ginger. Lemon peel may be used in place of ginger and spices in place of cinnamon.

CHILI RELISH
Mr. David D. Duggins

8 cups peeled tomatoes, or 12 whole
    cut into quarters

Cook slowly for 1 hour.

Chop up 2 whole onions
1 or 2 sweet peppers (red)
1 or 2 hot peppers (red, any variety)

Add to tomatoes and cook 30 minutes. Then add:

3/4 to 1 cup sugar (to taste)
1 tablespoon salt
1 teaspoon coarse ground pepper
3/4 cup vinegar
¼ cup water

Cook until desired thickness.

TOMATO CONSERVE

7 lbs. ripe tomatoes
5 lbs. sugar
2 lemons, sliced very thin
½ doz. each whole cloves, allspice
2 sticks cinnamon

Put all spices in cheese cloth and boil with tomatoes and lemons till the latter are transparent, then add sugar and cook until thick. Delicious with meat or used on toast like a preserve.

DELICIOUS SWEET PICKLES

Make a thick syrup by boiling the following:

1 cup brown sugar
¾ cup vinegar
1 cup water

cinnamon bark, a few whole cloves
1 teaspoon allspice in bag

Cut 6 dill pickles in any shape you like and cook in this syrup for 20 minutes. The pickle is improved by standing in the syrup several days before using.

GREEN ONION PICKLE
Mrs. Burton Dawkins

½ gal. small Bermuda pickling onions
2 lbs. sugar, ½ gal. vinegar
1 tablespoon each mustard, celery seed
1 teaspoon allspice

Make a brine strong enough to float an egg. Cover the onions, unpeeled, with this and allow to stand for twenty-four hours or longer (until the skins slip off easily). Remove peel and cover the peeled onions with ice water (with ice floating in it) and let them stand for three hours.

Make a syrup of sugar and vinegar and place the spices in it in a bag. Let this simmer slowly for ½ hour. Strain. Drain the onions from the ice water and pour the syrup over them and heat thoroughly but do not boil. Put in jars while hot and seal.

One teaspoonful of olive oil may be added to each jar.

GREEN TOMATO PICKLES
Mrs. Burton Dawkins

1 peck green tomatoes, sliced thin
6 large white onions, sliced thin

Place them in a bag with a teacup of salt poured over them, and let them drain for twelve hours. Place in a preserving kettle with the following:

1 lb. sugar or more, to taste
1 tablespoon powdered mustard
1 teaspoon black pepper
1 tablespoon celery seed
1 cup horseradish, freshly ground
½ cup mustard seed, 1 qt. vinegar
1 tablespoon allspice
1 teaspoon cloves, put in a bag

Cook the above mixture on a slow fire until tender, about thirty minutes. Put in jars while hot and seal.

KILN DILL PICKLES
Mrs. Joseph Merrick Jones, Jr.

5 cups water
6 cups white vinegar
½ cup rock salt
1 teaspoon alum
cucumbers, small preferred, but large
    may be used, washed and dried

Bring to a boil water, vinegar, salt and alum. Lower heat and stir until salt is dissolved. Let sit.

In quart jars pack the cucumbers, adding to each jar 1 clove garlic, 1 dried red pepper, ¼ onion sliced and 1 tablespoon dill seed. Do not cut the cucumbers. Re-heat brine and pour over the cucumbers. Seal and keep in sunlit place for a week.

SWEET CUCUMBER PICKLES
Mrs. George S. Frierson

9 lbs. large sour cucumber pickles
4 lbs. sugar
1 tablespoon each allspice, cloves
6 buttons garlic
1 cup Tarragon vinegar

In porcelain or glass container, put cucumbers sliced in rounds, layer of cucumbers and layer of sugar. Add other ingredients. Stir once a day for three days, then they are ready to be used. Not necessary to put in sealed jar.

Using this recipe dill pickles can be made by adding 1 oz. of dill seed and a cup of olive oil.

WATERMELON RIND OR RIPE CUCUMBER PICKLE
Mrs. Frank H. Lawton

1 gal. rind peeled and cut into strips
2 heaping teaspoons salt
    water to cover

Soak rind in brine over night.

Boil in this same salt water until tender. Drain, press all water from rind, with a tea towel. Place rind in stone crock. Make the following syrup and pour over pickles:

3 lbs. sugar, 1 qt. vinegar
1 oz. stick cinnamon, ½ oz. whole cloves

Place spices in bag and boil in syrup 15 minutes. On each day for 9 days thereafter pour off syrup, boil up with spices and add a little sugar or vinegar as necessary so as to keep syrup the same consistency as on the first day. Add a small quantity of spice to the spice bag as seems desirable for flavor. These pickles may be kept in the crock. If they are to be sealed in jars, on last day put rind in syrup and boil for 10 minutes.

WATERMELON AND RIND PICKLE
Mrs. Carl Marshall

rind from 1 large melon
    (select rind with large white area)
2 vials Lilly's slacked lime
2 gals. water

Make solution, stirring several times before adding rind. Prepare rind as thick and white as possible in cubes and oblongs. Weigh fruit, soak over night in lime water. Next morning rinse through several waters before boiling. Boil until transparent and easily pierced with toothpick. Put through cold water several times till chilled, then put into boiling syrup:

lb. for lb. of sugar and fruit
½ qt. vinegar
1 package each allspice, cloves and
    cinnamon bark
10 oz. ginger root (pounded and boiled
    a few minutes in little water. Add
    to syrup)

Cook rind in syrup for 1 hour or until syrup is of proper consistency. Fifteen minutes before finishing add vinegar.

SPICED WATERMELON RIND

3 pounds white portion of watermelon,
    cubed
5 cups sugar
2 cups cider vinegar
1 cup cold water
1 tablespoon whole cloves
1 tablespoon whole allspice
1 tablespoon whole cinnamon
1 lemon, sliced

Let watermelon stand in salted water to cover overnight (2 tablespoons salt to 1 quart fresh water). Drain, cover with fresh cold water, cook until tender. Drain. Combine sugar, cider vinegar and 1 cup cold water. Tie in a bag: cloves, allspice, cinnamon and lemon slices; add to syrup. Boil 5 minutes. Add watermelon and cook until transparent, about 45 minutes. Pack in hot, sterilized jars. Yield: 1 quart.

TOMATO JELLY

24 tomatoes, skinned and chopped
1 cup sugar to each cup of tomatoes
1 lemon sliced thin
4 or 5 sticks cinnamon

Boil all together to the consistency of jelly. A very slow fire must be used and it must be watched and stirred constantly. It will take two to two and a half hours. Do not strain. When proper consistency is reached put in jelly glasses and seal. Most unusual and delicious.

SWEET PEPPER RELISH

Mrs. Albin Provosty

12 each green peppers, red peppers
12 onions, medium sized
6 tablespoons salt
3 cups each sugar, vinegar
    cayenne pepper, celery salt, spices

Grind peppers and onions and allow them to drain well. Put on to boil with the vinegar, sugar and salt. Cook briskly about fifteen to twenty minutes. Add the hot pepper, celery salt and spices. Bottle while hot.

children's recipes

HOW TO PRESERVE CHILDREN

Mix together:

1 large picnic basket, filled
    to brimming
6 to 8 children
    large playground (field in country
    preferred)
    lots of sunlight
    tons of flowers
    few friendly doggies
    loads of laughter

Bake all in warm sun until well browned. When done, remove to one large soapy bath tup and douse well with all the tender loving care in the world!!

ACEY'S BISCUITS

Sylvie Schraeder

1 cup flour
1½ teaspoons baking powder
¼ teaspoon baking soda
1 teaspoon salt
1½ tablespoons oil or shortening
¾ cup buttermilk

Blend shortening with flour. Add remaining ingredients. Flour a cloth covered board. Knead dough three times. Roll to a thin layer with rolling pin. Fold the layer in half and roll very lightly with rolling pin so that layers will separate easier for buttering after baking. Cut with a biscuit cutter. Bake in pre-heated 400° oven for 15 minutes.

B. B.'S POMANDER BALLS

Misses Charlotte and Millie Corrigan

small thin skinned oranges
whole cloves
ground cinnamon

Stick whole cloves into the oranges until the outside is completely covered. Roll the oranges in the ground cinnamon, patting in as much of the cinnamon as will stick to the orange. Wrap the oranges separately in tissue paper and keep it for 8 weeks. Take out of paper and shake off excess cinnamon. Tie a pretty ribbon around the orange and hang it in your closet on a coat hanger. Your clothes will smell delicious. You may want to use these in your lingerie drawers and shelves. (Good for Christmas presents, too!!)

CANDLE SALAD

Miss Laura Ball

6 big lettuce leaves, washed and
    drained
6 slices of pineapple
3 bananas, cut in half
6 cherries
6 tablespoons juice from cherries, or
    Maraschino cherry juice

Put lettuce leaf on salad plate. Next put 1 slice of pineapple on the lettuce leaf, and in the hole in the pineapple slice stand up one half of the cut banana, standing the banana on the cut end. Use a toothpick for each cherry and stick it on top of the standing banana. Pour 1 tablespoon of the cherry juice or Maraschino over each salad. Keep cold until ready to serve. These can be done ahead of time and look very fancy. (Be sure you cut your bananas evenly, or they will not stand up.) Serves 6.

CHIP A DE DO DA CHICKEN

(Very simple)

Miss Lainey Jones

1 fryer, cut up, or 6-8 pieces of
    your favorite pieces

2 large bags of potato chips (if
   you like the Barbequed Potato
   Chips, this is very good, too.)
2 sticks of butter
1 tablespoon paprika
1 teaspoon garlic salt

Melt butter with paprika and salt.
Crush potato chips finely with a rolling pin. Wash and dry chicken on a
paper towel. Dip in the melted butter
mixture and then roll in the crushed
potato chips. Place on baking sheet
lined with tin foil, and bake in a 350°
oven for 1 hour.

CINNAMON TOAST
WITH THE MOST

Misses Susu and
Keppy Laudeman

4 slices bread, toasted and cut into
   finger pieces
butter, cinnamon, and sugar

Cut crusts from the toast, and butter well, Sprinkle generously with cinnamon and sugar and cut into finger
pieces. Place under broiler briefly to
crisp. Watch carefully, it burns easily.

DULCE DE LECHE

Misses Molly and Sarah Selman

Place a can of condensed milk in a
pot of water to cover. Boil over a slow
fire for 4 hours, keeping the can
covered with water. When cool, open
both ends of the can and slide out.
Keep in covered dish in icebox. This
can be sliced or eaten with a spoon. It
may also be served hot with sliced
French Bread. This is the way it is
served in Argentina.

FATHER'S DAY CAKE

Miss Lynne Johnson

1 box packaged devil's food cake mix
1½ cans beer
   frosting of your choice

Follow the directions on the package of cake mix, substituting beer for
the required amount of water. Bake as
usual, and frost with icing of your
taste.

FRUITY FRINKY
SHERBET

Miss Ria Zander

2 cans sweetened condensed milk
   (28 ozs.)
4 cans (12-oz. size) fruit flavored
   soda pop (strawberry, grape, or
   orange)

Combine ingredients and pour into
electric ice cream freezer. Follow
operating instructions for your own
particular freezer.

THE DEVIL'S EGGS

The Misses, Lisa, Michelle
and Sissy De Russy

6 hard boiled eggs
Durkee's Sauce
paprika
salt and pepper

Peel and slice eggs lengthwise. Remove yolks and mash with fork in
bowl adding enough Durkee's sauce to
make a pasty consistency. Season with
salt and pepper. Stuff yolk mixture
into egg white cavity. Sprinkle with
paprika. Chill. Makes 12.

EASY BLENDER MOUSSE

Miss Elizabeth Keenan

¼ cup packed light brown sugar
2 egg yolks
2 eggs
6 squares semi-sweet chocolate,
   melted and cooled
3 tablespoons orange juice
1 cup heavy cream
2 packs ladyfingers, separated

Combine first 4 ingredients in blender and whirl until light and foamy.
Add next 3 ingredients. Continue to
whirl until well blended. Place separated lady fingers upright around sides
of individual molds. (custard cups may
be used.) Gently pour in chocolate
mixture and chill until set.

FRENCH FRIED ONIONS

Miss Heidi Hayne

1 cup milk
1 cup buttermilk pancake mix

1 egg
1 teaspoon salt
¼ teaspoon pepper
1 tablespoon oil
2 large yellow onions, sliced
    thickly and separated into
    rings
    peanut oil for frying

Whirl all ingredients except onions in blender. Dip rings in batter right from blender and fry in hot peanut oil.

HAPPINESS IS: KEPPY AND SUSU'S BROWNIES

Misses Keppy and SuSu Laudeman

1 stick butter
3 squares unsweetened chocolate
4 eggs, beaten
2 teaspoons vanilla
2 cups sugar
1 cup flour, sifted
1 cup chopped nuts

Melt chocolate and butter in top of double boiler. Remove from heat and stir in everything else. Pour into greased baking pan. Bake at 325° for about 35 minutes. Center should stay moist. Cool before cutting.

JELLY JUMBLES

Mere Laudeman

½ lb. butter
2 cups sugar
4 eggs
½ pint sour cream (to which add 1
    teaspoon cooking soda)
5 cups sifted cake flour
1 teaspoon salt
1 teaspoon nutmeg
1 teaspoon vanilla
2 jars currant jelly (9 oz. size)
    confectioners sugar

Mix first eight ingredients as you would prepare a cake batter. Drop teaspoonfuls onto an ungreased cookie sheet. Bake in 400° oven only until brown around the edges. Fill two cookie sections together like a sandwich with currant jelly and roll in confectioners sugar.

JOSEPH STREET TUBE STEAKS

Misses Kappy and Susan Calhoun

1 pack refrigerated Crescent
    Dinner Rolls
6 hot dogs
6 slices American Cheese
    mayonnaise and yellow mustard

Remove rolls from package. These are made in triangles. Take two of the triangles and place them long flat side together and press the long sides together with your fingers. You will now have a square.

Slice your hot dogs down the middle, but do not cut all the way through. For each hot dog, break one piece of cheese up and stuff into the hot dog. Spread mayonnaise and mustard to your taste on the uncooked rolls, and place hot dog, stuffed, in the roll diagonally, each end of the hot dog should touch a corner point of the roll. Fold the other ends of the roll around the hot dog and pinch together. Bake in 350° oven until roll is light brown.

MARSHMALLOW POPCORN BALLS

Miss Coco Eshleman

½ cup unpopped corn
3 tablespoons butter
1/3 cup white corn syrup
½ cup white sugar, firmly packed
1½ cups marshmallows

Pop corn and put into large mixing bowl. Put rest of ingredients into sauce pan, and stir over medium heat until hot and bubbly. Pour syrup over corn, and butter your hands well. When slightly cool shape into balls with hands. Gooey, but good.

MELT IN YOUR MOUTH PRALINES

Miss Sally Huger

2 cups white sugar
1 teaspoon baking soda
1 cup buttermilk
2 tablespoons butter
2½ cups pecan halves
    pinch salt

Let all ingredients boil together in a heavy pot until the mixture forms a soft ball when dropped in a cup of cold water. Remove from heat until creamy. Drop by large tablespoonfuls on a greased cookie sheet. Let harden and hide them from the neighbors!!

MERRY GO ROUND CHEESE BITES

Miss Lainey Jones

1 cup grated American cheese
2 tablespoons cream
3 tablespoons softened butter
2 tablespoons mayonnaise
1 teaspoon salt
¼ teaspoon cayenne
6-8 slices bread, crusts removed

Mix first 6 ingredients together until well blended. Roll each slice of bread with a rolling pin until about half its size in thickness. Spread each rolled slice with about 2 tablespoons of the cheese mixture. Gently roll up like a jelly roll, and cut crosswise in thirds. Place on baking sheet, and heat in a 350° oven until cheese starts melting out of the ends.

NEAT LOAF

Miss Fifi Benjamin

2 lbs. good ground beef
2 eggs
1 finely chopped large onion
¼ cup minced celery
½ teaspoon baking powder
4 tablespoons bread crumbs
2 large tomatoes from a can
4 bacon slices

Put everything except bacon in a bowl and mix thoroughly. Put in baking dish and lay bacon slices over the top. Bake 1 hour at 350°.

ORANGE LOLLIPOPS

Miss Susu Lane

2 cups granulated sugar
2/3 cup light corn syrup
½ cup water
3-4 tablespoons orange extract
  orange food coloring

Put sugar, corn syrup and water in

sauce pan and cook over medium high heat (higher at end of cooking) until candy thermometer registers 305°. Take off heat and add orange extract. Drop a tablespoon of the hot syrup one at a time onto a greased cookie sheet. Press a lollipop stick (popsicle sticks or ice cream sticks can be used, but they are kind of big) into each tablespoon of syrup. Wait until they get hard and then pop them off the sheet.

PICNIC TOMATOES

Master Benjie Eshleman

6 large tomatoes
2 cups grated American cheese
½ cup ground or finely diced ham
  enough mayonnaise to hold
  mixture together

Cut tops off of tomatoes and scoop out a big tablespoon from inside of the tomato. Stuff with cheese-ham mixture, piling as high as you can. Put each tomato on double thickness of tin foil square and fold foil up around top. Place on grill with daddy's hamburgers. These will take about ½ hour for the cheese to melt and tomatoes to warm through. (May also be placed in a 350° oven for 30 minutes.) Serves 6.

FAT PIGGIES

Misses Liz and Karen Stierman

4 hot dogs
1 cup mashed potatoes
4 bacon strips, cooked
1 cup (4 ozs.) sharp cheddar cheese,
  grated
mustard

Boil hot dogs for 3 minutes. Slice almost through lengthwise. Open and spread with mustard. Mound with mashed potatoes, top with cheese and bacon strips. Bake in 375° oven till warmed throughout and cheese melts, about 20 minutes. Serves 4.

PETITE PIZZA

Mimi Gundlach

1 frozen pizza pie
  olive slices, anchovies, crumbled
  bacon, mushrooms or boiled shrimp

Allow pizza to thaw slightly for ease in cutting. With small cookie cutter cut out pizza rounds, top with olive slices or other of the above. Arrange on cookie sheet and bake according to package directions. Makes 2 dozen hors d'ouevres size pizzas.

PANE OF GLASS (ROCK CANDY)
Mrs. B. S. Nelson

½ cup granulated sugar
2 tablespoons water
1 pan cold water

Procedure:
1. Start with paper box that frozen vegetables come in. (Remove vegetables from box by running warm water over the box.) Rinse box.
2. Place box in dry skillet.
3. Put approximately ½ cup granulated sugar and 2 tablespoons water into box.
4. Put medium flame under skillet.
5. Heat the skillet (with box in it) for approximately ten minutes. Watch for the sugar to begin to turn brown at the edges.
6. Lift box from the skillet and float it in a pan of cool water so that the candy may cool and harden.
7. Peel candy from box and eat.
Variations: Add food colorings or oil base flavorings.

PINWHEELS
Miss Melissa Douglass

1 large pack Philadelphia Cream
  Cheese
2 tablespoons cream
1 teaspoon paprika
1 teaspoon garlic salt
1 large stalk celery

Cut bottom end off celery stalk. Cut top end off, too, about where the green leaves start. Take stalk apart and wash separate stalks. Fill each stalk with the cheese mixture. Replace stalk as it was before you started, sticking it together with the cream. (You may have to turn some stalks around so the fat ends are not all together.) As you put the stalk together, fill in the holes with the extra cheese. When finished,

wrap in waxed paper and chill in refrigerator for 2 hours. Slice crosswise to serve, and you will have about 12-16 pinwheels.

POPCORN CRUNCH
Miss Elizabeth Crusel

3 quarts freshly popped corn
1½ cups pecan halves, or nuts of
  your choice
1 cup firmly packed light brown sugar
¼ cup honey
1 teaspoon vanilla
½ cup butter

To pop proper amount of corn:

½ cup unpopped corn
3 tablespoons salad oil

Heat oil; when one kernel used for testing pops, add the rest of the corn. Put cover on pot or you will have popcorn all over the kitchen. Shake pot around, lifting from the heat from time to time. When the sounds of the corn popping almost stop, remove from the heat and turn into a shallow roasting pan. Do not add salt or butter.

Sauce:

In a 1 quart sauce pan over low heat melt the butter; stir in brown sugar and honey. Over medium heat bring to a boil, stirring constantly. Then let boil for 5 minutes without stirring. Remove from heat; stir in vanilla. Pour mixture over the popped corn and nuts, and stir until well mixed. Bake in pre-heated 250° oven, stirring every 15 minutes for 1 hour. Cool completely. Break apart and store in tightly covered container. Makes 3 quarts.

RICE IS NICE
Miss Liz Huger

1 cup Uncle Ben's converted rice
1 can onion soup
1 stick butter
1 can water chestnuts, sliced
  salt and pepper
  water to make 2½ cups liquid

Combine ingredients in baking dish. Cook in 375° oven till rice is tender and liquid is absorbed, about 30-40 minutes.

RINK TUM DIDDY
(Ground meat and noodle casserole)
Miss Lydia Campbell

2 pints fresh tomatoes or 2
   No. 2 cans
3 medium onions, diced
1 lb. grated American cheese
2 lbs. ground round steak, or good
   hamburger
2 teaspoons salt
1 large pack wide egg noodles
1 cup sliced mushrooms, cooked
   (optional)

Fry ground meat in margarine or bacon fat until it is well browned. Boil noodles 10 minutes in salted water. Drain and mix all together with ½ of the grated cheese. Put in casserole and put the rest of the cheese on the top.

SOMEMORE'S
Camp Green Cove, North Carolina
(Through Lainey Jones)

graham crackers
Hershey bars
marshmallows

Put graham crackers on baking sheet. Cover with squares of Hershey bars, and then top with a marshmallow. Heat in 300° oven until melted. When done over the open campfire, these are placed in a skillet over the campfire until melted. Yummy!!

MOCK STROGANOFF
Miss Alicia Chandler

1 cup onions, chopped
1½ lbs. ground beef
1 clove garlic, crushed
3 cups tomato juice
1 teaspoon salt (or to taste)
1½ teaspoons celery salt (or finely
   chopped celery)
2 teaspoons Lea and Perrins sauce
   dash of pepper
3 cups (about one 12-oz. package)
   uncooked egg noodles
1 cup chopped green pepper
1 cup sour cream
1 large can mushrooms

Cook onions, ground beef and garlic till "grey." Add tomato juice, salt, pepper, celery salt, Lea & Perrins, and uncooked egg noodles. Stir gently and cook covered for 20 minutes. Add chopped green pepper, simmer 10 minutes. Add sour cream and mushrooms. Serves 4-6.

WATERMELON SNOWBALLS
Miss Cabbie and Mimsie Huger

2 cups sugar
3 cups water
3 cups seeded crushed-up watermelon
2 egg whites, beaten stiffly
   juice of 1 lemon

Add sugar, water and lemon to the crushed watermelon. Fold in the stiffly beaten egg whites. Freeze in ice trays and mound high in cone shaped paper cups. A super summer cooler!!

INDEX

COFFEE, TEA AND BEVERAGES

Absinthe Frappe.........4
Absinthe Suissesse.......4
Air Mail Special.........5
Anchors Aweigh.........5
Berta.................5
Blackberry Cordial.......5
Blackberry Wine.........5
Cherry Bounce.........7
Cherry Bounce,
  Liquer De Merise.......7
Cocktails
  Alexander...........5
  Ash Blonde..........5
  Audubon...........5
  Bermendania.........5
  Bloody Bull..........5
  Bloody Mary Special....5
  Bloody Mary (3).......6
  Bull Shot...........6
  Cameo Kirby.........6
  Candado Rum Drink....6
  Champagne.........6
  Daiquiri............7
  Folklore............8
  Guerrero...........9
  Honduras...........9
  Louisiana...........9
  Manhattan..........9
  New Iberia.........10
  New Orleans........10
  Sazerac...........12
  Selina.............6
  Strawberry.........12
  Sugar Bowl........12
  University.........13
Coffee:
  Cafe Au Lait.........1
  Cafe Brulot (2).......1
  Cafe Brulot (3).......2
  Cafe Diable.........2
  Cafe Royale au Rhum...3
  Coffee Creole, Dripped..1
  Creole Coffee.........1
  Irish (2)............3
  Rum Coffee.........3
Contradition, The.........6
Egg-Nog...............8
Egg-Nog,
  George Washington.....7
Fizzes:
  Apricot Fizz au Georges.8
  Gin Fizz............8
  Gin Fizz "Ramos".....8
  Green Fizz..........8
Flaming Youth..........8
Galatoire's Special.......9
Goodnight Stinkers......12
Highball, Diamond Fizz...8
Highball, Garden of Eden...9

Hot Tom and Jerry.......13
Kick-off...............9
"Mickey Special".........3
Milk Punch.............9
Mint Julep Beauregard....9
Mint Julep to Keep
  on hand.............9
Mint Julep, St. Regis.....10
Mint Julep, San Domingo..12
O'Jen................10
Orange Brulot...........3
Orange Cooler.........10
Orange Flower Syrup.....11
Peaches A-Glow.........11
Planter's Punch.........11
Rum Special...........4
Sangria...............12
Simple Syrup..........12
Standard Bar Measures....5
Summer Special.........12
Taglio Limoni..........4
Tea:
  Iced Tea.............3
  Jamaica Afternoon Tea..4
  Russian Tea..........4
  Spiced.............4
  Spiced, Mr. J's........4
  Tea a la Russe........4
Tender Trap, The.......13
Tom Collins...........13
Tropic Cooker.........13
Whiskey Sour.........13
Whiskey Toddy,
  Belle Chasse.........13
Zephry...............13

APPETIZERS AND HORS D'OEUVRES

Admiral's Golden Buck...16
Anchovy Canapes.......15
Artichoke Leaves, Stuffed.15
Avocado or Guacamole Dip 20
Avocado..............21
Bacon Wrapped Chicken
  Livers, Oysters, Olives..15
Beurre d'Anchois.......16
Bouchees d'Anchois.....16
Bouchees Souffles.......17
Bouchees Surprises......16
Boulettes de Saucisson...27
Broccoli Dip...........21
Canape Egyptian........16
Celery Farci...........16
C'est la vie Whip........21
Cheese-Olive Appetizer....18
Cheese:
  Balls (2)............17
  Chili Con Quotis......17
  Crescents...........17
  Crumbles...........18
  Pecan Wafers........19

Puffs...............19
Roll................19
Straws (1)..........19
Straws (3) 1..........20
Chicken Bits in Beer Batter 20
Croquettes de Camembert.18
Croquettes de Saucisse...27
Eggplant Appetizer......22
Galettes au Roquefort....18
Italian Meatballs........22
Jellied Appetizers, small...15
Liver Paste.............22
Mushrooms:
  Cheese Stuffed.......23
  Crabmeat Stuffed....23
  Italian Stuffed.......23
  Marinated..........24
  Oyster Stuffed.......24
  Pickled............24
  Rounds............24
  Toothpick..........24
Mustard Butter Toast.....24
Old Faithful Cheese
  and Onion Puffs.......18
Oysters:
  Deviled (2)..........25
  Fried Po-Boy.........25
  Rockefeller.........25
  Smoked............25
Pate de Foie Gras Biscuits
  with Bacon.........26
Pate, Epicure..........26
Pate in Jelly..........26
Pate Paysan..........26
Petite Quichesa la Red....26
Pierre's Appetizer.......17
Pin Wheel Sausage Rolls...27
Pork Sausage..........27
Roquefort Cheese.......19
Roquefort Roll Waldorf...19
Sara's Cheese Bits.......17
Shrimp Appetizer.......27
Shrimp, Marinated.....27
Spinach Dip..........21
Swedish Meatballs.....22
Tango Cream.........22
Tulane Footballs.......20
Vegetable Dip..........21

EGGS, CHEESE AND GRITS

Cheese:
  Fromage...........36
  Souffle.............35
  Souffle au Fromage...36
Eggs:
  A La King..........31
  A La Purgatoire......32
  Benedict...........30
  Benedictine.........30
  Black Butter, In......30

Casserole for Brunch . . .30
Creole 31
Danish Roe 31
De Luxe 31
Egg and Cheese
Casserole 30
En Cocotte 31
Fried Eggs Provence 31
Huevos Rancheros 32
Russian 32
St. Denis, Eggs 32
Sardou Galatoire's 32
Scrambled Eggs Benoit .32
Shirred A La Stanford . .33
Shirred, Old English 33
Snowdrift Eggs 33
Venetian Eggs 33
Grits:
Cheesy Fried 36
Garlic 36
Souffled 36
Omelets:
Au Four 33
Bacon-Mushroom 34
Crab 34
Mushroom 34
Oyster 34
Oyster Omelette Pascual
Manale 35
Quiche Lorraine 35
Rum 35
Sunday Morning Kiln . . .34
Wootie's Wiener 35

HOT BREADS, PAN-
CAKES AND WAFFLES

Biscuits:
Beaten 38
Cheese, Mittie's 38
Four O'Clock 38
Sticky 38
Bread:
Banana 38
Batter 38
Brown 39
Brown, Steamed 41
Carrot 39
Dilly Casserole 39
Nut, English 39
Orange 40
Pumpkin 40
Quick Delivery, Hot 40
Southern Egg 40
Spoon 40
Squaw 41
Whole Wheat, Mittie's . .41
Brioche 41
Buttered Bread Crumbs . . .41
Cake, Danish Egg 42

Calas Chiffon 42
Calas Tou' Chauds 43
Cheese Brioche 39
Coffee Cake 43
Corn:
Bread, Tante Mathilde's .43
Dodgers 43
Mexican 40
Muffins, Plantation 43
Pones, Indian Pumpkin .44
Pones, Old Fashioned . .44
Puffs 44
Coush-Coush, Acadian 44
Croissants Parisian 44
Fritters, Cornstarch 45
Fritters, Rice 45
Kennedy's Calas Tout
Chaud 42
Muffins, Polk 45
Nut Sticks 45
Owendaw 46
Pain Perdu (2) 46
Pain Perdu, Petie's 46
Pancakes 46
Pancakes:
au Bayou Teche 46
Buckwheat (2) 47
Creole 47
French 47
French, Bringier 47
Griddle, aux Miettes . . .48
Pecan Loaf 48
Popovers 48
Rolls (2) 48
Rolls, Cinnamon 48
Sally Lunn 49
Toast Cinnamon 49
Waffles, Chocolate 49
Waffles, Plantation 49
Waffles, Sour Milk 49
Wheat Fluff 50

SALADS AND SALAD
DRESSINGS

Artichoke, Mousse (2) 52
Artichoke Aspic 52
Artichoke In Tomato
Aspic 53
Artichokes Sharon 53
Avocado 53
Avocado Aspic 53
Avocado Mousse 53
Borsch, Jellied 57
Chicken (2) 54
Club 54
Cole Slaw 54
Crab 55
Crab, Marinated 55
Crab Meat, Roquefort
Dressing 54

Cranberry 55
Cucumber, Cream of 56
Cucumber with Sour
Cream Dressing 56
Dessert 56
Egg Mousse 56
Fish Aspic 58
Frozen, Teneriffe 56
Fruit 56
Gazpacho 57
Ground Artichoke
Mousse 57
Leek 58
Lettuce Chapon 58
Lobster Mousse (2) 58
Mandarin Orange 59
Mirliton (Vegetable Pear) . .59
Mushroom 59
Onion, Begue 58
Pate de Foie Gras
Aspic 59
Pear, Jellied Bartlett
Beet 57
Peas and Sour Cream 59
Pegasus 60
Potato, Hot 60
Raspberry Jelly 60
Shrimp Mousse 60
Shrimp, Congealed 60
Sour Sweet 61
Three Star Special 61
Tomato Dill Aspic 61
Tomato, Restacked 61
Tomato, Spiced,
a la Jones 61
Turkey 62
Creole French Mustard 62
Dressing:
A L'Italien 65
Cooked 65
French (2) 62
French, Unusual 63
Fruit Salad 63
Green Goddess (2) 63
Honey Poppy Seed 63
Kolb's 63
"Mignon" 64
Mrs. Sel's 64
Pastorial 65
Poppy Seed 64
Roquefort Cheese 64
Russian 64
Salad 64
Mayonnaise, Caviar 62
Mayonnaise, Quick 63
Mayonnaise, Waring Blender64
Vinaigre Aromatise 65

BISQUES, GUMBOS AND SOUPS

Avocado 67
Crawfish 69
Crayfish 67
Crayfish 68
Madame Begues's
  A L'Ecrevisse 68
Onion 69
Shrimp 70
Tomato 70
Borsch Creole 76
Bouillabaisse 74
Bouillon 76
Bouillon Oyster 80
Broth, Oyster 80
Butter Balls for Soup 74
Consomme, Jellied
  DeLuxe 77
Consomme, Royal 77
Courtbouillon 75
Courtbouillon
  Barataria 75
Courtbouillon Fish 74
Crabmeat Stew 85
Gumbos:
  Chicken Okra 70
  Crab (2) 70
  Creole Seafood 71
  File 71
  "Gumbo Z'Herbes" 73
  Okra, Crab and Shrimp .72
  Oyster 73
  Quick 73
  Scoop's Irish Creole
    Saturday Night 72
Kathleen's Fruits of
  The Bayou 74
Roux 67
Soups:
  Almond 75
  Bean, Famous House of
    Representatives
    Restaurant 75
  Bean, Famous Senate
    Restaurant 76
  Black Bean 75
  Brain Soup Bonne
    Femme 76
  Chicken Curry 76
  Chicken Soup Onorato .76
  Corn (2) 77
  Corn, Cream of 77
  Crab, Cream of 77
  Mushroom 78
  Onion 78
  Onion, Cream of 78
  Oxtail Soup, A La
    Lucie 78
  Oxtail Soup – for
    Eight Persons 79

Oyster (2) 79
Oyster 80
Oyster, Crescent City
  Style 80
Oyster Soup Lafayette ..80
Red Bean 81
Split Pea (2) 81
Soup Gauloise 78
Tomato Soup Frappe ...81
Tomato Soup Martin ...81
Turtle (3) 82
Turtle Soup
  A La Mardi Gras 83
Turtle, Lockport 82
Turtle, Mock 83
Vegetable 83
Vegetable, Belair 84
Vegetable, Deep South .84
Vichyssoise 84
Vichyssoise, Cold 85
Vichyssoise, Quick
  Mock 85

FISH AND SHELLFISH

Codfish Cakes 87
Cod Roe and Bacon 87
Crabby Elizabeth 89
Crabs:
  Chops a la Nouvelle
    Orleans 87
  Fricassee 87
  Halves in Wine Sauce,
    Hard Shell 89
  Meat Au Gratin 88
  Meat, Baked 88
  Meat with Sauce, Lump .88
  Meat Newberg 88
  Meat Sycamore 89
  Meat Timbale 89
  St. Jacques 88
  Upside-Down 89
Crawfish Etouffee 90
Crayfish, Boiled 90
Filet of Sole
  Veronique 95
Fish:
  Boiled 91
  Charpentier, Broiled ...91
  Creamed 91
  Glace 93
  Martinique 92
  Mousse 93
  Ring, Cold 95
  Souffle 96
  Timbale 96
Flounder A La
  Marseilles 92
Flounder Louis 15th 92
Flounder, Stuffed 92
Kedgeree 93

Les Ecrevisse
  De Gaulle 90
Lobster, Crab Meat or
  Crayfish A La Newburg .91
Oysters:
  Abbevile 99
  A La Bechamelle 100
  Alexandria 99
  Baked Oysters
    Bourguignonne 100
  Baked Oysters Emile ..100
  Benedict 101
  Bohemian 101
  Broiled in Brown Sauce 101
  Caribbean 102
  Cocktail Oysters A La
    Rascal 102
  Curried 102
  Fairview 102
  Farcis 103
  Fried 103
  Poached 103
  Poulettes 103
  Rockefeller 103
  Rockefeller Sauce 104
  Roffignac 104
  Scalloped 104
  Scalloped, Grand Isle ..105
  Steamed 105
  Stuffed (2) 105
Oysters and Artichokes ..100
Oysters and Artichokes
  Sunset Farms 100
Oysters and Crabmeat
  A La Bonne Femme ...102
Oysters and
  Sweetbreads 105
Oyster and Sweetbread
  Pies 106
Oysters with Bell
  Peppers 101
Pompano En Papillote ...94
Red Fish Shah of
  Persia 94
Red Snapper, Coldd
  Boiled 95
Seafood, Wilder Than
  Who?? 106
Shrimp:
  Barbequed 106
  Barbequed A La
    Manale 106
  Boiled River Shrimp
    "Belair" 107
  Creole (2) 107
  Fried 107
  Newburg 108
  Pie 108
  Remoulade 108
  Rossi 108
  "Shrimp Orleans" 108

Souffle 109
Supreme 109
Victoria 109
Shrimp and Mushrooms . .107
Stewed Terrapin 96
Trout 97
Trout:
  Almondine with
    Seedless Grapes 97
  Barbequed 97
  Duglere, Filet of 97
  Emily 97
  En Papillot, Filet of . . .98
  Marguery 98
  Meuniere Amandines . .98
  Plauche 98
  Veronique 98
Trout with White Wine
  Sauce 99
Turtle Au Gratin 99
Vol-Au-Vent Bercy 94

POULTRY, GAME AND
DRESSINGS

Chicken:
  Acadian 111
  A La Pierre 117
  Avocado 111
  Baked (Broilers),
    Mushroom Stuffing . .111
  Baked 111
  Breast of, Hawaiian . . .115
  Broiled in Wine 112
  Croquettes with Brains
    and Mushrooms 112
  Curry (2) 112
  Curry, Hawaiian 113
  De Luxe 114
  Esther 115
  Fricassee with
    Dumplings 115
  Ganymede 115
  "La Louisiane" 116
  Oriental 116
  Paprika 116
  Pie 117
  Scalloped 118
  Smothered 118
  Souffle 118
  Tureene 119
  Valmont 119
Chicken in Sour Cream . . .119
Coq Au Vin 112
Coquilles De Volailles 114
Curry Luncheon 113
Dressing:
  German Turkey 124
  Oyster 124
  Rice 124

Ducks:
  Breasts, Sauteed 119
  Halved 119
  Mallard Duck 120
  Pot Roast Duck
    Au Coon Ass 120
  Roasted Wild Mallards .120
  Smoked 120
  Wild Duck A La Fell . .121
  Wild 121
Fried Chicken
  A Merveil 115
Galatine of Goose 121
Honey Bun's Chicken
  and Dumplings 114
Hot Jellied Chicken 116
Poulet A La
  Raphael 117
Poulet Saute A La
  Bordelaise 118
Quail in Sherry 122
Quail with Truffles 122
Rabbit Aux Fines
  Herbes 123
Roasted Chicken 117
Roast Pheasant with
  Cress 122
Stuffing:
  Chestnut 124
  Oyster for Turkey 125
  Oyster, Old Fashioned .125
  Pecan 126
  Sausage 125
  Turkey 125
Turkey:
  Baked 123
  Hash 122
  Wild 123
Venison En Casserole 124
Venison Steak 124

MEATS

Bacon, Baked
  Canadian 128
Beef Burgundy 128
Beef Buschelone 128
Beef And Pork
  Barbeque 129
Beef Carbonados,
  Flemish 129
Beef Steak and
  Kidney Pie 130
Beef Stew,
  Bourguignonne 130
Beef Stroganoff 130
Beef Stuffed Pork 129
Boeuf Provencale,
  Estouffade de 131
Brains Au Fromage 131

Calf's Feet
  Ravigote · 132
Chile Con Carne 132
Chile Con Cornie 132
Cutlets de
  Villeneuve 132
Daube Glace (1) 132
Daube Glace (3) 133
Daube Glace (1) 134
Daube Glace
  Clemenceau 134
Daube Pot Roast 134
Daube, Roasted Beef 134
Daube, Vieux Carre 135
Filet Supreme, Stuffed . . .135
Grillades (2) 135
Grillades Pannees 136
Grillades Pointe
  Coupe 136
Ham:
  Au Marquis . . . . :. .136
  Baked 136
  Mousse 137
  Pontalba, Baked
    Stuffed 136
  Stuffed 137
  Virginia 138
Hash, Baked 138
Jambon Au Champagne . .137
Jambon, Mousse Au 137
Jerky 138
Kidneys, Curried 139
Kidneys, Flambes,
  Lamb 139
Lamb:
  Alsatian 139
  Lamb L'Anglaise,
    Boiled 139
  Parslied Leg of 140
Liver Aux Vingt-Cinq
  Piastres 140
Liver with
  Sweetbreads 140
Meat Balls A La Russe,
  Glorified 140
Meat Loaf A La
  Von Fronk 141
Meat Loaf, Cranberry 141
Mouton, Gigot de 139
Mutton with Cabbage 141
Mutton Chops Au Diable .141
Pork Roast 142
Pork Sausage 142
Saucisse,
  Croquettes de 142
Sauerbraten 142
Steak, Barbequed a la
  General Trousdale 142
Steak, Charcoal Broiled
  a la Earl 142
Steak, Gentleman's 143

Stew, Brunswick 144
Sweetbreads, Artichokes
  and 144
Sweetbreads and Fresh
  Mushrooms 144
Sweetbreads and Ham . . .145
Tongue 145
Tournedos Royal 145
Veal, Lamb or Chicken,
  Blanquette of 145
Veal:
  Blanquette De Veau . . .146
  Cutlets Maintenon 146
  Marinated 146
  Panne a la
    "Boo Bird" 146
  Roast with Orange
    Sauce 146
  Stuffed (Veal) Pocket .147
  With Wine 147
Wiener Schnitzel 147

VEGETABLES, PASTAS,
JAMBALAYAS & CASSE-
ROLES

Apples Dorothy Dix 149
Apples, Fried 149
Artichoke:
  Bottoms Stuffed with
    Ground Artichokes . .149
  Casserole 149
  Casserole, Artichoke
    and Ham 150
  French 149
  Hearts and Asparagus . .150
  Mousse 150
  Ring 150
  Stuffed (2) 151
  Stuffed with
    Sweetbreads 151
Asparagus:
  Amandine 151
  Casserole 151
  French Fried 152
Bananas In Jackets 152
Bananas, Orleans Club . . .152
Baked Barley &
  Mushrooms 152
Beans:
  Baked 152
  Barbequed 153
  Louisiana Style, Red . .153
  String with Corn 153
  String, Italian 153
  String with Mushroom
    Sauce 153
Beets, Piquante 154
Bell Peppers, Stuffed 154
Bell Pepper, Crayfish
  Stuffed 154
Cabbage, Stuffed 154

Carrots Au Sucre 154
Carrot Ring 155
Casseroles:
  Chicken and Ham 170
  Chicken or Turkey 111
  Fish 172
  Meat with Noodles 172
  Mother Goose 172
  Pork Chop 173
  Shrimp and Cheese . . .173
  Toulousain,
    Cassoulet 173
Cauliflower, Baked 155
Cauliflower with Shrimp
  Sauce 155
Chou-Croute Garnie 171
Chou-Croute Garnis 171
Corn:
  Pudding (2) 155
  Pudding, Quick 155
  Souffle 156
Cucumber Ring 156
Cushaw 156
Cushaw, Candied 156
Eggplant:
  A L'Olin 156
  Casserole 157
  Crabmeat Cheese
    Topping 157
  Farcis 157
  Souffle 157
  Souffle 158
  Tomato with Cheese
    Sauce 158
Jambalaya 169
Jambalaya:
  Creole 170
  Louisiana, A La
    Kolb's 170
  En Famille 170
Ham and Potatoes
  Au Gratin 172
Macaroni Pie 167
Mirliton:
  Farci 158
  Stuffed (2) . . . . 158 & 159
Mushrooms:
  Stuffed 159
  Stuffed with Brazil
    Nuts 159
Noodle Ring 167
Noodle Ring 168
Okra, Corn and
  Tomatoes 159
Onions, French Fried 160
Onion Pie 160
Peas, New 160
Plantains, Fried (2) 160
Potatoes:
  Au Cordon Bleu de Paris,
    Soufflees 161
  Duchesse 160

Puff 161
Raw Potato Pancakes . .160
Strata 161
Sweet, Balls 161
Sweet, En Casserole . . .161
Sweet Potato Pudding,
  Plantation 162
Sweet Souffle 162
Rice:
  Cajun 162
  Carolina Curried 162
  Dirty 163
  Las Vegas 163
  Lou's Dirty 163
  Octavie 163
  Spoon Bread 163
  Wild 164
Souffle Aux Epinards 165
Spaghetti:
  A La Aimee 168
  Chicken Spaghetti
    Dinner 171
  Michele 168
  Oysters, and 168
  Rolling 169
  Supreme 169
  White House 169
Spinach
  "Au Bain Marie" 164
  Au Gratin 164
  Casserole (2) 164
  Creole 165
  Pudding 165
  Spinach Stuffed Squash 165
  Spinach with
    Artichokes 165
Squash Casserole with
  Shrimp 166
Tomatoes:
  A La Creole 166
  Felecie 166
  L'Aigre-Douces 166
  Stuffed 166
  Stuffed with Cheese . . .167
Turnip or Mustard Greens 167
Yams with Fruit 167

SAUCES FOR MEATS,
POULTRY, FISH AND
VEGETABLES

Anchovy Sauce 175
Arnaud Sauce 175
Arnaud, Sauce 175
Avocado Sauce 175
Barbeque Sauce (2) 176
Barbeque Sauce (2) 176
Barbeque Sauce for
  Fresh Pork 176
Barbeque Sauce,
  Heavy's Super 176

Barbeque Sauce For
   Poultry, Pinhead's 182
Bechamel Sauce 177
Bearnaise Sauce (3) 177
Bearnaise Creole,
   Sauce 177
Black Butter Sauce 177
Chili Sauce 178
Cocktail Sauce 178
Cocktail Sauce
   Bonfouca 178
Cream Sauce 178
Curry Sauce 178
Curry:
   Accompaniments with
    Curry 175
English Horse-Radish
   Sauce 178
Epicurean Sauce 178
Fish Sauce 179
Fish, Sauce for
   Boiled 179
Fish Sauce Mere 179
Fish or Shrimp, Sauce
   for 179
Ham Sauce 179
Ham, Sauce for Baked ...179
Hollandaise Sauce (2) 179
Hollandaise Sauce 180
Hollandaise Sauce,
   Easy 180
"Hollandaise", White 180
Hollandaise Sauce,
   Mock 180
Hot Mustard 175
Hot Sauce for
   Broccoli 177
Lamb or Game, Sauce
   for 180
Lamb, Mint Sauce
   for 180
Marchand de Vin,
   Sauce 180
Marguerite Sauce 180
Oysters Rockefeller
   Sauce 182
Oysters Rockefeller
   Sauce 183
Paradise Sauce for
   Ducks 182
Remoulade Sauce 182
Shrimp, White Butter
   Sauce for 183
Spaghetti Sauce
   de Luxe 184
Spanish Sauce 184
Steak Sauce 184
Tartar Sauce 184
Tartar Sauce, Sour
   Cream 184
Tomato Catsup 184
Touraine, Sauce 185

**DESSERTS, CANDY
AND ICE CREAM**

Apples, Candied 202
Apricot Glaze 202
Bananas Flambeaux 187
Bananas Foster 187
Big Sink Specialty 187
Blackberry Bread 187
Blackberry
   Roly-Poly 187
Brulot Bread Pudding 188
Butterscotch Brown 188
Carmel Mousse Au
   St. Aubin 188
Caramels, Honey 202
Charlotte Russe 188
Cherries in the Snow 188
Cherries Jubilee 189
Chocolate Dessert 189
Chocolate Fudge 203
Chocolate Ice Box
   Dessert 189
Chocolate Roll,
   Frozen 189
Chocolate Sponge
   Viennois 200
Chocolate Tart
   Pudding 189
Coffee Cream 190
Coffee Delight 190
Coffee Frappe 190
Compote, Frozen
   Fruit 190
Corn Flake Ring 190
Couer A La Creme 190
Cream Cheese,
   Frozen 191
Creme Brulee 191
Creme Brulee 191
Creole Puffs 191
Crepes:
   Brulees............192
   Crepes (Basic) 191
   Cooking Crepes 191
   Fitzgerald 192
   Suzette 193
   Suzette Gauloises 193
Crystallized Pumpkin 202
Cup Custard 193
Date Loaf 202
Devonshire Cream 208
Eggnog Ring 193
French Nougat 203
Frozen Buttermilk 206
Fudge, Easy 203
Grapefruit Aspic 194
Grapefruit Glace 203
Green Grapes 194
Hot Weather Special 194

Ice:
   Apricot 206
   Lemon 206
   Watermelon 206
Ice Cream:
   Au Caramel 205
   Caramel 205
   Crunch............194
   Ginger 206
   Pistachio 206
   Pontchartrain's
    Famous Pie, The ...194
   Praline 206
Lemon and Chocolate
   Frozen Pie 195
Lemon Sponge, Frozen ..195
Lucinda's Surprise 195
Marrons Glaces 203
Marzipan 203
Mocha Creme 195
Nuts, Spiced 203
Omelet Souffle 195
Orange Mousse 196
Peaches:
   Aglow 196
   Au Chateau 196
   Brandy 196
   Dumplings 193
   Frozen 196
   Super Melba 196
Pears Au Cointreau 196
Pecans:
   Orange Sugared 204
   Salted 204
   Spiced 204
Pots De Cremes 197
Pralines:
   Pralines (Basic) (2) 204
   Deborah's 204
   Pecan (2) 205
   Tournes 205
Prunes or Dates,
   Stuffed 205
Pudding:
   Butterscotch 197
   Carrot 197
   Chambliss 197
   Coconut 197
   Marshmallow 198
   No Name 198
   Plum, English 198
   Rice, Creamy 198
   Rice, Frozen 198
   Rum 198
   Rum Chestnut (2) 199
   Sponge 199
   Waldorf Steamed 199
   Walnut Date 199
Sabayon 199
Sauce:
   Blackberry 207
   Brandy 207

Cabinet 207
Chocolate (2) 207
Chocolate, Sherry's ...207
Chocolate, Yum Yum .208
Eggnog.............208
Hard 202
Orange 208
Praline Sauce, Vieux
Carre.............208
Savarin 200
Sherbet, Banana 207
Sherbet, Orange 207
Strawberry:
Casseroles 200
Celeste 200
Cream 200
Mousse 201
Shortbread 201
Tart Angelique 201
Tezcuco Plantation
Nougat 204
Trifle, Tipsy 201
Trifles, Queen of 201
"Zabayon" 201

CAKES, SMALL CAKES, COOKIES, FROSTINGS, PIES AND PASTRIES

Baisers Creoles 217
Batons Des Noix 217
Brownies 217
Brownies 218
Butterscotch
Brownies (2) 218
Butter Dough 218
Cakes:
Almond Cakes No. 1 ..217
Almond Cakes No. 2 ..217
Banana 210
Cheesecake 210
Chocolate Almond ...210
Chocolate Cakes 218
Chocolate, Easy 210
Chocolate Fudge 211
Chocolate Ice Box ...211
Chocolate Nut 211
Eggnog Cakes........220
Emilia's Spice 216
Fluff Cakes
Meringues 220
Fruit (2) 212
Fruit, Brazil Nut 212
Fruit, Cake Hermione .212
Fruit, White 212
Fudge Cake Square,
Au Parisien 220
Fudge Pie Cake 213
Jam 213
Jam, Old Fashioned ...213

Layer Cake A La
Cajon 211
Lemon 214
Nut 214
Orange Cake A La
Evelyn 215
Pecan and Raisin 215
Pound 215
Sour Cream 215
Spice 215
Sponge (4) 216
Strawberry 216
Tea Cakes 223
Upside Down 217
White 217

Cookies:
Coconut Kisses 219
Coconut Kisses,
Blanches 219
Corn Flake Kisses ...219
Cream Puffs 220
Croquignoles 220
Danish 220
Drop Nut 220
Ginger Snaps 221
Hello Dolly 219
Ice Box 221
King's 221
Kitten's Tongue 221
Lebkuchen 221
Les Oreilles de
Cochon 222
Love Wreaths 221
Meringue Shells 222
Nut-Butter Cookies ...222
Oatmeal, Thin 222
Point Coupee 222
"S" 223
Sand Shells 223
Sesame Seed 223
Spritzenkuchlein 223
" 'Ti's Gateaux" 223
Wafers, Chocolate Nut .219
Wafers, Christiana ...219
Wafers, Vanilla Tea ..224
Empanadas 213
Fillings:
Cream 224
Lemon (2) 224
Lemon Jelly 224
Frostings:
Chocolate Nut Minute .225
Chocolate Pecan 225
Marshmallow, A
La Mamie 225
Seven Minute 225
Gingerbread Au Vieux
Temps 213
Icings:
A La Lucie 225
Chocolate 224

Chocolate Marshmallow
Pecan 224
For Fudge Squares 225
Mocha Icing and
Filling 225
Orange Glaze 225
Quick White 226
Jelly Roll 214
Lemon Bunkuchen 214
Pastry:
Chess 226
Hot Water 226
Kiechen 226
Pie Crust Infallible ...226
Pies:
Black Bottom 227
Cherry, Mock 228
Chess 228
Chocolate 228
Chocolate Chiffon ...228
Chocolate Meringue ...228
Cream Cheese 228
Creme de Menthe 228
Grasshopper 229
"Jefferson Davis" ...229
Joan's Easy 229
Lemon (2) 229
Mince Meat 230
Molasses 230
Mystery 230
Orange 230
Peach Surprise 231
Pecan 230
Pecan (2) 231
Plantation Pecan 231
Pumpkin 231
Rhubarb 231
Rum 231
Strawberry Cream ...232
Tarts:
A L'Apricot 227
Fruit 227
Pastry 237

CONSERVES, PRE-SERVES AND PICKLES

Chili Relish 234
Chow-Chow 234
Chutney 234
Cranberry Conserve 234
Cranberry Jelly, Quick ...235
Cranberry Relish 235
Cranberry Sauce 235
Cucumber Pickles, Sweet .239
Dill Pickles, Kiln 239
Fig Preserves 235
Ginger Pears 235
Kumquat Conserve 235
Marmalade 235

Marmalade, Economical .235
Marmalade, Orange and
    Peach 236
Olives, Spiced 236
Onion Pickle, Green 238
Oranges de luxe 236
Peaches, Brandied 234
Peach Conserve 236
Peach and Pear
    Pickle 237
Peach Preserves 237
Pear Butter 237
Pear Conserve 237
Pumpkin Preserves 237
Tomato Jelly 240
Tomato Pickle, Green 237
Tomato Pickle, Green 238
Sweet Pickles,
    Delicious 238
Sweet Pepper Relish 240
Watermelon and Rind
    Pickle 239

Watermelon Rind or Ripe
    Cucumber Pickle 239
Watermelon Rind, Spiced .239

CHILDREN'S   RECIPES

Acey's Biscuits 242
B. B.'s Pomander
    Balls 242
Candle Salad 242
Chip A De Do Da
    Chicken 242
Cinnamon Toast 243
Dulce De Leche 243
Father's Day Cake 243
Fruity Frinky Sherbet . .243
Eggs, The Devil's 243
Easy Blender Mousse 243
French Fried Onions 243
Happiness Is: Keppy and
    Susu's Brownies 244

How To Preserve
    Children 242
Jelly Jumbles 244
Joseph Street Tube
    Steaks 244
Marshmallow Popcorn
    Balls 244
Melt In Your Mouth
    Pralines 244
Merry Go Round Cheese
    Bites 245
Meat Loaf 245
Orange Lollipops 245
Pane of Glass 246
Picnic Tomatoes 245
Piggies, Fat 245
Pizza, Petite 245
Pinwheels 246
Popcorn Crunch 246
Rice Is Nice 246
Rinktum Diddy 247
Somemore's 247
Stroganoff, Mock 247
Watermelon Snowballs . . .247

Full Size 11" X 13"

prints of each illustration including The Loner
are available from the artist

These exact reproductions are all signed
and suitable for framing

ALL PRINTS ARE $3⁰⁰ Each
(please specify by Chapter Heading)

Send Check or Money Order to:

Robert Seago
3411 Octavia Street
New Orleans, LA 70125

3 Week Delivery

ORDER FORM

Published & distributed by —
CLAITOR'S PUBLISHING DIVISION
3165 S. Acadian at I-10, P.O. Box 3333
Baton Rouge, La. 70821

Date _____

Phone orders TOLL-FREE 800-535-8141 (La. customers 504-344-0476)

Please send: __ copy(ies) Jones GOURMET'S GUIDE TO NEW ORLEANS Creole Cookbook and Restaurant Guide @$7.95. *
__ copy(ies) Jones RECIPES FROM MISS LOUISE @$8.95. *
__ copy(ies) Akin THE CRAWFISH COOKBOOK: Cajun, Creole @$4.95. *
__ copy(ies) Akin INTERNATIONAL CRAWFISH CUISINE COOKBOOK: @$8.95. *
__ copy(ies) Babin NATURAL COOKING CAJUN CREOLE STYLE @$7.95. *
__ copy(ies) American Cancer Society A LOUISIANA SAMPLER @$6.95.
__ copy(ies) Guidry From Mama To Me: ACADIAN-CAJUN RECIPES OF CHURCH POINT, LA. @$4.95. *
__ copy(ies) Land LOUISIANA COOKERY @$4.95. *
__ copy(ies) Vidrine LOUISIANA LAGINAPPE @$8.95. *
__ copy(ies) Vidrine QUELQUE CHOSE de DOUX (Acadian Recipes for the Sweet Tooth) @$3.50. *
__ copy(ies) Vidrine QUELQUE CHOSE PIQUANTE (Spicy Acadian Recipes) @$3.95. *
__ copy(ies) Vidrine QUELQUE CHOSE POUR UN JOYEUX NOEL (Acadian Recipes for Christmas) @$2.95. *
__ copy(ies) Vidrine BEAUCOUP BON @$4.95. *
__ copy(ies) La. Federation of Women's Clubs A TASTE OF LOUISIANA @$8.95. *
__ copy(ies) COOK WITH MARIE LOUISE @$4.95. *
__ copy(ies) Bardwell MODERN MEATLESS MENUS COOKBOOK @$3.50. *
__ copy(ies) Uhler CAJUN COUNTRY COOKIN' @$5.95. *
__ copy(ies) Uhler ROYAL RECIPES FROM THE CAJUN COUNTRY @$4.95. *
__ copy(ies) BRUSHY BAYOU RECIPES @$9.95. *
__ copy(ies) Elstein & Wilkenfield DIETER'S ULTIMATE COOKBOOK @$11.95. * 'Microwave conversions by Ruth Comingore.
__ copy(ies) Ramsey JUST A MOUTHFUL COOKBOOK. 1978. @$4.95. *

☐ Check enclosed, including tax plus $1.00 per book delivery & ins.

☐ Charge my established account
(Acct. # if known _____

☐ Charge my VISA or Master Card

VISA
Acct. No. _____ (expires _____)

or Master Card
Acct. No. _____ (expires _____)

FOR FASTEST SERVICE
CALL WITHOUT CHARGE
800-535-8141
Except La. 504-344-0476

Name _____
Address _____
City _____ State _____ Zip _____
*Add tax as appropriate